To
Continue
the
DIALOGUE

The Living Issues Discussion Series

*T*HE LIVING ISSUES DISCUSSION SERIES IS EDITED by Michael A. King and published by Pandora Press U.S. as well as sometimes copublished with Herald Press. Pandora Press U.S., in consultation with its Editorial Council as well as volume editors and authors, is primarily responsible for content of these studies, which address "living issues" likely to benefit from lively and serious discussion.

1. To Continue the Dialogue:
   Biblical Interpretation and Homosexuality
   Edited by C. Norman Kraus, 2001
2. What Does the Bible Really Say about Hell?
   Wrestling with the Traditional View
   By Randy Klassen, 2001

To
Continue
the

DIALOGUE

Biblical Interpretation and
Homosexuality

Edited by C. Norman Kraus

Foreword by Richard A. Kauffman

Living Issues Discussion Series, Volume 1

Pandora Press U.S.
Telford, Pennsylvania

Pandora Press U.S. orders, information, reprint permissions:
pandoraus@netreach.net
1-215-723-9125
126 Klingerman Road, Telford PA 18969
www.PandoraPressUS.com

Library of Congress Cataloguing-in-Publication Data
To continue the dialogue : biblical interpretation and homosexuality /
edited by C. Norman Kraus.
    p. cm.
    Includes bibliographical references.
    ISBN 1-931038-01-5 (alk. paper)
    1. Homosexuality--Religious aspects--Mennonites.
    2. Homosexuality--Biblical teaching. I. Kraus, C. Norman (Clyde Nor-
man), 1924-

BX8128.H67 T6 2001
261.8'35766--dc21

                                                                    2001032873

10 09 08 07 06 05 04 03 02   10 9 8 7 6 5 4 3 2

Contents

Foreword by Richard A. Kauffman   7
Series Editor's Preface by Michael A. King   12
Editor's Preface   13
Introduction by C. Norman Kraus   17

PART ONE: THE NEED FOR CONTINUING DIALOGUE

  1   The "H" Words: *Hermeneutics* and *Homosexuality*   •   25
      C. Norman Kraus

  2   Psychological Dynamics: Being Gay or Lesbian   •   45
      Marcus Smucker

  3   Homosexuality: Biblical, Theological, and Polity Issues   •   62
      David Schroeder

  4   A Pastoral Plea   •   76
      Paul M. Lederach

  5   The Story of the Listening Committee   •   81
      Melanie Zuercher and Edward Stoltzfus

  6   Mennonites and the Homosexual Issue:
      A Recent History   •   92
      Lin Garber

  7   Mennonites Shift Focus from Morality to Who Belongs   •   111
      Michael A. King

PART TWO: FRAMING THE THEOLOGICAL QUESTIONS

  8   Why Does the Bible Divide Us? A Conversation with Scripture
      on Same-Gender Attaction   •   121
      Don Blosser

  9   The Biological Basis of Homosexuality   •   148
      Carl S. Keener and Douglas E. Swartzendruber

10 Homosexuality:
   A Call for Compassion and Moral Rigor • 174
   A. James Reimer

11 Six Perspectives on the Homosexuality Controversy • 187
   Theodore Grimsrud

12 What Can We Do When We Don't Agree?
   Christian Tolerance in Romans 14:1–15:6 • 209
   Reta Halteman Finger

13 Fruit of the Spirit or Works of the Flesh?
   Come Let Us Reason Together • 223
   Mark Thiessen Nation

14 Commanded to Keep
   Wrestling and Wrestling and Wrestling • 245
   Carolyn Schrock-Shenk

15 Making Theological and Ethical Decisions:
   Contextualizing the Bible • 256
   C. Norman Kraus

16 Responses • 280
   Mary Schertz, John A. Lapp, Willard M. Swartley, Sheldon Burkhalter, Richard Showalter, Elsie Steelberg and Donald Steelberg, Elaine K. Swartzentruber, George R. Brunk III

*Appendix A: Report of Listening Committee
              for Homosexual Concerns   303*
*Appendix B: Entering the Homosexuality Discussion:
              A Guide For Congregational Dialogue   323*
The Contributors   328
The Editor   332

Foreword

NOT SO LONG AGO A GROUP OF CONSERVATIVES in the Presbyterian Church USA "invited" the liberals in their denomination to leave. The conservatives were chagrined that these liberals were advocating ordination of "practicing gays" and performing same-sex covenantal unions. The liberals, not surprisingly, were incensed. This is our church too, they said, and we're not leaving.

The pressing issue in the Mennonite Church is different: acceptance into church membership of non-celibate gays and lesbians. But the group dynamics are increasingly becoming politicized, in ways similar to what is happening among mainline Protestants.

I winced when I first saw a "Welcoming Letter" which appeared as an ad in the *Mennonite Weekly Review* (February 17, 2000). Neither the content of the letter nor the signatories were what bothered me. The arguments were familiar to me, and I found it interesting to observe who signed the letter (and who didn't dare despite agreement with its content), some of whom I consider personal friends. Further, I knew the perspective represented in the letter wasn't very welcome in official Mennonite discussions and publications. Thus resorting to an ad no doubt emerged from frustration at finding no better way to gain a hearing. But I also knew every action elicits an equal and opposite reaction. My wait was not in vain: though signed by a single critic, the reaction came in the form of another paid advertisement rebutting the welcoming letter.

I asked myself then, Is this the way we do church? Do Mennonites deal with a hot, contentious issue which seems to be ripping the church apart by carrying out a paid advertising campaign in an independent Mennonite newspaper? Although I didn't say it there, this question was the inspiration for an article I wrote for *The Mennonite*, "A Third Way between Fight and Flight" (May 2, 2000).

Should we not, as a people of peace, I asked then, find another way for finding our way through this sticky wicket? And because I think there should be a third way besides fight and flight, I consented to write the foreword to this book—though not because I agree with all perspectives represented in these pages. That would not a dialogue make.

My interest in engaging in such dialogue is this: I fear unless we take another tack, Mennonites may be headed for the same terms of engagement as mainline denominations. For instance, when Gregory Dell, a United Methodist pastor in Chicago, was tried by his conference for "marrying" a gay couple, all three parties involved in the case hired public relations experts: Dell's church and supporters, his opponents in the United Methodist Church, and the church itself. Each PR person tried to win the war of public opinion through the secular media, especially in the Chicago area. Eventually, this case became the subject matter for a Northwestern University-sponsored symposium on how the media become involved in and are used by contentious ecclesial combatants.

Perhaps this is an extreme example, but a lesson for Mennonites in any case. If we avoid face-to-face conversation, debate, and discernment and use instead the politics of confrontation, than we, supposedly a historic peace church, will have found no more redemptive a way forward than denominations seemingly ready to engage in Holy War.

What this issue should be about is discernment: trying to discern the will and way of God on this matter at the threshold of the third millennium of the Christian Era. I know, others will disagree with this premise. For some, the issue is standing up for an oppressed minority; for others, it is standing up for the truth as they know it. (Is there any other?) But if we can't step back from our own positions long enough to hear the perspectives of others, then dialogue, if not discernment, is foiled. Then I see no way around the fight-flight syndrome.

Further, here is how I would frame the issue for discernment (others will disagree here, too): the biblical norm for sexuality is that a man and woman are commanded to leave their mother and father and join in lifelong union with one another. This was decreed before the Fall and was reaffirmed by Jesus (Matt. 19:5; Gen. 2:24; cf. 1 Cor. 6:16 and Eph. 5:31), despite the fact that he relativized the Levitical Holiness Code. The dilemma we are faced with is that, for reasons we still don't entirely understand, a small portion of the population has a same-gender orientation or affection. Such people are incapable of or find it unbearably difficult to be attracted to persons of the opposite sex; instead, they are drawn toward persons of the same sex.

The ethical issue, then, is not whether to change the norm. The Bible makes clear, it seems to me, that this norm is to be male-female attraction and marriage. The issue, rather, is how we respond to these exceptional cases. Do we demand that gays and lesbians try to change their orientation? Do we expect that they remain celebate, despite the fact that they, like most heterosexuals, burn with sexual passion (to paraphrase the apostle Paul)? Or would the Holy Spirit bless our making some exceptions enabling persons with fundamental same-gender attraction to enter monogamous, covenantal, lifelong, same-sex unions? Practically speaking, these seem to be the options facing us. And dividing us.

It is true that Mennonites have had a history of people pealing off on their own, of conservatives bolting because they think the church is moving too fast or making compromising changes; of liberals leaving because they think the church is too bound to the past, thwarting liberating or energizing changes; or of pietists of various stripes moving on amid claims the church is not spiritual enough. In many such cases, the schismatics are putting their own convictions, ideas, and religious experiences—egos, too—ahead of the unity of the body and this treasure we call peoplehood. Whereas I am not comfortable with the current struggle over the "H-issue," as one chapter in this book calls it, I am even more discontent with the flight option.

What I plead for, instead, is a commitment to the common struggle of discovering God's will for us. To do this, we need at least the following: confession, empathy, humility, patience, and prayer.

Confession: Here's mine: I am hopelessly and helplessly heterosexual. Try as I might, I can't imagine what it must be like to experience same-gender attraction or to be marginalized as a sexual minority. Further, I never chose to be heterosexual, although I enjoy it tremendously and can't remember a time I didn't feel attracted to the opposite sex. In fact, some of my earliest childhood memories involve feelings of attraction toward women. My experience no doubt colors how I approach same-sex orientation.

Empathy: Whatever stance I take, it must be tempered with awareness that the person whose sexuality I am discussing might be—hypothetically speaking—one of my children or a best friend.

Would that make a difference? More radically, what difference would it make if I were the one whose sexuality is being openly and vigorously debated?

Empathy, take two: We ought to be as empathetic in our responses to those with whom we disagree as toward persons experiencing same-gender attraction. Aristotle, I believe, was the one who said the mark of an educated person is to be able to argue a position with which one disagrees. Perhaps that is also a trait of a Spirit-filled Christian who longs to lovingly search for the truth.

Humility: It's trite to say that none of us has the whole truth. But still true. Moreover, I wonder how we will be judged a generation or two from now. Given how different many matters look different now than they once did, that question should give us all pause. We should all try to look back at ourselves from some historical perch about fifty years hence. Will we judge who we are now as too harsh? Too lax? If awareness of the potential for future judgment doesn't make us humble, what will?

Patience: We need patience, not just with each other, but also with a process which doesn't seem to yield either quick or easy solutions.[1] Patience is a fruit of the spirit; fractiousness is not.

Prayer: What would happen to us if we devoted as much time to this issue, personally and corporately, as we give to debate over the issues? I wouldn't expect bolts of lightning to pierce the heavens on account of my prayers or those of all of us. But the terms of our engagement and the attitudes we bring to it might alter. I pray God it might happen. Soon.

Experts in "polarity management" point out that, whereas problems can be solved and conflicts resolved, polarities can only be managed. Perhaps this is an issue for which there is no resolution. We can only work at managing the polarities, by which I mean maintaining an emphasis on both the love and holiness of God, both justice and righteousness in the covenant community, both forgiving and enabling grace. Unfortunately, not many of us are capable, as individuals, of holding such polarities in creative tension. That is why we need each other in the church. And why we need to keep persons of varying perspectives in dialogue with each other.[2] May the dialogue continue.

—*Richard A. Kauffman, Pastor*
  Toledo (Oh.) Mennonite Church

Notes

1. Alasdair C. MacIntyre's comment about moral argument in general is applicable to this issue: "The most striking feature of contemporary moral utterance is that so much of it is used to express disagreements; and the most striking feature of the debates in which those disagreements are expressed is their interminable character. I do not mean by this just that such debates go on and on and on—although they do—but also that they apparently can find no terminus. There seems to be no rational way of securing moral agreement." *After Virtue: A Study in Moral Theory* (Notre Dame: University of Notre Dame Press, 1984), 6.

2. Mennonites, being a singing people, ought to keep two hymns in focus amid these discussions: "There's a Wideness in God's Mercy," especially verses three and four; and "Teach Me, O Lord, Thy Way of Truth."

Series Editor's Preface

*B*ECAUSE HOMOSEXUALITY OR SAME-GENDER sexual affection is a "living issue" that deserves serious discussion and an examination of various ways Christians understand the topic, *To Continue the Dialogue* is an an appropriate volume with which to inaugurate the Living Issues Discussion Series. All books in the series provide guidelines for discussion as well as comments from respondents who begin the conversation through freedom not only to affirm but also to disagree with perspectives offered by authors or editors.

Special thanks are due to the many persons, both named and unnamed, who through involvement with *To Continue the Dialogue* helped launch the series. First to deserve credit is John A. Lapp. When he sent his response to the book, he suggested that such a series might be useful and that *Dialogue* was already nearly in such a format. Convinced, we immediately began to establish the series parameters and to polish this book into series format. Of course C. Norman Kraus, editor of *Dialogue*, deserves thanks for his many months of hard work on the book and for modeling, in his work with authors and publisher, the type of vigorous and candid taking of positions combined with flexible readiness to learn from the other we hope the series will help support. We also thank those who first suggested that a book on homosexuality be developed.

That is not to imply *Dialogue* is perfect. We wish, for example, that more of the writers asked to add their voices to the discussion underway in these pages had felt able to do so. Nevertheless, we are grateful for the many who have contributed insightfully, respectfully, and with some diversity of viewpoint to matters so frequently divisive. We pray that the discussion they help move forward will continue to unfold with the care they model.

—*Michael A. King, Living Issues Discussion Series Editor*

Editor's Preface

*T*HIS BOOK IS A SYMPOSIUM, THAT IS, A COLLECTION of chapters contributed by different people with varying points of view. It is important for readers to keep this in mind as they move from chapter to chapter. This means, among other things, that individual authors should not necessarily be held responsible for what other writers have said. And it certainly means that the editor does not necessarily agree with all that has been written. The chapters do not present an argument laid out in a rational order leading to a final conclusion. Rather they are like windows which give us varying perspectives on a common subject.

One might well ask what then gives the book its unity. What, beside the common subject of homosexuality, provides a connecting thread for the beads on this necklace? There are two strands. First is the concern for biblical interpretation or hermeneutics, broadly defined as both determining the meaning of the text and its ethical application (contextualization) in different cultures.

Second is the conviction that the church is not yet ready to declare a dogmatic conclusion to the contentious debate that swirls around the subject of human sexuality. The last word has not been spoken on either the meaning of biblical texts or the scientific nature and origin of sexuality, either hetero- or homosexuality. We do not yet adequately understand how differences in sexual attraction arise. While all the writers agree that any form of abusive, promiscuous sexual expression is immoral, we are not entirely certain how to assess ethical values in all homosocial expressions. Some authors lean one way and some another.

If there is an implicit position we are advocating, it is that the church may need to live with some ambiguity on this subject in the next decades. Even though we essentially agree on the exegetical

13

interpretation of the Scripture text, we may still legitimately differ on its contextual implementation. We may hold to the same basic sexual morality and "family values" and still differ in local applications of these values. Accordingly, we well may need to adjust the church organization to accommodate such differences, much as has happened in some contexts in relation to divorce and remarriage, and has happened among Mennonites, formally committed by confession of faith to a peace church position, when some who serve in the military also become church members.

My own chapters assume this necessity. While I contend that they present a legitimate and authentic reading of the texual meaning, I would not argue that they present the only possible reading. But so long as there are such legitimate differences, we need to be prepared to exercise respectful tolerance and acceptance of one another in the body of Christ. Some of our authors speak of the need not to be too certain or dogmatic in our "firmly held convictions." Others plead for putting person ahead of dogma, while still others present the different options which genuine and competent Christian scholars have adopted. It is not the intention of any of the authors to argue that there is only one indisputable solution for the church to adopt.

The interpretative process does and must go beyond scriptural word study and determining the historical meaning of the text. There are no revealed applications of textual meanings that can be translated into dogmatic social practice and directly applied universally to each situation. Contextualization inescapably introduces an element of subjectivity. The significance of social practices differ widely from culture to culture and locality to locality because individuals and local communities have their own idiosyncratic experience of culture. Further, anthropologists have discovered that cultural meaning is dynamic and constantly changing. It is this cultural dynamic and flux, not the ambivalence of Scripture, that makes the continual mid-course cultural adjustments necessary. And for guidance in that task we rely on the presence of the Holy Spirit of Jesus.

Because the data are not all in, and because human lives and well-being are at stake, this symposium advocates that the church's stance should remain one of "dialogue." Our stance, as Mennonite denominational documents of the 1980s urged, should continue to be an experiential one of study, examination, and exploration as we seek the mind of the Spirit both in biblical understanding and congregational life. A number of church documents have begun to use the phrase "teaching position" to describe the Mennonite denominational stance on homosexuality. This is a happy phrase if it describes the true spirit of the teaching process which requires continuing openness to new information and experience.

Although we have sought balance wherever feasible, the word *dialogue* in the title should not lead the reader to expect that this volume fully balances views pro and con on the issues involved. Dialogue is not polite adversarial debate. Neither have we tried to balance representative institutional views. We have, in fact, avoided advocacy papers which argue explicitly either for or against the acceptance of monogamous homosexual unions in the church. Thus we have aimed not simplistically to pit the "traditional" against the "innovative," the "exclusive" against the "inclusive" positions. Our authors vary in their point of view on this issue while frequently pleading for a continuing openness to developing understanding both of biblical and experiential data.

Those who take an absolutist position on either side of the question will naturally see this as weakness. We hope, however, that our readers will be persuaded that there is room in the church for Christians of both persuasions who remain open to continuing the dialogue.

I would be remiss if I did not point out that this symposium is the result of a close collaboration between the editor and Pandora Press U. S. publisher Michael A. King. He not only encouraged and nurtured the process but has also helped shape its content. All of us, editor and authors, owe him a special debt of gratitude. In addition Michael and I are grateful to colleagues behind the scenes who encouraged and supported the project with both words and money. And we are indeed grateful to our authors for their generous and timely contributions.

—*C. Norman Kraus, Editor*
Harrisonburg, Virginia

Introduction

*T*HROUGHOUT THE WORLDWIDE CHURCH, Christian denominations and groups have been long wrestling with what stand to take on homosexuality. Among them have been Mennonites, whose own difficult conversations have given rise to this book. The hope is that these chapters may provide fresh resources not only for Mennonites but also for any Christians looking for ways to move beyond the impasse so many conversations on these matters seem to reach.

One key turning point in the Mennonite journey came in 1985 when, after four years of prayerful research and study, the General Conference Mennonite (GC) and Mennonite (MC) churches mandated the publication of a working document on *Human Sexuality in the Christian Life* to stimulate study and dialogue in the congregations. Besides speaking to the broader definitions and issues of sexual relationships, the report devotes a long section to the biblical teaching on homosexuality yet leaves the final solution open. The report states that "While the committee could not come to one mind as to openness to all of the alternatives above [abstinence or covenant union], it does urge the church to continue to uphold the traditional sexual ethic which does not allow promiscuity or sexual relationships outside of a covenantal relationship" (p. 116).

The following years, 1986 and 1987, both Mennonite denominations agreed on statements which declare homosexual "orientation" a non-issue for church membership but make celibacy or monogamous heterosexual marriage the only moral options for expression of sexual intimacy. These statements call for continuing dialogue, but the denominations (now in the process of becoming the Mennonite Church USA as well as Mennonite Church Canada) have not launched further official study of the hermeneutical, ethical, or theological issues involved in the question.

Instead, and on the MC side, after some eight years of ambiguity the Mennonite Church General Board asked its Council on Faith, Life and Strategy, a churchwide committee originally appointed as a prophetic voice within the institution, to clarify the meaning and scope of "loving dialogue." In response the CFLS declared that dialogue should not be understood to mean that the "homosexual issue is unresolved or that the position of the church is in question."[1] Rather, they defined the area of dialogue as "pastoral care" of homosexual persons and their families. Thus the calls for serious study and discussion of the substantive biblical and theological issues by the Study Committee (1980-1981) and the Listening Committee appointed in 1992 were defined as "pastoral" concerns.

In the meantime some conferences have taken action to exclude or otherwise discipline congregations which accept homosexual persons in covenanted relationship with each other. An informal dialogue of sorts has continued in the church papers as readers address letters to the editors. The emotional pitch of this dialogue-turned-debate has intensified. Some are writing that dialogue itself is compromise and therefore inappropriate.

It is difficult to understand how anyone aware of the complexities of sexual definitions and regulations in both church history and biblical interpretation can call for an end to the dialogue. Through the centuries the church has not spoken with one unified voice on the issue. In fact, it has been sensitive to the cultural differences and legal definitions of the societies in which it found itself. Furthermore, there has not been one fixed interpretation of the biblical texts. For example, even within the biblical texts themselves there are differing interpretations of the sin of the Sodomites.

Many of us are not familiar with the history of this social issue in the Christian church. As the church began to establish itself in the Mediterranean and Near Eastern cultures, it had to contextualize its message regarding many issues, like slavery and gender roles, in Graeco-Roman law and custom. Even within the Roman Empire there was no standardization of custom and practice. Gender roles and expectations differed from one national-language group to another. The definition and regulation of marriage and sexual relationships in general differed from culture to culture. Contrary to common assumptions, the church did not develop a universal orthodox ethic and practice with regard to these matters.

Definitions of gender roles conditioned attitudes toward homosocial and homosexual practice. In the ancient and medieval worlds the female role was assumed to be one of subjection, passivity, and reception. Male relationships were valued above male-female relationships. In heterosexual relationships males were the *subjects* in a sexual liaison and females were *objects*. Homosocial unions among heroes of the past which included homoerotic and homosexual aspects were idealized. There are even examples of this within the medieval church, such as the seventh century couple, Saints Serge and Bacchus.[2]

Thus defining legitimate homosocial relationships (same-gender unions) was a significant part of the church's task which involved different patterns in different times and places. In premodern European cultures the church even formulated ceremonies for same-sex unions to regulate and sanctify them. These ceremonies emphasized the monogamous, lifelong, homosocial and homospiritual relationships but did not explicitly rule out homoerotic aspects.

Social attitudes toward and regulation of same-sex relationships are integrally connected to definitions and expectations of heterosexual relationships, and both have varied over the centuries. At present, European cultures differ significantly from East to West in their homosocial patterns—their understandings of how persons of the same sex are expected to relate to each other. In Latin American cultures a lingering male machismo (at least as viewed from within a more feminist perspective) affects attitudes. In Africa tribal beliefs and practices clearly influence gender roles and relationships.

In North America definitions of gender roles and attitudes have changed and remain in flux. During the life times of many, the centrality of the nuclear family, the importance of bearing children, the value of romance and erotic passion in married love, the role of physical sexual expression in marriage, the public expression of same-sex friendships, the propriety of nudity in homo- and heterosexual company have all changed significantly. Indeed within recent decades attitudes and social-legal policies toward homosexual practice have taken new turns. Clearly such changes do not automatically legitimate revisions of the church's sexual ethic. They do, however, require us to reexamine our traditional assumptions about human sexuality and our biblical rationale for regulating it.

Calling attention to this historical-cultural variation, even within the church itself, highlights the complexity of the social-religious issues involved and suggests the need for continuing study, research, and dialogue. We are dealing with subjects of profound ethical and religious values. Our personal self-definition as human beings is involved. For Christians this involves understanding God's intention for humanity as it is disclosed in the Hebrew-Christian Scriptures. The authority of Scripture is not in question. What that authority is saying and how it applies to our twenty-first century situation is in debate, however.

As mentioned in the preface, the goal of this book is not to call the church to adopt a particular position. Although individual writers may lean in one direction or another, the book as a whole includes a diversity of perspectives and encompasses chapters which sensitively reaffirm a relatively traditional stand and may undergird the church's current position. What the book does call for is continuing dialogue on the biblical and cultural questions involved in addressing homosexuality. Authors are convinced that as a church we do not yet have an adequate understanding of the nature of the problem or the biblical and cultural issues involved to reach a final solution. Thus dialogue which seeks to further common understanding is still called for.

Some have objected to the word *dialogue*, supposing that it implies compromise, and have suggested that in relation to this book's discussions we use *conversation* instead. After carefully considering the options, we have decided to continue with dialogue, the word used in the 1980s denominational documents. While dialogue is a form of conversation, it suggests a seriousness of purpose that conversation does not necessarily have. One dictionary definition of dialogue reads, "3. an exchange of ideas or opinions on a particular issue especially with a view of reaching an amicable agreement," and "6. to discuss areas of disagreement frankly to resolve them" (*Random House Webster's College Dictionary*).

Dialogue by its very nature demands careful listening. In dialogue one does not listen as an adversary while preparing a rebuttal. Dialogue is not competitive debate to be settled by a majority vote such as we witness on the national political scene; rather, dialogue requires both respect and trust in the opponent's integrity and competence. It also requires humble recognition that we may not have the whole truth and a willingness to learn from the other person even while we forthrightly present our own position. Such a stance is not compromise. It assumes the possibility of arriving at a resolution different from that envisioned by either competing side.

Dialogue is the way the church deals with differences in understanding and conviction among its members.[3] Dialogue, not monologue, is the way of seeking consensus in the community of the

Spirit. Churchly consensus does not come by dictation from the top. True spiritual unity is not achieved by decree. This position, of course, assumes the presence and power of the Holy Spirit as the "go-between God" who makes all real communication possible. Indeed, dialogue is a miracle of the Spirit!

Dialogue in the institutional church will require postponement of an ultimate resolution while we work with interim solutions. To preserve the authenticity of churchly dialogue, all participants must be equally recognized as full members of the body of Christ. They must be free to follow their own convictions under the lordship of Christ. Those who cannot in good conscience fellowship with same-sex oriented individuals living in mutual covenantal relationships should not be required to do so. Vice-versa, those who cannot in good conscience exclude such individuals from church fellowship should not need to go against their conscience. As Gerald Biesecker-Mast has observed, it is precisely this dialogue of grace under the aegis of the Holy Spirit that constitutes us as a "church" seeking to find agreement.[4] These essays plead for this kind of dialogue.

Notes

1. See Michael A. King, chapter 7 in this book, as well as *Fractured Dance: Gadamer and the Quest for Understanding amid Conflict* (Telford, Pa.: Pandora Press U.S., 2001), for a more detailed account of these events.

2. See John Boswell, *Same-Sex Unions In Premodern Europe* (New York: Villard Books, 1994). Boswell holds that the church in medieval Europe did not take a unified position against such relationships until the fourteenth century. Other scholars would disagree with that interpretation of the data. In any case, Boswell's data documents the fact that cultural differences existed and the church operated within these differences.

3. Dialogue, as Gerald Biesecker-Mast has put it, "is not merely a means to an ethical end, . . . [In this case] for example, [dialogue is not] an intermediate process on the way to proscribing or legitimating certain sexual practices. Instead, genuinely open-ended and mutually persuasive dialogue is precisely the condition of possibility for any appropriate or credible sexual ethic for Christian communities." See Biesecker-Mast, "Mennonite Public Discourse and the Conflicts Over Homosexuality," *Mennonite Quarterly Review* 72 , no. 2 (April 1998): 297.

4. Biesecker-Mast, 297.

PART ONE

The Need
for Continuing
Dialogue

Chapter 1

The "H" Words:
Hermeneutics and
Homosexual

C. Norman Kraus

I'M OLD ENOUGH TO REMEMBER WHEN GAY MEANT lighthearted. And of course I didn't know the word *lesbian*. Indeed I remember rather clearly when I first distinguished between the meaning of lesbian and thespian. "Homo," "hetero," and "hots" were simply not part of my generation's everyday vocabulary. Sexual passions were "temptations" not "fantasies," and of course such temptations were triggered by the bodies of the opposite sex. Anyone who did not feel such passions was simply "queer." I'm admitting this sixty years later. At the time to be socially and religiously correct we did not admit our sexual feelings for either the opposite or same gender. One might say that both homoerotic and heteroerotic feelings were kept "in the closet"!

Sex functioned as a four-letter word. Sending information about condoms and birth control through the United States mail was illegal. Intercourse—oh yes, we did have some other words for that, but my dad threatened to wash my mouth out with soap if he ever heard me use them! The one acceptable rationale for sexual intercourse was procreation. Of course it was also quite enjoyable—that could not be helped, as Saint Augustine admitted already in the fifth century. But the idea that sexual activity could enrich loving relationships was never mentioned, if in fact it was believed. Sex education, given in segregated gender groups, warned about the psy-

25

chological dangers of masturbation, and prescribed cold showers for boys as the remedy for sexual arousal.

I didn't know the word *hermeneutics* either. I learned that only when I went to seminary. The Greek words *hermeneuo* and *exegesis* mean to explain or interpret, and they are transliterated and used to refer to biblical interpretation. Hermeneutics, then, is the discipline of biblical interpretation. The task of interpretation, as we were taught, was to correctly translate the original text and give it a common-sense reading. The basic questions we were taught to ask of the text were "What do the words mean?" or "What does the text say?" Giving a critical explanation of the words of the text was exegesis. Volumes of excellent biblical word studies lined the library shelves, and those of us studying the New Testament in its original language used our Greek-English lexicons liberally.

There was an argument among some of our teachers about which of the above questions was the right one to use in addressing the text. Does it simply mean what it "says"—does the meaning lie in the literal grammatical interpretation of the text? Or do we have to go beyond the literal words to determine what they "mean"? After we know the grammatical-historical meaning of the words, do we still have to determine whether they should be interpreted literally or spiritually, with spiritually in this case meant symbolically as in the case of the millennium? I remember the textual advice of one of my teachers who said, "If the literal meaning of the text makes sense, it is nonsense to give it any other sense."

If the literal meaning of Scripture was clear, then the only things left to do were to believe and behave it. We confidently quoted the line, "If the text says it, I believe it; and that settles it." A literal interpretation implied the direct transfer of the command or theological opinion from the cultural setting of the Bible to our present modern culture. We understood hermeneutics, meaning interpretation, to be simply a matter of grammatical and historical meaning of words, and most of us considered these words "inerrant."

In most of our Mennonite and some strict Holiness circles the question of cultural adaptations, or "contextualization," simply was not at issue. If the Levitical code said that a woman should not "wear that which pertaineth to a man," that meant no slacks. If the New Testament epistles said that followers of Christ should not wear gold, then gold glasses frames as well as rings and other decorations were to be rejected. If Jesus said not to swear oaths, then one must "affirm" instead. If he said no divorce, then one might argue over the "exception phrase" in Matthew, but even that seemed to be evading the clearer direct command stated in Mark. If the Gospels said or inferred that evil spirits cause sickness, modern distinctions between healing and exorcism were projected back into their pages (a contextualization in reverse), but there was little or no room for exploring how this ancient view of disease and its causes translates into modern medical terms.

This straight-line application of the doctrines and commands of Scripture covered a wide range of subjects, including gender specific issues like the role of men and women in marriage, the place of women in public worship, matters of cultural separation such as dress patterns and attendance at worldly amusements, worship patterns (a cappella singing), sacramental ordinances to be observed in the church, sexual morals, and social mores. When the biblical text spoke on any such issues, disobedience became "sin," and variations in interpretation became serious business! Of course this did not settle all the differences in understanding the meaning, but it did furnish an agreed-upon hermeneutical base.

Bishop George R. Brunk, my home pastor and bishop, used to say that the trouble with Fundamentalism was that it was not fundamental enough. By that he meant that fundamentalists were selective in what biblical admonitions they applied to modern North American society. He referred to the more extensive list of literal biblical commandments which Mennonites attempted to obey as "the all things." Fundamentalists did not keep the "all things." Of course, Mennonite applications of biblical teachings to the early twentieth-century American culture were selective too, but they followed a different interpretative formula.

The differences in biblical applications among Mennonite groups generally involved obvious differences and even contradictions in the biblical texts, and/or different cultural definitions and backgrounds. An example of the first is the conflicting texts about allowing women to speak in the public church services and of the second whether a wedding band is ornamentation, or wine is allowable in moderation, or how much and what kind of sexual expression is morally allowable before the marriage ceremony. Although an earlier generation of Mennonite scholars did some of what we now refer to as contextualization, they were not consciously aware of the process. They simply taught what they understood the Bible to say. They defined marriage, dress codes, fornication, oaths, and more in terms of the inherited nineteenth-century

American culture. In effect, the Bible read in King James English became a nineteenth-century American book.

Then came the 1960s and 1970s. Mennonite communities had largely escaped the cultural-moral revolution of the 1920s but were hit squarely by the whirlwind of the 1970s. Their cultural-moral definitions of an earlier era underwent rapid and radical revision, and their boundaries of social nonconformity proved to be lines in the sand.

In the 1921 Mennonite Church confession entitled *Christian Fundamentals,* under the article "Of Separation," the church is admonished to "keep itself aloof from all movements which seek the reformation of society independent of the merits of the death of Christ and the experience of the new birth." Today such periodicals as *The Mennonite* and *The Mennonite Weekly Review* as well as promotional literature explain the organizational strategy for the new "transformed" denomination (referring to the merger-in-progress of two previously separate Mennonite denominational bodies). In such materials, cooperation with people of other faiths and even with those who profess no religion is advocated as a goal for peace and service ministries. Attitudes toward divorce have radically altered. Concepts of sexuality and what is morally and spiritually acceptable in sexual practice between married partners have been vastly revised. Even what is tacitly permitted in premarital relationships has changed.

The Hermeneutical Lag

All of this, of course, is obvious and well known. What I want to point out is that as we shifted our cultural, religious, and moral definitions and practices, we did it without benefit of a careful review and revision of our assumptions and methods of biblical interpretation. In other words, we did not pay adequate attention to hermeneutics. Our scholars and teachers cautiously discussed the issues in our seminaries and colleges, but most of our attention was focused on clarifying the nature and meaning of the text in its historical context. Historical in this case indicated a literal rather than allegorical or symbolical meaning. Cultural factors surrounding the original text played little part in understanding the significance of ancient practice, and underwhelming attention was given to updating the concepts and language of our belief and practice for life in today's world.

For fear of raising controversy we did not adequately explain the reasoning behind the shifts which were being made in our understanding and practice. What had changed, how, and why? Was it the Bible? In the *1963 Mennonite Confession of Faith* the word *inerrant* is omitted from the description of the biblical message. Did the Holy Spirit no longer speak through Scripture with a consistent unchangeable message? Or was it the modern cultural situation that was changing? Certainly North American culture was changing, but were we also becoming more assimilated to it and acquiescing to the interpretations of "worldly" churches? Had the church leaders and scholars of an earlier generation been wrong? Were we modifying our moral principles and reinterpreting our biblical interpretation accordingly? Or were we simply adjusting biblical principles to speak to a changing culture? The spurt of assimilation was disquieting!

Why should shifting cultural patterns change our understanding of so many explicit biblical doctrines and regulations? Why, for example, when Paul so specifically and explicitly tells the Christian women of Corinth to keep their hair long and wear a covering on their heads during public worship (1 Cor.11:1-17), was it no longer necessary to do so? Why was it now okay for preachers to wear flashy neckties and gold rings even in the pulpit?

Why did life insurance no longer indicate "lack of filial trust in the heavenly Father" as the 1921 *Christian Fundamentals* stated? Why was the communion service, which had been open only to "those who share a like precious faith," now open without further examination to anyone who made some profession of belief and had been baptized? Why was the moderate social use of alcoholic drinks now in some (not all) church circles a matter of personal discretion? Why did movies and other worldly entertainment become not only accepted but advertised in our media and referred to in our pulpits? And what about the rather radical shift from admonition and discipline according to biblical prescriptions to "pastoral counseling" and toleration of dissent?

I am not raising objections to all these changes, although I doubt they all represent spiritual improvement. What I want to call attention to is the lack of a thoughtful revision of our hermeneutical assumptions and methods that could have given us a rationale and guidance in making the changes. Emphasis upon following Jesus' way of life implies a cultural and ethical as well as a theological mandate. *Following* Jesus requires a process of conscious cultural adaptation of biblical practices and norms as they are applied from age to age and place to place. Thus for those in the Anabaptist tradition of *Nachfolge Christi* (following Christ) this deficiency was and remains a serious handicap.

This is where the second "H" comes in. It is my contention that we simply have not developed an adequate, consistent hermeneutic to deal with the changes we confront in our rapidly changing world. This omission has seriously confused our denominational discussion of issues like interracial marriage in the 1950s, divorce in the 1970s, women's role in the home and church in the 1970s and 1980s, peace and nonresistance in the 1980s and 1990s, and currently the issue of homosexuality. It seems a long time ago now, but in the 1950s we actually had to make the biblical case for racial equality and especially for "mixed marriages!"

Although we could focus on any of a number of cultural-moral issues around which to organize the hermeneutical questions, today the most troubling issue in both the church and society is homosexuality. Further, the nature of the biblical references to and prohibitions of same-gender sexual activity raises distinct problems of interpretation and application. Most of those advocating a given position appeal to and want to be faithful to the Bible, but we have not agreed on the rules of interpretation and contextual application. Biblical scholars are not in agreement regarding what kinds of sexual activities are being addressed in Scripture touching on homosexuality. Neither has our culture, with its emphasis on scientific inquiry, come to a final consensus on the nature and moral status of homosexuality in contemporary society. While the second factor complicates the problem, this essay is focused on the issues involved in understanding and applying the biblical data on the subject.

What assumptions and methods can guide us in interpreting the message of the Bible for our day? If we no longer need to take literally the explicit instructions and reasoning of Paul in 1 Corinthians 11, why do we need to do so for the explicit instructions in the Holiness Code of Leviticus 18 concerning homosexual acts?

If we do not need to literally apply Jesus' teaching against violence and killing to every act of homicide, why must we do so with Paul's harsh criticism of homosexual practice among the pagans as he understood it (Rom.1:26-27)? What are the guidelines for deciding whether the condemnation of "male prostitutes [and] sodomites" in first-century Corinth (1 Cor. 6:10) applies to all homosexual relationships in twenty-first century America?

What, for example, is the reasoning behind the statement in the controversial "Welcoming Open Letter," published February 17, 2000 in *Mennonite Weekly Review*, that biblical texts against same-sex relationships "do not address homosexuality as we understand it today"? *What hermeneutical factors need to be taken into account in answering these questions?*

Hermeneutics and Contextualization

Interpretation of Scripture in the church requires more than a simple study of grammatical syntax and the original meaning of words. To know what the Bible meant in its literary and historical context is not sufficient. For those who believe that the Bible is an authoritative guide for life in the church today, hermeneutics must include the cross-cultural transfer of meaning from the original context to the present. What in the two different cultures is comparable? This necessitates a careful critique both of biblical cultures and our own.

Such a critique must begin by recognizing that the Bible was written in antiquity for the ancient cultures to which it was originally addressed. It is an old and historical book, not a modern and philosophical-theological one. Its message from and about God is given in the literary form of a story reporting ancient Israel's interaction with Yahweh. It is not a philosophical essay presenting theological and ethical concepts based on rational inquiry. It is a collection of documents of very different kinds written in three languages, collected, edited, and copied over a period of more than 1500 years. It is both inspired and inspiring yet nevertheless comes to us in the human guise of an ancient culture. This has significant hermeneutical implications for the transfer of its message to our modern and postmodern societies.[1]

The writers of the Bible presuppose the ancient pre-rational world view which some scholars refer to as "mythical" and "sacral"; on the surface, at least, these views become part of the message. Certainly the writers do not accept in full the world views of the nations around them, which they often challenge or aim to transform. They do, however, express themselves in the genres of their day, just as they might express themselves in North American imagery and vernacular if writing in our day.

To give just a few examples: The Bible's sexual ethics are predicated on a physiology of procreation which scientific examination has shown not entirely to fit contemporary understandings.[2] The writers' presuppositions about human relations and patriarchal family systems cast the husband-father in a dominant role and allowed for a double ethic we have obviously modified. Their notions of the causes of disease influence the "biblical" view of moral consequences—and are sometimes called into question even in the Bible itself, as when Jesus in John 9 does not blame blindness on sin. Their conception of God as immediately involved in the natural and historical processes, that is, fighting against Israel's enemies or causing drought, assumes a theocratic religious rationale and sanction for Israel's social and moral systems.

Thus all of Israel's legal and social codes of conduct have a religious basis, and their violation is defined as sin. Our concepts of secular law and rational ethics are virtually unknown. Biblical writers operate in a sacred, rather than profane or secular, cultural context. They assume that Israel's ethical and legal traditions are based on the direct commandments of God. Actions are wrong because they dishonor and are detestable to God. They are shameful and make the offender unclean in God's sight. No sharp distinction is made between the ethical and the religious. God's covenant with Israel is the final rationale for all behavioral rules, and God's punitive authority is their basic sanction. Punishment for wrongdoing is experienced as shame and defilement, and the social penalty is isolation, banishment, or death which is the ultimate expulsion.

By contrast, in today's secular culture we make a distinction between the secular and sacred, between religious, moral, cultural, and legal codes and the sanctions which enforce them. Thus today we must determine to which category the various biblical injunctions belong and what this tells us about how we should implement them.

Further, the Bible uses ancient literary forms to present its message. It is composed of stories, historical records, legal codes, holiness or "purity," codes (sacred taboos), proverbs, prophetic oracles, poetry, recorded visions, parables, myths (meaning, in this case, not untrue story but one whose meaning is even larger than life), the Gospels, apocalypses, and personal correspondence to churches in the New Testament. These by no means can all be interpreted and applied to our twenty-first century in the same way. The literary genre, as well as cultural definitions and assumptions of any given passage, must be taken into account when interpreted for application to today's issues.

The historical character of God's self-disclosure opens the Bible to changing interpretations and applications even within the Bible itself. Its own pages reflect the changes in the cultural characteristics and presuppositions over the thousand years it was in writing. Prophetic interpretations modify the more legal characteristics of the Mosaic code. For example, the prophets even challenged the whole sacrificial system. Rabbinical Judaism adapted and applied its requirements to the changing situation of the Jewish Dispersion throughout the Roman Empire. The "New" Testament does not hesitate to interpret and use the Hebrew Scriptures in keeping with its own further understandings in Christ. For a Christian hermeneutic, of course, the changes in interpretation implicit in the historical revelation in Jesus are crucial.[3]

This process of contextualization must continue into the present, since the New Testament has more in common with the culture of its preceding Hebrew society than it has with our modern Western culture. Indeed, Jesus' word in John 14:26 indicates that he is leaving a dynamic rather than a literal legal guide for his followers as they move into the future. Through the centuries the Holy Spirit has continued to enlarge and modify our understanding and application of Scripture's message (see 2 Cor. 3:6).

The task of hermeneutics involves a critique of our contemporary culture and discernment of what corresponds to and expresses the essential meaning of the ancient text. This involves us in both a critical historical and a theological process. Transfer of authentic meaning across cultures, whether historically or geographically modified, is not merely a matter of finding corresponding words. As any good translator will tell you, it is a far more subtle and complicated process of understanding both the cultures from which and to which the message is being transmitted.

The experience of the Mennonite Church of Hokkaido, Japan, when it confronted the 1 Corinthian 11 passage about women having their heads covered, provides a good example of this process. The Japanese Christians pointed out to the missionaries that the custom had no precedent or symbolism in their culture. This led to an intensive and extended study that took months and the help of a sensitive biblical scholar before they decided how authentically to obey it.

In contrast, the response of the church in India was quite different. In the Indian culture it was the custom for women to cover their heads with the shawl end of their saris when they appeared in public. Today many Indian women still cover their heads during the church services.

Factors in Contextualizing
Sexual Morals and Practice of the Bible

In this section it is not my intention to argue for or against receiving into church membership those who engage in homosexual practice. Approval or disapproval is the issue yet to be resolved. The question here is rather *how to arrive at a biblical assessment* of the moral and spiritual implications of homosexual orientation and its physical-social expressions in Western society. More particularly, what is the "mind of Christ" on this issue as disclosed in Scripture?

Our concern then should be to achieve a more adequate understanding of the cultural settings which must be taken into account when we search for an authentic biblical resolution of such issues. What in the ancient social milieu parallels or matches the issues involved in the present homosexuality debate? Obviously the writers of Scripture disapprove of homosexual practice as they observe it in the pagan world. What kind of homosexual practices do they have in mind, and for what reasons do they oppose them? What kind of innovations in sexual practice do they allow and justify? These questions must involve us in a more general look at sexual morals and social codes, particularly as they relate to religious regulations.

Let me gently remind those who want to settle such issues with appeal to a few inerrant biblical texts that it was precisely a process of rational, moral critique that led the church to make the traditional distinctions between "ceremonial" and "moral" regulations in the Hebrew Torah. Accordingly many ritual taboos having to do with sexual/genital activity found in Israel's covenant law have been dropped. For example, nocturnal emission of semen made a man unclean, as did a woman's menstrual period. The New Testament itself encourages us to make spiritual and moral discernment rather than simply to apply traditional codes literally and legally (2 Cor. 3:6). The Jerusalem Council (Acts 15) had to make judgments between such items of the Holiness Code as eating meat offered to idols, eating non-kosher meat, fornication, circumcision, and more as the Christian message crossed cultural boundaries.

Acceptable gender roles and sexual practices reflect the varying cultural definitions of human societies and have changed greatly over the centuries. Polygamy, divorce, and men visiting prostitutes

were at least tacitly approved in ancient Israel. Of course, in a patriarchal society rules were different for women. They could not initiate divorce, be prostitutes, or have more than one husband! Such
actions would disgrace the men to whom they belonged, namely,
husbands and fathers. Jesus and Paul leveled the playing field for
men and women (Gal. 3:25-28). While they did not consciously
change the gender roles, they placed the two genders on an equal
social and spiritual level. In the following centuries while the church
officially continued to hold these values, at the same time it continued to sanction a double standard for sexual morality.

While incest was consistently forbidden, its definition varied.
Bestiality—using animals to satisfy sexual arousal—was strictly forbidden to both males and females. Same-gender sexual liasons
among males were associated with pagan customs (pederasty), religious rites (cultic prostitution), and often with violence (rape of
slaves, foreigners, and defeated enemies) and was consistently forbidden in Hebrew-Jewish culture. For a male to be cast into a passive "female" role in a sexual liaison was shameful and humiliating. Homosexual rape was a violent way of humiliating a conquered
enemy and showing dominance and power. The master's use of female slaves for sexual purposes was carefully regulated, and such
use of male slaves was forbidden.

Interestingly, no mention of lesbianism is made except in Romans 1:26. Apparently it did not occur to ancient males that women
might enjoy homoerotic relations, and if they did, it was little threat
to their masculinity and blood lines. Fathers "gave" their daughters
to be married, and husbands determined if children were born. In a
strictly patriarchial society women's sexual orientation was simply
irrelevant to their use as sexual objects by males.

Masturbation is only incidentally mentioned, in disapproval of
"spilling of seed" (Gen. 38:8-9). Onan was put to death not for mas-
turbating as such, but because he defied Yaweh's command by self-
ishly refusing to impregnate his dead brother's wife. The account
reflects a view of sexual relationships quite different from ours. We
would consider it morally inappropriate for an Onan to have sexual
relations with the wife of his deceased brother!

Modifying the Sexual Rules

Even on a superficial reading one can see that these sexual regulations reflect a view of sexual relationships quite different from

our own. Further, the moral-religious rationale for these regulations differs markedly from the reasoning the Christian church uses today. Not only have there been changes between old and modern worlds, but ancient Israel also made significant changes in its interpretation of the Mosaic law during its own history. Indeed, the prophets' role was to interpret and apply the word of the Spirit to the developing situations. And after the time of the prophets, the rabbis worked out a detailed casuistry for applying the regulations to the new cultural situations.

The changes become most obvious in the ministry of Jesus and the apostles following him. Jesus' messianic mission, to inaugurate the rule of God, changed the focus from Israel to the world. This change of focus in itself transformed the rationale for regulating human relationships. As Paul put it so forcefully in Galatians 3:28, "There is no longer Jew or Greek . . . slave or free . . . male or female; for all of you are one in Christ Jesus." (Compare Col. 3:11, where this new human reality is spoken of as a renewal of the image of God.) With this new focus, a new standard of agapeic (loving) respect as the basis for *shalom* (peace and wholeness) replaced the Mosaic regulations that defined shalom in Israel. As Paul put it, Christ is our peace (Eph. 2:14).

This new standard is most clearly demonstrated in the early church's revised attitudes toward and practice of Israel's holiness taboos.[4] This is hermeneutically significant because the proscription of homosexual acts is a part of the Holiness Code (Lev. 18:22; 20:13). Peter's struggle with the taboos against intimate association with "unclean" Gentiles epitomizes this shift from legal regulations to agapeic respect. The religious-cultural taboo against intimate association with Gentiles, whom Jews referred to as "dogs," incited the same kind of emotional response in first century Judaism as our taboo on homosexual intimacy.

The fact that Peter's story is told three times in the Acts, and that later mention is made of the difficulties of Jewish believers at Antioch, indicates how extreme their feelings about this issue were. Indeed, the controversy split the first generation movement between Gentile and Jewish churches.

Closely related to the holiness taboos was the practice of circumcision, the sexual symbol of the Jews' religious identity and separation from pagans. Sexual and religious identity were intimately interwoven. Circumcision is a religious requirement, not strictly a moral one, and the strong convictions associated with it had been bred into the Jewish psyche through generations of conditioning. Consorting with Gentiles and not requiring circumcision were radical innovations. To break down these lines of purity and separation from pagan culture seemed a rejection of Yahweh's covenant!

Immediately important for our present reflection is the question of the apostolic rationale for such innovations. Their rationale is not explicitly developed, but the implicit indicators are fairly clear. Perhaps most significant is the word from Jesus that "the Sabbath was made for humankind, not humankind for the Sabbath." The Sabbath law was the most sacred Jewish institution, far more important than the taboos of the Holiness Code, yet Jesus insisted that its regulation must consider the human situation and need.

A second indication that Jesus and his followers established a new rationale can be seen in the changes in patterns of male and female relationships which underlay the content of sexual regulations. In general, physical conditions related to sexual functions such as menstrual flow in women, or ejaculation and genital deformity in men, ceased to have religious and hence moral significance. Jesus refused to be bound by the purity taboos of the Holiness Code.

Jesus demonstrated clear disregard for rabbinic tradition based on biblical texts with regard to association with women, even those who were social outcasts because of divorce or prostitution. His relaxation of the harsh penalty for people caught in fornication and adultery is a third factor pointing toward a basic shift in attitude regarding sexual violations. This indicates not indulgence of unfaithfulness but an altered understanding of its nature and resolution. In short, Jesus' injunction that we are to love one another as he has loved us sets a new perspective, approach, and standard for dealing with areas of moral, religious, or cultural tensions.

None of these factors give us an immediate answer to our questions about modern sexual practices, but they do give us a spiritual-moral perspective and context within which to make adaptations to changing cultural norms and practices. With this in mind, let us look at our modern Western cultural scene to see how things are both different and the same.

Contemporary Social-Ethical Context

The current Western cultural climate is quite different from that of the ancient Middle Eastern societies. In the following paragraphs I list several comprehensive changes in our culture and contemporary world situation that have greatly affected our perspective on sexual relations and the way in which we interpret and apply biblical injunctions.

First, democracy and respect for the privacy and rights of individuals to follow their own lifestyles have greatly reduced what is accepted as the legitimate scope of social-political control of sexual practice. Private sexual activity among "consenting adults" is considered an individual, "personal" matter. The accepted limits of public regulation are much narrower now than even a century ago. Supreme Court decisions have raised privacy to a constitutional right, and the legal regulation of sexual morals by the state is strictly limited to what may have criminal public consequences. The churches are free to advocate a moral standard, but they have little authority beyond an appeal to religious sanctions. In the religious sphere one can cite as an example the Roman Catholic Church's inability and reticence to enforce its birth control regulations.

Evangelical Protestant churches have also championed the right to privacy in sexual morals, and what was once strictly prohibited is now accepted as blameless if not virtuous. Procreation is no longer the sole justification for erotic stimulation. The standards for heterosexual stimulation no longer include severe condemnation of practices like oral sex and mutual masturbation. I mention these because traditionally they were considered "dirty sex"—an abomination—and entirely inappropriate for Christians. Now any form of heterosexual erotic stimulation that is mutually enjoyable and enriching is sanctioned and even praised. The blessing of such sexual techniques illustrates how radically the moral and religious climate has changed and puts the question of homoerotic stimulation in a new context.

Second, overpopulation has made controlling the world population far more crucial than replenishing the earth with human habitation. In the ancient world, and even during the medieval and early modern period of European history, the threat of population depletion was serious enough to affect the regulation of sexual practices. Childbearing was the fundamental justification for sexual gratification. The basic purpose of marriage which defined and legitimated it was to produce progeny. If the couple could not have children, the binding quality of the marriage was in jeopardy. There were times when the Church even discouraged men and women from joining the monasteries because of the need to repopulate Europe after wars or plagues.

Today with the opposite problem of overpopulation we have a different view of the moral significance of birth control and sexual practices which might reduce the birth rates. Today, without recrimination, couples may choose not to have children. Sexual companionship, not childbearing, defines marriage. Such changes do not necessarily argue for or against homoerotic sexual companionship, but they do radically change the cultural environment in which the question is to be considered!

Third, equality of men and women before the law and respect for women as fully human beings in God's image have changed moral attitudes toward polygamy, divorce, and the female sexual role in coitus, as well as woman's role in the family. Further, scientific understanding of the procreation process makes her a co-creator and not simply the passive carrier of the male's "seed" which reproduces children. Women, as well as men, have the right freely to choose their sexual partners. Again, although not an argument for lesbianism, this change radically affects the cultural parameters for social-moral assessment.

Fourth, through our modern scientific techniques we have discovered what we now call a "homosexual orientation." The word *homosexuality*, denoting a physical-psychological predisposition, was first used in the 1890s. Since then scientists have explored the nature of this phenomenon, not only in humans but other animals as well. While we do not yet fully understand the roots and causes of such an orientation (indeed, we do not know the root causes of heterosexual orientation either), we do know it is not merely a perversely chosen lifestyle. Evidently homosexual orientation has both genetic and environmental—"natural"—causes, and commonly manifests itself quite early in life, before blame can be attached for a moral choice.

Finally, in contrast to traditional "pre-rational" cultures, our modern rational cultures make an ethical distinction between religious and moral codes. When we make ethical judgments today, we take into account the actor's knowledge, intention, physical and mental ability, social consequences, and more. We do not decide what is moral simply by looking for a literal command from God as understood in the religious tradition. We may use religious convictions and beliefs about God as motivations and sanctions for moral action, but we do not equate morality with religious regulations. This distinction is generally agreed upon in the definition of some commandments as ceremonial or cultic rather than moral. Thus in the modern context moral questions involved in homosexuality and its expression cannot be satisfactorily resolved simply by appeal to the religious tradition.

This has particular significance for the hermeneutical process. In the theocratic culture of the Bible the covenant commands covered both religious and moral categories without making obvious distinctions. The rationale giving both categories their force is that they are the words of Yahweh; that is, the sanction is religious not moral. When behaviors are proscribed as "an abomination" or "unclean" the sanction is religious and ritualistic, not necessarily moral. For example both sexual intercourse during a woman's menstrual period and the moral prohibition against rape are given as religious taboos. Both are detestable in God's sight. Thus arguing that "the Bible says" cannot adequately establish the ethical character of a behavior, because from today's perspective biblical norms cover both commands we still see as valid and also those we no longer observe.

Today in the church as well as in society at large we discriminate between moral and religious aspects of an activity for ethical and legal purposes. We define moral and immoral activity in terms of its consequences. That which creates a virtuous personal character and contributes to social well being is considered to be moral (ethical). Some of the commandments of God like "You shall not steal or commit adultery" are both religious and moral. Others such as the Sabbath law, and many of the Levitical taboos are, according to common contemporary understanding, primarily religious in character.

Obviously in religious traditions these categories overlap, since religious disciplines are often understood to contribute to moral character. And traditionally in Christendom, where church and state overlapped, sharp lines were not drawn for the purposes of social legislation. However, we must ask today how purity taboos—religious prohibitions—translate into our modern ethical categories.

Since the Bible explicitly classifies homosexual activity as an "abomination," our interpretation and application of the Levitical rule prohibiting it involves this kind of hermeneutical discrimination. We must ask what if any moral grounds, other than the religious taboo, undergirded the original prohibition and penalty for homosexual acts. This involves a theological-ethical evaluation of the ancient rationale as well as the taboo itself. Do we have a touchstone for such an evaluation beyond the immediate textual taboo? I am convinced that in the life and message of Jesus Christ we do.

Today, even those who strongly oppose same-gender sexual activity object to the death penalty for such activity. This already indicates that we are bringing a different standard of evaluation to the cultural transfer of the text. We are making modern theological and ethical judgments beyond what the Bible says explicitly. This is a necessary hermeneutical step in making decisions about issues like this one. We need to be aware and own the process under the guidance of the Holy Spirit of Jesus.

A Biblical Rationale for Contextualizing Sexual Regulations

Thus far I have tried to show that the hermeneutical process must involve us in cultural critique of both the ancient culture underlying biblical injunctions and our modern culture. We can no longer simply do word studies and quote Bible verses as a rationale for our ethical decisions. To be truly biblical we must go beyond the literal commands and doctrines as understood and applied in the ancient cultures. We must attempt to understand their intent and ask how they functioned in their cultural context. Then, after we have understood our contemporary cultures, we must ask how that intent can be authentically expressed in our situations.

To give one example, it is not enough to quote "an eye for an eye and a tooth for a tooth" as the biblical rationale for retaliatory justice. We must see the command in its ancient context, where it limits the blood feud as the way to achieve justice. Further, as Christians we must press the point a step further in the spirit of Jesus and Paul to insist that we are to return good for evil.

In regard to sexual practice we do well to remind ourselves that the Bible itself has influenced many of the changes in our ethical guidelines for today. It is the Bible, especially the example and teachings of Jesus, that has raised the status of women, giving them personal worth equal to that of men; that has insisted on mutual respect and caring for the sexual welfare of each other; that has accented the personal worth of each individual; that has insisted on monogamy as the standard for sexual companionship; that has made the welfare of children a priority; that has eradicated the taboos of "clean and unclean"; that has erased the demands for literal legalistic obedience to the traditional religious commands. The new attitudes, issues, and questions related to sexuality and sexual practices do not stem only from immoral passions and the increased license of our modern secular society but stem also from profound changes Jesus and his followers introduced.

A biblical rationale should begin with the theological understanding of humans as creatures in God's image before turning to specific regulations. Modern individualism interprets this image in Stoic terms as a spark of reason in each individual that gives unique worth to each person. While this is not entirely wrong, the biblical concept is a corporate social one. Humanity, in its social solidarity under God, is "in God's image." The Genesis text reads "male and female God created them in the image of God." This can be read to mean that each one separately is in God's image, but it also strongly suggests that the image is expressed in the human social relationship. Some would go further, believing the text infers that it is specifically in the male-female sexual bonding that the image is expressed, but this is not clearly indicated.[5]

In any case the Bible does not equate the identity and worth of individual human beings with their sexual identity and orientation. Unfortunately, the contemporary tendency to equate human and sexual identity has greatly exacerbated the issues surrounding the discussion of sexuality. Humans, "male and female," are in God's image. One's sexual orientation does not alter that, although the exercise of sexual desires does reflect on that image.

Ephesians 4:24 speaks of God's likeness or image in moral terms as "true righteousness and holiness." The image is disclosed in our personal social relationships (righteousness) and in our relationship to God (holiness). Such an ethical-spiritual conception of the image, and not a physical-sexual one should be the controlling image for a biblical rationale. The questions then are, What defines "true righteousness and holiness" in the sphere of sexual relationships? What is the measure of a "truly devout and pious life pleasing to God"? (That is what the word translated "holiness" means.) The contrast here is to the "old self, corrupt and deluded by its lusts" and abandoned to licentiousness and indulgence in every kind of impurity (vv. 23, 19). In contrast to such a profligate, self-centered life, Paul urges a genuinely devout life shaped by the example of Jesus (vv. 20-21). What then does this suggest for our own patterns of sexual expression?

Within this framework let me suggest five conditions all sexual activity should meet to qualify for "true holiness."

1. *Take place within monogamous faithfulness.* Sexual activity should be engaged in within the boundaries of covenanted relation-

ship with monogamous faithfulness. Unfaithfulness and irresponsible sexual practices contradict the image of God and degrade our true humanity under God.

2. *Contribute to God's purposes.* Sexual activity should strengthen commitment to God and Christ's rule of peace and justice (the kingdom of God). Both Jesus and Paul put the kingdom ahead of sexual companionship and family.

3. *Deepen spirituality.* Sexual activity should enhance social-spiritual development, deepen personal relationships, and give joy to both partners. Put in biblical terms, it should enhance the expression of God's image.

4. *Strengthen family and community life.* Sexual activity should build family relationships and strengthen the social community.

5. *Heighten love of others.* Sexual activity should strengthen respect and compassion for fellow human beings. God's covenant with humanity is a covenant of "life and peace" (Mal. 2:5). That which destroys human life and community breaks Jesus' command to love one another as he loved us and is sin.

In both biblical-theological and scientific studies, questions about homosexuality remain unsolved. Many of these cannot be immediately answered. We need time and sober judgment to make the kinds of linguistic and cultural evaluations called for. Equally devout, committed, and competent students of the Bible differ on how it should be understood and applied. At the least, faithfulness to Christ requires that we take the time and effort to come to consensus on our hermeneutic principles before we divide the church over an issue like homosexuality. We should remember that some theological and ethical issues took centuries to be resolved, including the question of which writings should be included in the Bible we quote so earnestly to prove our case.

Notes

1. This plea for what Paul Hiebert has called "critical contextualization" as part of the interpretative process is simply dismissed as "liberal" by some who equate the contemporary English text with "the Word of God for today." For example, one well meaning but uninformed pastor was heard to exclaim, " I don't care what the original words meant to their original readers. The Bible [as we have it today] is the Word of God for today!" Or again, Gerald Martin in a letter to the *MWR* Readers Say column equates the "absolute truth of Scripture" with his literal reading of the biblical texts on the subject of homosexual relationships and suggests that further dialogue,

which presumably includes biblical interpretation, is " a direct challenge to the Bible's truthfulness" (June 22, 2000, 4).

2. For example, in the Wisdom of Solomon 7:1-2 the conception process is described as follows: "In the womb of a mother I was molded into flesh, within the period of ten months, compacted with blood, from the seed of a man and the pleasure of marriage." The contribution of the ovum was unknown.

3. On the issues surrounding sexuality, an appeal to what John Howard Yoder called the "concreteness of Jesus" in his *Politics of Jesus* still leaves us with questions about how his example is to be followed. Jesus lived a celibate life. His relationships with both males and females are well within the bounds of first century Jewish patriarchy although he demonstrates a clear disregard for rabbinic squeamishness about association with women other than their wives and about purity taboos in general (Mark 7:19). He strengthened the ideal of monogamous faithfulness in marriage as the original intent of God in creation. However, he did not make marriage and family a foundational value in the kingdom of God (Matt. 19:3-11). The subject of homoerotic or even homosocial relationships is never raised. Martti Nissinen concludes, "The only sources, the Gospels, do not provide material for far-ranging hypotheses." See *Homoeroticism in the Biblical World* (Philadelphia: Fortress, 1998), 118 ff.

4. The Holiness Code is only one of the law codes contained in the Pentateuch. Millard Lind observes that "the Pentateuch contains no fewer than three law codes: the Covenant code (Exod. 20:22–23:33), the Deuteronomic code (Deut. 12–26; 28), and the Holiness code (Lev. 17-26). . . ." See "Law in the Old Testament," in his collected essays, *Monotheism, Power, Justice* (Elkhart, Ind.: Institute of Mennonite Studies, 1990), 61 ff. The Holiness Code deals with ceremonial and religious taboos which defined Israel's relation to God.

5. The ancient church fathers who used Genesis 1:27 to locate the image of God in the male and female relationship did not relate it to the literal physical bonding. In Ambrose, for example, "The image of God resides in the human mind, which is made up of a 'higher' part (reason) and a 'lower' part (the senses and their appetites). These parts correspond to the typical attributes of male and female, respectively." Thus the true image exists in the proper relation of reason and desire. See John L. Thompson, "The Survival of Allegorical Argumentation in Vermigli's Old Testament Exegesis," in *Biblical Interpretation in the Era of the Reformation*, ed Richard A. Muller and John L. Thompson (Grand Rapids, Mich: Wm. B. Eerdmans, 1996), 258 ff. The very idea that heterosexual bonding is somehow related to the character of the image is itself based upon the modern concept of sexual orientation.

Chapter 2

Psychological Dynamics: Being Gay or Lesbian

Marcus G. Smucker

Introduction

This chapter is about homosexual orientation, often refered to as gay or lesbian. The material comes largely from my own reflections and encounters: listening to stories of persons who are gay or lesbian, reading autobiographical writings of gay persons, and my experience as a parent of a daughter who is lesbian.

Through exploring first my own reflections and then the psychological dynamics related to same-sex orientation, I hope to help heterosexual readers understand, in part, what it's like to be a person with a homosexual orientation in our society. And I hope to reflect briefly on how gays and their families can move toward self-acceptance despite the obstacles.

I feel particular tension in writing this chapter. On the one hand, it is necessary to begin to portray the struggle and trauma that can accompany being a sexual minority. On the other hand, amid some of the generalizations offered in this chapter it is important to recognize that each person's experience is unique. For some the journey is one of intense struggle, even ending in suicide; for others the journey is less difficult. Overall, it must be said that being gay or lesbian in this society can cause great pain for gay and lesbian persons and their families. This chapter describes some of that pain.

In this chapter I do not address biblical/ethical issues, church positions, the controversy over whether change of orientation is possible, or most such issues so intensely pursued in our social and church worlds today. My purpose is solely to contribute to better understanding of the experience of being a person of same-sex orientation so issues related to gay and lesbian people can be addressed more faithfully and effectively, with appropriate compassion and wisdom.

Personal Reflections

During her mid-twenties, Deb (whose story is being told in consultation with her) began to wonder about her sexual orientation. Her experience during high school and college had been confusing. She wanted to enjoy romantic relationships like her friends but often felt more attraction to girl friends than boy friends. In time she had to face the challenge of being a person with same-sex orientation. How should she see and feel about herself? How would others respond and react to her? How would family and church regard her? What would her life be like as a lesbian?

For three years she wrestled with herself as she sought to come to terms with this. With the help and support of a good friend, she was finally able to accept herself as a person with a same-sex orientation. Fortunately she was able to find other friends who were not only supportive but also valued and affirmed her as a person.

It took another year before she could bring herself to talk with us, her parents, about it. She knew we too would struggle with this. She did not want us to experience pain because of her. When she discussed this with us, she encouraged us to meet with a support group to help us with our struggle. We did indeed experience deep pain for a time. We too would now face the personal, societal, and church challenges that same-sex orientation brings in this culture.

Later we recognized earlier signs that Deb might grow up with a same-sex orientation. Already in her preschool years, her total disinterest in dolls was a frustration to her same-age girl friends. As a child she protested vigorously when expected to wear dresses to church or other such occasions. As a teenager she had many friends, male and female, but never dated. Like others, Deb's sexual orientation was not matter of a choice; it was something given to her. But unlike the experience of most people, her sexual orientation has presented her with some major challenges.

So what is it like to be a gay or lesbian person? What is the experience of being a parent of a gay or lesbian person? What are the challenges of having a same-sex orientation in our Western culture today?

As a pastor, professor, and pastoral counselor, I have had numerous sessions with persons struggling with their sexual identity and orientation. Through these conversations I have become increasingly aware of the intense personal, psychological, and spiritual struggle common to people with a same-sex orientation.

Nevertheless, I was unprepared for the impact on my own life when my daughter disclosed her sexual orientation to my wife and me. Suddenly homosexuality was interwoven into our family experience. Even though for some years I had wondered about my daughter's sexual orientation, the actual disclosure brought a swift, visceral pain that stayed with us for days. I was amazed and awed at the depth of our reaction and the nagging questions we encountered about ourselves as persons and parents and about our daughter. Facing these questions was hard and at times depressing, but it also brought our daughter and us to new levels of personal strength, care, and mutual regard for each other.

Later my awareness of this experience deepened when I met with twelve persons for several hours and listened to them describe their experiences of being gay or lesbian. In that conversation it became apparent that self-acceptance is a major challenge. Their comments included the following. When you are a person who is gay or lesbian, you tend to—

- see yourself as perverted, twisted, mentally unstable, inappropriate, inadequate, not deserving respect;
- fear disclosing yourself even to close friends;
- feel dread and fear in "coming out" to your family;
- expect to lose emotional support from family and friends;
- hesitate or avoid sharing your experience with others when you feel attraction to another person;
- have few, if any, positive images for living your life;
- be viewed by people as being sick or twisted;
- have your sexual orientation equated with sleazy sex;
- keep hearing messages from society that you are not acceptable, not okay, worthless, scum.

Obviously coming to accept oneself is a major struggle and an extraordinary task for those of same-sex orientation. Stanley Siegel writes, "The gay man's inevitable internalization of society's view of his homosexuality as either a defiantly spiteful preference or a pathological deviation adds to the individual's already percolating fear and hatred of himself."[1] Yet without self-acceptance, one cannot have a genuine sense of personal well being. Instead, one tends to loathe or dread oneself. Without self-acceptance one cannot have a healthy, nurturing relationship with God. Instead a person of homosexual orientation will tend to experience guilt and despair when seeking God.

The negative messages from society are generally so pervasive—in home, church, and public arena—that gay or lesbian persons must develop extraordinary inner strength before it is possible to believe in themselves again. This is an arduous journey. Some never arrive at this point. The journey is particularly difficult for teenagers and is the source of a significant percentage of teenage suicides.

The severity of this struggle for self-acceptance becomes apparent as we explore the impact of the five psychological dynamics described below.

Psychological Dynamics

Ultimately, gay and lesbian persons who persevere in their journey toward personal authenticity and self-esteem can find profound personal and social gains. Their struggles often endow them with extraordinary gifts and creativity. This chapter, however, does not focus on that aspect of gay or lesbian experience. Rather we explore the nature of a gay person's struggle to come to inner freedom and self-esteem—an outcome that is not certain because of the murky waters that must be navigated on the way to self-acceptance.

The five psychological dynamics described here are experienced primarily by persons who are gay or lesbian but also in a secondary way by their families, whether or not the families accept their son or daughter. The journey of a same-sex orientation is not only a personal one; it is also inescapably a journey taken by the whole family. For the sake of simplicity and clarity, however, we will focus on these dynamics as experienced by the gay or lesbian person in our culture.

Dislocation: personal, familial, societal, and spiritual

To be gay or lesbian in our culture is to experience dislocation at all levels of one's existence. Life seems "out of joint" with family, friends, society, the church, and God. Gay or lesbian persons must either hide the truth of their orientation from themselves and their family and friends or risk derision and rejection.

The dislocation begins with the dawning awareness, sometimes already in childhood, of being different. This was driven home to me when I visited my friend Ray, who in his fifties was dying of AIDS. Ray had been my friend for many years, and earlier I had been his pastor. Through all these years he had kept his secret, but on his deathbed he told me, "I always knew I was different, but I tried to fit in and do what was expected."

In that moment I knew, as his friend and former pastor, that I had participated in a conspiracy of denial that resulted in deep pain for Ray. If he had revealed his true self to me when I was a young pastor, I would not have known what to do. Yet his secret was kept at great cost. Holding his secret alone made his life and journey far more difficult and unwieldy. Ray was successful in his profession, a respected leader in the church, a husband and father of several children. Although he refrained from same-sex relationships until toward the end of his life, through all those earlier years he experienced an excruciating dislocation within himself and with the world about him.

This dislocation may begin already in childhood but becomes more severe in the adolescent experience. "Gay youths, Stanley Siegel writes,

> are not entitled to a typically unsophisticated adolescence, during which they can legitimately and openly date . . . during which they can stumble and fumble through the protocol of social gathering, grouping, pairing and coupling. Gay boys cannot learn or experience any of their true social adolescence while they are living in their parents' house; they are too busy hiding from themselves and then from the world of their families. They often are too preoccupied with the discomforts inherent in pretending to experience what they feel they ought to be experiencing.[2]

The sense of spiritual dislocation can also be profound. Mel White writes about his spiritual journey as an accomplished evangelical Christian writer and closeted gay person:

> Still afraid that my homosexuality was some kind of punishment from God, I couldn't possibly accept myself. Instead of falling back into the loving arms of my creator, instead of loving and trusting myself, I went on fighting and denying the

very longings that would lead me home. In my frenzy to please God, to honor my commitments, to support my family, and to keep distracted from my needs and desires, Valium became my only real source of comfort.[3]

Family, church, and society encourage such dislocation in many ways. Language to describe gays is often derisive, and social attitudes and actions frequently identify gays and lesbians as worthless, worthy only of being harassed or even tormented and bashed. Even Christians frequently portray disdain and disgust of the gay person in their language and actions. For the person who is gay or lesbian this sense of dislocation is pervasive—in the person's inner life, in the intimate circle of family and friends, in the spiritual realm of God and the church, and in society in general.

Shame

For the person and the family, experience of homosexual orientation can bring profound shame. Shame is the sense of being exposed to the very core of our being. In shame we feel utterly and completely exposed and conscious of being looked at. One is visible even though not ready to be visible and has a growing sense of feeling small. In the moment of shame, the person can only wish for invisibility.[4]

When shame is toxic we have the urge to cover up, to become a false self, to cease to be authentic. This can lead to complex and disturbing inner states such as depression, alienation, self-doubt, loneliness, inferiority, and a profound sense of inadequacy or feeling of failure. Internalized shame spreads throughout the self, ultimately shaping one's whole life and identity. When we have a positive identity, we have a vital sense of who we are as individuals. We can embrace our worth, our adequacy, and our very dignity as human beings. But all this can be obliterated through protracted shame which leaves us feeling naked, defeated, and intolerably alone. For many, this describes the experience of being gay or lesbian, especially in their earlier years.

This shame is reflected in the comments of the twelve gay and lesbian people I met with to inquire about their experience. It was present in their early fears about themselves, expressed in thoughts of themselves as perverted, twisted, mentally unstable, and not deserving respect. They were afraid to reveal their orientation even to close friends. Herein lies the experience of feeling over-exposed, small, wanting to vanish.

The rage that often accompanies such unrelenting toxic shame is vividly described in the diary of a teenager who bitterly struggled with same-sex orientation and ultimately ended his journey in suicide. The diary reads as follows:

> I am evil and wicked. I want to spit vulgarities at every one I see. I am dirt; harmful bacteria grows inside of me. . . . I was innocent, trusting, loving. The world has raped me till my insides are shredding and bleeding. My voice is small and unheard, unnoticed. Damned. . . . Gentle springtime weather surrounds me but a fierce unrelenting storm rages within. . . . How much longer? How much more can I take? Only time and a million tears of bitterness. . . . I wish I could crawl under a rock and sleep for the rest of time.[5]

Excerpts from Bobby's diary demonstrate that the shame experienced by people with a same-sex orientation is rooted in who they *are*, not primarily in what they *do*. Shame pervades "surface and depth, conscious and the unconscious" and becomes a way of experiencing one's self and shapes how one behaves. Certainly most, if not all, gays and lesbians in our culture will face shame at some time in their journey. In what follows we will explore three arenas which become sources of shame for the person who is gay or lesbian.

One is the shame linked with *the sense of being different* early in life. Chastity Bono, describing her own experience, says, "As a child I always felt there was something different about me. I'd look at other girls my age and feel perplexed by their obvious interest in the latest fashions, which boy in class was the cutest, and who looked the most like cover girl Christie Brinkley."[6] In time this was accentuated by her mother's disapproval of her dress and behaviors and her displeasure and anxiety over Chastity's tomboyishness.

Ultimately this felt like disapproval of her as a person. Increasingly she felt ashamed for being different. Later she discovered this to be true of others also. She says, "In my conversations with gays and lesbians over the last few years, I began to uncover a similar map in their stories: first we feel different, then we are criticized or receive negative feedback, then we internalize the criticism and become ashamed of who we are."[7]

Puberty and adolescence are a second arena of shame for the young person aware of being gay or lesbian. The reasons for this are fairly obvious. Not only must gay or lesbian persons face the feelings of awkwardness that usually come with the emergence of puberty, but they must also face the dawning awareness of their sexual attractions and urges that are deemed unacceptable and taboo by family, friends, and society in general.

The gay person feels compelled to face what seem like the demons of his sexuality alone. His dawning sexuality cannot be explored and celebrated as with his heterosexual peers. For fear of the shame of exposure, he must keep his sexuality a secret, often hidden from himself as well as from others. At some level he lives with a pervasive sense of being a bad person. This can readily become a toxic shame.

Having one's inner life exposed is a third arena of shame. The sexuality of gays and lesbians tend to be brought into the public arena, targeted, and exposed in ways that are demeaning. Normally any of us are embarrassed if our sexual attractions, urges, experiences, or practices are unduly exposed. Our sexual expressions are personal and private matters. When a heterosexual teenager enters puberty she is discretely recognized as a person with sexual interests, potential, and attractions. Her inner life is hers, and her family and peers identify with her and in one way or another approve and celebrate her new status.

But it is not so with persons of same-sex orientation. If for the sake of integrity and authenticity gay or lesbian individuals "come out," they will likely encounter pain, resistance, and disapproval from family and friends. Their sexual orientation becomes the focus of fear, sorrow, disappointment, sometimes long discussions, and often intense attempts to help them change. Who they are may be held up for ridicule and rejection in society, and they may even face the loss of home or work. Even in the arena of church their sexuality becomes an embarrassment, the focus of hours of discussion, public debate, and angry interactions among church members.

The experience of shame is a critical factor in the life of a gay person. Some gay and lesbian persons turn the shame of feeling different toward themselves and become self-destructive. Because of the close connection between the awareness of difference and shame, being gay or lesbian inescapably often marks homosexual persons as lesser in their own eyes and in the eyes of society. Others will try to hide their true identity from themselves and the world by thrusting themselves into what are considered "normal" patterns of life. Later in life they may feel compelled to come out. Some ultimately overcome the shame and move on with their life.

In any case, it becomes apparent that the journey for the person with a same-sex orientation is vigorous and demanding. To learn to cope with these inner and outer obstacles and become a productive and mature person requires considerable inner strength, creativity, and a strong sense of identity and purpose in life.

Isolation

Shame obviously brings isolation. Personal and social isolation is one of the demons gays and lesbians face while they remain hidden from themselves and/or society. They also frequently experience isolation during their process of accepting their "new" identity and while coming out to family and society. During this time it is hard for gays or lesbians to be at home with themselves and with family and friends. The dread and fear they encounter usually has to be faced alone.

The severity of this experience is clear in an excerpt from Bobby's diary: "I can't ever let anyone find out that I'm not straight. It would be so humiliating. My friends would hate me. They might even want to beat me up. And my family? I've overheard them. They've said they hate gays, and even God hates gays, too. Gays are bad and God sends them to hell. It really scares me when they talk that way because now they are talking about me." Later Bobby wrote this poem:

> I've locked myself out
> And don't have the key
> I blew the light out
> And now I can't see . . .
> Afraid of answers I don't have
> And might not ever know
> I wonder in which direction my life will go?[8]

This sense of isolation often begins in early childhood. Siegel writes that a gay child almost always knows, much earlier then society gives him credit for knowing, that "in a profound and fundamental way he is not the same as the majority of the children in his family, room, group, playground, school, community and, ultimately, world."[9] The child becomes aware of the observer's perspective, internalizes the view, and begins to feel decidedly different and uncomfortable about it.

Some will use isolation as a way to cope with their shame. In its more severe form, isolation can become the gay or lesbian person's primary strategy for coping with being so different and may ultimately lead to social and emotional separation from family and peers and withdraw into internal isolation. Others may cope with shame by becoming confrontational about the attitudes and actions of family and friends in response to them. This too isolates the gay or lesbian person in his or her social context.

Loss and grief

When one becomes known as being gay or lesbian, it may mean loss of self-image and self-acceptance, loss of family, loss of friends, loss of work, loss of being safe in society, loss of affirmation, loss of positive recognition and appreciation, and even a sense of loss of church and God. Loss is, without a doubt, a significant part of the gay and lesbian experience. Kenneth Mitchell et al. talk about six types of losses people experience: material loss, relationship loss, intrapsychic loss, functional loss, role loss, and systemic loss.[10] I will highlight three of these: (1) relationship loss; (2) intrapsychic loss; and (3) role loss as relevant to the gay or lesbian person's life.

Relationship loss

Mitchell writes, "Relationship loss is the ending of opportunities to relate oneself to, talk with, share experiences with, make love to, touch, settle issues with, fight with, and otherwise be in the emotional and/or physical presence of a particular other human being" (38). When death ends the opportunity to engage in relationship with another, the loss is obvious. But relationships may be cut off also by ridicule, disdain, ostracism, isolation, and rejection. These too may rob the gay or lesbian person of the emotional dimension of relationships and sometimes even the physical presence.

When it becomes known that individuals are gay or lesbian, their significant relationships change. Sometimes old friends are lost and new friends must be sought. At first family relationships tend to become strained and painful. Meaningful church relationships tend to be lost because the gay or lesbian person no longer feels welcome in church.

Intrapsychic loss

According to Mitchell and Anderson,

Intrapsychic loss is the experience of losing an emotionally important image of oneself, losing the possibility of "what might have been," abandonment of plans for a particular future, the dying of a dream. Although often related to external experiences, it is an entirely inward experience. (40)

The first experience of intrapsychic loss is most likely to happen in adolescence. The loss of self-image, the dying of a dream, and the significant change in one's life and place with others are inner losses. These losses are often kept secret.

Bobby writes about this in his diary:

> During the early years of my life (up to about 11 or 12) I was in fact happy and free. I liked who I was. I knew I was very individual and maybe even a little different in the eyes of my friends. But that didn't stop me from being ME. . . . But as I grew up and became more and more conscious of others and what they wanted, I think I maybe began to see the difference between myself and those around me. I felt rejection before. . . . now I was older and really felt a strong need for acceptance. So . . . slowly I began to lose touch with who I really was."[11]

Intrapsychic loss can have a severe psychological impact on a person. It disrupts the rhythm of mutual recognition and the relationship between inner and outer experience. It creates serious disequilibrium with one's self-image and self-acceptance. If unresolved, the inner world moves toward profound disturbance or emptiness.

Role loss

Persons with a same-sex orientation often experience severe role loss. "The loss of a specific social role of one's accustomed place in a social network is experienced as role loss," write Mitchell and Anderson. "Disorientation is a powerful part of the sense of loss at this point. It involves the sense that one does not know how to behave in social situations."[12]

Loss and grief are an inevitable part of human experience. Mitchell and Anderson, describing the process of loss and grief in terms of human attachment and separation, write that

> the genesis of grief lies in the inevitability of both attachment and separation for the sustenance and development of human life. The biological connection necessary for the survival of the fetus before birth continues in social forms throughout life. There is no life without either attachment or loss: hence there is no life without grief. (21-22)

> Adult attachments are straightforward continuations of childhood affectional bonds. Adult attachment is not an infantile need we outgrow or a regression to infantile dependency. The desire to be loved and cared for is fundamental to human nature in adults as well as children. (28)

The grief we experience from major loss evokes panic, anxiety, shock, sorrow, anger, and even guilt. Grief, by nature, is personal; it is a very lonely task only the individual can fully experience. But the resolution of grief requires the presence of other persons to hear and "feel with" these emotions. Grieving is, in part, an interpersonal process. If we become isolated in our grief, we tend to get stuck with it.

What often makes grief and loss unique for persons who are gay or lesbian is isolation. Often they must face this radical change in their life, this radical discontinuity, when they become isolated from some of their most significant supporter persons. This is because being gay often means being severely marginalized, if not rejected, in family, church, and society. Thus the experience of loss and grief is greatly intensified.

Homosexuality is also a significant loss for parents and family, no matter how accepting they are of their son or daughter, brother or sister. Bono says, "That parents grieve is natural; when a parent replaces his or her private expectations of a child with the reality, there is loss involved."[13]

When parents discover that a child is gay, they must give up significant hopes and dreams for that child. They exchange the known for the unknown. They enter a new and strange world. As a family they experience deep intrapsychic loss. There is, for a time, loss of social and ecclesial comfort. Sometimes even parents experience loss of acceptance among friends in society and in the church.

Extraordinary Developmental Challenges

The psychological dynamics described above obviously interfere with the essential process of human development. In the emerging infant there is a process of "mutual regulation" which fosters the child's growth and development. As parent and child interact in ways appropriate to one another's needs and capacity, the infant moves from an inner imbalance and immaturity to an increasing sense of internal and external familiarity and consistency.

It is essential that the maturing child's inner life continue to be matched with external recognition, appreciation, and challenge. This helps her develop a sense of inner sameness, goodness, self-acceptance, and a growing ability to love and work in her family and society. As the child experiences congruence between her inner and outer worlds, she learns to trust herself and others. This includes trust of her inner life, the ability to cope with her own urges, and the ability to see herself as a trustworthy person.

This process is easier to understand and describe in infancy than adulthood, but we humans never outgrow the need for mutual regulation and mutual trust. We all need positive mirroring in intimate relationships and recognition in the social environment. These are essential for health and well-being throughout life. Yet it is this process that is disturbed for persons who are gay and lesbian in their adolescence and adulthood. Family and friends tend to have strong negative reactions toward certain deep and fundamental inner urges of gays and lesbians, and society again and again rejects them as persons.

Siegel helps us understand even more poignantly how the developmental process of gays and lesbians is disrupted.

> Our society almost always aborts or derails the gay man's development early, either directly by oppression and ostracism, or indirectly through the self-hatred and self-limitation that constant oppression and ostracism so successfully incubate and nurture. . . . [This] interrupts, if it doesn't absolutely prevent, a smooth process of growth and self-acceptance. The ostracism and oppression become a part of the person's psychic drama, and the battle goes on inside the individual as well as outside, throughout his entire life, as the dominant society poses new challenges and new condemnations every day.[14]

In light of this, it takes great courage for gay or lesbian persons to come out to themslves, let alone to family and society in general. Yet so long as a gay person remains hidden to self and society, significant elements of personal identity remain diffuse or even distorted. In human development, personal identity emerges from a reasonable degree of self-awareness and the experience of knowing and being known in society.

It becomes evident, then, why the stages of growth for the person with a same-sex orientation differ severely from that of a heterosexual person. They cannot follow the routine path of human development but instead have to pioneer their own paths to maturity. This often begins with a long period of emerging self-awareness and self-acknowledgment, followed by a period of struggle with self-acceptance, then a time of coming out during which they begin to assume a gay or lesbian identity.

Frequently this occurs during adolescence and young adulthood. If so, the routine developmental tasks (identity formation, the capacity for intimacy and generativity) are often disturbed and destabilized by this experience. After gay or lesbian persons assume a gay identity, they can take up developmental tasks with new clarity but with the awareness that they must now work out identity and lifestyle in the context of lifelong social marginalization. Gay or lesbian persons will never again be viewed as just average members of society. As they now continue the journey of maturing, they will be forced to tap exceptional strengths and creativity to cope with the ridicule, ostracism, and rejection that always lurk in the shadows around the next turn in the road. For some this will have a life-long crippling effect. For others it will inspire inner strength, creativity, and resilience.

Implications for the Church

In light of what I have been describing, what are implications for those of us who are Christian and want to be a faithful church ? I observe five requests I believe the Spirit is making of us who wish to be take up the challenge to represent Jesus Christ in the world though the church.

To go beyond the leper syndrome

This means to explore a more immediate awareness of the experience of gay and lesbian persons and their families. The tendency to want to disassociate from our children who are gay and lesbian tends to breed isolation and ignorance among church members and alienation for those who are homosexual. We as church members need to express interest in the life and spiritual well-being of the gay and lesbian children who emerge from among us. For many of us it would be easier if they would just go away. Few Christians personally and specifically invite their gay and lesbian sons and daughters to faith and participation in the life of the congregation. The church tends to want to discard gays and lesbians like lepers.

To go beyond simple myths and personal prejudice

This means being willing to encounter and understand the complexity of this issue. Often when I hear church people talk about gays and lesbians, it becomes apparent that they have not done much to inform themselves concerning this very complex issue. All too often in Mennonite and other denominational circles the subject is addressed with condemnation, deep hostility, ignorance, and prejudice. True, it is hard work to read the conflicting literature and seek to become informed. It may be distasteful and disconcerting for some to be exposed to open, direct, respectful, and non-polemic conversation with those who are gay and lesbian. But the church cannot be faithful in its call to continue the redemptive agenda of Jesus without encountering and understanding the experience of those who are gay and lesbian.

To go beyond self-righteous posturing

The call to the church is to active spiritual and theological engagement with the "children of the church" who are gay and lesbians. All too often we seem to feel that when we have pronounced homosexuality sin, we have taken care of our responsibility. Sometimes we want the doctrinal agenda to be whole agenda. But it is not. Unless church members engage in direct dialogue with our children who are gay and lesbian, the church may well have culpability in the day of judgment for the souls of our gay and lesbian children. To fail to pray for them, to neglect to engage them in dialogue with what the church believes to be God's truth, is to ignore God's heartfelt desire for the salvation of all those who are gay and lesbian.

The difficulty, of course, with biblical and theological dialogue is that it is a reciprocal process We not only get to say what we believe to be true but we also need to listen to what the other person other believes and say., This can be hard work. It can be threatening. But we cannot dialogue effectively on behalf of God without respecting the other person in the process.

To go beyond safe and convenient distancing

This involves active pastoral care for gay and lesbians and their families. Frequently, when the church pronounces a person or persons wrong, it no longer feels any responsibility for the well-being of that person or those persons. When we pronounce other persons wrong, we tend to want to turn away from them, to ignore them rather than allow God to call us to walk with them and to support them in their journey. Yet this chapter identifies the keen challenges and potential struggles a gay or lesbian person will have in society. The church needs on God's behalf to develop ways to walk with our children who are gay and lesbian.

Conclusion

As we have seen, the experience of being gay or lesbian presents some unusual challenges on the journey of human development and maturity. The psychological dynamics of growing up are different for the gay person than the heterosexual person. The possibilities for self-destruction or social degradation are real. The extraordinary inner and outer obstacles for the person with a same-sex orientation require extraordinary strength to successfully cope and mature.

Many with same-sex orientation rise to the challenge. Those who oppose them often do not get to see their integrity and strength of character because of the disdain they hold for persons who are gay and lesbian. In our currently polarized political, social, and ecclesial atmosphere, persons in the gay and lesbian community will only be seen and heard as persons with a deviant sexual orientation, not as persons to respect and love.

As a parent of a lesbian daughter, I have seen what a difference love and respect can make in contributing to a person's stability and well-being. Being gay or lesbian can be a fundamentally destabilizing experience. Without care and support from family and friends, the destabilizing impact can be greatly accentuated. As a father and a Christian, I consider it my responsibility to care for those on this journey in whatever ways I can.

In this chapter I address the dynamics of same-sex orientation. In doing so I hope to generate more awareness of the experience of being a gay or lesbian person.

As one committed to the church, I have wrestled for years with the issues the church faces in its positions on homosexuality. As the father of a daughter with a same-sex orientation, I also identify with the pain and frustration of the gay community. Therefore I understand the debate quite well on both sides.

From either perspective, however, I am often deeply offended by the rhetoric I hear and the things written by my brothers and sisters in the church. I find the attitudes expressed, the lack of respect and care for the gay and lesbian person, disappointing and at times very painful. Too many times people speak on this subject out of ignorance. Too many who speak have never held a significant conversation with gay or lesbian persons in order to understand their experience and to care for them. Too many of our gay and lesbian sons and daughters in the church have no one in the church who cares for them as persons, no one who prays for them, no one to express interest in their spiritual life.

Instead, I hear people in church circles again and again reflect the anger, fear, and disgust of our society. When I as a parent hear judgment without genuine care for the person, I feel deep disillusionment and grief.

We need to invest time and energy in learning to know gay and lesbian people and in beginning to understand their experiences. People with a same-sex orientation do not need our pity—any more then they need our disdain—but they do need our understanding and respect.

Notes

1. Stanley Siegel and Ed Lowe, Jr. *Uncharted Lives: Understanding the Life Passages of Gay Men* (New York: Dutton, A Plume Book, 1994), 29. This is a remarkably clear description of one gay man's developmental journey.

2. Siegel, 24-25.

3. Mel White, *Stranger at the Gate* (New York: Dutton, A Plume Book, 1994), 184.

4. Erik Erikson, *Childhood and Society* (Hammondsworth, Middlesex, England: Penguin Books, 1963), 244-246.

5. Leroy Aarons, *Prayers for Bobby: A Mothers Coming to Terms with the Suicide of Her Gay Son* (San Francisco: HarperSanFrancisco, 1995), 24.

6. Chastity Bono, *Family Outing* (New York: Little, Brown and Company, 1998), vii, 11-12.

7. Ibid.

8. Aarons, 75.

9. Siegel, 54.

10. Kenneth R Mitchell and Herbert Anderson, *All Our Losses, All Our Grief's: Resources For Pastoral Care* (Philadelphia: Westminster Press, 1983), 36-42.

11. Aarons, 55-56.

12. Mitchell and Anderson, 42.

13. Bono, 235.

14. Siegel, 29.

Chapter 3

Homosexuality: Biblical, Theological, and Polity Issues

David Schroeder

*T*HE BIBLE HARDLY DISCUSSES HOMOSEXUAL BEHAVIOR. As is often noted, it is mentioned much less often, for example, than economic issues. If we treated the texts on the dangers of wealth the way we treat the texts on homosexual activity, we would first of all give away all our possessions, then radicalize these texts to make them even more stringent than they already are. We would simply say it is impossible for a rich person to enter the kingdom of God!

But what do these texts about homosexual behavior actually say? The answer depends on what kind of an approach we take to the Bible and its message. If we want to get at what the Bible says to us today about homosexuality, we need to pay attention to more than careful exegesis of the text. We need also to do careful analysis related to biblical and systematic theology.

In *exegesis* we seek to establish what the text said and meant in its original language and context. In *biblical theology* we try to get at the beliefs and assumptions of the writer that caused the writer to say what was said. In *systematic theology* we seek to understand what this would mean in our time given the way we understand the world today.

Let me illustrate. In 1 Peter 3:3 Peter tells wives they should avoid outward adornments such as braided hair, gold jewelry, or fine clothes. There is no problem of exegesis here. Wives were not to braid their hair or wear gold jewelry or fine clothes. But this is generally disregarded today. Why? To answer this we need to turn to biblical theology. What did the writer know and believe that made him give this prohibition?

The gospel made women accountable to God the way men were accountable to God (Gal. 3:28). It had given them the status of "free" women, and Peter is addressing them as such. We now know who Peter was alluding to when he told Christian or free women not to ornament and display themselves. The usual free women (*hetaerae*) in that society were princesses who had been conquered in military exploits and were now consorts of political leaders and appeared with them in public. These women were free to own property and dolled themselves up with braided hair laced with gold threads and so forth. What Peter was insisting on was that Christian women not express their freedom by conforming to worldly free women in their make-up and dress.

If we ask what this mean for us, we need to inquire not about braided hair or jewelry but about those things and areas where we are in danger of conforming to the world about us. It may have nothing to do with braided hair at all when applied to our situation yet be a biblically correct application of the gospel to life.

Exegetical Notes

To elucidate the significance of our three-step approach to Scripture—exegesis, biblical theology, systematic theology—I will first note briefly the exegetical aspects of our study. Then we will look at biblical and systematic considerations.

Genesis 19:1-29

This text does not speak *directly* to homosexual activity. The men of Sodom are intent on gang rape. They do not want these men to be given the city's hospitality. The men of Sodom break the law of hospitality. Both Abraham (18:1-8) and Lot (19:1-3) kept this law, whereas all the men of Sodom did not. All of these men were considered to be heterosexual and not homosexual. Their intended actions were wrong whether directed at men or women, whether done by heterosexuals or homosexuals. This is thus not a text that speaks to consensual same-sex relations. No one legitimizes rape, let alone gang rape. The clearest biblical interpretation of the sin of Sodom is found in a long list of sins mentioned in Ezekiel 16:49.

Leviticus 18:22 and 20:13

These texts are part of the Holiness Code and its laws of clean and unclean. Male-to-male sexual activity is prohibited. But nothing is said about comparable female activity. In both Leviticus passages various prohibitions are given, among them male same-sex sexual activity. In 20:10-16 the penalty for most such sins is death.

This prohibition would have an unambiguous application if it were not for the fact that we do not keep many of the laws of the Holiness Code today. Jesus himself relaxed many of them (Mark 7:1-23). For instance, we do not use the death penalty for a disobedient or rebellious son (Lev. 20:6) or as punishment for adultery (Lev. 20:10). Whether these laws are kept or not depends at least in part on whether they are in some way restated in the New Testament.

1 Corinthians 6:9-10

The passage begins with a list of those who will not enter the kingdom of God: "fornicators, idolaters, adulterers, *malakoi, arsenokoitai,* thieves, the greedy, revilers and robbers." We skip very quickly over this list and focus only on the two italicized words, the meaning of which are not as clear as we would like them to be.

Translators have difficulty with these terms. The *Jerusalem Bible* renders them "catomites, sodomites"; NIV "male prostitutes and homosexual offenders"; Authorized Version "effeminate and abusers of themselves with mankind"; RSV "sexual perverts"; NEB "homosexual persons"; NRSV "male prostitutes and sodomites."

We might note by way of contrast that we well know what the word *greedy* means. What if we treated the greedy the way we treat homosexuals?

The term *malakoi* is not a technical term for a homosexual person. It appears in Hellenistic literature as pejorative slang to describe the passive (soft) partner in a homosexual relationship. These were most often boys. The term *arsenokoitai* is not found in any Greek text before this New Testament references. Robin Scroggs claims (and Hays agrees) that the word was used to translate Leviticus 18:22 and 20:13 (lying with a male).[1] If this reading is correct, and I believe it is, then this text would seem to support the Levitical condemnation of same-sex sexual activity.

1 Timothy 1:10

The 1 Timothy 1:10 passage uses *arsenokoitai* along with the lawless and the disobedient, the godless and sinful, the unholy and profane, those who kill their father or mother, murderers, fornicators, slave traders, liars, perjurers, and all that is against sound teaching. Again we should note the long list of sins included. If it simply refers to all male same-sex genital intimacy,the list supports the Levitical text.

Acts 15:28-29

Here the term in question is *pornia*, fornication. This has a much broader range of interpretation. Homosexual activity could be included under the term, but it does not refer to same-sex sexual activity as such. It refers to all illicit sexual activity.

Romans 1:18-32

Paul speaks about homosexual activity in a specifically theological context in this Romans text. The passage is introduced by 1:16-17 where he speaks of the power of God unto salvation, and the righteousness of God that is revealed to humankind. And he adds that the righteous shall live by faith.

Then in 1:18 he speaks of the "wrath of God" revealed from heaven against all ungodliness. God has created and revealed the moral order. God has so ordained that that which serves life and furthers life is good, and that which harms, counters or destroys life is evil. God is sovereign Lord and evil will not succeed in the end. It will be judged both now and in the future. This is what is meant by the "wrath of God" that is becoming manifest against all evil (v. 18).

God does not force but *invites* people to do the will of God. God even makes it possible for us, through the strength of the Holy Spirit, to choose to do what is right and good. At the same time, God allows humans to make wrong choices and from the time of Adam and Eve they have done so.

Paul seeks to explain that moral perversion is the result of human choices—choices of death rather than life. As Ernst Käsemann comments, moral perversion is the result of God's wrath, not the reason for it; the reason for it is the rejection of God and God's will, i.e. human rebellion.[2] God simply allows us to reap the consequences of our rebellion against God.

According to Paul, the consequences of our human rebellion, which is "the manifestation of God's wrath," are the following:

> people became futile in their thinking (1:21)
> they became fools, idolaters (1:22-23)
> they lusted after the impure (1:24)

believed lies rather than the truth (1:25)
and began to worship the creation rather than the creator.

When this happens, sexual relations become idolatrous. Paul also indicates that because of human rebellion against God, people's passions were degraded. Women exchanged natural intercourse with unnatural, and men did the same. (This is the only place where female same-sex relations are mentioned.) Human sin led to wickedness of all kinds (1:29-30).

It is clear from the above that homosexual activity is not the focus of the passage. Paul focuses on human sin, or the rejection of God, and one illustration among others is that the rejection of God results in the rejection of the created sexual roles or order. Same-sex sexual relations are clearly named as one of these transgressions.

Biblical Theology

As we turn toward biblical theology, it is important to note, first of all, that the Old and New Testaments agree same-sex sexual activity (coitus) is wrong. In the Old Testament this prohibition is applied only to male same-sex relations, probably because women belonged to their fathers and husbands and were to be protected by them. In the New Testament where women have become responsible persons themselves, lesbian relations are mentioned as well, in that women are accountable in the same way men are.

In both Testaments, that is, in both Hebrew and Greek societies, all persons were held to be heterosexual. All adult men and women were expected to marry and to produce offspring. Homosexual relations were thus seen and evaluated within the context of heterosexual persons (mainly married men) having homosexual relations. Neither Greek nor Hebrew had a word for persons with same-sex orientation. They thus speak of homosexual activities, not persons.

Neither Testament addresses the questions we now bring to Scripture. These questions are—

(1) What advice do the Scriptures have for persons who have a same-sex sexual orientation? Many persons claim that they did not at any point choose their orientation. It was a given in their lives.

(2) The claim is made that persons who have a same-sex orientation need to express sexuality in a same-sex covenant relationship parallel to a heterosexual marriage. Is this forbidden in Scripture?

It is clear from the above that the Bible cannot be used to condemn persons who claim to have a same-sex sexual orientation. It does address the question of sexual activity, but sexual orientation is simply not addressed in Scripture. Persons with a same-sex sexual orientation have been present in the church throughout the ages. Often they were married and raised a family. But always they were expected to remain celibate or to be faithful to their wives. They have made good contributions to the church.

By the same token, since Scripture does not give advice for those of homosexual orientation, it cannot be used to justify same-sex sexual relations on the part of those with a same-sex orientation. The Bible does not speak to the issue, since all persons in biblical times were seen as heterosexual in nature.

Given that the particular questions we bring to the text are not addressed in the text of Scripture, we have to develop a theology on the basis of the biblical record that answers the questions asked. To do this is to develop a systematic theology, or to apply a biblical theology to our day. We have done this in many areas, such as whether to buy insurance, belong to a union, use birth control, or participate in a capitalist economic order. None of these issues is directly addressed in Scripture.

Systematic Theology

Thus far, the Mennonite Churches (in denominational deliberations held at Saskatoon, Sask. and Purdue, Ind.) have recognized that persons who have a same-sex sexual orientation should be permitted to be full members in the church so long as they do not engage in same-gender sexual activity. The church has thus answered the first question we asked earlier about persons who have a same-sex sexual orientation.

No one is arguing for promiscuous sexual relations for either heterosexual or homosexuals. This means the only thing we are really debating is whether same-sex sexually oriented persons should be permitted to enter a same-sex sexual covenant parallel with heterosexual marriage. If the church were to affirm this, it would need to work out a theological rationale based on the Scriptures. The difficulty is that, by and large, neither the church nor the Christian homosexual community has thus far done this.

Neither the church nor the Christian homosexual community has worked out a proper theology to support each group's particular actions and expectations. The churches have made a formal statement that allows same-sex oriented persons to be members of the church as long as they do not engage in same-sex sexual activity. But they have not said this loudly or made it easy for members of the church to come out of the closet. Nor have they given a clear picture of how such persons can participate in the community of faith and its mission.

Persons of same-sex orientation have asserted their Christian faith and have given their testimony about being accepted by Christ even if not by the church. However, in my opinion, they have not developed a satisfactory theology of same-sex covenants. They have not offered a rationale that adequately takes into account the creation of human beings male and female for the continuance of the human race.

At present the theology of the various Mennonite church denominational streams is not acceptable to the gay and lesbian Christians and the theology of the gay and lesbian Christians is not acceptable to the church. This is why further discussion is needed, and this is what the discussion should be about.

The question of genetic determinism

In our theological quest we must face the question whether there is any extra-biblical information that needs to be taken into account in making a decision. Do the physical or social sciences shed any further light on the questions we are asking? It seems clear there is some kind of determinism at work, at least for a small percentage of people, that causes their same-sex orientation. There is no agreement, however, on what the root of this determinism is. Is a genetic, psychological or sociological determinism at work? What would change if we knew the answer?

If there is determinism at work, then we already know that persons who have a same-sex sexual orientation cannot be faulted. They are not to be held morally responsible for the orientation they have received. This is why the church has not acted against persons of same-sex orientation but only against same-sex sexual relations.

If the determinism is totally genetic, then no one is at fault. But even then we cannot say that the orientation is God-given or normal. We simply do not know that. Just because it is genetic does not make it good or, for that matter, of God.

If the determinism is totally psychological, then those persons most closely or deeply associated with persons of same-sex sexual orientation may share some responsibility for its occurrence. If the determinism is totally sociological, then the whole society shares some of the responsibility for having created the conditions or culture that give rise to same-sex sexual orientation. In each case, therefore, to the degree determinism is at work, the persons concerned cannot be faulted.

It would be safer to assume, however, that whatever determinism is at work is a mixture of genetic, psychological, and sociological factors rather than totally one or the other. It would also be proper to assume that persons involved are not totally without choice. The question of determinism turns out to be much more complicated than at first supposed.

The nature of same-sex attraction

There has been a tendency to lump all homosexual persons and activities together. It does not seem right to do so. Most likely the three possible causes—genetic, psychological and sociological— could all play a part in different combinations in each person. Brian Cunningham, a Toronto psychotherapist, lists ten different types of cases having to do with homosexuality.[3] If he is right, then we have not yet learned to distinguish one case from the other, even though we need to make theological-ethical decisions in this area. Were we able to make such distinctions, we would need to handle each case on its own merits as we do in situations of divorce and remarriage. Thus far we have not been willing to consider this in the cases of homosexuality.

Making Decisions about New Questions

Who makes the decision?

By "new questions" I mean those not explicitly spoken to in the context of biblical culture. As we cross different cultures, or as our own cultures change, new questions arise which the church under guidance of the Holy Spirit must decide. As we have noted, there are questions about the nature of homosexual orientation to which the biblical admonitions do not speak.

Our church (Mennonite Church Canada) polity has been congregational. The local congregations set the guidelines for church membership and make decisions binding on the members of the congregation. It stands to reason, therefore, that the primary decision regarding whether to accept persons in a same-sex covenant relationship as members of the church would rest first with the local congregation.

Such a polity has several advantages. First, no local congregation is forced to accept as members those whom they believe do not comply with basic standards binding on congregational members. Second, decisions about individuals are made in the context where people know each other intimately. Decisions can then be made on a personal rather than legalistic or theoretical basis devoid of contextual considerations.

The local congregation, however, does not stand alone. It belongs to a union of congregations—area conferences or districts and national bodies. A conference or district of churches can affirm or call into question the decisions of a local congregation. It can do so in a number of different ways as mentioned below.

How new decisions are made

The New Testament church faced many new questions. We do well to observe how the apostles dealt with these new questions. Paul accepted as authoritative the Old Testament, the words of Jesus (1 Cor. 7:10), and the tradition of the apostles (1 Cor. 15:3-5; 11:2; 2 Thess. 2:15). Since the Gospels and the epistles are based on the apostolic tradition, this is roughly equivalent to the Old and New Testament as we have them today. But Paul recognized that some things had not been addressed in any of these sources. In such cases Paul clearly indicated that he spoke differently to such instances than in relation to questions where there was "a word from the Lord" (1 Cor. 7:6, 10, 12).

Where Paul had no word from the Lord he gave his opinion or judgment as one who had the Spirit of God (1 Cor. 7:25, 40). We can distinguish between two types of situations where Paul speaks to questions not mentioned in his sources. The first relates to *applying the gospel in new settings,* such as eating meat sold on the open market (1 Cor. 8:1-13). In these contexts Paul indicates that Christians are free to eat meat offered to idols but should respect the conscience of those not totally freed from the power of idols. If such Christian brothers or sisters are present, they should not eat meat offered to idols. Paul asks us, in other words, to take the situation into account when applying the gospel.

The second type of decision *involves a new understanding of the nature of the gospel.* In working with the Gentiles, Paul had received a special insight into the nature of the gospel which indicated that gentile Christians need not be circumcised (Gal. 1 and 2). Circumcision had been a sign of the covenant of Israel with God from the time of Abraham (Gen. 17:9-11). But in working with the Gentiles who were accepting Christ as Savior and Lord, Paul realized that the gospel did not require Gentile Christians to be circumcised. They did not have to become Jews first to become Christian. This was such a departure from tradition that Paul's insight had to be confirmed by the entire church at Jerusalem (Acts 15). Paul made the decision on the basis of his understanding of the gospel. It was made on the mission field, then confirmed by the larger church.

The Church a Loosing and Binding Fellowship

Jesus commissioned the church to be a loosing and binding fellowship (Matt. 16:13-20, 18:15-20; John 20:23), and in the New Testament church we see this process at work. The church is to help set people free from bondage, that is, to be a loosing or freeing fellowship. In the same way the church is to be a binding fellowship. That is, the church is to bind itself to follow Jesus and that which is God's will for life and peace.

This mission of the church is modeled for us by God in the exodus. God liberated the Israelites who were in bondage in Egypt and then at Sinai, God promised to be Israel's God and asked the people to bind themselves to keep God's commandments. The same action is modeled for us in Jesus Christ. When we call Jesus "Savior," we are speaking about how he has saved us from bondage to sin; when we call Jesus "Lord," we indicate that we have bound ourselves to do his will.

The church seeks through its worship and decision making to loose and bind church. But the members of the church do not always agree on what belongs to Christian freedom or bondage. In such cases, members of the church need to be patient with each other as they seek, over time, to know the will of God and the leading of the Spirit. What is the church to do when for one set of members "loosing" means setting persons free from their same-sex orientation, and for the other members it means freeing the church from homophobia? Such a situation requires patience from all members if they are to reach some kind of understanding of what each is saying and to discern together the promise of God for the church.

If we follow Matthew 18:15-23, we will speak personally to the individuals involved as members of a congregation. We will not first establish rules that keep people out, so we need to deal personally with "offenders." We will rather seek to find some kind of understanding or resolution before it is brought before the congregation.

In any case, the first point of discussion and decision is in the local congregation even though the local congregation works in mutual accountability to other congregations. Mutual accountability does not mean, however, that one congregation exercises authority over the next congregation or that one area conference or district has direct power over any other conference or district. Accountability means rather that each congregation respects the other congregations and is willing to give and to receive encouragement, exhortation, and admonition for the purpose of discerning together the will of God for the believers.

In a similar way, conferences or districts become members of a national body. As part of that body, conferences and districts are accountable to each other, even as all the congregations of their regional bodies become accountable to each other. As a consequence, conferences or districts can address issues related to other conferences through the national body. *To follow this line of accountability takes time, and the more difficult the issues, the longer it takes to come to agreement on what actions to take and what actions not to take.*

Why same-sex covenants are a stumbling block

One reason same-sex covenants prove difficult for the church is that they pit two basic Christian actions against each other: hospitality (love) and discipline.[4] *Discipline*, because we have always bound ourselves to monogamous heterosexual marriages and worry that any other covenant is unwarranted and needs to be excised from the fellowship. *Hospitality*, because the stance of the church toward all people is to be open to everyone who confesses Jesus Christ as Lord. We cannot move totally to one pole or the other without denying the gospel in some way.

Another reason we are at odds is that we want to be demonstrably Christian. We want not only to do what is right but also to be seen as doing what is right. The problem is that at this point the issues are not as clear as we would like them to be. Neither inclusion nor exclusion seems the full answer, yet these are the only two options typically considered. We therefore need to look for other alternatives. What might these be?

One alternative might be to declare that we are not yet ready to give a final answer to the problem of inclusion or exclusion of Christians who have made a same-sex covenant. We would declare this to be something we are working on and agree that people need to search together for what will have saving power for all. The assumption implicit in this option is that we do not know now and will not for some time be sure what this saving solution is. This option involves trust that with time we will come to know the leading of the Spirit and are committed to bind ourselves to that which is of the Spirit. We need time to work at a new theology based on the Scriptures and on our understanding of the nature of the gospel.

In Judaism the Scribes were asked to do the loosing and binding for the people. They were to study the Law of Moses and from that Law determine what people were free to do (loosing) and what people were required or forbidden to do (binding). Any scribe could suggest a law or an interpretation of the law. The other scribes would then try to show that, under certain situations, the law or ruling suggested did not stand up to scrutiny. If no one could find a reason why the ruling should not become binding, it was considered to have the approval of all the scribes and became binding.

In those instances where the scribes could not agree, no binding word was given. On divorce, mentioned in Deuteronomy 24:1-4 for example, they could not agree. The Shemmites held that only in the case of adultery could a husband divorce his wife. The Hillelites claimed that a husband could divorce his wife if he found any "indecency" in her. As a result the people had to live without a final word on this matter, and it is not surprising that they came to Jesus to see if he could help. Jesus indicated that they were both wrong. Divorce was never what God intended (Mark 10:1-12). Jesus' words imply that they need yet another approach to the question!

What is significant here is that they did not presume to have a final word until they could come to some form of agreement. More homework was needed. But the Scribes fully believed that with time God would give them insight and understanding that would lead to resolution of the problem.

In the meantime?

First and foremost we need to be Christian in relation to others with whom we disagree. Especially in times of disagreement we should let the fruit of the Spirit be manifested in our love, joy, peace, patience, kindness, goodness, faithfulness, gentleness, and self-control (Gal. 5:22). None of these should be missing in our response.

Procedurally, we could allow individual congregations to make local decisions *without immediately assuming that they are the position of the conference or implying that other congregations should do the same.*

If we follow such an approach, local situations can become cases to be observed to see whether God is blessing this new decision or whether it leads to judgment. This will be a way to test what is of God. It also offers a way to gain further knowledge and understanding of all that is involved in any decision. Churches that have chosen to deal differently with the situation will need to be observed. This includes churches that have withdrawn or been forced from area or national bodies, as well as those that have excommunicated persons in same-sex covenants. All such churches will help us see what God is blessing and what God is judging.

Whatever a congregation's stand, however, one that has undertaken a responsible discernment process should not have a position imposed on it from the outside. Only as a congregation is in dialogue with other congregations, that is, in area or national bodies, should such local situations be resolved.

As soon as one church makes a decision that other congregations in the area body do not agree with, it becomes an item for consideration within the area and then the denominational body. The broader church thus becomes involved and further considerations are engaged in that may lead to resolution. Through such a procedure a third way satisfactory to all the churches may be found.

Once we feel secure enough to share in open dialogue we can invite those still in the closet to feel free to declare who they are and where they stand. This will not happen until people who are now members of the church feel they will be treated in a Christian manner, not pre-judged for their stand.

The challenge of the moment

Some believe the homosexual issue is gaining urgent attention among Mennonites now as a result of the process, underway as of this writing, of integrating the General Conference and Mennonite Church denominational bodies. Although homosexuality has entered the discussion about membership in the new Mennonite Church USA and is often used as a litmus test to check on the sincerity of the dialogue partners, merger is hardly the only reason the issue is coming into such sharp focus at this time. Regardless of how matters are worked through in the integration process, the question of Christian same-sex covenants will not go away until all churches or denominations have seriously dealt with the problem. If it is not properly dealt with, it will divide churches and families against each other. We will do untold violence to one another in the process.

I believe the Spirit of God brings things to the surface for the church to address when the church is ready. It is the same as in our personal lives. When we have suppressed things that are too difficult for us to handle, they arise to consciousness at a time we are able to deal with them. Thus it is that in our day the question of the peace position has arisen for many denominations in a new way. Thus it was with the question of women in ministry for many churches. And I am hoping the time will come for our churches to consider their involvement in the economic sectors of our society from a Christian and not only from an economic point of view. At present we are not yet open to that, but perhaps sooner than we expect, the Spirit of God will force us to consider this as well.

I have faith that the church is now ready to deal with homosexuality in a way that avoids either-or solutions of inclusion or exclusion. What the precise solution will be, I do not know. I only know that if all participants in the discussion sincerely search for God's will, the Spirit of God will lead us on.

In terms of chronological time (*chronos*) we do not know how long this will take. If people on both sides of the discussion choose to be stubborn and more intent on convincing people than trying to hear what God is saying, we may never come to resolution. In terms of God's time (*kairos*), we have some idea of what can happen. If we together search for the promise of God this situation presents to us, and if we do so with all our hearts, then the time will come when we say with the church in Paul's day, "It seemed good to the Spirit and to us. . . ." Then we will know what is of God. May God give us the grace to look for the promise of our Lord.

Notes

1. I basically agree with the exegesis of Richard B. Hayes, *The Moral Teachings of the New Testament* (San Francisco: Harper Collins, 1996), 379-406. The reference to Scroggs is 382.

2. See Hays, 385.

3. Listed by J. W. McCormick, M.D. Toronto in *Focus* 5, no. 4 (Spring 1988). This is a publication of the Christian Medical and Dental Society.

4. Gerald W. Schlabach, "Deuteronomic or Constantinian: What is the Most Basic Problem of Christian Ethics?" in *The Wisdom of the Cross*, ed. Stanley Hauerwas, Chris H. Huebner, Harry J. Huebner, and Mark Thiessen Nation (Grand Rapids, Mich.: Wm. B. Eerdmans Publishing Co., 1999), 466ff.

Chapter 4

A Pastoral Plea: "Welcome one another, as Christ has welcomed you" (Rom. 15:7)

Paul M. Lederach

*H*OW SHALL THE CHURCH RELATE TO PERSONS IN OUR midst who are not heterosexual? My concern is especially for the sons and daughters of our Mennonite congregations who have discovered they are "different." They are not heterosexual like the vast majority among us. They have a homosexual orientation, but they long to follow Jesus and be part of his body.

Most of them grew up in Christian homes. They were active in congregational life. They attended Sunday school, went to vacation Bible school, participated in boys and girls clubs, and church camps. Many attended church-related elementary and high schools. They accepted Christ at a young age and were baptized. As they grew toward maturity they realized they were homosexual, something they sensed but were unable to define from early childhood. They experienced the distress of admitting this reality to themselves and then to parents and family.

They feared to tell the congregation, for all too often this admission led to responses of anger, judgment, and rejection. Insensitive persons with Bibles in hand were quick to utter the sure word of God's judgment. How shall the church relate to these persons in our midst? Let me be bold enough to make a few suggestions.

Maintain an Appropriate Sense of Proportion

Heterosexual Christians must ask themselves why this issue has become such an emotional and divisive matter. Obviously, more than Bible verses are involved. When Jesus' teaching about greed or love for enemy are ignored or rejected, there is no comparable vigorous and sustained rejection of the persons doing so. All of us are sexual beings. Sexual behavior is a critical aspect of our innermost, secret selves. For many heterosexual persons, homosexual activity is repulsive. That reaction, however, is personal rather than scriptural. This helps to explain why individuals and congregations seem ready to accommodate greed and rejection of nonresistance (about which Jesus taught in word and deed), but are unrelenting in rejecting gays and lesbians who profess faith (even though Jesus said little that relates to them).

Since for heterosexual people, homosexual activity is so repugnant, it is not difficult to call it sin. Some even go so far as to call it "the vilest of sin." However, in the New Testament catalogs of sins (1 Cor. 6:9-10; 1 Tim. 1:9,10), the Greek words thought to refer to homosexual activity are not given special emphasis.

Homosexual persons form a small portion of human society, and even a smaller portion have any interest in the church (which is not hard to explain). As a small portion of human society, their effect on society is constantly overblown. They not only lack power but also become the scapegoats for undermining marriage, family, and morality. Heterosexual Christians must be careful to maintain an appropriate sense of proportion.

Share Personal Faith and Experience

Sexual orientation is morally neutral and not well understood. How either heterosexual or homosexual orientation occurs is not clear. It is a complex mix of biological and environmental factors that are largely beyond personal and social control. From earliest times there have been persons whose primary sexual attraction is to persons of the same gender. These persons also bear God's image, and God loves them. It follows that heterosexual Christians, who are in the vast majority and who have power in the church, have a profound obligation to engage in conversations with (not just about) gay and lesbian individuals who desire to follow Jesus and fellowship in his body. We need to learn from each other. Spiritual journeys and experiences of faith are to be shared.

Include Believers of Homosexual Orientation in Our Biblical Discernment Process

How one's sexual orientation is expressed, whether hetero- or homosexual, has ethical implications both personally and socially. People of both orientations face the same kind of personal and social moral issues in expressing their sexuality. Believers, regardless of orientation, are on a continuum between celibacy on one hand and promiscuity on the other. Celibacy is an option open to both groups equally (1 Cor. 7:8). Promiscuity is out of the question for both! The New Testament defines appropriate heterosexual behavior for Christians in fairly specific detail. In brief, genital contact is not permitted outside of a permanent, monogamous, marriage relationship.

Appropriate homosexual behavior is not so considered. The concept of "homosexual orientation" was unknown when the New Testament was written. When Paul mentions same-sex activity he views it as the degenerate behavior of heterosexual individuals who knew God but refused to recognize God's goodness and authority. They were unthankful. Claiming to be wise, they became idolatrous, worshipping the creature rather than the Creator. At the bottom of the downward spiral, they engaged in "unnatural" sexual activity with others of the same sex (Rom 1:21-32). This picture is a far cry from the experience of homosexual persons in our midst who grew up in our congregations, have given their hearts to Jesus, and long to fellowship in congregations of God's people.

The heterosexual majority has tried to achieve consensus regarding appropriate behavior for persons with a homosexual orientation without their participation. Heterosexual believers have insisted that believers with a homosexual orientation must be celibate or become heterosexual to remain in church fellowship. In this way many believing homosexuals are locked out of the kingdom. Exclusion takes precedence over inclusion, judgment over mercy, and law is elevated above grace. Jesus warned that those who try to make others in their image end up keeping themselves, and those they try to mold in their image, out of the kingdom (Matt. 23:13-15).

Affirm a New Testament Understanding of Holiness

The New Testament understanding of holiness must be reaffirmed. In the Old Covenant holiness was tied to rituals, to observance of feasts and holy days, to sacred areas, and to exclusion of what was considered "unclean." Jesus and the apostles reinterpreted the Holiness Codes. For them, at the heart of holiness was love and acceptance.

Jesus included love for neighbor in the Deuteronomy 6:4 command to love God. He added, "There is no other commandment greater than these" (Mark 12:29, 30). Another time Jesus said, "*Whoever* comes to me I will never drive away" (John 6:37 NIV; emph. added). Jesus invited *all* to come to him to find rest, since he is both gentle and humble, and his yoke is easy and his burden is light (paraphrase of Matt. 11:28-30).

Both Paul and James affirm this emphasis. Paul summed up the whole law in a single commandment, "You shall love your neighbor as yourself" (Gal 5:14). James wrote,

> You do well if you really fulfill the royal law according to the Scriptures, "You shall love your neighbor as yourself." But if you show partiality, you commit sin and are convicted by the law as transgressors. . . . So speak and act as those who are judged by the law of liberty. For judgment will be without mercy to anyone who has shown no mercy; mercy triumphs over judgment. (James 2:8-13)

Peter writes that those who call God "Father" are to be holy like God is holy, and he adds that impartiality is a characteristic of God's holiness (1 Pet. 1:13-17). Peter learned this in his contact with "unclean" Cornelius. Certainly Peter and fellow believers did not consider Cornelius and his gentile household likely candidates for a major outpouring of the Spirit. But God's impartial judgment was not according to the old Holiness Codes of clean and unclean. Luke records the event three times and each time repeated, "What God has made clean, you must not call profane (or unclean)" (Acts 10:15, 28; 11:9). When Peter saw the work of the Holy Spirit, he simply said, "Who was I that I could hinder God?" (Acts 11:17).

Recognize and Honor the
Work of the Holy Spirit Among Us

Jesus sent the Holy Spirit to guide the church into all truth, which suggests that he will work through the experience of believers in interpreting and applying Scripture to the changed situations. Jesus knew the church would face issues like slavery in ways unanticipated in his day, and he gave the church great latitude to discern his will and way. Indeed, he went so far as to say, "Whatever you bind on earth will be bound in heaven, and whatever you loose on earth will be loosed in heaven" (Matt. 16:19). This suggests that the church needs to honor the work of the Spirit in the lives of homosexual believers and include them in discerning how to exercise the keys of the kingdom.

The Holy Spirit will lead persons with a homosexual orientation who believe in Jesus and want to follow him to discern an appropriate expression of their sexuality between celibacy and promiscuity. Since heterosexual genital contact is appropriate only in marriage, perhaps persons with homosexual orientation should engage in genital contact only in monogamous, lifelong commitments. If this is their discernment, this may be difficult for heterosexual Christians to accept. However, heterosexual Christians must be careful not to place burdens on others they themselves are unable to bear.

It is time to listen to believers in our midst who have a homosexual orientation. The harassment of homosexual persons and their families must be addressed as unworthy of the Name. To hate, to fear, and to reject these persons reveals the spirit of the world that is not characteristic of the community of the Spirit. In Christ's body there is compassion, patience, justice, mercy, and love. How people are received reveals our commitment to redemption, to reconciliation, and to peacemaking.

The question of same-sex practice within the bounds of committed, lifelong monogamous relationships is not an issue on which faithfulness or fellowship stands or falls. To make it so is to elevate sexual orientation to a level it does not deserve. While miraculous changes of orientation may or may not occur, breaking down the walls of hostility can become a reality. Our Lord longs to create one new humanity, built upon the foundation of the apostles and prophets. A step in this direction is to welcome one another as Christ has welcomed each of us.

Chapter 5

The Story of
the Listening Committee

Melanie Zuercher and Ed Stoltzfus[1]

The Task and the People

In 1990, the General Boards of the General Conference Mennonite Church (GC) and the Mennonite Church (MC) mandated formation of a Listening Committee for Homosexual Concerns. The boards saw this as a response to the call to remain in "loving dialogue" that was part of human sexuality position statements passed by the two denominations in 1986 and 1987.[2] It followed the pattern of an MC regional body which had had Listening Committees attached to several conventions. The Listening Committee was to work under the GC Commission on Education (COE) and the MC Mennonite Board of Congregational Ministries (MBCM).

The Listening Committee was given three tasks: to care for gays and lesbians and their families by "listening to their alienation and pain in the church and society"; to "encourage and help dialogue" between the various perspectives on homosexuality; to "foster continued theological discernment in the church" on homosexuality; and to make recommendations on policy, program, and church life to deal with the hurt and alienation experienced by gay and lesbian people and their families.[3] The recommendations were to go to COE and MBCM, which reported to the General Boards.

Eight people were named to the Listening Committee. Sue Goerzen, Harrow, Ontario; Dorothea Janzen, North Newton, Kansas; Earl Loganbill, Newton, Kansas; and Bernie Wiebe, Winnipeg, Manitoba, represented the General Conference. The Mennonite Church was represented by Edward Stoltzfus, Harrisonburg, Virginia; Delphine Martin, Waterloo, Ontario; Vern Rempel, Lancaster, Pennsylvania; and Ann Showalter, Oak Park, Illinois.

Some serving on the group were pastors and others had pastoral experience. One was a therapist; one led a program of conflict management at a university; one was a theologian. Some had gay or lesbian relatives or family members. A representative of the appointing boards met regularly with the committee.

The committee soon realized that it was ill-advised to exclude from their number anyone of same-sex orientation. According to the chairman, Ed Stoltzfus, they felt they needed the added perspective and helpful information such persons could add. With this in mind the committee requested that Doug Basinger of San Francisco and Ruth Wenger of Philadelphia be added to the committee.

Although their travel expenses were paid, committee members volunteered their time over the next two years to listen to individuals and groups from the entire spectrum of the Mennonite church, in a number of settings. They met initially in Newton on November 16-17, 1990. They had four pre-assembly sessions before Eugene '91, the General Assembly of the Mennonite Church in Oregon. They met a third time in Philadelphia, June 12-13, 1992, and finally before and in connection with Sioux Falls '92, the Triennial Sessions of the General Conference Mennonite Church in South Dakota. At both conventions, Listening Committee members staffed a room where individuals and groups came to share concerns, stories, opinions, and beliefs about homosexuality in the Mennonite church.

The Report: "None of Us Is the Same"

The Listening Committee issued a progress report to COE and MBCM, its appointing boards, in 1991, then submitted a final report on August 30, 1992. In a cover letter, Committee members wrote that

> Our journey has been an arduous one which has left none of us totally the same today as we were when we began. . . . We joined people in our various Mennonite communities and found this issue present wherever we went. Numbers vary, but the excruciating pain and utter alienation are common.

The context in which the Listening Committee was asked to work included the statements on human sexuality in the Christian life that were passed by the GC delegate body in Saskatoon, Saskatchewan, in 1986, and by the MC delegates in West Lafayette, Indiana, in 1987 (a general assembly known as Purdue '87). In addition, Mennonite theologians and scholars were at work on a *Confession of Faith in a Mennonite Perspective*, which would be accepted by both Mennonite denominations when they met jointly in 1995.

The so-called "Saskatoon statement" said this:

> We understand the Bible to teach that sexual intercourse is reserved for a man and woman united in marriage and that violation of this teaching is sin. It is our understanding that this teaching precludes premarital, extramarital and homosexual sexual activity.[4]

The Purdue document's wording was similar, but added that

> We covenant with each other to take part in the ongoing search for discernment and for openness to each other. As a part of the nurture of individuals and congregations, we will promote congregational study of the complex issues of sexuality, through Bible study and the use of [other] materials.

Both statements pledged to remain "in loving dialogue with each other in the body of Christ."[5] The Confession of Faith would eventually contain this statement: "According to Scripture, right sexual union takes place only within the marriage relationship."[6]

The Listening Committee recognized that "many of our GC and MC people feel that the Saskatoon and Purdue statements settle the parameters of this dialogue on [homosexuality] and should also settle this issue."[7] In their summary statement attached to the final report, however, committee members offered observations based on what they had heard over the past two years:

> It seemed that—in many cases—the less individuals, families, congregations and conferences had entered into personal dialogue with people affected by [homosexuality], the more convinced they are that the issue hardly exists or else does not need to exist. . . . It seemed that—in most cases—the more individuals, families, congregations and conferences entered into dialogue with people affected by this issue, the more they became convinced that the previous statements [i.e., Saskatoon and Purdue], while helpful to some, are not adequate treatments of biblical teaching or adequate responses to actual experience.[8]

The Listening Committee's final report was twenty-six pages long, plus a four-page appendix detailed the congregational discussion of Waterloo North Mennonite Church in Waterloo, Ontario, on whether or not to exclude gay and lesbian people from membership. The report described the committee's procedure and then listed a number of observations arising from its experience as a committee over two years.

Among these observations, they noted,

> Our committee listened and observes [that] there is widespread, apprehensive concern on the subject of homosexuality in our church. . . . that this issue places many conscientious members at the painful, grinding edge between two cardinal emphases in our theology and practice, [namely] unconditional Christian care and love, particularly for socially marginalized ones, and confrontation with moral judgment on these persons for acts they consider sinful; . . . [that] members of our church are not sure what homosexuality is and do not share a common understanding of important words and ideas used in discussing the subject. . . . which cause confusion in our conversations with each other; . . . [that] there are strong differences of opinion among us on the sources or causes of homosexuality which give rise to different views for resolving the question; . . . [that] many in our church are hard pressed with homophobic fears . . . because our thinking on this subject has been shaped by popular myths [false impressions and misconceptions] about it [homosexuality].[9]

They noted that, by extrapolating from general population percentages, we know there are many homosexuals in our congregations, and "more who do not reveal their homosexual orientation than who do."

Then as now, many people were asking what the Bible says about homosexuality. Others were asking what aspects of homosexuality were sinful. In this confused and tense situation both denominational leaders and our congregations were becoming cautiously involved with several approaches to questions raised, and the committee observed that the experience from this involvement would be crucial for churches in the years ahead.[10]

The report concludes with one program recommendation, namely, "that the Mennonite Church and the General Conference Mennonite Church intensify its efforts to help congregations study homosexuality to discern how homosexuals can relate to the church's life and ministry." This is followed by several "enabling" recommendations addressed to the General Boards, COE and

MBCM along with other denominational institutions, congregations, and pastors suggesting ways for carrying the study forward.[11]

The Outcome

The final report was given to COE and MBCM, the initiating committees, in August 1992. In early December 1992, Norma J. Johnson, executive secretary of COE, and MBCM executive secretary Everett Thomas wrote to Listening Committee co-chairs Goerzen and Stoltzfus, listing the actions taken by their respective groups. Both COE and MBCM accepted the report "with thanks" and indicated they would pass it on to the two denominational General Boards. "It seems inappropriate to release the final report of your committee to the public before both General Boards have had the opportunity to discuss it," the letter explained.

> Providing for an integrated (GC/MC) response to the Listening Committee's recommendations is the highest priority for us as we proceed with this task. This means that the recommendations of the Listening Committee will probably not be released in either GC or MC circles until after the responses from both General Boards in March 1993.[12]

When the GC General Board met in mid-March 1993, it, too, accepted the Listening Committee's report and recommendations "with thanks." However, the board also stated, through general secretary Vern Preheim, that it did not agree with the wording of the recommendation, particularly the call to each denomination to "intensify its efforts to help churches study homosexuality."

Therefore the General Board decided that the recommendation section of the report would not be made available to churches, and that only those congregations that requested the report would receive one. If and when they did, they would be sent a copy of the final report *without the recommendation section*, plus a copy of the Saskatoon statement on human sexuality, and the General Board's resolution in response to the Listening Committee's report.

Mennonite Reporter quoted Preheim as saying that "[General Board] members wanted to be clear that the board is being guided by the 1986 Saskatoon conference resolution of 'Human Sexuality and the Christian Life,'" according to a March 19, 1993, General Conference Mennonite Church News Service release written by Carla Reimer. "While General Board members appreciated the listening committee recommendations and tried to capture the essence in their action, they feared many would find some of the wording in the listening committee recommendations offensive," Preheim added.[13]

The MC General Board, meeting a month later, also received the Listening Committee's report "with thanks." It reaffirmed the 1987 Purdue statement "as the current denominational position on this question." Following the lead of the GC General Board, it agreed "to make the report of the Listening Committee (without committee recommendations)" available by request.

However, its action differed from that of its GC counterpart in that it encouraged "congregations and conferences to continue dialogue and study of human sexuality" and assigned denominational responsibilities to MBCM for providing consultation resources on homosexual concerns for congregations and pastors."[14]

The Boards' decision not to release the Listening Committee's recommendations caused something of a stir in the church. Listening Committee members themselves were disappointed with the decision and at least one passed a copy of the entire report, with the recommendations intact, to Paul Schrag, editor of *Mennonite Weekly Review*. In an editorial in the May 6, 1993 *MWR*, Schrag wrote,

> The General Boards of the Mennonite Church and the General Conference Mennonite Church are attempting to suppress part of a report prepared by the MC/GC Listening Committee for Homosexuality Concerns. This shows a lack of confidence in church members' ability to make their own decisions about how to respond to homosexuality.

Schrag continued,

> Church members should have the opportunity to decide for themselves what they think of the recommendations. The General Boards could have released the recommendations without endorsing them.
>
> Church members should have a chance to evaluate all the committee's work. What some find offensive, others might find encouraging. The boards do not need to protect people from being offended. And of course no congregation is forced to pay attention to the report and the recommendations at all.
>
> The recommendations do not contradict the 1986 and 1987 GC and MC resolutions that say homosexual activity is sin. They suggest ways to fulfill the resolutions' mandate for the church to study sexuality. . . . The issue is freedom of information. Let the people decide.[15]

Schrag's challenge notwithstanding, the decision of the General Boards' stood. The only way "the people" could decide was to obtain a complete copy of the Listening Committee's report with recommendations through unofficial channels. Both MBCM and COE sent out copies of the Listening Committee's report without its recommendations to all persons requesting it. In addition effort was made to assemble a "packet of resource material and sell this material to congregations as requested."[16]

Clearly denominational leaders perceived the growing importance of the homosexual issue in the church. But neither denomination initiated study programs to lead the church in working through the issue—this despite the MC's formal promise in their 1987 Purdue statement to "promote congregational study of the complex issues of sexuality, through Bible study and the use of [additional] materials."

In the absence of denominational initiative, various conference assemblies, leadership groups, and pastors hoped to meet the increasing discussion of homosexuality and settle the issue either by smothering it with "benign neglect," or by appealing to the Saskatoon and Purdue statements as the final word of the church. Some conferences issued additional position statements reaffirming the sinfulness of "homosexual practice" guided by the Saskatoon and Purdue texts. Others initiated a variety of disciplinary actions in congregations directly involved with homosexual persons.

In November 1993, at the request of the MC General Board, the MC Council on Faith, Life and Strategy opined that "regarding homosexuality, further study and discussion is not for the purpose of reviewing or changing the position of the church."[17] This effectively quashed further official study on the causes and moral nature of homosexuality. The final official statement made in the *Confession of Faith in a Mennonite Perspective* pronounced all homosexual sexual activity to be sin. Thus the call of the Study Committee on Human Sexuality and the Listening Committee for more sensitive and intense study of the issues was effectively muffled.

A Gathering Storm

But debate on homosexuality did not stop. A cacophony of voices arose from several fronts. It arose from gay and lesbian church members who had dared to make their sexual orientation public knowledge. These members, wanting to maintain connection with the church, tried to initiate open discussion of homosexuality in the church. Debate also arose from the action of several congregations welcoming gay and lesbian members, thereby precipitating discussion on whether those congregations should continue as members of their respective conferences. And debate unfolded through an onslaught of writing in church periodicals, especially in letters to editors. Ironically, protestations of those who opposed official church study and discussion only roused more debate.

In the 1990s, one by one congregations that accepted non-celibate gays and lesbians were disciplined in one form or another. Indeed, already in November 1987, the Ames Mennonite Church of Ames, Iowa, had been put out of Iowa-Nebraska Conference (MC) because of its willingness to accept non-celibate homosexuals as full members of the congregation.

On March 18, 1995, the home missions committee of Northern District Conference (GC) voted to end the conference's financial support of St. Paul Mennonite Fellowship in St. Paul, Minnesota, stating the "need to uphold the standard of the larger Mennonite church on issues of faith and practice." The conference's executive committee affirmed the home missions committee's action later in the month, and delegates upheld it during their 1995 sessions in Freeman, South Dakota. St. Paul was known to be a church that openly accepted non-celibate gays and lesbians as members.

During their April 7-8, 1995, sessions, delegates of Illinois Conference (MC) voted to place Oak Park Mennonite Church of Oak Park, Illinois, and Maple Avenue Mennonite Church of Waukesha, Wisconsin, on probation because of each congregation's acceptance of non-celibate gay and lesbian people as members. At delegate sessions a year later, March 29-30, a vote to expel the congregations failed by the narrow margin of three delegate votes.

On July 27, 1996, *MWR* published a front-page article focusing on the release by the Supportive Congregations Network (SCN) of a list of the ten Mennonite and Church of the Brethren congregations affiliated with the group that were willing to describe themselves as "publicly affirming" in their acceptance of gays and lesbians.[18] The article's publication coincided with the first SCN conference, "Dancing at the Table: Re-Imagining the Church," held July 28-30, 1996, in North Manchester, Indiana.

One of the publicly affirming congregations named in the article was Rainbow Mennonite Church in Kansas City, Kansas. The *MWR* article set in motion a chain of events within South Central

Conference (MC) that finally resulted in a ballot vote on expulsion by the conference delegates in late October 1997. The results of the vote, made public on March 11, 1998, showed a simple majority in favor of expelling the congregation from the conference. The decision took effect March 1, 1999. (In July that same year at conference sessions in St. Louis, delegates passed a by-laws change that would require a two-thirds majority for passage of votes on expulsion.)

Earlier in 1997, in July, Southside Fellowship of Elkhart, Indiana, and Assembly Mennonite Church of Goshen, Indiana, were informed by letter from the executive committee of Indiana-Michigan Conference (MC) that their conference voting privileges had been suspended for two years.

On October 14, 1997, Franconia Conference (MC) officials made public the results of a ballot vote expelling Germantown Mennonite Church in Philadelphia. The congregation had been on associate (non-voting member) status for the previous two years because it welcomed non-celibate homosexuals as members. By this action, the oldest continuously meeting Mennonite congregation in America was expelled from Franconia, effective January 1, 1998.

Southeast Mennonite Conference (MC) delegates voted on December 5, 1998, to put Atlanta Mennonite Fellowship on "non-member participant status" (no conference voting privileges and no members in conference leadership positions). Both Southeast leaders and Atlanta members described the outcome as a "third way"— neither full membership nor expulsion. Iowa-Nebraska Conference (MC) followed the same pattern in an action on June 24, 1999. A seventy-seven percent majority voted to put Faith Mennonite Church of Minneapolis, Minnesota on "sanctioned member status." Similar action has been taken in the case of the South Calgary Inter-Mennonite Church in Alberta, which is subject to discipline from Northwest Mennonite Conference (MC).

Ensuing Complications

All these congregations, except St. Paul Mennonite Fellowship, were dually affiliated with the Mennonite Church and the General Conference Mennonite Church. This has caused complications in the process of integrating the two denominations. The MC and the GCMC have had different polities regulating how congregations are members of the denomination. GC congregations are directly joined to the General Conference Mennonite Church through the

Congregational Delegate Session of the denomination, while MC congregations are joined to the Mennonite Church through membership in area conferences. This has resulted in different denominational patterns of disciplining congregations. To date, neither the GCMC nor any GC area conference has formally endorsed the discipline imposed on the congregations by MC conferences.

What will happen to these congregations in the new integrated Mennonite Church USA projected to become a legal entity in 2002? The proposal being submitted to the delegates of the conjoint assembly planned for Nashville, Tennessee, in July 2001, is that congregations are to be members of the Mennonite Church Unites States through area or district conferences. If this polity arrangement is agreed upon, as is expected at the date of writing, this will place the question of congregational status in the new Mennonite Church USA in the hands of the various conferences.

In the meantime, some congregations have withdrawn, or are considering withdrawal, from the denominations because they believe that the denominational position and action against homosexuals is not clear and stringent enough. In early 2001, the Cornerstone district of Virginia Conference (MC) withdrew from the conference assuming that Virginia will elect to become a part of the integrated Mennonite Church Unites States.[19] The Hopewell district of Atlantic Coast Conference (MC) is likewise deciding whether to withdraw from the Mennonite Church because of differences emerging initially from interpretation of charismatic reality and expression, but clearly influenced by the homosexuality issue. Several congregations in Eastern District (GC) are considering withdrawal based on the belief that Mennonite Church USA has an inadequate view of Scripture; but again biblical interpretation on homosexuality exacerbates their hermeneutical objections.

All this raises the question whether the church leadership's decision in the early 1990s not to follow through with the calls for continued study and discussion of the biblical, theological, and moral dimensions, as well as the "pastoral" aspects, of the homosexuality question, was ill-advised. On the other hand, the paradoxical stance of both the GC and MC General Boards, which pronounced all homosexual sexual intercourse sin, and at the same time called for continuing study and openness on the subject, may have posed an "impossible possibility," to quote the late theologian, Reinhold Niebuhr. In any case, given the history reported above, is it not time to listen again to the Listening Committee's recommendation?

Notes

1. An original article by Zuercher was taken from http://welcome-committee.org. Zuercher's work has been augmented with more recent developments by Stoltzfus and editor Kraus.

2. See "A Call to Affirmation, Confession and Covenant Regarding Human Sexuality," adopted by Mennonite Church General Assembly, July 8, 1987 (Elkart, Ind.: MC General Board, 1987); or "Resolution on Human sexuality," adopted at the Triennial Session of the General Conference Mennonite Church, July 1986 (Newton, Kan.: GC General Board, 1986).

3. See "Final Report: Listening Committee for Homosexual Concerns," August 20, 1992 (Newton, Kan.: Commission on Education of the General Conference Mennonite Church, 1992).

4. See "Resolution on Human Sexuality."

5. See "A Call to Affirmation, Confession and Covenant Regarding Human Sexuality" or "Resolution on Human Sexuality."

6. Article 19, "Singleness and Marriage," *Confession of Faith in a Mennonite Perspective* (Scottdale, Pa.; Herald Press, 1995), 72.

7. See "Final Report: Listening Committee for Homosexual Concerns," August 20, 1993 (Newton, Kan.: Commission on Education of the General Conference Mennonite Church, 1993).

8. "Summary Report of the MC/GC Joint Listening Committee for Homosexual Concerns," August 1992.

9. "Observations from the Joint Listening Committee for Homosexual Concerns," excerpted from the report presented to COE and MBCM, August 20, 1992. See Appendix 1. This paragraph summarizes the report items 4-8, 7-13 of the original report.

10. "Observations," 9-13.

11. See Appendix 1 for a full account of the recommendations.

12. Letter to Sue Goerzen and Ed Stoltzfus from Norma J. Johnson, executive secretary of the Commission on Education of the General Conference Mennonite Church, and Everett J. Thomas, executive secretary of Mennonite Board of Congregational Ministries of the Mennonite Church, Dec. 3, 1992.

13. Reimer, Margaret Loewen, "Conference has mixed response to report on homosexual concerns, " *Mennonite Reporter* (April 19, 1993), 1.

14. Letter to Ed Stoltzfus from Everett Thomas, June 29, 1993.

15. Schrag, Paul, "Entire Homosexuality Report Should be Public," *Mennonite Weekly Review* (May 6, 1993), 4.

16. Letter to Ed Stoltzfus from Everett Thomas, June 29, 1993.

17. Minutes of the MC "Faith, Life and Strategy Committee," Nov. 1993.

18. Preheim, Rich, "Churches Make Public Their Views on Gays," *Mennonite Weekly Review* (July 6, 1996), 1.

19. Reporting in the *Sword and Trumpet* (January 2001), 19, Ken Gonyer wrote, "The decision was precipitated by the apparent intent of the conference to join the Mennonite Church USA without clear membership guidelines pertaining to churches that accept and promote the homosexual [lifestyle]."

Chapter 6

Mennonites and the "Homosexual" Issue: A Recent History[1]

Lin Garber

*I*N JANUARY 1998 THE OLDEST MENNONITE CONGREGATION in North America was expelled from one of the two district conferences of which it was a member. A few months later the other conference with which that congregation was affiliated, which had no mechanism by which to expel a member church, rejected the ministerial credentials of that congregation's new pastor. Both actions were in response to the congregation's acceptance of some members of sexual minorities into full membership.

This treatment of Germantown Mennonite Church in Philadelphia by Franconia Conference of the Mennonite Church (MC) and the Eastern District of the General Conference Mennonite Church (GCMC) occasioned outcries from members and sympathizers of the sexual minorities in question. Those outcries in turn stirred equally loud support for conference actions from people who thought such sexual minorities had no place in their denominational circle. "What is the Mennonite Church coming to?" was the question asked by *both* sides in this dispute.

About the same time, this problem of sexual minorities in relation to faith communities was making news on the world scene. The World Council of Churches, meeting in Zimbabwe in December 1998, was addressed by Robert Mugabe, president of the host country, who spoke disparagingly against gays and lesbians. A few months earlier the world convocation of Anglicans had voted over-whelmingly to condemn the intimate relationships of members of the same sex, by a tally that showed a polar divergence of opinion between two-thirds-world clergy and most of those from Anglo-American countries. In India, leaders of orthodox Hinduism violently protested a film which portrayed a mother- and daughter-in-law forming a lesbian relation which challenged the traditional patriarchal order.

The view from within each one of these societies and faith communities can obscure the universality of the conflict. Anglican or Zimbabwean or Mennonite gays and lesbians can easily feel unjustly treated by their own people, as if *their* community is the oppressive exception to a tolerant world. As a matter of fact, one could have visited almost any country in the world during the last years of the second millennium or the early years of the third and found similar examples of religious and political leaders wrestling with the issue.

Much has been and is being written about the broad historical and geographical scope of the oppression, both real and perceived, and the way it waxes and wanes over time and across latitudes and longitudes. However, for purposes of this chapter, I concentrate on how these matters play out among Mennonites in North America. In looking at the Mennonite churches in relation to this subject, I want to explore where they are now and how they got there. I hope to be balanced in my approach. At the same time, in an effort not to perpetuate exclusion or silencing of persons of same-gender affectional orientation (SGAs), I want to give ample attention to how matters look when viewed from the SGA perspective.

Among Mennonites, the issue is often *who* can be members of the church. In contrast to the "catholic" traditions, where all inhabitants of a community were typically deemed members of the church and only admission or non-admission to the rites of communion created a distinction, in the Mennonite faith tradition membership is voluntary. The Anabaptist-Mennonite idea is that church membership entails a commitment to certain standards of faith and practice agreed on by the entire church community. It further entails commitments of mutual assistance in time of need, mutual counsel, and submission to the will of the whole "body" of faith.

It is not hard to see why such concepts can produce anxiety about the nature of those with whom one is in such intimate association. The necessary accompaniment to such communal mutuality is an energetic and intentional process of discernment, of careful and considerate reciprocal listening. These processes, especially among the relatively assimilated and institutionalized Mennonite bodies that are now moving toward merger, have often taken second place to considerations of institutional survival and efficiency. Consequently there has been an importation of consultants, facilitators, and resource persons where there used to be, at least in the idealized fantasies about the good old days, prayers for the guidance of the Holy Spirit.

All of this has meant that new notions of membership have come into play. Not the "weak and heavy laden," but those who contribute to the overall health of the institution seem sometimes more welcome than those who might be disruptive, especially those who might tend to repel the "stronger," more affluent members.

To place the problem in context, we need to look at the policies of other religious denominations in regard to SGAs. While some mainstream denominations, such as the United Methodists and the Presbyterians, are embroiled in controversy over whether their gay and lesbian members may be ordained to the clergy, or whether they may have "services of union" or similar analogs to marriage blessed by the denominational clergy or performed on church property, among most Mennonites the controversy has been over whether to admit such people into membership in the first place.

Denominations such as the United Church of Christ and the Universalist-Unitarians place no restrictions at all, at least on the national level, on membership and full participation in leadership. Yet even where denominations have no official position against the membership of gay and lesbian people, barriers exist against such membership that vary from congregation to congregation, parish to parish, or diocese to diocese.[2]

Celibacy, Promiscuity, or Committed Monogamy?

Until well past the middle of the twentieth century, the heterosexual majority considered "homosexual orientation" a psychological illness, and churches ignored it or dealt with individual cases as a sinful predilection. The heterosexual majority, both outside and inside the churches, considered the difference "queer," unfortunate, even shameful, and responded accordingly. The orientation itself was considered the problem. (The language of "sexual brokenness and bondage" is still used in "pastoral" guidelines of the Mennonite

Church.) Many SGAs either hid their difference and conformed to the community's mores or left the church and often the community.[3]

Certainly single people are not to be assumed to be SGAs, yet undoubtedly some have been, and many maiden aunts and bachelor uncles lived peaceably and with integrity in the Mennonite communities. However, to the extent that hiding their difference was in fact practiced, the principal method of concealment was to enter a heterosexual marriage under the heavy, sometimes coercive, persuasion of people in the churches. The result has been a tragedy of unhappy and broken families.

Of particular concern are the depressed or burdened spouses and former spouses, especially wives and ex-wives of gay men. There are few, if any, support groups or systems within the Mennonite churches, and almost none in any other, or even in secular psychotherapy, for these women told by the church that all this man needs to change is the love of a good woman—or vice-versa. When change did not occur, spouses left by the other could only conclude this was because they were not a good woman (or man).

[Editor's note: More recently, since the issue is out of the church closet, the question of continuing membership for those of same-gender affectional orientation living in committed monogamous relationships has been raised. This has led in some cases to formulations by denominational bodies of an ethical distinction between *orientation* and *practice* (in the face of arguments by dissenters that such a distinction is not viable).[4]

Further, for church discipline purposes, distinctions between "practicing"and "non-practicing" gays have been projected. People with same-gender affectional orientation are welcome so long as they promise to remain celibate (at least theoretically, according to some official statements, yet see below for contrary realities in practice). The argument is that the Bible mandates that sexual relations are to be confined to marriage, and marriage is reserved for a man and a woman. Thus same-sex unions are by definition promiscuous and sinful.

[For many in the SGA community, the distinction between practicing and nonpracticing has not been a crucial moral distinction. Rather it has been between promiscuous and committed monogamous relationships.] SGAs had for many years been trying to convey that long-term, committed, covenant relationships do exist among them. These relationships follow the ideal model of marriage required of opposite-sex couples, complete with vowed lifelong fidelity and mutual support. Such relationships were cited as the biblical, ethical, moral alternative to the promiscuity that many people in the dominant community thought was prevalent, especially among gay men.

This emphasis on the committed monogamous relationship backfired on SGA church members in a startling and unexpected way when it became the lightning rod for anti-gay polemics in the church press. One kind of reference equates such relationships with such immoral and criminal acts as adultery, stealing, and drunkenness.[5] By definition people in committed monogamous relationships are practicing their "homosexual lifestyle," and put in the same category as those who sexually act out in bathhouses, bars, public restrooms, and other settings for promiscuous behavior.[6]

Although the exclusion of same-gender attracted individuals in responsible, monogamous unions is problematic to the gay community, the fact that acceptance of celibate SGAs is now viewed in many denominational contexts as officially approved (if not always evident in given settings) seems to represent an advance in attitudes over the past two decades. In 1989 Kauffman and Driedger reported that an average of 32% of respondents from the five Mennonite bodies surveyed (ranging from 28% to 44%) would not accept "homosexual" persons "not engaging in homosexual acts" as members of their congregations. Eighty percent would not accept such persons as leaders, and 88% would apparently deny the possibility of ordination to persons of acknowledged homosexual orientation even if they were celibate. To say it another way: only 20% of Mennonites would have accepted even celibate homosexuals as leaders (only 12% would ordain them), and just over two-thirds would have accepted even celibate homosexuals as church members.

On the other hand, it should be noted that a significant minority of the two integrating denominations (22% of the MCs and 32% of the GCs) were willing to accept "persons engaging in homosexual acts" into membership, although 97% of the former and 94% of the latter appeared unwilling to consider them for ordination.[7]

Bipolar Responses to the Issue

Same-gender attracted people experience a wide range of responses among North American and European Mennonites today. (The rapidly growing population of two-thirds world Mennonites presents complications of its own.) There is virtually total acceptance in the Netherlands, including ordination to the clergy and the performance of commitment ceremonies in the churches. At the other end of the continuum are those groups or congregations in the United States most closely aligned with American Fundamentalism or the "Religious Right." In these groups there is virtually absolute ostracism.

These two extremes can also be found in the North American mainstream Mennonite denominations. On the one hand some district conferences of the MC, while proclaiming "pastoral concern," continue to describe same-sex attraction, in or out of a "covenanted relationship," as lust and temptation to sin. And on the other hand, the Supportive Congregations Network (SCN), which is affiliated with the Brethren-Mennonite Council for Lesbian and Gay Concerns (BMC) makes it its mission to affirm the spirituality of gay, lesbian, bisexual, and transgender people and encourage their acceptance in the churches. It should be noted, however, that BMC has been struggling throughout its existence for any kind of recognition by the official church groupings, so the pole of response that it represents actually lies beyond the denominational planet.[8]

One of the most pervasive aspects of the fundamentalist approach is the advocacy of what are called "transformation ministries" by their adherents, or the "ex-gay" movement by its detractors. Within the realm of psychiatry there are so-called "reparative" or "conversion" therapies, which have been repudiated by almost all major professional associations in the field.[9] This point of view is often promoted at official denominational levels.

In a study guide adopted by Lancaster Conference (MC) in September 1997 called "The Church and Homosexuality," the last page provides "Resources for Additional Help." The four listed entities, Day Seven Ministries, Exodus International, Homosexuals Anonymous, and Regeneration Books, are all related to the "ex-gay" movement.[10] BMC and SCN are conspicuously absent, as is "Connecting Families," a Brethren-Mennonite version of Parents and Friends of Lesbians and Gays (PFlag, itself absent). Even any reference to such authorities as the American Psychiatric Association and the American Psychological Association, with their multitude of resources, is missing. In fairness, that is not too surprising, since those organizations have issued statements opposing psychiatric and reparative or "conversion" therapy.[11]

This position, that all homosexuals can and should change if they wish to be members of the church, crops up in the official statements of some other conferences also, while referrals to ex-gay organizations are recommended in others, most notably in the "clarifications" issued by the MC General Board in 1991 (see text at http://www.ambs.edu/ljohns). The Virginia Conference follows this same tack in its pamphlet, "A Pastoral Approach Toward Persons with a Homosexual Orientation" (1999).

Although the Lancaster document is called a "study guide" and is subtitled "A Paper for Study and Discussion," it spells out the most restrictive position adopted by any MC district conference. The September 1997 conference assembly that adopted the statement explicitly approved the inclusion of the following preemptive declaration by an overwhelming margin (greater than 98%). "Congregations who justify homosexual acts preclude themselves from continued fellowship with other congregations in Lancaster Conference."

Among Mennonites there is a tendency for those who agree with them to appeal to such statements as the authoritative last word. Those who have questions, then, may find themselves silenced. Such statements are often seized on by anti-gay partisans as church pronouncements which make no further discussion necessary. The most telling example of this phenomenon is found in the nearly identical statements adopted by the GCMC (Saskatoon 1986) and the MC (Purdue 1987). These documents are full of language of repentance and apology for past mistreatment of gay people and call for continuing dialogue and prayerful discernment over the acknowledged disagreement that remains. Yet the single reference in these statements to homosexual genital contact as sinful is repeatedly invoked by anti-gay polemicists as "the official position of the Mennonite Church."[12] The earlier calls of official denominational study and listening committees for continuing serious study have been virtually ignored.[13]

In the psychiatric circles of the 1960s, Drs. Edmund Bergler, Irving Bieber, and Charles Socarides were the most prominent exponents of the idea that homosexuality in males was a disordered condition usually caused by a dominant mother in combination with a physically or psychologically absent or distant father, and that it could be cured by psychotherapeutic means. This view has survived within a fringe of the profession and been embraced by the religious right.

Occupying a comparable position within Mennonite circles has been Dr. Enos Martin, affiliated with Hershey Medical Center and a bishop in the Lancaster Conference. He has been the leading Mennonite spokesperson for the "ex-gay" point of view for many years, and his influence has been pervasive, especially in southeastern Pennsylvania.[14]

At the other pole are the Brethren-Mennonite Council for Lesbian and Gay Concerns and its subsidiary group, the Supportive Congregations Network (SCN). BMC originated in the mid-1970s, founded by Martin Rock, a gay male member of the Church of the Brethren employed by a Mennonite agency until his orientation was disclosed.[15] The SCN consists of more than twenty congregations in the Mennonite Church, General Conference Mennonite Church, and Church of the Brethren that have declared themselves "Open and Publicly Affirming" of their gay and lesbian members, plus another fifty or so who are either welcoming or are exploring the question, but who have not yet agreed to make their positions public.

The existence of these groups, plus the fact that nineteen percent of the Mennonites polled by Kauffman and Driedger would accept homosexuals "engaged in homosexual acts" for membership in the church, makes it inaccurate to say that practicing homosexuals may not be accepted into membership of Mennonite churches. At least a dozen Mennonite churches openly declare their dissent from any such assertions, and a good many more are working on it.

There continue to be gradations in both directions between these poles of opinion. Pressures from anti-gay congregations and individuals within the conferences have led to expulsions of four congregations (Ames, Germantown, Rainbow, and Atlanta) and to the disciplining of five (Oak Park, Maple Avenue, Assembly, Southside, Faith, and South Calgary Inter-Mennonite). Some congregations have withdrawn because they considered the discipline inadequate. More recently, Cornerstone congregations, centered in Virginia, and the Hopewell congregations of the Atlantic Coast Conference began negotiations for separation from their conferences in protest against the "Membership Guidelines for the formation of Mennonite Church USA" approved by the Executive Board September 23, 2000.[16]

Growing Churchwide
Awareness of the Gay Issue

Before 1969, Mennonites subscribed to the attitude of the general population regarding same-gender affection. They functioned as if it did not exist. Little, then, can be said to be a distinctively Mennonite history of the gay issue before that time. To be sure, the phenomenon presented some problems for those in charge of church institutions such as colleges that had populations of young people segregated by sex. But again, those were problems shared by all of North American society. The prevailing mood was "don't ask, don't tell," much as it was toward pre-marital cohabitation, abortion, and even birth control.[17]

Change began with the Stonewall incident of June 28, 1969, when a gay bar in Greenwich Village called the Stonewall Inn was raided by the police.[18] For much of the general population, this intrusion of an uncomfortable subject into their awareness was the final insult of the freewheeling, rebellious 1960s.

This was certainly true for most Mennonites, yet enough Mennonites had been exposed to the counter-culture movements of the period, or had actively participated in its various liberation and civil rights movements, that it was possible for them to include the newly visible cause of "gay liberation" in their sphere of sympathy and concern. This was especially the case in the growing populations of young Mennonite professionals and academics who were moving into university communities and metropolises, such as Philadelphia, Chicago, New York, Washington, D.C., Minnesota's Twin Cities, and San Francisco. [19]

The Mennonite fellowships that formed in these new urban settings were diverse. They included representatives from across the smorgasbord of Mennonite sectarian expressions, ranging from Old Order Amish to General Conference Mennonites, and typically affiliated with two or three of the existing denominational organizations instead of just one. They also included a wider range of household types than previously—from single persons living alone to unrelated persons living together. Also included were the occasional mixed-gender but unmarried couple, people living in communal arrangements, students sharing group living quarters, and a scattering of traditional nuclear families. Missing was the old extended family embracing grandparents, maiden aunts and bachelor uncles that many of them had experienced in their developing years.

These fellowships, for all their counter-cultural aspirations, also tended to be somewhat uniform in their whiteness (their ethnicity tended toward the Swiss-German or Dutch-Russian strains of their communities of origin), middle-class status, and level of educational achievement. But they engaged in dialogue with their urban settings in ways that would have scandalized many of their home communities had they known about it. Not least of these ways was acceptance of gay people (an acceptable blanket term in the 1970s) into full participation and membership (though membership itself was often a somewhat amorphous concept for these groups).

At the same time, many of the metropolitan areas where such fellowships arose were home to "mission churches" established by more theologically conservative emissaries, generally from more rural churches. It was not unheard of for the same family to have one member going to a metropolitan university and engaging in some of the exact "scandalous" or "sinful" behaviors another member might be trying to combat from a mission "station" in that same city. The tensions between the social and theological conservatism of the missionizing groups and the openness to free inquiry that characterizes the academics continue to play out to this day, especially on the subject of same-gender relationships.

Statements by some representatives of Mennonite African-American and Latino communities to the effect that the gay issue is a "white middle-class problem" have been a source of tension in some areas when disciplinary measures have been debated and voted upon. From the perspective of some members of communities of color, the concern has been to speak clearly against what is viewed as sin. To SGAs, that has been a denial of the existence of their black and Latino gay and lesbian brothers and sisters, as well as of the commonality of oppression shared by all these communities. However, some of the minority spokespeople have said that the problem to which more of this energy needs to be devoted is racism, a sentiment with which many SGAs agree.

A chronology of discourse

The 14 June 1977 issue of *Gospel Herald* contained an article by Kevin Linehan with the title "A Pastoral Response to Homosexuality."[20] An anonymous letter published in response to that article more than two months later, in the August 23 issue, contained the following paragraph:

> Now that you have opened the door to a discussion of this important issue, I feel it is mandatory for you to publish an article giving a sympathetic, balanced view to the question of the church's relationship to the homosexual. Perhaps you may want to contact persons such as John Howard Yoder for suggestions.

It has not been possible to track all the subsequent references to the subject in the letters-to-the-editor pages of all the church papers, but it is certain that this evocation of his name led a reluctant John Howard Yoder to fruitful delving into its ethical and theological underpinnings. Unfortunately much of his resulting work, cut short by his untimely death, has not been cleared for wider dissemination. However, given how little serious study has been undertaken by Mennonite scholars, here was an important move toward giving the issue careful scholarly attention.

It may be that the 1978 statement by the then Rainbow Boulevard Mennonite Church of Kansas City, Kansas, welcoming gays and lesbians into church membership, helped force the issue on to the agenda of the denomination-wide agencies. In any case, that was the year in which the Mennonite Medical Association held the first of two consultations on the general subject of homosexuality. John Howard Yoder zeroed in on the principal weakness of the event's format: "Here we come to a point where I must confess the severe limits of carrying on a conversation in the absence of the people we want to care about."[21]

At the second consultation the next year, the former wife of a gay man told her story, but no contribution from a gay or lesbian Mennonite was included. There is no indication in the published proceedings that any gay person was present, although conflicting reports would have either one "ex-gay" or two gay men, one not a Mennonite, as having been there.

In May 1980, a consultation was held at Laurelville Mennonite Church Center in Pennsylvania.[22] A group of invited educators, church agency employees, and theologians was commissioned to wrestle with the topics of singles and sex, extramarital sex, and homosexuality in a tightly scheduled weekend. The new factor here was that several openly gay and lesbian Mennonites were invited to attend and to contribute to the discussions. But even here none was asked to serve as a resource person. Some of the people who had made presentations at the MMA consultations were again front and center at this event.

In 1981, the MC General Assembly met at Bowling Green, Ohio, and a forum was scheduled for the discussion of homosexuality, but attendance was explicitly closed to any openly gay people. The event was under control of Dr. Enos Martin, the promoter of the "ex-gay" Day Seven Ministries discussed above. There were protests against this procedure which did not yield change.

In 1982 there was a seminar at the Associated Mennonite Biblical Seminaries in Elkhart, Indiana, at which John Howard Yoder continued his wrestling with the theological foundations of the ethics surrounding the church's treatment of gay and lesbian people. By the time of the 1983 Joint Assembly of the GCMC and the MC at Bethlehem, Pennsylvania, the frustration of some gay and lesbian people and their supporters at the silencing of the people most concerned and most informed about this topic began to be heard.

From the point of view of the institutional church, the tendency toward a policy of exclusion and silencing makes sense: the church is struggling to maintain its boundaries by declaring SGA "practice" sinful. Meanwhile SGAs find it difficult to explain such a policy without reference to homophobia. While on the one hand it is important not to fling the term around carelessly, the fact remains that homophobia does exist as a clinical phenomenon, characterized by fear and loathing of any kind of contact with gay, lesbian, bisexual, and transgender people—those whose existence challenges the gender identities of the majority of the population.[23] The great pressures placed on the denominational leaders to keep "those people" away from the gatherings of the faithful must have been driven in part by such fears.

At the Bethlehem General Assembly, the BMC set up a display with the initial approval of the governing boards, but the display was ordered dismantled after a few hours. The Mennonite Women's Caucus then provided display facilities at its booth, and the BMC was assigned a private room within the convention facility to which drop-ins were welcomed. A workshop session, with a sympathetic theologian and a sympathetic psychiatrist leading, was held with an overflow crowd in attendance. The Region V Listening Committee conducted a session at which several gay men were invited to contribute.

The episode of the booths has been played out at every assembly since then, in one form or another. It seems to have become almost a ritual. BMC applies for display space, and after "due consideration" the request is denied for one reason or another. BMC then books space in some nearby facility where it may receive inquiries and hold meetings. But there have been officially sponsored workshop sessions on the programs of most subsequent assemblies, and the procession of parents, an "ex-gay" speaker (for the required "balance"), and one or two openly gay or lesbian people, shepherded by a church functionary, has made the names and faces of some members of the Mennonite SGA community quite familiar to those who make a practice of attending these assemblies.

As early as 1980 (GCMC) and 1981 (MC), the general assemblies of the two largest Mennonite denominations called for a study of the issues that cluster around the subject of homosexuality. The resulting document was officially approved in 1985 and 1986 after a four-year study by a committee from both denominations made up of biblical scholars, medical doctors, and church leaders, both male and female. It was approved and recommended by the administrators of both denominations as the foundation for further study and ultimate action.

The report, *A Working Document for Study and Dialogue: Human Sexuality in the Christian Life* is remarkable.[24] This early product of desktop printing was promoted "as a working document," not "as a position statement" (Foreword, p. 3), and the administrators who issued it urged that "this study guide be used seriously in its totality." It provided the framework from which were developed the Saskatoon Statement of 1986 (GC) and the Purdue Statement of 1987 (MC), and it is referred to frequently in the report of the Listening Committee for Homosexual Concerns mandated by the same two denominations in 1990. (See the chapter by Melanie Zuercher and Ed Stoltzfus as well as the summary of the report in the appendix.) The recommendations of the administrators were not followed.

The "readers" debate

The liveliest and most copious discourse on the subject in Mennonite forums has been that in the letters-to-the-editor columns of the church papers, at least until the recent emergence of the electronic forum called MennoLink. From January 7, 1995, the date of a conference between congregations that accepted gay and lesbian members and officials of the MC and GCMC General Boards, until August 29, 1995, there was a crescendo of such letters. On that second date, the editor of the *Gospel Herald* announced, "After this issue, we will discontinue printing letters on homosexuality for a time. We will make an exception if a letter addresses something we print."

Following the expulsion of Germantown from Franconia Conference in November 1997 there was a de facto lifting of the moratorium by the *Gospel Herald*, since letters could be justified as "address[ing] something we print." What follows is based on examination of those letters printed in the *Gospel Herald* from January through August 1995, and those in issues of December 1997 and January 1998.

Much could be learned from analysis of this correspondence, but one aspect of it that seems especially worth calling attention to is the use of Scripture to prove one's point. I have done a crude classification of the letters by whether they take a stance favorable to or opposed to SGAs. In the "anti" column I have placed letters advocating "transformation" or "change" as conditions for their acceptance along with those that speak of "hating the sin but loving the sinner," and those which claim that all would be well if only SGAs would be celibate. Few letters could be placed in a neutral category.

Without going into a statistical breakdown, it becomes clear that the two sides appeal to different Scriptures to support their position. The antigay polemicists rely heavily on two passages of Scripture as support for their position. One is 1 Corinthians 6, with writers citing anything from the whole chapter to the specific verses 9 and 10. The second is 1 Corinthians 5.

What surprised me, and what I will focus on here, is that 1 Corinthians 5 was invoked more often than any other passage to show how terrible "homosexuality" is and why the church has a right to expunge it from its midst. Whenever the subject of disfellowshipping or excommunicating members or expelling congregations from conferences arose, this text was appealed to as scriptural precedent for the practice. But most uses of this passage failed to note that the "sin "for which Paul recommended expulsion was a *heterosexual* offense, namely, "a man is living with his father's wife," and the expulsion was of a single individual, not a congregation. Yet this incident was brought up no fewer than eight times in the group of letters studied. (1 Cor. 6 was cited six times, while the other familiar texts from Leviticus and Romans were mentioned no more than three times each.)

One sample of how the passage was applied occurs in a letter by Paul O. King in the April 4, 1995, issue. While he does not make a direct reference to "homosexuality," there can be no doubt about the intended target of the letter. He writes, "Paul's words were sharp: 'Hand that man over to Satan. Don't associate with anyone who calls himself a brother who is sexually immoral or greedy, an idolater, or a slanderer, a drunkard, or a swindler.'" This is a selective paraphrase, taking words from verse 5 and skipping to verse 11. The words omitted give the conditions and goal of the action under which such drastic action is to be taken: "When you are assembled, and my spirit is present [Paul is referring to his own spirit here], with the power of our Lord Jesus . . . for the destruction of the flesh, that his spirit may be saved in the day of the Lord Jesus." The letter also omits the final condition of the discipline, namely, "not even to eat with such a one." Was the writer reluctant to remind readers that he was quoting the passage used by Menno, and today's Old Order Amish, to justify shunning?

Another letter makes explicit the supposed connection between Romans 1 and 1 Corinthians 5. "God assures us in Romans 1:26-28 that he didn't change his mind about homosexuality. And in 1 Corinthians 5 we discover that it is still our responsibility to 'cut off' such from God's people, lest the church is defiled."[25] On the other hand, SGA defenders resorted most often to two passages in Acts: the story of Peter's vision ("God has shown me that I should not call anyone profane or unclean") in 10:28, and the enlargement of the early church's boundaries to include the uncircumcised in chapter 15. Clearly this represents two different understandings of the moral nature of same-sex affectional orientation and two different approaches to interpretation and application of Scripture.

What remains to be done is to make available to the church as a whole, through official Mennonite organs and institutions, the serious study being done on the relevant Scripture passages. An excellent start was made in *Human Sexuality in the Christian Life* (1985) referred to above. To my knowledge, this has not been widely used as a congregational study guide in the churches. Likewise the Listening Committee Report, which urged further empathetic study of the subject, did not receive wide distribution (see more on this in the Zuercher and Stoltzfus chapter). There has been a veritable flood of books published, from all perspectives and out of many denominations, giving intensive attention to these passages, but studies with a particular Anabaptist-Mennonite perspective, such as found in this book, are only beginning to emerge in Mennonite circles. Much remains to be done to heal the divide among us.

Notes

1. This chapter was first prepared for a symposium to be published by the Welcoming Committee. The present version has been edited and slightly revised with the author's permission. The original document can be found on the WC website at

http://www.welcome-committee.org/chapter-garber.htm

Readers with access to the World-Wide Web may use the following URL for resources that will illuminate much of what is said in this chapter. See http://www.ambs.edu/ljohns/glbmenu.htm. Grateful thanks are due to Professor Loren Johns for an excellent piece of work.

2. One example of that last case comes in the Episcopal Church, within which there is a collection of churches that publicly express their welcoming stance, similar to such collections as the Reconciling Congregations of the United Methodists, or the More Light Congregations of the largest Presbyterian body. But the only Episcopal churches in that grouping, called "Oasis," are in the dioceses of San Francisco and Newark, N.J. The latter is the diocese of the now-retired Bishop Spong, famous for his advocacy of lesbian and gay rights, and the former is of course the location of the most established gay population in the U.S. Yet there are many welcoming Episcopal parishes scattered throughout the country.

3. Once a term of opprobrium, in recent years the word *queer* has been appropriated with pride by transgender and intersex people and others who don't really fit the category of "same-gender affection," or gay or lesbian, yet who emphatically suffer from as much or more discrimination and misunderstanding as they do. Increasingly it is also used in academia as an umbrella term for *all* sexual minorities. *Homosexual* and its derivatives are avoided as much as possible in this chapter. It is set within quotation marks unless found in quoted material. The more that is learned about the diversity of human sexual nature and expression, the more obvious it becomes that there is not a meaningful category of orientation that can be designated by this single word. To SGAs and other "queer" people, *homosexual* now carries much the same emotional force as the word *nigger* does to an African-American, and people who wish to be accurate will not use it when alternatives are available.

4. See, for example, the 1983 Virginia Conference statement that was reaffirmed by the Council of Faith and Life (overseers of the conference districts) in 1997: "2. We believe that it is necessary to distinguish between 'homosexual orientation' and 'homosexual practice'" in *A Pastoral Approach Toward Persons with a Homosexual Orientation*, published by the conference, 1.

5. In a letter from Arnold Reimer, Beatrice, Neb., the writer said, "For those who think that a monogamous homosexual relationship is not wrong, would they hold the same position that if two people commit adultery or steal or get drunk, then it is not wrong, but if more than two are involved in the activity, then it becomes wrong?"(*Mennonite Weekly Review*, December 11, 1997). The first appearance of this pejorative usage to come to my attention was in connection with the public discussion of Franconia Conference's action against Germantown Church, in a process that became official in 1995 when Germantown was first placed on a kind of probation. I am not aware that the terminology came into question in earlier cases, such as Ames in 1988, or in contemporary controversies, such as those surrounding four congregations in Illinois and Indiana-Michigan Conferences of the MC.

6. It has not been possible to trace the first uses of some of these terminologies, but it would be most instructive to do so. There is a persistent vo-

cabulary used in anti-gay polemics that is unique to the genre, pointing to a common source. Groups studied by Didi Herman in *The Antigay Agenda: Orthodox Vision and the Christian Right* (Chicago: University of Chicago Press, 1997), would seem to offer a fruitful starting point for investigation.

7. *The Mennonite Mosaic*, J. Howard Kauffman and Leo Driedger (Scottdale, Pa.: Herald Press, 1991), 198.

8. This history, as it pertains to denominational groupings, will be confined largely to the GCMC, MC, and CMC (Conference of Mennonites in Canada), which are integrating into two binational body as of this writing. With only the most minutely nuanced variations, the stance of all the remaining bodies can pretty well be summed up as complete and total rejection of membership for SGAs who have not promised to remain celibate. The abbreviations MC, GC, and CMC are being used here to refer to the bodies that existed prior to the 1999 formation of Mennonite Church USA and Mennonite Church Canada.

9. A statement (hereafter APA statement 1998) adopted unanimously by the Trustees of the American Psychiatric Association in December of 1998 concludes thus: "Several major professional organizations including the American Psychological Association, the National Association of Social Workers and the American Academy of Pediatrics have all made statements against 'reparative therapy' because of concerns for the harm caused to patients. The American Psychiatric Association has already taken clear stands against discrimination, prejudice and unethical treatment on a variety of issues including discrimination on the basis of sexual orientation."

10. This document can be found at http://www.ambs.edu/ljohns/Lancaster.htm.

Day Seven Ministries is the Mennonite wing of Exodus International, headquartered in Lancaster Conference and spearheaded by Dr. Enos Martin, a psychiatrist who is also a Lancaster Conference bishop. Exodus International, the second listed resource, is simply the umbrella group to which Day Seven adheres. Homosexuals Anonymous, as its name implies, treats same-sex orientation as an addiction, and Regeneration Books is described as "a ministry similar to Day Seven."

11. APA statement 1998.

12. The statements are compared side by side at http://www.ambs.edu/ljohns/Resolutions.htm.

13. "Final Report: Listening Committee for Homosexual Concerns." Memorandum from the Joint Listening Committee for Homosexual Concerns, August 20, 1992, directed to Commission on Education, General Conference Mennonite Church and the Mennonite Board of Congregational Ministries, Mennonite Church [hereafter "Final Report"], p. CL 20. The document is at http://www.ambs.edu/ljohns/LCReport.htm.

14. For the positions of Bergler, Bieber, and Socarides, a useful commentary can be found in Duberman, Martin, *Cures: A Gay Man's Odyssey* (New York: Dutton, 1991), 53-54 for Bergler, and 64-67 for Bieber and Socarides.

15. Martin Rock's personal story can be found in *From Wounded Hearts* ed. Roberta Kreider (Gaithersburg, Md.: Chi Rho Press, 1998), 1-7.

16. At one end of this middle ground of conferences who have not adopted the "preemptive strike" strategy of the Lancaster Conference statement are six district conferences of the MC that have taken action to "discipline" such congregations, four of which have finally moved to expel them: Iowa-Nebraska (Ames, 1988), Franconia (Germantown, 1997), South Central (Rainbow, Kansas City, Kans., Mar. 1998/Mar. 1999), and Southeast (Atlanta, Dec., 1998). Illinois and Indiana-Michigan have "disciplined" but not yet expelled congregations (Oak Park, Ill., and Maple Avenue, Waukesha, Wis., in the case of the former, and Southside and Assembly, in Elkhart and Goshen, Ind., respectively, in the case of the latter).

Two SCN-listed Mennonite congregations affiliated with MC district conferences have not been acted against: First Mennonite of San Francisco (whose district conference, Pacific Southwest, is itself an integrated body as of 1995), and Mennonite Congregation of Boston, which retains dual membership in Atlantic Coast Conference of the MC and the Eastern District of the GCMC.

Another congregation, Faith of Minneapolis, although not on the SCN publicly affirming list, is well-known as accepting of gay and lesbian people. An action brought to discipline Faith at the Iowa-Nebraska Conference in 1998 failed to get the required two-thirds majority vote, but a repeat attempt in 1999 succeeded when the wording of the resolution was changed from "discipline" to "placing under sanction."

Other SCN Mennonite congregations are not affiliated with a conference that is exclusively MC: Boulder and Arvada in Colorado belong to the Western District of the GCMC, but not to Rocky Mountain Conference of the MC. Circle of Hope Mennonite Fellowship, a new congregation in Goshen, Ind., has decided to defer any conference affiliation for the time being. St. Paul Mennonite Fellowship in Minnesota belongs only to the Northern District of the GCMC. (An awkward situation arose when Iowa-Nebraska Conference attempted to expel St. Paul and was informed that the group had never joined!) In Canada, the Olive Branch congregation in Waterloo was formed only at the time when the two conferences in Ontario were well on their way to integration.

17. There are certainly dramatic and poignant individual stories that could be told of Mennonite experiences prior to Stonewall, but they would have to be recovered via oral history or other private means; because they were not recorded in any available public documents they are beyond the scope of a paper like this one.

18. There are many accounts of this incident, whose details are only peripherally relevant here. One is in Charles Kaiser, *The Gay Metropolis* (San Diego: Harcourt Brace & Co., 1977), 196-202.

19. The Canadian situation is not strictly comparable, in that cities like Kitchener, Vancouver, and especially Winnipeg, had long had substantial Mennonite populations that simply grew along with the expansion of these once-small cities into metropolises, while Toronto's growth engulfed a traditional Mennonite community in the Markham area.

20. For Kevin Linehan's intense but short-lived involvement in the Men-

nonite Church as an "ex-gay" pastor, see his book *Such Were Some of You* (Scottdale, Pa.: Herald Press, 1979).

21. "Is Homosexuality a Sin? How not to Work at a Question," in the proceedings of the Mennonite Medical Association Consultations on Homosexuality that were held at Schiller Park, Ill., in 1978 and 1979. Unfortunately I no longer have a copy of those proceedings.

22. I have misplaced my correspondence regarding this event, so at this writing I cannot verify under what sponsorship it was held.

23. The following are a selection of articles regarding homophobia as a clinical phenomenon: Henry E. Adams et al., "Is Homophobia Associated With Homosexual Arousal?" *Journal of Abnormal Psychology* 105, no. 3 (August 1996), 440-45; Walter W. Hudson and Wendell A. Ricketts, "A Strategy for the Measurement of Homophobia," *Journal of Homosexuality* 5, no. 4 (1980), 357-72 (this paper presents the Index of Homophobia or IHP, one of the standard measurement tools used by clinicians); Eric de Kuyper, "The Freudian Construction of Sexuality: the Gay Foundations of Heterosexuality and Straight Homophobia," *Journal of Homosexuality* 24, nos. 3/4 (year not stated), 137-44; Glenn Wagner et al., "Integration of One's Religion and Homosexuality: A Weapon Against Internalized Homophobia?" *Journal of Homosexuality* 26, no. 4 (1994), 91-110; Paul Van de Ven, "Comparisons Among Homophobic Reactions of Undergraduates, High School Students, and Young Offenders," *Journal of Sex Research* 31, no. 2 (1994), 117-24; Richard Seltzer, "The Social Location of Those Holding Antihomosexual Attitudes," *Sex Roles* 26, nos. 9/10 (1992), 391-98.

24. Newton, Kan., and Scottdale, Pa., 1985. The complete document is on the web at http://www.ambs.edu/ljohns/HSCL-cl.htm

25. Letter from Duey Matthews, Pryor, Okla., in *Gospel Herald* (March 21, 1995), 5.

Chapter 7

Mennonites Shift Focus from Morality to Who Belongs

Michael A. King

*D*URING 1997-1998 I STUDIED THE DELEGATE CONVERSATIONS that led to the 1998 excommunication of Germantown Mennonite Church from Franconia Conference, a Mennonite denominational body to which Germantown up to that point belonged.[1] As part of that study, I prepared the history offered here of how conversations in the larger denomination and eventually at Germantown gradually shifted from morality to polity. As I examine below, the debate moved from the morality of same-sex sexual expression to whether persons or congregations whose theology of homosexuality was more inclusive than that of the denomination should be included or excluded as members—or whether a third way between these poles might be found.

This is by no means to suggest that discussion or discernment of moral issues has ceased to take place. Obviously homosexuality continues to generate much ongoing wrestling with matters of morality. At the same time, my suggestion is that the leading edge of the conversation has over time shifted somewhat from what is right or wrong to what, amid the continuing moral tensions, the polity options shall be.

My history begins with 1987. Of course starting the narrative here is potentially an arbitrary decision; what happened in 1987 was shaped by previous currents of church polity and conversation. But for my purposes starting with events in 1987 seems less than arbitrary, because the Franconia conversations, as well as most denominational discussion, have been explicitly shaped not so much by what preceded 1987 as by the ripples sent out from and defined in Purdue.

The Purdue 87 Statement

At "Purdue 87," held at Purdue University in Lafayette, Indiana, the Mennonite Church, through a biennial North American assembly of delegates, attempted to define its stance on homosexuality. The Human Sexuality in Christian Life Committee, a denominational committee charged with helping Mennonites over six years to discuss and clarify their stand on homosexuality, had produced a report which included concern to love "those with a different sexual orientation" but also attempted to clarify the boundaries of acceptable sexual expression. Delegates voted to approve the report. These key words were later to become those meant whenever the Purdue 87 statement was referred to and remained so significant they were reproduced in the 1997 Franconia delegates booklet:

> We confess our fear and repent our absence of love toward those with a different sexual orientation and our lack of understanding for their struggle to find a place in society and in the church.
>
> We covenant with each other to study the Bible together and expand our insight into the biblical teachings related to sexuality. We understand the Bible to teach that genital intercourse is reserved for a man and woman in a marriage covenant and that violation even in the relationship, i.e. wife battering, is a sin. It is our understanding that this teaching also precludes premarital, extramarital, and homosexual genital activity. We further understand the Bible to teach the sanctity of the marriage covenant and that any violation of this covenant is sin.
>
> We covenant with each other to mutually bear the burdens of remaining in loving dialogue with each other in the body of Christ, recognizing that we are all sinners in need of God's grace and that the Holy Spirit may lead us to further truth and repentance. We promise compassion and prayer for each other that distrustful, broken, and sinful relationships may experience God's healing. (*Praying for the Church Beyond Us*, 1997, 29)[2]

That the delegates' adoption of this statement was a defining moment in an ongoing flow of effective history but not a damming of the current seems evident in this news report:

> Some delegates—especially those with a hardline position against homosexuality—seemed frustrated that six years of work had still not produced a clear denominational stand. A few others, like Sam Steiner of Ontario/Quebec, argued that the Bible itself "is not that clear" on homosexuality. Martin [chair of the Human Sexuality committee] pleaded for compassion and tolerance, and Moderator-Elect Ralph Lebold asked the delegates to accept the fact that there are differences among them on the subject.
>
> David Thomas of Lancaster suggested that the affirmation/confession/covenant section of the committee's report could be used as "a statement that we can take back to our congregations." The delegates agreed—by a large majority. (Gay and lesbian Mennonites in attendance at Purdue 87, through a statement they issued later, said they felt rejected by the action.) (Shenk, 1987, 533)

The plurality of delegate viewpoints, the call even by the Moderator-Elect (the denomination's top elected leader) for acceptance of different viewpoints, and the fact that a delegate helped turn what had been a "report" into a "statement"—such factors point to the inherent ambiguity of the delegates' action. What had they done? Had they approved rules binding on all Mennonites? Or a more informal report to their congregations? In addition, whatever the official or unofficial status of the statement, it called for Mennonites to "remain in loving dialogue . . . recognizing that . . . the Holy Spirit may lead us to further truth and repentance." What did this mean? Was the statement a provisional one, to be revised as further truth was glimpsed?

For eight years the status of the statement as well as the meaning of the "loving dialogue" phrasing remained unresolved. Precisely this ambiguity then became a resource for those who preferred that the church stance not be interpreted solely in exclusivist terms or as having churchwide authority. Ensuing tensions between rival interpretations led to a denominational need to lessen the ambiguity.

Efforts at clarification then involved such moves as a January 1995 consultation of Mennonite church leaders reported on by J. Lorne Peachey. There General Secretary (highest denominational staff position) James M. Lapp responded this way to questions about the role of the statement: "General Assembly statements have the authority conferences attribute to them. . . . If conferences accept them as authoritative, they are" (Peachey, 1995a).

In contrast, Mary Burkholder, the executive secretary of the Mennonite Conference of Eastern Canada (one of the conferences, or regional clusters of congregations, to which Lapp was referring), noted this: "I would have thought that when a statement is passed by General Assembly, it has authority for the life of the church" (Peachey, 1995a).

Other participants in the consultation noted the difficulty of determining at which level of denominational life accountability was finally lodged. No definitive conclusions were reached, but participants "agreed the answers need not come as 'either-or' in resolving the questions and tensions." They explored a range of options conferences had in "dealing with churches that adopt a practice different from the formal position of the Mennonite Church on homosexuality." These options included the following (1) terminating a congregation's conference membership or encouraging the congregation voluntarily to seek membership elsewhere; (2) accepting a congregation without question; or (3) continuing a relationship with the congregation while placing restrictions on it—such as by demoting it from full to "associate membership" in the conference. Additional possibilities included allowing "practicing homosexuals" to be congregational members but not leaders at any denominational level, or establishing a few "congregations of refuge" permitted to accept practicing homosexuals (Peachey, 1995a).

In this consultation report can be seen the continuing ambiguity regarding the denomination's position on homosexuality and what range of freedom congregations and conferences had to determine their own stand on the issue. Also evident in the report, however, are moves toward clarification, particularly in the outlines of the three options—exclusion, inclusion, or inclusion with restrictions—for conference handling of dissenting congregations that were to emerge as key in the Franconia discussions.

The report on these options marks a key shift in the denominational discussions. Here a significant move is being made from questions of whether or in what ways homosexuality is sinful to *how different stances should be dealt with*. This is evident in responses to the report by writers who hold contrasting positions but who focus on the managing of differences. On the one hand, Ryan Ahlgrim is disappointed that consultant participants did not address the possibility that a congregation could have homosexual members but not be at odds with the denominational positions. He contends that this could be the case, because the Purdue statement "identifies homosexual genital activity as a sin, but it says nothing about forbidding church membership to homosexuals" (1995). On the other hand, Ruth and Timothy Stoltzfus Jost "are dismayed and deeply concerned that our church would consider approving, or in any way accepting, any practice the Bible calls sin" (1995).

For some months, the *Gospel Herald* records show, ambiguity fostered continuing discussion along similar lines. Ambiguity persisted even as some conferences began to make decisions regarding congregations which accepted practicing homosexual members. In April 1995, Illinois Conference delegates "took steps toward the exclusion of two . . . congregations" even as a guest speaker "cautioned against rushing to judgment" (Hockman, 1995). In May, as Cummings reports, Franconia Conference delegates acted to place Germantown Mennonite Church on associate member status for two years, meaning that the congregation "may send nonvoting delegates to conference assemblies and members serving in conference capacities may complete their terms." During that period Germantown was asked

> not to advocate for a position on homosexuality different than the conference, refrain from sanctioning same-sex covenantings, and support the conference in upholding the ideals of heterosexual relationship and marriage. (1995)

Both conference actions prompted numerous letters continuing the debate regarding the status of the Purdue statement and its meaning. Thirty-nine people signed a June 1995 open letter asking that "the efforts to expel churches that have gay and lesbian members be discontinued" because "Our church statements on homosexuality have not required exclusion from membership but, rather, openness to dialogue" (Ahlgrim et al., 1995). In early August, ten more persons added their names to the original 39, noting that the "Mennonite church statement on homosexuality calls us to openness to dialogue, not exclusion" (Borntrager et al., 1995).

In contrast, on August 29, fourteen members of a men's Bible class supported the Franconia action, contending that "sin must be purged from among us if we expect God's blessing as a Mennonite Church" (Bachman et al., 1995). Twenty-seven members of another congregation expressed their strong concern "about the way that some people apparently desire to use Scripture to justify including practicing homosexuals into church membership" (Byrne et al., 1995).

The multiple-signatory letters were perhaps the last straw for *Gospel Herald* editor Lorne Peachey, who on August 29 (1995b), in the same issue in which he published the final such letters, declared a moratorium on letters to the editor on homosexuality except "if a letter addresses something we print." Peachey noted that up to that point all letters had been published in keeping with the "Mennonite Church official statement on homosexuality—which calls the practice sin but also urges continued discussion with those who disagree. . . ." But now perhaps a period of silence would be more beneficial, "to allow us to catch our breath" and "pray, study the Scriptures, and listen to what God may be saying to the church" (1995).

Still ambiguity persisted. Then, according to a December news report (*Gospel Herald*, 1995), a "news story in the church press about 12 Mennonite and Brethren congregations which have publicly stated that they welcome gay, lesbian, and bisexual people as members" led to a sharp clarification of lines. The Mennonite Church General Board asked the Council on Faith, Life, and Strategy (CFLS), which reports to it, to resolve the ambiguity. CFLS indicated that the Purdue statement "is the position of the Mennonite Church as well as of CFLS and the General Board" and stressed that

> the words "loving dialogue" found in this document should not be construed to mean that the homosexual issue is unresolved or that the position of the church is in question. . . . Rather, "loving dialogue" relates to the area of pastoral care in terms of biblical teaching on the denominational position, care of families and individuals who are touched by this issue, admonitions to those with a homosexual orientation, sponsorship of ministries that are directed toward calling persons out of homosexual practices and restoration in the body of believers, and dialogue that reflects the love of Jesus. (Council on Faith, Life, and Strategy, 1995)

Despite such efforts to reduce ambiguity, the fullest tests of the church's position continued to unfold in the conferences. The key debate continued to be how differences should be managed. *Gospel Herald* summarized 1996 developments this way:

> Three area conferences deal with homosexuality in annual meetings. Recommendation to oust two churches who [sic]

don't make homosexual practice a test of membership fails by three delegate votes at Illinois Conference meeting. Indiana-Michigan Conference delegates pass statement on sexuality and membership, and Southeast Conference moves toward separation with congregation which accepted into membership a gay couple living in a covenanted relationship. (1996)

On April 15, 1997, precisely while the Franconia cluster conversations on which my study focused were under way, a significant event took place. As *Gospel Herald* reported, by a roughly three-fourths vote Illinois Conference, whose earlier vote to expel two congregations had failed, agreed to place the congregations "under discipline" (Sommer, 1997). This was a new form of sanction delegates had created by amending their previous constitution. Such discipline stopped short of expulsion of congregations while removing from them conference voting privileges, possibly conference funds if they were receiving them, and the right to serve on conference commissions. Then late in 1997 Franconia did decide to expel Germantown congregation, effective in early 1998.

In the years since, as various chapters in this book amply document, the struggle has continued to define who shall be considered in or out of an area conference or the emerging Mennonite Church USA and on what terms. The end of the story may lie years or even decades ahead.

Notes

1. The study is reported in full in King, 2001. This chapter is adapted from that work and is used by permission of Pandora Press U.S.

2. Although most chapters in this book follow MLA endnote style, this chapter and chapter 9, which are among those more oriented toward social science, follow the author-date style more common for social scientific writing.

References

Ahlgrim, Ryan. 1995 (Feb. 7). [Letter to the editor]. *Gospel Herald*, 5.

Ahlhgrim, Ryan and Stanley Bohn, Marjorie Reimer Ediger, Eldon E. Esau, Calvin Flickinger, Matthew C. Friesen, James Gingerich, Steven Goering, Susan Ortman Goering, Gary Harder, Elfrieda Hiebert, Rhonda Horsch, Dorothea Janzen, LeRoy Kennel, Pauline Kennel, Kathy Landis, Weldon Nisly, Bonnie Neufeld, Chuck Neufeld, Brenda Sawatzky Paetkau, Miles Reimer, Steven G. Schmidt, Myron Schrag, Earl Sears, Ann Showalter, Joyce M. Shutt, Marlene Smucker, Stan Smucker,

Muriel T. Stackley, Rod Stafford, Donald R. Steelberg, David Swartz, Jerry Toews, Leann Toews, Dorothy Wiebe Johnson, Steve Wiebe Johnson, John Waltner, David M. Whitermore, Bruce Yoder. 1995 (June 20). "An open letter to the Mennonite Church and the General Conference Mennonite Church." *Gospel Herald*, 4.

Bachman, Charles and Isaac Beiler, Howard H. Hanna III, Isaac Lapp, Jonathan Lapp, Melvin G. Lapp, Walter Martin, Earl E. Mast, Kenneth Mast, John Smoker, Mel Smoker, Clair Umble, David M. Weaver, Samuel Yoder. 1995 (Aug. 29). [Letter to the editor]. *Gospel Herald*, 6.

Borntrager, Naomi, and Merritt Gardner, Ruth Ann Gardner, Suella Gerber, Nancy S. Lapp, Steven L. Mullet, Dorothy Yoder Nyce, John Nyce, Arden Shank, Meribeth Shank. 1995 (Aug. 1). [Letter to the editor]. *Gospel Herald*, 4.

Byrne, Geoff and Joan Byrne, Bradley J. Fair, Linda M. Fair, Lu Ann Horst, Annabelle Hoylman, Arthur S. Hoylman, B.D. Hoylman, Ed Kehr, Doris Martin, Wilmer G. Martin, Cheryl Mickley, Gary Mickley, Glenn E. Musselman, Lois Musselman, Leona Musselman, Melvin Musselman, Mildred Musselman, Diane Rider, Douglas Rider, Michael L. Rider, Roxanne Rider, Earl Schmidt, Elizabeth Schmidt, Dick Shaffer, Helen Shaffer, Lois Whisler. 1995 (Aug. 29). [Letter to the editor]. *Gospel Herald*, 6.

Council on Faith, Life, and Strategy issues statement on meaning of "dialogue." 1995 (Dec. 12). *Gospel Herald*, 10.

Cummings, Mary Lou. 1995 (May 9). Franconia designates Germantown as associate member. *Gospel Herald*, 10.

Hockman, Cathleen. 1995 (April 18). Ilinois Conference wrestles with future of churches accepting homosexual members. *Gospel Herald*, 8-9.

King, Michael A. 2001. *Fractured dance: Gadamer and the quest for understanding amid conflict*, C. Henry Smith Series, vol. 3. Telford, Pa.: Pandora Press U.S.

Peachey, Lorne. 1995a (Jan. 17). "Conference leaders explore various options for work with differing views on homosexuality." *Gospel Herald*, 9.

——— 1995b (Aug. 29). "For everything there is a season." *Gospel Herald*, 16.

*Praying for the church beyond us.*1997. [Semi-annual report, Franconia Mennonite Conference, Spring Conference Assembly, April 26].

Shenk, Steve. 1987 (July 28). "Mennonites condemn militarism, apartheid, homosexual practice." *Gospel Herald*, 532-534.

Sommer, Susan. 1997 (April 15). "Illinois Conference places two churches 'under discipline.'" *Gospel Herald*, 9.

Stoltzfus Jost, Ruth and Timothy. 1995 (Feb. 21). [Letter to the editor]. *Gospel Herald*, 8.

PART TWO

Framing the Theological Questions

Chapter 8

Why Does the Bible Divide Us? A Conversation with Scripture on Same-Gender Attraction

Don Blosser

*T*HE BIBLE IS THE BASIC SOURCE OF GUIDANCE AND AUTHORITY for Christian faith. When there are issues to be resolved, we ask, "What does the Bible say?" We assume that when we read the Bible, we will then know what to do. Why, then, do we have such confusion over what the Bible says?

Traditionally in the church we have depended on pastors and Sunday school teachers to tell us what the Bible means and have accepted their interpretation without carefully checking the text for ourselves. More recently, through radio and television, we have been exposed to many other persuasive interpretations, not to mention a multitude of different translations that do not always agree. Gradually, our attitudes toward the Bible and toward authority have changed. We do not always want to be told what the Bible says. We want to study it and decide for ourselves.

Consequently we do not always agree on what the Bible says. Denominations, area conferences, congregations, and individuals argue about the Bible. Often we quickly accuse each other of not being "biblical." Then we refuse to work together at finding resolution for our differences, choosing instead to condemn and talk about each other, often in the end separating. Tragically the very Scriptures God gave to unite us tear us apart, causing pain for all involved.

We have intense feelings about the Bible; that is good. But sometimes our intensity causes us to use the Bible in ways that hurt. We have good intentions. We believe we are being faithful to the biblical message, but often we do not recognize how or who we are hurting. This only adds to the pain, because the persons being hurt are in our own congregations, our circle of friends, or even our own families.

How Do We Read the Bible?

In 2 Timothy 3:16 we are told that the Bible is "profitable for teaching, for correction and for training in righteousness." But how do we decide what should be taught, who needs to be corrected, what behavior is righteous?

Some Christians argue that the Bible must be taken literally as direct words from God. The words of the Bible carry an eternal significance separate from the culture in which they were written. These words are not merely human; they are God's. The text, as well as the meaning of the text, does not change over time. What the Bible says is what the Bible means.

Other people, equally committed to the Scriptures, ask, "What did the words mean when Paul or Moses used them?" They believe the task of the biblical scholar is to get as close to the mind and culture of Paul as possible. We can best know the intention of God if we understand the situations Moses and Paul were facing as they spoke to this issue. What were the images in Paul's mind as he wrote to the church at Corinth? Are these the same images that come to our minds as we read the text today? Our use of language is different from Paul's, and our understandings of science and culture more complex than those of first-century culture. Therefore we must know the context of the biblical message to apply it faithfully in our own culture.

Which Direction Does the Bible Point?

Some see the ancient biblical culture as the normative ideal to which God is calling all cultures. This approach holds that the faithful church should be calling persons back to that first-century culture in which God gave the Scriptures. The ideal is to replicate the biblical culture in today's societies.[1] Since God is unchanging, they argue, the meaning of God's Word never changes. They fear that "contextualizing" the Bible tampers with the meaning. It allows everything to become relative and causes people to stray from its truth. According to this approach, then, the mission of the church is to hold to the truth "once for all delivered to the saints."

Others in the church emphasize that God is not simply "back there." God is "out there," ahead of us, calling us to new expressions of the historic biblical faith. The meaning of the Bible is not tied to one culture. For these persons, the model for the faith community is not the ancient culture of the Bible, but the eternal culture of the heavenly community. Accordingly the mission of the church is to share the message of God's eternal mercy and grace with all humanity in every culture. This requires contextualization.

These people believe that we do not have to duplicate the specific ethical or religious practices of the first century to be faithful to the will of God today. They ask what God's intentions were behind the specific guidelines given in biblical culture. What did God want to accomplish in that setting? Faithfulness then means applying biblical principles to our lives in ways that give faithful contemporary meaning to these eternal truths. Models for this can be found in the Bible itself, since much of Acts and Paul's writing records early Christians' efforts faithfully to apply God's principles in new settings as the gospel began to spread.

Awareness of different ways we approach the Bible may help us understand why we have experienced such deeply felt tensions. We come to the Bible asking different questions. We are standing back to back, looking in opposite directions, even as we each sincerely believe we are facing God. No wonder we do not come out at the same place. Our biblical knowledge would be greatly enhanced if, rather than facing away from each other, we at least met face to face and talked with each other, sharing what we see so everyone might benefit from the combined wisdom.

When we have the courage to talk with those who interpret the text differently, the experience can expand our own understanding of the text and encourage us to be more accepting of others even when we strongly disagree. In the following studies, we look at how various groups read the text in hopes of better understanding our differences and gaining a stronger basis for talking together.

Reading the Bible Together: The Old Testament

Genesis 1-2

The Genesis accounts refer to God's creation of male and female for the purpose of bearing children and perpetuating the human race. (The idea of romantic love develops much later.) Some students of the Bible believe this proves heterosexual relationships are normative because God created humanity as male and female and gave them the charge to "be fruitful and multiply" (Gen.1:28). Further, Genesis 2:24 says that a man should leave his parents and become "one flesh" with a woman, thus proving God's intention that sexual intercourse should be an exclusive male-female relationship. Accordingly, all other sexual activity is in violation of the way God created us to be, and any alternate expression must be sinful.

It is easy to understand why this explanation is persuasive. It is a simple, straightforward reading of the English text. However, Hebrew language scholars question whether this explanation reflects either the spirit or the content of what the text actually says. They tell us that Genesis 1:26-28 simply presents the biological identity of Adam and Eve as male and female, not as husband and wife. The purpose of the text is to identify the special status which these male and female creatures have above the rest of creation. They are made in the image and likeness of God. In sharp contrast to other ancient creation accounts that depict humanity as inferior and created to serve the fickle whims of the gods, they are elevated above other creatures and have a dignity and responsibility matching that of the creating God. The text, however, does not address the sexual role or sociological relationship of these two creatures.[2]

God intends for humanity to perpetuate itself ("be fruitful and multiply"), but this sexual function of procreating children is not the defining human element. All the animals are given the same mandate. People who are childless are certainly no less human than those who have families. Neither is heterosexual union the central defining element of humanity. Persons who are celibate are fully human. Indeed, Paul says some very positive things about remaining single in 1 Corinthians 7. Procreation is not a command of God that must be followed to be fully human.

In the sparsely populated Old Testament world, infertility was regarded as a curse and even attributed to divine affliction. Today the current problem is over-population, and it is no longer appropriate to apply that theological assumption.

The passage in Genesis 1–2 reflects an ancient sexual view of humanity. Humans were viewed as simply "male and female," that is, separate entities with no indication of mutually shared characteristics. Today we recognize that each of us possesses both male and female characteristics. Such characteristics exist on an overlapping continuum in every individual human being.

We have a rapidly expanding knowledge of genetics and the developmental basis of human sexuality. Although one's environment provides influences on later sexual expression, one's sexual orientation now appears to have deep biological roots. Patterns of sexual orientation begin to be formed in the developing fetus before birth. This being the case, the faith community is called to accept all persons without regard to their specific genetic structure. The desire to "fix it" because it is seen as an aberration defies God's creating activity and places us in the position of being judge over God's activity. Unfortunately, the people of God have a long history of wanting to play judge over persons whom they perceive to be different from the majority of the community.

Genesis 19:1-29

The story of Sodom is a tragic account of an ancient culture at its worst, including abuse of strangers and offering women as a sacrifice to save men. Richard Hays, professor of divinity at Duke University and author of *The Moral Vision of the New Testament,* states that "this text is irrelevant to the topic of same-gender sexual issues. There is nothing here on which to base any judgment about the morality of same-sex behavior."[3] But since perception of reality can be as powerful as reality itself, this story must be considered.

Two angels come to the city. Lot, a recent immigrant who is not fully accepted, insists that they stay at his house. That evening every man of the city, young and old, comes to Lot's house and demands that Lot bring the strangers out "so that we may know [*yadah*] them." Lot attempts to protect his guests by making a despicable decision to offer his two virgin daughters as a sexual alternative, but the men refuse and threaten Lot if he does not turn his guests over to them.

The traditional explanation is that Sodom was overrun with sexual immorality. With the arrival of the strangers, the men of Sodom see the opportunity for new sexual partners, so they go to Lot's house demanding sexual intercourse (*yadah*) with them. This approach also argues that the men of Sodom refused to accept Lot's offer of his daughters because they wanted men (not women) as sexual partners, and they saw the two visitors as offering a creative new sexual experience.

This interpretation is based on a narrow (but technically acceptable) reading of *yadah*, which is translated "to know." This same word is also used as a euphemism for sexual intercourse, and those who hold this view argue that the sexual meaning is clearly implied in the following sentence where Lot offers his daughters who "have not known" (*yadah*) a man. Thomas Schmidt, in his book *Straight and Narrow*, argues that this sexual meaning of *yadah* in verse 8 controls the sexual meaning of *yadah* in verse 5, thus proving that homosexual fervor was the driving force behind the mob action, and that for such behavior the city was condemned by God.

Schmidt then links Ezekiel 16:49 "Sodom did abominable things before God" with Leviticus 18:22 "you shall not lie with a man as with a woman for it is an abomination." He concludes that the abomination of Sodom was the fact that men were having sexual intercourse with other men.[4] He refers also to Philo and Josephus who indicate that Sodom's sins were sexual in nature.[5]

Other biblical scholars take serious issue with this approach. They agree that *yadah* sometimes means sexual intercourse but insist that such a translation is rare and does not express the most common meaning of the word. *Yadah* occurs 1048 times in the Old Testament. Of these occurrences 933 have the meaning "learning to know someone as a person." In only eleven cases (slightly more than one percent) does it serve as a euphemism for sexual intercourse.[6]

The text contains additional information that suggests the need for a more careful reading of the story. The text is precise in stating that "every last man in the city, both young and old" (v. 4) came to Lot's house. Does this mean every man in the city was a homosexual looking for sexual satisfaction? That assumption is statistically problematic if not totally impossible. In ancient culture, sexual intercourse was a private experience. It violates the most basic cultural norms of virtually all societies to argue that several hundred men would gather to satisfy their homosexual passions with these two strangers. It also seems clear that Lot does not think the group has same-gender sexual attraction, for he offers them a heterosexual option (his two daughters) which the men refuse because sexual activity is not their issue.

What, then, would bring *every man* in the city to Lot's house under these conditions? Two strangers have come to the city and are staying with Lot. Lot is already suspect because he has no history as a member of the community. The men of the city are worried about the security of their homes and families. "Who are these strange men? We want to know them" (v. 5). The story reports mob action by men who were worried about their security. They tried to protect the city by intimidating and terrorizing the visitors. They wanted to be absolutely certain these spies did not perceive them as being weak or vulnerable, so they threatened to brutalize them.

Fear about city security was a common experience in the ancient world. Stories of spies who infiltrated cities and then reported on wealth, military defenses, numbers of men, and city layouts as precursor to military attacks are told throughout the ancient world (see Josh. 2). The men, all of whom are responsible for the common defense of the city, want to know whether the presence of these visitors poses a threat to the safety of their families.

Hays is correct when he says this is not a sexual story, and to read it this way does not address the issue at hand. Martti Nissinen, who has done a careful study of the ancient scene, also agrees that modern interpreters have erred in speculating about the homosexual motives of the Sodomite men. They were not motivated to satisfy sexual lust but to intimidate threatening strangers by showing their supremacy and power over the guests.[7]

There is an even more compelling reason to doubt the sexual interpretation of this story. Jesus referred to Sodom on three occasions (Matt.10:15; 11:23-24; Luke 17:29, plus parallel readings). In each reference the sin Jesus identifies with Sodom is greed, luxury, and refusal to accept the stranger. According to Ezekiel, the sin of Sodom was "pride, excess of food, and prosperity without showing compassion for the poor and needy" (Ezek. 16:49). Jesus affirmed the Ezekiel tradition to explain the destruction of Sodom.

Jesus certainly would have known current rabbinical explanations regarding Sodom, but he chose not to accept them. For followers of Jesus this is an important lesson. When we make Sodom a story about sexuality and God's condemnation of the city, we ignore the interpretation Jesus gave and use extra-biblical interpretations to support our own agenda.[8] That is a dangerous hermeneutical practice.

Judges 19

The story in Judges 19 has many thematic and linguistic parallels with the Genesis story. A Levite was returning home with his concubine; they needed to stay overnight in the village of Gibeah. They camped in the village square because "no one took them in to spend the night" (19:15). That in itself was a violation of local cultural hospitality. An old man from the city found them in the square and invited them to his house. That night some perverse men of the city surrounded the house demanding that the visitor be turned over to them "that we might know [*yadah*] him" (19:22). Attempting to protect his guest, the host offered his own virgin daughter and the Levite's concubine as bribery to leave the guest alone. The men gang-raped the concubine throughout the night. The next morning she was found dead on the front steps.

The behavior of the men (both her husband and the men of Gibeah) toward the women was despicable and inexcusable.[9] This is a story of gang rape, whether of a male or a female, to shame and humiliate a stranger who sought their protection. The sole basis for making it a story of same-gender atrocity is the translation of *yadah* in verse 22 to mean sexual intercourse, and this translation loses credibility when the details of the story are examined.

The men of the city asked that the male visitor be given to them so they might know his identity and purpose. Nissinen suggests that their motivation for brutalization and sexual intimidation was based on a fear of the stranger, and thus was an offense against the honor of the guest. Thus the issue is city security and male honor, not homosexual satisfaction.[10] The fact that they accepted the concubine and gang-raped her to death supports this understanding. Had they been asking for male sexual partners, the substitution of the concubine would not have been acceptable.

This story condemns the social inhospitality of strangers, and sexual abuse. Neither homosexual lust nor activity is present in this story. That is a creation of later tradition that is read back into the story, and is therefore inappropriate.

Leviticus 18 and 20

The only two forthright statements against male same-gender intercourse appear in the Holiness Code: "You shall not lie with a man as with a woman." This act is given as one of the sexual offenses for which the death penalty is prescribed. Since it is listed as an abomination, some argue that there is no room for further dialogue about same-gender sexual activity under any circumstances. We should simply label it as sin and obey the command of God. Any attempt at discussion is immediately suspect because discussion is seen as an attempt to destroy the clear and obvious meaning of Scripture in order to promote a sinful agenda.

It is very difficult to talk about a topic when simply talking together is labeled sinful. Honesty requires that we examine the text, validate the context, accept the message, and look for an appropriate, biblically faithful, contemporary application. One core element in interpreting this text for today is the relationship of the Old Testament Levitical laws to Christian ethical behavior. From its beginning, the church has distinguised between Old Testament moral law and ceremonial law. Not all the Levitical guidelines are automatically retained in Christian faith. There are also other Old Testament guidelines that were either deemed obsolete or simply disregarded by the New Testament Church: circumcision (Acts 15), purity laws (Mark 5), unclean food (Acts 10), inclusion of marginalized people (Luke 14), and even Sabbath observance (Mattt. 12:1). We must look at the purpose behind the laws, then determine how that purpose can be given faithful expression in our own experience.

Preservation of the nation as a special people of Yahweh was crucial to Israel. Children were valued as vital to the community's security, which was achieved through providing male children who would defend the country against invading forces. This led to specific and severe punishments for sexual behaviors that interfered with conception. For example, withdrawal of penis during intercourse, masturbation, or other activities that "wasted" semen were condemned because those actions precluded the possibility of reproduction. They were considered a violation of the will of God whose intention was to protect the security of the family by providing children who would care for the parents in their old age.

In the Old Testament, the community was a constant focus of concern in the experience of the individual. Sexual behaviors that could never expand population were condemned because they endangered the tribe's very survival. Heterosexual intercourse was primarily for the purpose of bearing children who would support family and nation. Thus homosexual activity threatened the security of the community and was forbidden, while heterosexual prostitution, which preserved the possibility of childbearing, was tolerated. Sexual "orientation" was not considered a factor in the regulation of sexual behavior in most ancient cultures. Today, we give far less consideration to the community consequence of individual acts.

The major cultural and demographic changes of our contemporary period raise the question whether literal obedience to these biblical rules still maintains the same principle. Population has now become a matter of opposite concern. The earth is in serious danger of overpopulation. While some Christian traditions still understand the biblical mandate to apply today, most do not condemn couples who choose not to have large families. We do not charge childless couples with living in violation of God's will.

Further, many scholars think the prohibition in Leviticus 18 and 20 should be understood as a directive to Israelite men to avoid the cult prostitution of Canaanite worship. They point out that Canaanite worship was heavily sexual in nature. Ceremonial prostitutes, both male and female, functioned as priestly agents through whom one participated in divine activity. The spiritual powers of the gods were tapped through these sexual acts, leading to fertility and abundance in the agricultural realm. This effectively united worship, sex, and prosperity into one act. If this is the meaning of the prohibition, it would also explain the severe consequence of death for such sexual activity; namely, the necessity of keeping the community free from all infiltration of pagan influence. This concern is identified with severe commands to obliterate those religious influences that challenged Israel's faith (see 1 Kings 18:40).

The church is confronted with the difficult task of discerning which of the laws that governed Israel should be transferred to the new faith community of Jesus. Church members do not agree on how these Old Testament stories should be interpreted. These stories involve explicit sexual abuses of the most destructive kind, behaviors that should never be found in the life of a Christian.

What is the relationship of the sexual abuses in the original stories with sexual expression in our modern situation? Is it valid to place these horrific stories of sexual abuse under the umbrella of vague, general terminology, then apply them to a specific contemporary sexual expression that has nothing whatever to do with the abuses of the original stories? How can we recover the centrality of the biblical message about how we treat persons who are oppressed, abused, or simply different from us in one specific way? This was the focal point of Jesus' teachings—love for the neighbor, the oppressed, the alien, and the enemy.

Reading the Bible Together: The New Testament

The New Testament opens a more familiar and often more intense area of discussion. While reading what others have written on this topic, I began to notice that although the study of the Bible should shape our beliefs, not a single writer admitted to having changed her or his beliefs as a result of study. In all cases, the writers held theological or sociological beliefs that guided their study, and the work they did in the biblical text only proved the correctness of the beliefs they had before they began! This is not intended as a criticism of these writers, since we all share in this tendency, but as an observation that the Bible is often used to support what we already believe rather than as a source of instruction.

What are the basic concepts of God that influence how we think about God, about the Scriptures, about life, and about how God relates to us as God's children? If we can keep these questions in focus and acknowledge their influence, they might help us better read the texts together, learning from each other what God is saying to us.

Jesus

Although Jesus frequently loosed his disciples from the legal taboos of the Holiness Code,[11] there are no recorded words of Jesus on the topic of same-gender orientation. Scholars argue vigorously among themselves about what this means; all claim that the silence of Jesus supports their beliefs. Some say same-gender orientation was such an obvious sin there was no need for Jesus to speak about it because all godly Jewish people knew such sexual activity was explicitly forbidden. Others argue that there were inevitably same-gender-oriented persons in the Jewish community and by his silence, Jesus accepted them. Thus they conclude that Jesus did not see same-gender orientation as a moral issue in the kingdom of God. Their conclusion is that followers of Jesus should not create an issue out of something Jesus has already indicated is not an issue.

Arguing from silence is always dangerous. Thus it would seem most appropriate simply to report that in the Scriptures we have no direct word from Jesus on this topic.

Paul

Three texts in the New Testament address this subject, all associated with the Apostle Paul: Romans 1:26-27; 1 Corinthians 6:9-11; and 1 Timothy 1:10. Since 1 Corinthians was written several years before Romans, we begin with this text. The text in 1 Timothy duplicates both the words and thought used by Paul in 1 Corinthians 6, so the discussion of specific words applies to both of the texts. It will not be necessary to repeat that discussion.

1 Corinthians 6: Who will inherit the kingdom of God?

Chapter 6 of 1 Corinthians opens with a discussion of differences within the congregation at Corinth and states emphatically that it is improper for Christians to sue one another in the public courts. Rather, we should settle differences within the congregation by talking together. That counsel has somehow been lost as we now talk *about* rather than *with* each other.

In verse 9 Paul begins with a theme statement: "Do you not know that the unrighteous will not inherit the kingdom of God?" Then he lists ten explicit examples of unrighteous behavior. Four of these are sexual offenses of which two are often assumed to refer to specific same-gender sexual contact. The NIV translates these last two words "male prostitutes" and "homosexuals;" and the NRSV translates "male prostitutes" and "sodomites" (6:9).

This makes it relatively easy to read the text and believe we know exactly what was in Paul's mind. In truth, however, English translators are uncertain about specific meaning of the original words. The words used are more descriptive of behaviors than of identity. The following chart shows the diversity of translation for the four sexual words in the list. The first two words are relatively simple, but the last two are much less precise, forcing translators to create their own descriptive meanings.

	pornoi	*moichoi*	*malakoi*	*arsenokoitai*
KJV	fornicators	adulterers	effeminate	abusers of themselves
RSV	immoral	adulterers	(-------- homosexuals --------)	
NRSV	fornicators	adulterers	male prostitutes	sodomites
Ox. RSV	immoral	adulterers	(------ sexual perverts ------)	
NIV	sexually immoral	adulterers	male prostitutes	homosexual offenders

The chart shows that *pornoi* "fornication" and *moichoi* "adultery" have a common, stable meaning, but that *malakoi* and *arsenokoitai* are much less precise. The RSV combines two Greek words, using one more general English word *homosexual* for the translation. A more careful look at these words is essential to determine more precisely what behaviors are being discussed.

Both *malakoi* and *arsenokoites* are masculine plural nouns. In first-century culture, they were used to describe men in terms that had pejorative sexist overtones against women which we today find offensive. I am aware of this; nevertheless it is important to report accurately how the words were used in that earlier culture.

Traditional interpretation of this text understands *malakos* primarily to mean "soft," as in soft, luxurious feminine clothing, or feminine-like in referring to soft smooth-skinned boys or young men before they had begun to show masculine traits such as whiskers. It was commonly used to refer to men or boys who attempted to look or act like women or who accepted the female role in sexual activity.

Since "effeminacy" carried the general meaning of degeneracy, or weakness of character (i.e., "similar to a woman" and was considered beneath masculine dignity), early English translators used it to translate *malakos*. A shift occurred in the mid-twentieth century translations when effeminate was no longer politically correct. "Effeminate" disappeared and "male prostitute" or "sodomite" began to be used to translate this word. *Malakos* developed the meaning of a man who assumed the woman's role in sexual activity, allowing the easy transition to "homosexual."[12]

Arsenokoites is made up of two Greek words *arsen* = male and *koites* = bed. Thomas Schmidt argues that Paul took the word directly from the Septuagint text of Leviticus 20:9 (*meta arsenos koitan gunaikos*, "a man should not lie "with a man as with a woman"). He insists that the same sexual meaning is clear and would have been widely understood.[13] Scholars who agree with Schmidt argue that Paul's use of these words shows the Christian church adopted the Old Testament teaching on sexuality, thus reaffirming the Holiness Code's condemnation of same-gender sexual activity in Leviticus.

He and other conservative scholars conclude that this text supports the belief that same-gender sexual activity is and always has been a violation of God's intention for humanity. They find compassion and hope for persons who are of homosexual orientation in verse 11, which reads, "This is what some of you used to be, but you are washed, sanctified, justified." They interpret this to mean that by the saving grace of God one can be freed from this sin and be transformed. They point out that the verbs used here are passive, emphasizing that this transformation is accomplished through the power of the Spirit of God. In short, they hold that the New Testament prohibition of same-sex relationships is deeply rooted in the Old Testament materials and is carried through into the New Testament with equal intensity.

Romans 1:26-27

The Romans 1:26-27 text is important because it gives a theological approach to the issue. Both males and females are included in the discussion whereas in the Corinthian discussion it is strictly a male issue. This passage has a three-fold condemnation of Gentile vices, each noting that because of these things "God gave them up" (1:24, 26, 28). Again, Schmidt represents the traditional view. Giving his interpretation a theological slant, he sees a direct connection between idolatry as lying about one's relationship with God, homosexuality as lying about one's relationship with your own body, and murder as lying about one's relationship with the life of another person.[14] Participation in such activity degrades the original image of God and gives clear evidence that such persons are no longer worshiping the true God. Such activities are a sure sign they are no longer godly people.

This approach to the text assumes Paul is describing perverse sexual conduct, not orientation. He is describing heterosexual (both male and female) individuals who have rejected their heterosexual identity to become involved in same-gender sexual behavior. (In modern terms we refer to this as "bisexual" behavior.) Individuals freely "exchanged," "gave up," "committed," and this conduct violated what was considered "natural." The sin was not in giving up heterosexual activity, but participating in same-gender activity. Implicitly this approach assumes that orientation is a voluntarily chosen sentiment; thus celibacy would be an acceptable option.

Paul uses the phrase "against nature" (*para physin*) to describe this kind of behavior. Traditional interpreters argue that "by nature" all individuals are either male or female. This implies that the "natural" order for sexual orientation is to be exclusively male or female. This puts all individuals (including bisexual and homosexual persons) into categories that reflect stereotypical heterosexual orientation. Individuals of same-gender orientation are classified as "not normal" by reason of the Adamic fall. Thus they are in need of healing (salvation) from their sinful condition.[15]

Schmidt, who holds this position, believes Paul made no distinction between same-gender orientation and voluntarily chosen same-gender behavioral patterns (a good point). He argues that Paul simply looked around and saw that the traditional distinction between male and female is the normal condition for humanity.

The unspoken implication is that since Paul, like all the ancient writers, did not recognize a category of involuntary homosexual orientation, the modern phenomenon is theologically and ethically unjustified. From creation, all same-gender sexual expressions are a perversion of the natural creation of God for human beings. The rejection of God's intention for male-female marriage creates an unnatural vacuum into which rebellious humanity inserts these defiant, sinful, same-gender-sexual behaviors.[16] When humanity turns its back on God, what emerges is false worship, false sexuality, and a false respect for human rights that leads to defiance of God and the loss of one's salvation.

In summary this position emphasizes the following:

- The Bible focuses on overt conduct. Since there is no mention in Scripture of "orientation," and no consideration of genetic causes for same-gender orientation, persons with same-gender attraction are assumed to be promiscuous in their sexual expression.

- The Bible contains a uniform condemnation of all same-gender sexual activity throughout. It is an abomination before God, it is unacceptable for Christians, and it should never be treated as an acceptable variation of human experience in the life of the church.

- Christian people can be healed or delivered from homosexuality. They can be set free to remain celibate or to enter into a normal heterosexual marriage relationship.

This position claims to accept the clear, obvious reading of the English Bible, and it projects unambiguous categories for making decisions about what is right and wrong. Given the assumption that such interpreters know what the text says, the only issue is whether we have the courage to be faithful to the text. But is the exegetical case this clear? Are we so sure what the first-century words are saying in our twenty-first-century terms?

Let's look at both texts again

Many other Christian scholars, who also care deeply about a faithful reading of the text, do not agree with the above interpretation of the New Testament. They also wrestle with the meaning of these words, arguing that a careful reading of the Bible provides a different set of conclusions that are actually more faithful to the basic message of Jesus.

What do they find? These scholars agree that *malakos* does have the meaning of "soft," but they point to evidence that it is used much more broadly than in a sexual context. Historically, *malakos* referred to persons who were cowards, or lazy, or specifically to men who lived a life of ease, decadence, and luxury.

Epictetus, the Stoic philosopher, used the word to describe men who "take life easy rather than endure the rigors of philosophic enquiry.[17] In classical Greek literature, *malakos* referred to men who "prettied themselves up" by shaving their bodies and using perfume to make themselves sexually more attractive to women, believing that women would prefer this more tender-appearing, sweeter-smelling male over the crude, unwashed, outdoorsman type.

Chrysostom, the fourth century church father, once wrote that the common folk refer to persons who love to study as *malakoi*,[18] much like small children today might call a young boy who would rather read a book than play football "a sissy." Josephus used *malakos* to describe a person who is "weak in battle," or "reluctant to commit suicide."[19] *Malakos* refers to men who exhibit feminine weaknesses that are presumed to be degrading to men, but it includes far more than a female sexual characterization.

Ancient cultures often expressed a distinct reaction against things feminine, implying that any sensible person would rather be dead than be a woman. This is seen in the first-century daily prayer of Jewish orthodox men: "Lord, I thank you that you did not make me a slave, a Gentile, or a woman." *Malakos* contained an oblique, if not direct, criticism of feminine (or effeminate) characteristics. When modern society no longer permitted identifying effeminacy as a moral category, translators began to associate the term specifically with gay and lesbian persons, and "effeminate" was dropped in favor of the more strident "homosexual."

Corinth was a thoroughly Greek city that gave free expression to sexual activity considered abusive and repulsive within the Christian community. One practice common in both Greece and Rome was pederasty. There are a disturbing number of references to philosophers and teachers who took young boys as students. In addition to teaching them the traditional subjects of history, math, and culture, they also "taught" them in the intricacies and techniques of sexual intercourse.[20]

These boys were required to be submissive and accepting when older men initiated the sexual activity and enjoyed the self-gratification they received. The relationship was terminated when the young boys matured (began growing beards) and were no longer pleasurable. The older men would then search for another *malakos*, while the young man, now reaching adulthood, would find his own *malakos* and the sexual cycle began all over again.

This practice flourished in Greece and Rome during the intertestamental biblical period, and there is substantial evidence that it continued through the New Testament period as well. The Greek culture justified it through believing the gods were sexually active in the same way. Greek mythology provides abundant examples of the gods engaging in sexual activity with young human males.[21]

Nissinen points out that Greeks "regarded it impossible for a man to have a deep, all-encompassing love relationship with a woman." He explains that since women were considered inferior to men, by definition a deep erotic relationship between men was considered superior. Plato, Plutarch, and other philosophers debated among themselves whether the love of a woman is superior or inferior to the love of a young boy, but they did not doubt that homosocial relationships were superior to heterosexual relationships.[22]

While a physically erotic relationship was possible between male and female, spiritual love could happen only between two males because in a male-female experience the partners were not equal. Sexual intercourse within marriage was for the purpose of bearing children, whereas "pure sexual enjoyment" was retained in the extramarital male-with-male relationships.[23] Thus same-sex erotic relationships were not necessarily terminated when a man was married.

Just as it is difficult to know the full extent of sexual prostitution in our own communities, it is difficult to know exactly how widespread the practice of male homosexual sex was in Paul's day, but there is sufficient evidence to show it was a common practice among the upper classes of Greek culture. Paul generalizes about an abusive sexual activity that people knew existed, and he identified it as a vulgar, dehumanizing practice that should have no place in the church.

The question that remains in dispute is whether this general biblical condemnation encompasses all forms of mutual, caring same-gender sexual relationships. What can be said with confidence is that the church should join with Paul in condemning all forms of sexual abuse, promiscuity, and slavery in our own culture.

Arsenokoites is a rare word in both biblical and cultural literature, but when it is used, the setting provides an important insight into its meaning. *Arsenokoites* usually appears in lists where sins of like character are clustered together. By noting what sins are linked together, we can learn a great deal about the nature of these sins. In most lists there are sexual sins (adultery, rape, prostitution), sins involving violence (murder, maiming, physical abuse), and economic or justice sins (stealing, destruction of property, etc.).

In these lists, *arsenokoites* does not appear with the sexual sins, but rather it is clustered with the sins of exploitation and economic justice. Biblical scholars are coming to the view that *arsenokoites* refers to a very specific form of sexual exploitation and abuse that is not necessarily related to same-gender attraction as commonly experienced today.

One of the clearest uses of this word comes from a Greek text dated about 100 years after Paul. It reads, "Do not accept a gift earned from doing unjust deeds, do not steal, do not betray information, do not *arsenokoiten*, do not oppress a poor man; pay the person who works for his wages, make provision for widows and orphans" (Sibylline Oracle 2.70-77).

Here *arsenokoites* appears in the middle of a list of economic sins related to oppression and exploitation. Later in the same writing, another paragraph contains a list of sexual sins: abortion, stealing the virginity of a young woman, promiscuity, adultery.[24] If *arsenokoites* was intended to condemn same-gender sexual behavior, one would expect it to appear here with sexual sins rather than with the sins of economic exploitation.

This leads to the conclusion that *arsenokoites* specifically prohibits economic exploitation through sexual activity (prostitution, child abuse, child pornography). It is helpful to note that first-century homoerotic practices most often involved exploitation of slaves and lower class youth by dominant males who held positions of social and economic power.

This same clustering principle is seen in the Acts of John, a second-century writing which condemns the rich men of Ephesus and specifically identifies the "poisoner, robber, swindler, *arsenokoites*, thief, tyrant, and warmonger" as being sinners. Here again, *arsenokoites* is listed with the economic and social sins of the day. The Acts of John has a later section that denounces sexual sins, but *arsenokoites* is not included in that list.[25]

Again, the conclusion reached is that *arsenokoites* refers to a sinful practice that should be condemned. All forms of sexual oppression and exploitation should be condemned by the Christian community, without specific regard to whether that oppression is homosexual or heterosexual in nature.

"Sexual Practice" and "Sexual Orientation"

We need yet to look at the ancient cultural assumptions about the root causes and nature of homosexuality. Biblical writers apparently had no concept of sexual "orientation"; they saw only sexual practices. Indeed, the word *homosexuality* first appears in English literature in the 1890s. The ancients believed all sexual practices were the result of conscious decisions made by persons who had freedom of choice. This belief is still held today by many Christians who assume that because the biblical writers thought of sexuality as a free choice made by the person, this must still be our position. They hold that biblical classifications must continue for all time as the authoritative base for our own thinking.

This raises a critical question. Is Christian faith locked into first-century scientific and medical understandings, or does the Spirit of God continue to empower us to learn more and more about how God created us and how we function as human beings? What is the proper role of contextualization, or the transfer of teachings and exhortations from their ancient settings to the present?

Jesus once said, "I still have many things to say to you, but you cannot bear them now. When the Spirit of truth comes, he will guide you into all the truth (John 16:12-13). On another occasion he said, "The one who believes in me will also do the works that I do, and in fact, will do greater works than these" (John 14:12). Jesus knew there were many things his followers would learn later that would lead to a positive extension of the work he was doing. It is appropriate to say that our knowledge of the world, of science, and of the human body goes far beyond what Paul and his contemporaries knew. Paul was a highly educated person but wrote within the first-century limitations of knowledge. God, working though Paul, honored these limitations in the inspiration process.

The exact causes of same-gender attraction remain a heated subject among theologians, psychologists, and scientists. As stated above, many Christians believe that sexual identity is freely chosen. Some who share this belief argue that same-sex orientation is the result of traumatic sexual abuse during early childhood, which emerges as an identity issue in later adolescence as the person responds to those unresolved destructive childhood experiences. They believe that while individuals do not freely choose their identity, and often have suppressed the painful events of their past which are having such a profound impact upon their present experiences, their sexual orientation can be changed (corrected or healed) through extensive therapy or spiritual healing.

On the other side of the debate, a growing number of scientists (many of whom have a strong personal Christian faith), think that both genetic structure and developmental interaction play a significant role in determining who we are. Scientific research suggests that the distinctive patterns of human sexual orientation and gender identity are shaped in the very early stages of human development. From their own counseling experience, prominent Christians in the fields of psychology and psychiatry, who are wrestling with the expanding world of formative genetic influence upon human development and personality, believe that for a certain percent of individuals there is little or no chance for profound change in sexual orientation. As yet there is no consensus. But the emerging evidence seems to lend support to this view as scientists identify a complex interaction of genetic patterns and developmental forces which contribute to the formation of human sexual identity.

In many instances the pattern of development seems relatively clear. Some children may have a vague feeling they do not fit in with the general expectations of their own culture. In their late teens or early twenties, these individuals begin developing sufficient internal ego strength to reflect on how they feel and who they are. Depending on their personal situations, they may feel forced to stifle their emerging self-understandings because of subtle or overt family, church, and community rejection. Others carefully begin to reach out, and when they find a safe, accepting friend or environment, they risk stating what they are feeling and discovering about who they are. They are not making a choice about their identity. They are simply finding the personal courage and community security to risk identifying what they have been feeling for years.

The distinction between male and female must be put on a continuum, rather than being seen as two separate, non-overlapping realities. This means there are individuals who find themselves near the center of this continuum, and given a particular environment, may feel confusing sexual identity signals within themselves. It is important to recognize that everyone's story will likely be different. It is therefore inappropriate to jump to conclusions, to use stereotypical language, or build on false assumptions about someone else's personal experience.

These emerging understandings of causation have profound theological implications. If sexual identity is shaped by a strong genetic contribution, then sexual orientation in itself is not sinful, for it is formed very early in life. What does it imply then when attraction to the same sex is equated with the sinful inclinations to anger or stealing? What does it imply when we refer to same-sex attraction as "abnormal" or "unnatural"?

Here it is essential that we understand how Paul is thinking when, in Romans 1, he talks about going "against nature." The first-century world used "nature" to express a fundamental cultural role, inborn character or instinct of a person, with no concept of genetic or biological meaning which the modern reader assumes. Paul's understanding of the natural male and female gender roles was not based on genetic formation. Modern genetic understandings were simply not part of his worldview. He labeled what he saw in the social order as "natural" (overwhelming majority) or "unnatural" (not meshing with the majority). He apparently assumed that gender attraction was instinctively heterosexual, and thus all other gender attractions were "against nature" (*para physin*). Accordingly, those who felt a same-gender attraction were actually violating their heterosexual identity given at creation.[26]

Today, we know that for a certain percentage of people (including those in our local congregations) reality is not that simple. We are ministering to people who find their sexual identity all along the continuum. Should we force same-gender-attracted persons to go against their own birth nature? Or have we the right to require them to remain celibate whether or not God has thus called them? Paul criticized those he assumed had a heterosexual attraction for rejecting their instinctive nature and experimenting with same-gender sexual activity. If we follow Paul's reasoning, what should we expect of those whose "nature" is homosexually oriented?

Within our faith communities there are young people who in late adolescence have genuinely committed themselves to following Jesus and have stated their desire to be members of the faith community with us. In most cases, their faith identity preceded any adult awareness of their own intricate sexual identity. Can we deny the integrity of their faith and reject them as brothers and sisters simply because their genetic formation differs from that with which most of us feel comfortable? I am convinced that the Bible would never permit us to reject or dismiss persons simply because of a genetic difference in their early identity formation.

When the Bible identifies specific abusive sexual behaviors we know were present in first-century culture, we should affirm the biblical instruction that these specific behaviors must have no place in the faith community. This is not in question. What is in question is the moral evaluation of the mutual caring expression of homo-erotic attraction in those who are homosexually oriented.

And as we have seen, the Greek words, like *malakos* and *arsenokoites* describing illicit first-century behavior do not speak un-ambiguously to this point. What we can say with certainty is that the call of faith is exactly the same for all persons, namely, to claim Jesus as Lord, to commit themselves to follow Jesus, to live holy lives, to work for justice and peace, to bring healing to a suffering world, to offer hope and salvation to all people.

When we do this, we demonstrate that we truly are the people of God, nurturing faith, expecting wholeness, purity, and maturity in Christ in our personal relationships, loving those people for whom Christ died, and living in the joy of the kingdom of God which has burst in upon us.[27]

A Word from the Early Church

Our differences in interpreting the Scriptures do not preclude their relevance or authority in our lives. The New Testament church itself struggled with different interpretations and applications of specific biblical texts. Within twenty-five years of its beginning at Pentecost, the church faced a crisis due to differing interpretations of religious experience. What began as a wonderful community of God's people gathered together in unity under the leading of the Holy Spirit, quickly became a community divided by sharp differences over who could be a member of the new people of God, and what kinds of membership regulations would be enforced. These sharp differences led to even sharper words of attack directed at others within the church.

There were a variety of strong voices stating their claims. One group, the Judaizers, argued that circumcision had always been the will of God and was still required for members in the new community. This meant placing some severe restrictions on Gentiles who might wish to become members. The second voice, coming from a more progressive group, argued that with the conversion of Cornelius and the affirmation of the Spirit upon that event (Acts 10:44-48), this requirement under the old covenant no longer applied.

Leaders from both groups met in Jerusalem to discuss this serious matter. Could a person be a committed follower of Jesus without first becoming culturally and religiously Jewish (being circumcised)? The meeting was tense, with both sides arguing that faithfulness dictated acceptance of their point of view. After hearing personal stories from Paul and Peter, and after long intensive debate, James, the leader of the Jerusalem church, reinterpreted the Old Testament Scriptures to acknowledge that the inclusion of Gentiles without special membership requirements had always been the will of God. He demonstrated this by quoting from Amos 9, Jeremiah 12 and Isaiah 45 (see Acts 15:16-18).

These texts had been in the Jewish Bible for centuries and presumably had been read in the synagogues. Yet no one had understood the texts to make this point until the experience of Cornelius forced the church to consider including gentiles. Only then did James recognize something in these texts never seen before. The experience of God's presence among these early Christians called them to re-examine how they had been reading the Scriptures. Only then did they understand the Scriptures to be saying that God had always intended the Gentiles to be included in the people of faith. The Scriptures had not changed, but God changed the hearts of the people reading the Scriptures to see God's will in a new way.

When the Jerusalem conference heard the experience of Gentiles who been saved by the grace of God, and when they heard these Old Testament texts confirming that this was God's will, they took the radical step of obedient faith and declared that they would accept people who previously had been unacceptable. They agreed they would no longer demand the ancient religious tradition of circumcision as a requirement for membership in the people of God. They did not forbid the practice of circumcision, but circumcision no longer controlled entry into the church.

In this situation, the church believed the Spirit of God was leading them in a new direction and was challenging a practice that had always been a central declaration of Jewish faith. What gave them that authority? The Holy Spirit confronted them in the form of persons who had experienced the grace of God. This challenged them to re-examine how they had been reading some specific texts in the Scriptures. As they read the texts in light of this new experience of God's grace, they came to a new understanding. Accordingly, they changed a specific practice. This guided them to include uncircumcised Gentiles into the faith community.

In his concluding remarks, James acknowledged that this had not been an easy decision. He implied that it would be difficult for more traditional groups to accept it. Therefore, he asked for understanding and sensitivity on the part of these newly accepted believers because "in every city there are those who proclaim the law of Moses, and have it read weekly in their synagogues" (Acts 15:21).

We look back at that event and say, "How simple it was, God's leading was so clear!" We wish it could be equally clear for the church today. But for members present in that conference, things were not as simple, pleasant, or harmonious as we may think. However, they did not separate from each other. They stayed in the process and saw the result as a wonderful indication of God's leading. Most of us (we who are the Gentiles) are now part of the faith community because of their courage to accept persons like us!

Observations for Talking Together

There are a significant number of ways in which the circumcision issue faced by the Jerusalem Council parallels our present situation. Circumcision was both a biblical and a highly sensitive cultural issue. It was the essential Mosaic mark of the covenant which proclaimed the Jewish male different from the Gentile male. It was not simply a ceremonial rite. It was a psychosomatic mark of cultural-religious "orientation." Those who did not have its identifying mark were "unclean."

The leaders at Jerusalem took the Scriptures very seriously. Indeed, the intensity of the different positions at the conference indicates how seriously they took its authority for their life. However, in light of the radical difference Jesus had made in their own understanding of the old covenant regulations and definitions, they accepted the Holy Spirit's work in their midst as an indication that change was called for. Peter's words, "Who was I that I could withstand God?" stated the mandate for accepting a new understanding of the Bible. The community agreed that they had to include people who were being saved by God's grace even though this grace had fallen on individuals they considered unclean and unacceptable.

Because of the extremely delicate nature of the situation, James urged tolerance and respect on both sides of the issue even though some participants did not fully understand or approve of what was happening. The leaders asked those breaking with the old regulations to be sensitive to the consciences of those who still clung to the old biblical interpretation. Even this cautious movement, however, did not keep the whole Jewish and Gentile church together.

Today we agree that the foundation for membership in the believing community is commitment to Jesus as Lord. We believe the Scriptures are God's Word and are authoritative for faith and life. We are committed to a high view of sexual morality as taught in the New Testament. We believe sexual intercourse belongs within lifelong covenant relationships, and sexual promiscuity and infidelity are violations of God's intention for all covenant relationships. But we differ over the Bible's evaluation of homosexuality, and whether ancient biblical attitudes and precepts are to be applied literally without adaptation to the present-day understandings of the homosexual phenomenon.

In this situation some among us believe that the work of the Spirit in the lives of our gay and lesbian brothers and sisters is indicating a new understanding of Scripture and calling for a new evaluation of homosexuality. No longer should we see our lesbian and gay brothers and sisters as "unclean." Rather, they should be accepted in the church so long as they give testimony to the healing grace of God and abide within the same sexual standards of monogamous fidelity required of heterosexuals.

Others among us insist that the homoerotic attraction itself is a moral perversion and Scripture requires that it must be changed or those of homosexual orientation must remain celibate. Of course the Bible does not state this explicitly, but those holding this position believe it is the only possible implication. This stand of course continues to deserve the same careful respect James called for in relation to the traditional understandings of circumsion.

How can we make it safe to study the Bible together and honestly share how the Scriptures speak to us without fear of being rejected or excluded—no matter what our position, whether in tension with or in harmony with the concerns emphasized in this chapter? Can we learn to share the depths of our own personal beliefs without declaring that our understandings of faith are the only possible correct understandings? Do we really want to say that we can have fellowship only with those who agree with us? If we can approach the Scriptures with a spirit of hope, love, and inclusion rather than judgment and separation, we might better hear our common foundations of faith that enable us to stay united in our diversity.

Can we acknowledge that we do not always know what we claim to know—that our understandings of Scripture have been (and still are) influenced by cultural and religious pressures that sometimes do not reflect the spirit of Christ? How can we make it safe to reach out and include others without being attacked verbally, or having our own faith questioned? Can we accept that the grace of God sometimes includes others in ways that we might not easily understand? Can we all accept that God is able to work in ways beyond what we understand from any given position, including our own (which needs to apply even to my comments in this chapter)?

If we can join together in worship and prayer, trusting the Holy Spirit to speak to us, both individually and collectively; if we can allow God's love and grace to flow through us to others, being thankful for what God has done for us, and pledging ourselves to be agents of grace in all human conditions; we can make it safe for anyone to come before God in humility and honesty so that together we might all find grace, healing and salvation.

Notes

1. This is the position of the most conservative Jews in the state of Israel. In their elementary schools, they spend five hours each day studying the ancient wisdom of Torah believing that these words reflect the never changing will of God for their lives today.

2. Choong Leong Seow, "Textual Orientation," in *Biblical Ethics and Homosexuality*, ed. Robert Brawley (Louisville: Westminster, John Knox Press, 1996), 26-27.

3. Richard Hays, *The Moral Vision of the New Testament* (San Francisco: Harper Collins, 1996), 381.

4. Thomas Schmidt, *Straight and Narrow* (Downers Grove, Ill.: InterVarsity Press, 1995), 86-88.

5. Philo, *Specialibus Legibus* 3.37-39, Josephus, *Antiquities*, 1.11.3, as in Schmidt, 89.

6. G. Johannes Botterweck, *"Yada"* in *The Theological Dictionary of the Old Testament* (Grand Rapids, Mich.: Wm. B. Eerdmans, 1975), 448-481. Botterweck identifies more than ten different uses of "yadah" in English translation. He provides very careful statistics and explanations for the various uses in the English Bible.

7. Martti Nissinen, *Homoeroticism in the Biblical World* (Minneapolis: Fortress Press, 1998), 49.

8. The book of Jude may be seen to counter this argument, but the author there draws on the extrabiblical Jewish traditions of Philo and Josephus to make his point about the historic sinfulness of Israel.

9. Seow, "Textual Orientation," 21. The modern reader is horrified by the actions of the Levite, as also with Lot in Gen. 19. This behavior is in accord with the Near Eastern hospitality codes of the day where protection of the stranger in one's house took precedence over the love of one's own children.

10. Nissinen, 50-51.

11. The imperative to replace the holiness of the law with compassion is

most clearly shown in Matt. 5:38-48 and Luke 6:27-36. These sections echo and modify the Holiness Code at crucial points. See Marcus Borg, *Conflict, Holiness and Politics in the Teachings of Jesus* (Harrisburg: Trinity Press, 1998), 135-155.

12. Dale Martin, "Arsenokoites and Malakos: Meanings and Consequences" in Brawley, *Biblical Ethics and Homosexuality*, 124-125.

13. Schmidt, *Straight and Narrow*, 95-96.

14. Ibid., 67.

15. William Consiglio, *Homosexual No More* (Wheaton, Ill.: Victor Books, 1991), and Mario Bergner, *Setting Love in Order* (Grand Rapids, Mich.: Hameworth Books, 1995), are two examples among a list of psychological/theological writers who promote healing and deliverance from the sin of homosexuality, believing that it is a freely chosen option.

16. Schmidt, *Straight and Narrow*, 81.

17. Epictetus: *Scattered Sayings*, 3.6.9, *On Freedom*, 4.1.25, cited in Abraham Malherbe, *The Cynic Epistles*.

18. Dio Chrysostom, *Discourses*, 66.25.

19. Josephus, *Wars of the Jews* 7.338, *Jewish Antiquities* 5.246 "some were eager to respond, and all but filled with delight at the thought of a death so noble, but other "softer-hearted" persons were moved with compassion for their wives and families." "Gaul was charged with "feebleness" in his encounter with Abimelech."

20. Martin, 127.

21. Nissinen, 58.

22. Plato, *Plato's Symposium*, 192A, Plutarch, *Plutarchs Moralia, v. IX, Dialogue on Love* 748-771E.

23. Nissinen, 65-68. Nissinen provides extensive discussion of the practice of pederasty in the culture, suggesting that Paul would have known about the practice and certainly would have opposed it.

24. Sibylline Oracle 2:70-77 in Charlesworth, *Old Testament Pseudepigrapha* (Garden City, N.Y.: Doubleday, 1983).

25. E. Hennecke, *New Testament Apocrypha*, vol. 2 (London: SCM Press), 224.

26. Nissinen, 106-107.

27. Miroslav Volf, *Exclusion and Embrace* (Nashville: Abingdon Press, 1996), develops this theme as a central element in the teaching ministry of Jesus in his chapter, "Gender Identity" (167-190). While Volf's discussion is much broader than our specific topic, his approach to faith and issues of gender is very helpful. See also Borg, 135-155.

Chapter 9

The Biological Basis of Homosexuality

Carl S. Keener and Douglas E. Swartzendruber

MENTION THE WORD HOMOSEXUAL IN ANY DISCUSSION after Sunday school and one will quite likely discover a wide range of responses and opinions. Indeed, few current issues have exercised the wisdom of the Church as homosexuality. Christians have widely divergent views about homosexuality to the point that many persons seemingly are unable to engage in any meaningful discussion. At times the shouting has become so intense that emotion wins over graceful rhetoric and reasonableness.

Nevertheless, we believe that any serious discussion of homosexuality requires an understanding of the possible origins of human sexuality. The aim of this chapter thus is to examine what we know at the present time about the biological bases of same-sex attraction. Some of this evidence remains controversial, and we need to remain open to counter-evidence. At the same time, we believe the total weight of evidence suggests that biological phenomena play a major role in the origin of same-sex attraction in many species of living things, including humans.

Science as a Way of Knowing

Scientists work with ideas—lots of them. But how do scientists decide which of their ideas, sometimes called hypotheses, theories, or conjectures, are better than others? The answer is *testability*, the ability to find out by critical tests and observations whether or not an idea is reasonably correct. Some philosophers of science, such as

Sir Karl Popper, insist scientists can only disprove an idea, never prove it (Popper 1962, 1972).[1] For example, consider the statement that all crows are black. This statement is true if and only if all crows have been observed and all are found to be black. In practice, however, to observe all living crows is probably impossible. So what scientists do is study a sample of crows, and then come to a tentative conclusion about the color of crows. However, if a scientist discovers that one crow is white, then the statement that all crows are black is false and thereby has been disproved. In such cases, the original statement must be modified, and in the example just given, one could state that most crows are black.

In general, scientists dislike the word *prove*, a term best left for mathematicians and logicians. In any case, the research of a scientist is not easy. Scientists begin with a problem, often stated as a hypothesis or conjecture, which is then investigated by methods suitable to solving the problem. Such studies are usually not simple because good research must deal with an adequate sample, a suitable comparison or control group, a clearly outlined experimental design, use of sophisticated statistical tests, consideration of rival explanations, and review of results by other experts in the field.

Moreover, scientists can investigate the natural world in several different ways. In some cases, the investigation proceeds by careful experimentation, often conducted within a laboratory with various types of instrumentation. This methodology attempts to establish repeatable chains of cause and effect. For example, questions concerning how animals digest sugars are answered by undertaking precise experiments. In other cases, scientific investigation is best conducted by means of critical observations and comparisons which often deal with complex and nonrepeatable events whose analysis generally results in less precise statements. For example, when a botanist decides that a group of plants should be recognized as an undescribed species, the supposed new species is carefully compared with closely related species.

Any scientific study of the nature of human sexuality is by its nature quite difficult. Human sexuality is certainly multifactorial, and thus both scientific observations and controlled experimentation may take place. The total weight of the evidence, however, becomes quite important.

Without a scientific background, some persons rely on anecdotal evidence—incidental stories that seem to support a given point of view. If many persons say that the earth is flat, well then, the earth is flat. However, interesting anecdotal evidence might be, it lacks the rigor of a carefully planned scientific investigation. Unless a scientist follows careful and repeatable procedures, the research will carry little scientific significance.

As examples, consider the following hypotheses: (1) a homosexual orientation is chosen; (2) hostile fathers "cause" their sons to become gay; (3) gays and lesbians can be "cured" of their homosexual orientation, thus gays and lesbians can become heterosexuals; (4) same-sex attraction has a heritable basis, and is fundamentally incurable; (5) ten percent of the adult population is either gay or lesbian.

How does one rigorously test these hypotheses? Will anecdotes suffice? How many cases should one observe for the hypothesis to be acceptable? Should it be more rigorously tested to eliminate possible errors? Would counter-examples disprove the hypothesis? How does one reach a reasonable conclusion about any of the hypotheses stated above? In brief, if homosexuality has a biological basis, what evidence would we expect to find? How would we begin to test the hypothesis that indeed homosexuality has a biological component?

John Moore (1993) has referred to science as a way of knowing, and Ernst Mayr (1982) has considered biological thought as a growth, an ever-enlarging expansion of human knowledge about how the world works. Although as scientists it is our aim to understand the natural world, any in-depth understanding calls for years of training, use of sophisticated technology, and a community of critical investigators who communicate with each other. One simply cannot be a very good scientist apart from years of training and a community of fellow critics!

Some Definitions

Before we review some of the current research dealing with the biological bases of homosexuality, we need to clear up a few definitions. The term *biological*, as we are using it, is an inclusive category. It includes *heredity*—our genetic makeup, the *physiological processes* involved in our development from a fertilized egg to an adult, and our *environment*. These are interacting components, and should be treated as part of an overall very complex system. In our view, it is impossible neatly to separate our heredity from our environment; both are important determinants in the person we have become.

(For more on this topic, see Seligman 1994, and Plomin et al. 1997.) As used in this chapter, the term *homosexual* is equivalent to the phrase "a person with a same-sex attraction" and refers to a person's sexual orientation only, not to human behavior or practice.

Too often the words *homosexual* and *homosexuality* are used loosely and may refer both to one's sexual orientation as well as to one's behavioral practices. For that reason, it is probably best not to use such terms as homosexual or homosexuality unless the context is clear (Drescher 1998b, 5). Moreover, we are using the word *gay* to refer to males with a same-gender attraction, and *lesbian* to refer to females with likewise a same-gender attraction.

Having said this, we believe that the words homosexual (or heterosexual), gay, and lesbian are more than a mere label aiming to control other persons (Halwani 1998; see also Pattatucci 1998a, and Stein 1998). The labels point to something real in the world of living things, and as scientists, we believe this world exists independently of our observations, invented labels, and the like (for more on this, see Searle 1995, 1998). Thus, it is our view that same-sex attraction occurs in humans no matter what name or label we give to describe this aspect of human behavior (for an additional analysis of this issue, see DeLamater and Hyde 1998).

Percentages of Gays and Lesbians

As indicated above, in this chapter we are distinguishing sharply between one's sexual orientation and one's sexual practices. However, it has never been easy precisely to determine a person's sexuality, and in fact some published research fails to indicate how gays and lesbians were ascertained (Fausto-Sterling 2000, 10). Moreover, it is difficult to eliminate certain biases, such as might occur in determining whether a person is gay or lesbian or bisexual, and in choosing one's sample for study. However, researchers in human sexuality are now addressing the problem of ascertainment bias (Zucker and Bradley 1995, 131; Bailey and Dawood 1998; Bailey et al. 1999).

Some researchers have developed a grid of key variables for determining a person's sexual orientation. For example, Fritz Klein suggests "sexual attraction, sexual behavior, sexual fantasies, emotional preference, social preference, self-identification, hetero/homo lifestyle" as a grid (Fausto-Sterling 2000, 10). Pattatucci (1998b), however, suggests four variables for determining one's sexuality, namely, self-identification, sexual attraction, romantic or sexual fantasy, and sexual behavior. We should point out that determining nonheterosexual persons is not a simple matter, and in reviewing any research dealing with gays and lesbians, one should note how knowledge of the sexual orientation was obtained.

Determining rough percentages of gays and lesbians has not been particularly easy either. Based on the widely cited studies by Kinsey and his colleagues a half century ago, ten percent of the male (and female) adult population has been considered more or less exclusively homosexual. However, by using his seven-point scale, Kinsey was measuring human sexual behavior only; he never classified humans on the basis of their sexual orientation. Thus as Mondimore (1996, 86) points out, the Kinsey data show percentages of certain sexual behaviors only, not percentages of persons with a same-sex attraction at all, and hence the misuse of Kinsey's data has resulted in a serious disservice to his research, however flawed statistically his research might have been.

Recent studies indicate that the ratio of gays to lesbians is roughly 2:1 (Pattatucci 1998b), and that bisexuality is relatively more common in women than men who appear to be more "bimodal," meaning either gay or straight (Pillard and Bailey 1998; Bem 2000). Recent estimates suggest that three to four percent of men and one to two percent of women in the United States are virtually exclusively gay or lesbian. Comparative studies of other societies suggest roughly comparable figures (Diamond 1993; Sell et al. 1995; Dixson 1998, Table 6.2).

Same-Sex Attraction as a Psychosocial Phenomenon

In a review at the end of a long and distinguished career, psychiatrist Judd Marmor (1998) assessed current views of the origins (etiology) of homosexuality, and noted that homophobia—irrational fear or dislike of gays and lesbians—rests largely on lack of knowledge about gays and lesbians. Moreover, Marmor maintained that societal homophobia rests on four basic assumptions:

(1) that homosexuality is sinful and/or immoral, an assumption largely based on religious grounds stemming out of the Judeo-Christian moral traditions;

(2) that homosexuality is unnatural, and thus basically unhealthy, a view sometimes based on the mistaken notion that in nature all species are inherently heterosexual;

3. that same-sex attraction is a chosen behavior, which can be "unchosen";

4. that homosexuality is potentially contagious, and thus can be acquired by seduction or bad role-modeling.

Unfortunately, one or more of these mistaken views has been the basis for justifying discrimination against gays and lesbians in our society as well as differential treatment by psychotherapists (for additional analyses, see Marmor 1998). Marmor believed that understanding the possible causes of homosexuality does have a critical importance in how psychotherapists treat their patients. In any case, a better understanding of the origins of homosexuality should also enable sensitive people everywhere to respect gays and lesbians as part of the significant variation among humans.

According to Marmor (1998), mental health professionals have suggested a number of explanations for homosexuality, including the following:

(1) Incomplete sexual development in which homosexuality represents a fixation occurring when the normal process of sexual development is arrested due to certain early life experiences, a belief based on Freud's research. Marmor noted that psychoanalytic formulations arising from Freud's work have been largely based on homosexuals in therapy.

(2) Homosexuals are narcissistic individuals.

(3) Male homosexuals dislike or even hate women because of "powerful unconscious *negative* feelings toward their mother figures" (Marmor 1998, 21).

(4) Male homosexuals identify strongly with their mothers, which is why they become erotically attracted toward men.

(5) Male homosexuality is the "outcome of pre-oedipal problems of separation and individuation from the mother" (Marmor 1998, 21), a view championed by Charles Socarides (1968).

(6) Homosexuality is "specifically induced by a parental constellation of a close-binding, seductive mother and a distant, unloving father" (Marmor 1998, 21), a hypothesis fostered by Bieber and his associates (Bieber et al. 1962).

As Marmor notes, all these "causes" can also be found in heterosexuals as well, and thus are not necessarily a definitive characteristic of homosexual development (see Isay 1996, 3). Although dysfunctional parenting is often blamed for "causing" the development of homosexuality in children and youth, we have yet been unable to find any peer reviewed studies using random samples demonstrating that dysfunctional parenting "causes" homosexuality. To date, there is some anecdotal evidence, but this is not the same as research involving careful sampling techniques and use of control groups. As Marmor observes, much of this evidence represents the fallacy of psychological reductionism, in which a disturbed relationship is believed to be the cause of the variant behavior.

LeVay, who has written about non-genetic factors and their possible role in human sexual development states that "what we know so far suggests that prenatal biological factors, including genetic factors in males, strongly influence sexual orientation. A role for postnatal environmental factors is possible but uncertain" (LeVay, 2000a). For more on the role of dysfunctional parenting and reparative therapy, see Nicolosi (1991), who advocates reparative therapy, and Drescher (1998a, b) who sharply criticizes this approach.

Marmor (1998, 21) concluded that

> over fifty variables in maternal, paternal and sibling family patterns have been found in male homosexuals–loving mothers, hostile mothers, loving fathers, hostile fathers, idealized fathers; sibling rivalries; intact homes; broken homes, absent mothers, absent fathers, etc.

The claim that a loving father would preclude homosexual development in a son is simply not true. As Marmor points out, he has treated a number of gays in therapy who have had a warm relationship with their fathers.

Furthermore, careful studies of non-patient heterosexuals with non-patient homosexuals have shown "*no* consistent relationship between the nature of the family constellation and subsequent sexual orientation" (Marmor 1998, 22). What is ignored in these various psychoanalytic assumptions is that one's personality structure may also have important biological bases as well.

Some Objections to a Biological Basis for Same-Sex Attraction

Although we firmly believe that biology plays a strong role in same-sex attraction, some persons believe that homosexuality has no biological basis whatsoever. This opinion is based on a number of widely held views, several of which are listed below:

(1) The belief that no compelling scientific evidence or critical "scientific" *proof* for a biological basis of homosexuality has been

demonstrated. This view is based in part on criticisms of apparent poor experimental procedures, inadequate sample sizes, sloppy experimental techniques, fudged data, experimenter bias, ascertainment bias, and the like (Byne and Parsons 1993; Byne 1995).

2. The belief that people become oriented toward same-sex relationships due to various environmental causes, such as bad nurturing by parents resulting in a disturbed early childhood relationship. Belief in environmentalism is typically associated with claims of cures for one's homosexuality. Accordingly, appropriate psychoanalytic and reparation therapies can change a person's same-sex orientation (Bieber et al. 1962; Socarides 1968, 1975).

3. The belief that people "choose" sexual orientation and are therefore morally responsible for this choice. Thus if persons choose a same-sex orientation, they can therefore choose an other-sex orientation as well. As Bieber et al. (1962, 319) stated, "heterosexuality is the *biologic* norm and that unless interfered with all individuals are heterosexual." Furthermore, "a heterosexual shift is a possibility for all homosexuals who are strongly motivated to change."

4. The belief that gays and lesbians are deviants (possibly demon-possessed), but certainly not created that way. Consequently, these "perverts" must be cured, banned, or destroyed. This belief accords with the view that in the Bible a few Scriptures suggest that homosexuality is a result of human sin and perversion and is therefore both pathological and evil. Hence, such persons must be reoriented ("cured") or destroyed (see Lev. 18:22, 20:13).

5. The belief that homosexuality is pathological, perhaps a result of some sort of social disintegration. Such perversions indicate that homosexuals are deeply disturbed persons. Socarides (1975) believes this pathology is traceable to early childhood fears (preoedipal ones occurring before the age of three) and is therefore induced by dysfunctional family dynamics. Although Socarides believes that same-sex orientation is pathological, it is one that can be cured with a proper psychoanalysis.

Moreover, Socarides maintains that

> homosexuality is not innate. There is no correlation between sexual instinct and the selection of sexual object, nor can any chemical imbalance determine the kind of partner preferred for sexual intercourse. Such selection is learned, acquired behavior; there is no inevitable genetic or hormonal inborn propensity toward a partner of either the same or opposite sex. (Socarides 1975, 99)

However, this view has gradually lost favor among many mental health professionals. The reader is directed to Bayer (1987) for a history of this shift (see also Drescher 1998a, b, and Friedman 1998).

An alternative view

In contrast to these beliefs, our initial observation is that most gays and lesbians knew they were different and that they were born that way (Isay 1989, 15ff., 1996, 5; Kreider 1998). Nevertheless, a crucial question for our Christian communities is how a person can become an "open" sexual minority (a GLBTI—gay, lesbian, bisexual, transgendered, intersexual person) within a social climate that regards same-sex orientation as deviant and sinful and in which rampant homophobia is all too prevalent (Gillis 1998).

However, according to Ellis (1996a), a belief that biology underlies human sexual orientation fosters more tolerance and acceptance of gays and lesbians than if a person attributes same-sex orientation to personal choice or learned behavior. Sadly, the suicide rates of gay and lesbian youth remain frighteningly high and account for perhaps 25 percent of all adolescent suicides. One study found that of 137 gay or bisexual boys, 30 percent had attempted suicide (Isay 1996, 184, n. 15; see also D'Augelli 1996, and Hartstein 1996).

Further observation cautions us to regard claims of cures with some degree of suspicion (Gonsiorek 1996; Haldeman 1996). To validate such claims requires asking how the relative degree of hetero/homosexuality was determined, whether or not the person believed he or she was bisexual, and whether or not the cure changed the pattern of behavior as well as the basic same-sex attraction itself. This is probably best judged by follow-up questions concerning the person's fantasies.

In a landmark study, Evelyn Hooker (1957) asked whether gay men fit the typical stereotype often accorded gays, namely, that they are neurotic, shallow, uniformly disturbed persons. She then administered a series of psychological tests (Rorschach, Thematic Apperception Test) to both gay and straight men (30 each, but paired with respect to education, intelligence, and age) with the aim to discover the overall psychological health of either group. The test results were given to three eminent psychologists who were asked to judge, on the basis of the test results, which person was gay and which was straight.

They simply could not tell any difference between gays and straights, and this failure marked a turning point among psychiatrists resulting in an eventual depathologizing of homosexuality. Hooker concluded that, in terms of their overall mental health, homosexual persons are no different than heterosexual persons (see Mondimore 1996, 89, for a sympathetic appraisal of Hooker's work). Nevertheless, Hooker's study was summarily dismissed by Bieber et al. (1962), whose views have considerably influenced many subsequent workers in mental health (Gonsiorek 1996).

Review of the
Biological Evidence for Same-Sex Attraction

The following discussion includes the more important lines of evidence that human same-sex orientation has important biological components. To be sure, none of these studies by themselves may be sufficient to persuade anyone that same-sex attraction has a biological basis. Indeed, certain traits suggest a correlation, not a direct cause. But taken as a whole, we think the evidence is compelling that human sexual orientation has a major biological component.

First, *pedigree studies* (family histories) look at family trees and thereby attempt to discover that certain traits also occur in one's ancestors. With respect to the human sex chromosomes (X, Y), genes for certain traits occur in either the X chromosome or the Y chromosome. Note that human males inherit their "X" chromosome from their mothers and their "Y" chromosome from their fathers (for differences between the X and Y chromosomes, see Jegalian and Lahn 2001). Specifically, for some male homosexuals, a gene (or genes) appears to be located in the X chromosome and is thus inherited through the mother which William Turner (1995) called "Homosexuality, Type I."

By means of comparative genetic studies of a number of pedigrees, Turner's research indicated that gene(s) for same-sex attraction of some homosexuals reside in the terminal region of the long arm of the X chromosome (Turner 1995; see also Hamer et al. 1993; Hu et al. 1995; Pattatucci 1998a, b). Moreover, both male and female homosexuality appears to run in families (Pillard and Weinrich 1986; Pattatucci and Hamer 1995a,b; Pillard 1996; Bailey et al. 1999; Bailey et al. 2000; Dawood et al. 2000), a conclusion also reinforced by studies of twins (see below).

In any case, recruiting subjects for any statistically significant research on homosexuality has been rather difficult, although with better sampling methods and more sophisticated analyses, a more accurate assessment appears to be emerging (Bailey et al. 1999). Although stated percentages of nonheterosexuals (i.e., gays and lesbians) vary, Pattatucci (1998b) claims that in her research (with Dean Hamer), the nonheterosexual base lines for men are roughly twice that for women.

Second, *twin studies* indicate that identical twins are twice as likely to share a same-sex attraction as fraternal (nonidentical) twins. In one study, Bailey and Pillard (1991) found the ratio to be 52 percent to 22 percent for men (see also Whitam et al. 1993; Turner 1995; Dixson 1998, 166; but see Bailey et al. 2000, for a revised downward estimate). Turner's work also discussed the problems with identical twins, one which is heterosexual, the other, homosexual, and showed there are biological reasons why identical twins are not always similar for the trait under investigation. Critics sometimes charge that because of these dissimilarities, same-sex attraction cannot be genetic, but Turner (1994, 1995) convincingly explains why these differences might occur and the reader is directed to his papers for additional study.

In a recent comprehensive study involving a large (N = 4901) cohort of twins in Australia, Kirk et al. (2000, 355) found "statistically significant support for the existence of significant genetic contributions to the trait of homosexuality." This study, along with that of Bailey et al. (2000), supports the view that both genetic and environmental variables are components of homosexuality, and that the genetic component is almost certainly due to more than one gene.

Third, *molecular biological* research by Dean Hamer and his colleagues suggested that male homosexuality might be a heritable trait (Hamer et al. 1993; Hu et al. 1995; Pattatucci and Hamer 1995a). Following a rather complicated investigation involving the techniques of molecular biology, Hamer claimed that quite possibly a gene (or genes) for male homosexuality was located at a specific region of the X chromosome. Hamer, however, never did claim to have found a specific gene for male homosexuality in the X chromosome, only that there was a strong probability that some heritable component (gene or genes) occurred in the X chromosome, which, in males, is inherited from their mothers.

Hamer's work has been criticized by, among others, Byne (1995), Byne and Parsons (1993), and Rice et al. (1999). However, Hamer has responded to an earlier report in 1995 by Rice (Hamer and Copeland 1998, 197). Although Rice and his colleagues attempted to replicate Hamer's work, the extent to which they were able to do this is not exactly clear. Had they actually replicated Hamer's research, they would have used Hamer's original samples, but this assumes that Hamer's blood samples would have been available. To the best of our knowledge, they only attempted to replicate Hamer's research by means of a different set of persons (see also Zucker and Bradley 1995, 134).

In an important, but often overlooked paper, William Turner (1995) claimed that what he called "Homosexuality, Type I" is determined by a gene (or genes) in the terminal region of the long arm of the X chromosome. As indicated above, Turner based his conclusions on evidence derived from pedigree studies, including finding a larger number of homosexual relatives in the maternal lineage as compared to the paternal lineage, higher rates of certain medical problems on the maternal side (spontaneous abortions, miscarriages, stillbirths, etc.), and a "distorted sex ratio in the maternal generation bearing male and female homosexuals" (maternal aunts greatly outnumbered maternal uncles, possibly a result of semilethal genes; see also studies by Bailey and Pillard, 1991).

Although Turner's work supports Hamer's research, Bailey and his colleagues (1999, 85) suggest that "X-linked genes account for relatively few cases of male homosexuality," and that a fairly large sample will be required to detect such a gene. Although their study "found no evidence that male sexual orientation is influenced by an X-linked gene," it did not provide "strong evidence against X-linkage" (Bailey et al. 1999, 84; see also Bailey et al. 2000).

Clearly additional studies on family pedigrees should be undertaken, but these are difficult and subject to various degrees of cooperation on the part of the families investigated. Thus the search for a clearly identifiable gene or genes for male homosexuality continues (Pillard 1997). Since there are thousands of genes (estimates vary from around 40,000 to 100,000) involved in human development and functions, it seems quite unlikely that complex characteristics such as sexual orientation and attraction would result from the action of a single gene.

Fourth, *brain anatomical studies* dealing with heterosexual and homosexual men showed interesting differences. The interstitial nucleus of the anterior hypothalamus (INAH3) located more or less in the center of the brain is two to three times larger in straight men than in gay men (LeVay 1991, 1996, 2000a). Other studies of the brain also showed structural differences between gay and straight men (Allen and Gorski 1992; Swaab and Hofman 1990). Although we are not at present certain how these differences arose, certain hormonal processes seem to be involved. For example, experimental studies over forty years ago at the University of Kansas showed that changing the levels of testosterone during fetal development of guinea pigs and rats could influence the sexual behavior of the adult. These manipulations also affected the size as well as the structural characteristics of the sexually dimorphic nucleus (SDN) in the brain (see LeVay 2000a). As Bailey and colleagues (1999, 84) state, the "most influential biologic theory of sexual orientation is that male homosexuality results from incomplete masculinization of relevant brain structures during prenatal development."

The origins of female homosexuality remain obscure (Bailey et al. 1999, 2000). Hu et al. (1995) agree, and concluded that the mechanisms underlying sexual orientation in men and women are at least partly distinct. Although the development of male sexuality may involve certain genetic factors in the X chromosome, to what extent female sexual orientation is influenced by genetic factors remains unknown. Clearly much more research remains to be done (Bailey et al. 1999; Bem 2000).

Recently, William Byne, an earlier outspoken critic of LeVay's work, has re-investigated LeVay's research by examining a new set of brain samples (LeVay 2000b). Byne reached a number of conclusions: The INAH3 indeed does exist; the cause of death (AIDS, etc.) does not affect its size; although the size differential between gay and straight men is not as large as that reported by LeVay in his 1991 paper, nevertheless the INAH3 is larger in straight men than in the gay men in Byne's sample. Byne discovered that, although the number of nerve cells in gay and straight men are the same, such differences as do occur arise later in fetal development.

What causes this difference is not known at present. As LeVay remarks, what is

> surprising about the gay/straight difference in INAH3, then, is simply that it is so localized and obvious, rather than being diffusely spread through the synaptic architectures [i.e., nerve cell connections] of the entire brain. This offers the hope that we will eventually be able to understand the origins of sexual orientation at a cellular level. (LeVay 2000b)

Fifth, *developmental hormone differences* in humans indicate that sexual identity exists on a continuum between male and female. Typically, an individual with XX sex chromosomes develops into a female, and an individual with XY sex chromosomes develops into a male. However, according to Fausto-Sterling (2000, 53), perhaps as many as 1.7 percent of all human births are intersexes of one type or another. This means that not all persons are sharply delimited males/females, a fact too often ignored in discussions of human sexuality.

For example, some children with XX chromosomes are born with enlarged adrenal glands. In such individuals, during the later part of fetal development, the adrenal gland secretes large amounts of male sex hormones, and thus these persons become masculinized females (Dixson 1998, 285). On the other hand, some XY children are borne with highly feminized genitalia due to being non-responsive to the masculinizing hormones, and thus develop psychosexually as women (Dixson 1998, 288). Both of these are genetically inherited traits, and often such individuals develop same-sex attractions in later life, thus underscoring a biological (and genetic basis) for same-sex attraction (Dittmann et al. 1992; Ellis 1996b; Pattatucci 1998b; LeVay 2000a).

Sixth, studies of *childhood behavior* show that young boys with highly feminine traits (often known as "sissies") in later life often become males with a same-sex attraction (Pillard and Bailey 1998; Bailey et al. 2000; Bem 2000; Dawood et al. 2000). These childhood trait and role differences typically show up in a child's life long before any sexual awareness occurs. Different roles associated with gender include "participation in aggressive activities, rough-and-tumble play, and competitive athletics, toy preferences, imagined roles and careers, cross-dressing, preference for same- or opposite-sex playmates, gender identity, and social reputation as 'sissy' or 'tomboy.' The group differences are generally larger for men (gay versus straight) than for women (lesbian versus straight)" (LeVay 2000a).

Daryl Bem (2000) has proposed an interesting theory (Exotic-Becomes-Erotic, or EBE), which suggests that "individuals can become erotically attracted to a class of individuals from whom they felt different during childhood" (Bem 2000, 533). Thus whatever the biological basis for same-sex attraction might be, the causation is not direct, but is mediated instead by gender nonconformist factors (see Bailey et al. 2000 for some support for this hypothesis). Moreover, Bem (2000, 537) suggests that "childhood gender conformity or nonconformity [is] the only significant childhood predictor of later sexual orientation for both men and women." In fact, one study (cited in Bem 2000) concluded that roughly 70 percent of both men and women reported "they felt different from their same-sex peers during childhood" (Bem 2000, 535). Moreover, Bem believes that "women's sexual orientations are more fluid than men's," and that "nonheterosexual women are more likely to see their orientations as flexible, even 'chosen,' whereas men are more likely to view their sexual orientations in essentialist terms, as inborn and unchangeable" (Bem 2000, 545).

There is some evidence that these gender nonconformist traits may be linked to different male hormone levels during fetal development (Berenbaum and Hines 1992; Berenbaum and Snyder 1995; LeVay 2000a). LeVay (2000a) notes that "gay people frequently experience anti-gay discrimination for years before they realize that they are in fact gay"(see also Rottnek 1999).

Seventh, differences in *throwing skills* between straight men and women and homosexual men have been studied. When comparing accuracies in throwing a ball to a target, straight men usually did better than straight women, a difference already exhibited in young children. However, gay men performed about as well as straight women, but much worse than straight men, a difference possibly the result of different neuronal connection patterns developed in the brain due to male hormone differences (Hall and Kimura 1995; LeVay 2000a).

Eighth, studies of *fingerprint ridge differences* in identical twins, one gay, one straight, show that the number of fingerprint ridges are left-shifted (i.e., there are more ridges on the left hand than on the right hand) in the gay twin as compared with the straight brother. Because fingerprint ridges are determined in the second trimester of pregnancy, such differences have a biological basis. The reasons for these differences remain unknown, but they cannot be due to post-natal environmental factors (Hall and Kimura 1994; LeVay 2000a; for a review of the possible importance of fingerprint patterns, see Zucker and Bradley 1995, 185).

Ninth, *otoacoustic emissions*—levels of weak sounds produced by the inner ear during the process of transforming incoming external sounds into electric signals—appear to be different between men and women. The relative strength of the emissions appears to be correlated with testosterone levels such that the higher the level of testosterone the weaker the signal, with men having generally weaker signals then women. However, in lesbians and bisexual women, the signals appear to be significantly weaker than in heterosexual women. These differences also appear to be correlated with the differing levels of male hormones during fetal development (McFadden and Pasanen 1999; LeVay 2000a).

Tenth, *anthropological data* indicate that homosexuality is probably universal in the human family. Following extensive fieldwork in the United States, Guatemala, Brazil, and the Philippines, Whitam and Zent (1984) concluded that gays and lesbians might be present in all societies. Many of these societies have institutionalized gender-discordant behavior (Dixson 1998, 164; Murray 2000). Moreover, Whitam and Zent (1984, 437) believe that the "pattern of the distant and hostile father . . . is the result of strong negative sanctions toward homosexuality in the Anglo-Saxon world, [and is] not the cause of homosexuality."

Eleventh, *gay ram studies* along with other *natural history studies* indicate that same-sex attraction exists also in the rest of the animal world. In her doctoral study at the University of California at Davis, Anne Perkins found that of the 2100 rams she studied, about 10 percent have a same-sex attraction. Perkins also discovered some important physiological differences between gay rams and non-gay rams. Moreover, the gay rams cannot be changed in their sexual orientation (Perkins and Fitzgerald 1997).

In a monumental work, Bruce Bagemihl (1999) showed that, ranging over the animal kingdom, many species exhibit homosexuality, and in some cases, homosexual pairs appear to be more lasting than heterosexual ones. Both Perkins' research and Bagemihl's review illustrate that same-sex attraction is not confined to humans, nor can it be said to be "unnatural," whatever moral lessons one wishes to draw from these examples (see Dixson 1998,146ff.). In a word, nature is prolific, diverse, and not easily subject to human classification (Fausto-Sterling 2000).

Even with all these collective data, we cannot be certain what the sexual orientation of a given individual will be. Simon LeVay has remarked that "genes and prenatal factors have only so much to say about our sexuality: there still could be some role for parenting, for life experiences or even for that bugaboo of many gay activists—choice" (LeVay 2000c).

In an arresting summary, Richard Pillard (1998, 83) maintained that

> in the end, it may turn out that even the most exact knowledge of sexual orientation development will give us no more than a guess about the outcome in a particular individual. There is

now evidence that neural connections in the brain are imprecisely directed. As neurons in a fetus sprout and grow, there appears to be only a statistical chance of their hooking up at an exact destination. Thus it seems plausible that we may never be able to predict, even knowing the specific genes, the particular family circumstances, and the cultural milieu, what will be the sexual orientation of a specific individual. *The outcome for any particular person may always be, in some measure, a matter of chance."* (italics added)

Alan Dixson (1998, 314) agrees:

At this time we are far from understanding all the factors which govern the development of gender identity and sexual orientation in human beings. In the current state of knowledge it would . . . be premature to conclude that a single developmental pathway leads to homosexuality.

Finally, Pattatucci (1998b, 34) points out that

although investigating genetic sources of variation in sexual orientation is a crucial endeavor for understanding the role of families, perhaps the most exciting frontier for family research lies in studying nonshared environmental sources of variation.

Children are often very different, even within the same family, but the question is why. Why does one child become a gay or lesbian adult and another child a heterosexual adult?

Increasingly, it is now apparent that the nonshared environment, such as different friends, sports interests, food and clothing tastes, hobbies, and the like, as experienced by children, is far more important than the shared environment such as going to the same church, living at the same address, having the same parents, etc. However, disentangling these components—genetic factors, shared and nonshared environments—is complicated, but constitutes important directions for future research. (For more on this, see Pattatucci 1998b, and Bailey et al. 2000.)

Implications for the Christian Community

Persons with same-sex attractions are very much a part of the church. The question now exercising Christian communities is how to respond to our GLBTIs—our gay, lesbian, bisexual, transgendered and intersexed sisters and brothers. Without exploring fully this question, this study does point the way toward a more humane view with respect to our sexuality. First, we suggest that all of us respect the self-identity of nonheterosexuals. When such persons claim they were born gay or lesbian, we should respect their views.

Second, we should cease claiming that same-sex attraction in itself is pathological or evil, and that the only solution is for gays and lesbians to seek some sort of cure, then marry a person of the opposite sex. If our review has merit, it should give us pause before we hunt for dubious moral alternative explanations as to why certain people are gay or lesbian, and that our acceptance of nonheterosexuals is based on their attempts at cures.

This is not to say that all non-biological approaches lack merit but that the findings shared in this chapter deserve consideration. Much research, of course, still needs to be done, especially in establishing clear genetic links to both human homosexuality and heterosexuality, as well as investigating the role of the nonshared environment in the development of persons within one family.

Summary

On the basis of the evidence presented in this chapter, we conclude that same-sex attraction does have a significant biological component. This does not mean that environment has no role. Explaining human sexuality is far too complicated for it to be reduced to easy formulations and patterns. Whatever the "cause" of a person's sexuality, what one does in response to one's sexuality and sexual attraction is a matter of human choice. But as for the attraction itself, it appears that, in many persons, this is beyond their immediate control.

Consequently, we believe that one of the initial steps in understanding same-sex attraction is to examine what is known about the biological bases of homosexuality. The call to the Christian community therefore is to find ways to help persons with a same-sex attraction accept themselves as they are, and to find ways to find fellowship and companionship within a Christian community.

As psychoanalyst Richard Isay states (1996, 175), "Opposing discrimination in a prejudiced society is good for the psyche. It directs anger away from ourselves to where it rightfully belongs. But it is love that makes us know who we are. And let no individual, no organization, and no institution try to take that away!"[2]

List of Important Reviews

The following list of papers and books directs the reader to current reviews dealing with the biological aspects of same-sex attraction. All papers and books listed are cited in the reference section. Some important journals publishing current research on homosexuality include the following: *American Journal of Psychiatry, Archives of General Psychiatry, Archives of Sexual Behavior, Behavior Genetics, Biological Psychiatry, British Journal of Psychiatry, Journal of Gay & Lesbian Psychotherapy, Journal of Homosexuality,* and *Nature Genetics.*

Papers

Bailey (1995)—short overview of the biology of homosexuality.

Bailey and Dawood (1998)—discusses behavior genetics and environmental influences (in this context environment does not equal social influence).

Diamond (1993)—includes surveys dealing with percentages of homosexuality.

Ellis (1996a)—reviews various theories of homosexuality.

Gladue (1993)—reviews various lines of evidence: genetic, hormonal, neuroanatomical, neuropsychological, etc.

LeVay (2000a)—compact review of key evidences that homosexuality has a biological basis.

Marmor (1998)—understanding the origin and causes of homosexuality (etiology) is crucial in relating to gays and lesbians.

Pattatucci (1998a)—reviews nature/nurture arguments, behavior genetics, environmental variables, etc.

Pattatucci (1998b)—fine presentation of the classification and genetics of sexual orientation, and concludes with an overview of directions for future research.

Pillard (1997)—good review of the history of research on sexual orientation.

Pillard (1998)—review of biologic theories of homosexuality.

Pillard and Bailey (1998)—overall review of evidence for a heritable component to human sexual orientation.

Weinrich (1995)—critique of studies with an anti-biologic bias.

Books

Bagemihl (1999)—major text reviewing the wide range of animal homosexuality; required reading for anyone claiming that same-sex attraction is not natural, i.e., doesn't occur among animals other than humans.

Burr (1996)—accounts for the major research efforts into the origins of human sexuality.

Cabaj and Stein (1996)—important reference of fifty-five chapters, most of which were written by psychiatrists and psychologists representing a major shift in views of human same-sex attraction from crime to illness to difference ("homosexuality is not an illness and is not psychopathological").

Dixson (1998)—detailed comparative study of the patterns of sexuality among primates; an important reference including material on sociosexual behavior and homosexuality in humans.

Drescher (1998b)—important book dealing with gay identities, origins of homosexuality, and various problems concerning therapies by a psychoanalyst.

Fausto-Sterling (2000)—challenges the simplistic notions of femaleness and maleness, nature vs. nurture, etc.

Hamer and Copeland (1998)—readable account of important investigations by molecular biologists showing crucial links between our genes (DNA) and who we are as persons. Hamer's research claimed to show that possible genes for male homosexuality are located in the Xq28 region of the X chromosome (i.e., the terminal region of the long arm of the X sex chromosome).

LeVay (1996)—excellent account of research on sexuality by a scientist who studied differences in human brain structures among females and males, including gays.

McKnight (1997)—a discussion of the evolution and biological underpinnings of human sexuality that argues for a biosocial perspective on human sexuality and its variations.

Mondimore (1996)—a careful review of homosexuality dealing with the history, biology, and psychology of same-sex attraction by a psychiatrist; required reading!

Murray (2000)—outstanding thorough treatment of age-structured homosexualities, gender-stratified organization of homosexuality, and egalitarian homosexualities occurring in various cultures.

Savin-Williams and Cohen (1996)—twenty chapters dealing largely with the developmental aspects of gays and lesbians over their life span, written especially to enlighten young adults as they attempt to understand their identity within modern cultures.

Seligman (1994)—strikes a sensible balance between the genetic and environmental aspects of human development; contains an excellent chapter on human sexuality distinguishing among sexual orientation, preference, and performance (behavior).

Wright (1998)—reviews recent studies concerning the genetics of human behavior; supports the view that both heredity and environment influence human behavior.

Zucker and Bradley (1995)—chapter 6 contains a fine comparative review of biological research dealing with gender identity disorders.

Notes

1. Although most chapters in this book follow MLA endnote style, this chapter, among the most oriented toward social science, follows the author-date style more common for social scientific writing.

2. The following persons commented on various drafts of this chapter, but all remaining opinions and statements are entirely our responsibility. Special thanks are due to Joe Blowers, Willis Breckbill, Thomas Chamness, Ted Grimsrud, Philip Hertzler, Dorothy Keener, Gladys Keener, Lois Kenagy, Willard Krabill, M.D., Norman Kraus, Roberta Kreider, Barbara Longenecker, Charles Longenecker, Ruth Conrad Liechty, John A. Lapp, Jay Martin, Elsie Steelberg, M.D., and Joyce Thompson.

References

Allen, L. S. and R. A. Gorski. 1992. "Sexual orientation and the size of the anterior commissure in the human brain." *Proc. Natl. Acad. Sci. U.S.A.* 89: 7199-7201.

Bagemihl, B. 1999. *Biological exuberance.* New York: St. Martin's Press.

Bailey, J. M. 1995. "Sexual orientation revolution." *Nature Genetics* 11: 353-354.

Bailey, J. M. and K. Dawood. 1998. "Behavior genetics, sexual orientation, and the family," pp. 3-18. In C. J. Patterson and A. R. D'Augelli (eds.), *Lesbian, gay, and bisexual identities in families: Psychological Perspectives.* Oxford University Press, New York and Oxford.

Bailey, J. M., M. P. Dunne, and N. G. Martin. 2000. "Genetic and environmental influences on sexual orientation and its correlates in an Australian twin sample." *J. Personality and Social Psychology* 78: 524-536.

Bailey, J. M. and R. C. Pillard. 1991. "A genetic study of male sexual orientation." *Arch. Gen. Psychiatry* 48:1089-1096.

Bailey, J. M., R. C. Pillard, K. Dawood, M. B. Miller, L. A. Farrer, S. Trivedi, and R. L. Murphy. 1999. "A family history study of male sexual orientation using three independent samples." *Behavior Genetics* 29: 79-86.

Bayer, R. 1987. *Homosexuality and American psychiatry.* Princeton, N.J.: Princeton University Press.

Bem, D. J. 2000. "Exotic becomes erotic: Interpreting the biological correlates of sexual orientation." *Arch. Sexual Behavior* 29: 531-548.

Berenbaum, S. A. and M. Hines. 1992. "Early androgens are related to childhood sex-typed toy preferences." *Psychological Science* 3: 203-206.

Berenbaum, S. A. and E. Snyder. 1995. "Early hormonal influences on childhood sex-typed activity and playmate preferences: Implications for the development of sexual orientation." *Dev. Psychology* 31: 31-42.

Bieber, I. et al. 1962. *Homosexuality: A psychoanalytic study*. New York: Basic Books.

Burr, C. 1996. *A separate creation: A search for the biological origins of sexual orientation*. New York: Hyperion.

Byne, W. 1995. "Science and belief: Psychobiological research on sexual orientation." *J. Homosexuality* 28: 303-344.

Byne, W. and B. Parsons. 1993. "Human sexual orientation: The biologic theories reappraised." *Arch. Gen. Psychiatry* 50: 228-239.

Cabaj, R. and T. Stein (eds.). 1996. *Textbook of homosexuality and mental health*. Washington, D.C.: American Psychiatric Press, Inc.

Dawood, K., R. C. Pillard, C. Horvath, W. Revelle, and J. M. Bailey. 2000. "Familial aspects of male homosexuality." *Arch. Sexual Behavior* 29: 155-163.

D'Augelli, A. R. 1996. "Lesbian, gay and bisexual development during adolescence and young adulthood," pp. 267-288. In R. P. Cabaj and T. S. Stein (eds.), *Textbook of homosexuality and mental health*. Washington, D.C.: American Psychiatric Press, Inc.

DeLamater, J. D. and J. S. Hyde. 1998. "Essentialism vs. social constructionism in the study of human sexuality." *The J. of Sex Research* 35: 10-18.

Diamond, M. 1993. "Some genetic considerations in the development of sexual orientation," pp. 291-309. *In* M. Haug, R. E. Whalen et al. (eds.), *The development of sex differences and similarities in behavior*. Boston: Kluwer Academic Publishers.

Dittmann, R. W., M. E. Kappes, and M. H. Kappes. 1992. "Sexual behavior in adolescent and adult females with congenital adrenal hyperplasia." *Psychoneurobiology* 17: 153-170.

Dixson, A. F. 1998. *Primate sexuality: Comparative studies of the prosimians, monkeys, apes, and human beings*. Oxford University Press, New York, Tokyo.

Drescher, J. 1998a. "Contemporary psychoanalytic psychotherapy with gay men with a commentary on reparative therapy." *J. Gay and Lesbian Psychotherapy* 2: 51-74.

Drescher, J. 1998b. *Psychoanalytic therapy and the gay man*. Hillsdale, N.J., and London: The Analytic Press.

Ellis, L. 1996a. "Theories of homosexuality," pp. 11-34. In R. C. Savin-Williams and K. M. Cohen (eds.), *The lives of lesbians, gays, and bisexuals*. Fort Worth, Tex.: Harcourt Brace College Publishers.

Ellis, L. 1996b. "The role of perinatal factors in determining sexual orientation," pp. 35-70. In R. C. Savin-Williams and K. M. Cohen (eds.), The
lives of lesbians, gays, and bisexuals. Fort Worth, Tex.: Harcourt Brace
College Publishers.

Fausto-Sterling, A. 2000. Sexing the body: Gender politics and the construction of
sexuality. New York: Basic Books.

Friedman, R. C. 1999. "Discussion of articles by Drs. Vaughan, Drescher and
Cohler." J. Gay and Lesbian Psychotherapy 3:91-98.

Gillis, J. R. 1998. "Cultural sexism and the family," pp. 249-269. In C. J. Patterson and A. R. D'Augelli (eds.), Lesbian, gay, and bisexual identities in
families: Psychological perspectives. New York: Oxford University Press.

Gladue, B. A. 1993. "The psychobiology of sexual orientation," pp. 437-455.
In M. Haug et al. (eds.), The development of sex differences and similarities in behavior. Dordrecht: Kluwer Academic Publishers.

Gonsiorek, J. C. 1996. "Mental health and sexual orientation," pp. 462-478.
In R. C. Savin-Williams and K. C. Cohen (eds.), The lives of lesbians,
gays, and bisexuals: Children to adults. Harcourt Brace College Publishers, Fort Worth.

Haldeman, D. C. 1996. "Spirituality and religion in the lives of lesbians and
gay men," pp. 881-896. In R. B. Cabaj and T. S. Stein (eds.), Textbook of
homosexuality and mental health. Washington, D.C.: American Psychiatric Press, Inc.

Halwani, R. 1998. "Essentialism, social constructionism, and the history of
homosexuality." J. Homosexuality 35:23-51.

Hall, J. and D. Kimura. 1994. "Dermatoglyphic asymmetry and sexual orientation in men." Behavioral Neuroscience 108: 1203-1206.

Hall, J. and D. Kimura. 1995. "Sexual orientation and performance on sexually dimorphic motor tasks." Arch. Sexual Behavior 24:395-407.

Hamer, D. and P. Copeland. 1998. Living with our genes. New York: Doubleday.

Hamer, D. H., S. Hu et al. 1993. "A linkage between DNA markers on the X
chromosome and male sexual orientation." Science 261: 321-327.

Hartstein, N. B. 1996. "Suicide risk in lesbian, gay, and bisexual youth," pp.
819-837. In R. P. Cabaj and T. S. Stein (eds.), Textbook of homosexuality
and mental health. American Psychiatric Press, Inc., Washington, D.C.
and London, England.

Hooker, E. 1957. "The adjustment of the male overt homosexual." J. Projec-
tive Techniques 21:18-31.

Hu, S., A. M. L. Pattatucci, C. Patterson, L. Li, D. W. Fulker, S. S. Cherny, L.
Kruglyak, and D. H. Hamer. 1995. "Linkage between sexual orientation and chromosome Xq28 in males but not in females." Nature Genetics 11: 248-256.

Isay, R. A. 1989. Being homosexual: Gay men and their development. New York:
Avon Books.

Isay, R. A. 1996. *Becoming gay: The journey to self-acceptance.* New York: Pantheon Books.

Jegalian, K. and B. T. Lahn. 2001. "Why the Y is so weird." *Scientific American* 284 (2): 56-61.

Kirk, K. M., J. M. Bailey, M. P. Dunne, and N. G. Martin. 2000. "Measurement models for sexual orientation in a community twin sample." *Behavior Genetics* 30: 3435-356.

Kreider, R. (ed.). 1998. *From wounded hearts.* Gaithersburg, Md.: Chi Rho Press.

LeVay, S. 1991. "A difference in hypothalamic structure between heterosexual and homosexual men." *Science* 253: 1034-1037.

LeVay, S. 1996. *Queer science: The use and abuse of research into homosexuality.* Cambridge, Mass.: The MIT Press.

LeVay, S. 2000a. "Sexual orientation: The science and its social impact." Unpublished paper to be published in Reverso, but currently available at LeVay's home page: http://hometown.aol.com/slevay/index.html).

LeVay, S. 2000b. "The science of sex: The 'gay brain' revisited." Unpublished paper. For source, see LeVay's home page, above.

LeVay, S. 2000c. "The science of sex: Fingers and fetuses." Unpublished paper. For source, see LeVay's home page, above.

Marmor, J. 1998. "Homosexuality: Is etiology really important?" *J. Gay & Lesbian Psychotherapy* 2: 19-28.

Mayr, E. 1982. *The growth of biological thought: Diversity, evolution, and inheritance.* Cambridge, Mass.: Belknap Press of Harvard University Press.

McFadden, D. and E. G. Pasanen. 1999. "Spontaneous otoacoustic emissions in heterosexuals, homosexuals, and bisexuals." *J. Acoustical Soc. Amer.* 105: 2403-2413.

McKnight, J. 1997. *Straight science? Homosexuality, evolution and adaptation.* London and New York: Routledge.

Moore, J. A. 1993. *Science as a way of knowing: The foundations of modern biology.* Cambridge, Mass.: Harvard University Press.

Mondimore, F. M. 1996. *A natural history of homosexuality.* Baltimore: The Johns Hopkins Press.

Murray, S. O. 2000. *Homosexualities.* The University of Chicago Press, Chicago and London.

Nicolosi, J. 1991. *Reparative therapy of male homosexuality: A new clinical approach.* Northvale, N.J.: Jason Aronson.

Pattatucci, A. M. 1998a. "Molecular investigations into complex behavior: Lessons from sexual orientation studies." *Human Biology* 70: 367-386.

Pattatucci, A. M. 1998b. "Biopsychological interactions and the development of sexual orientation," pp. 19-39. *In* C. J. Patterson and A. R. D'Augelli (eds.), *Lesbian, gay, and bisexual identities in families: Psychological perspectives.* New York and London: Oxford University Press.

Pattatucci, A. M. L. and D. H. Hamer. 1995a. "The genetics of sexual orientation: From fruit flies to humans," pp. 154-174. In P. R. Abramson and S. D. Pinkerton (eds.), *Sexual nature/sexual culture*. Chicago: The University of Chicago Press.

Pattatucci, A. M. L. and D. H. Hamer. 1995b. "Development and familiality of sexual orientation in females." *Behavior Genetics* 25: 407-420.

Perkins, A. and J. A. Fitzgerald. 1997. "Sexual orientation in domestic rams: Some biological and social correlates," pp. 107-127. In L. Ellis and L. Ebertz (eds.), *Sexual orientation: Toward biological understanding*. Westport, Conn.: Praeger.

Pillard, R. C. 1996. "Homosexuality from a familial and genetic perspective," pp. 115-128. *In* R. P. Cabaj and T. S. Stein (eds.), *Textbook of homosexuality and mental health*. Washington, D.C.: American Psychiatric Press.

Pillard, R. C. 1997. "The search for a genetic influence on sexual orientation," pp. 226-241. In V. A. Rosario (ed.), *Science and homosexualities*. New York and London: Routledge.

Pillard, R. C. 1998. "Biologic theories of homosexuality." *J. Gay and Lesbian Psychotherapy* 2: 75-85.

Pillard, R. C. and J. M. Bailey. 1998. "Human sexual orientation has a heritable component." *Human Biology* 70: 347-365.

Pillard, R. C. and J. D. Weinrich. 1986. "Evidence of familial nature of male homosexuality." *Arch. Gen. Psychiatry* 43: 808-812.

Plomin, R., J. C. DeFries, G. E. McClearn, and M. Rutter. 1997. *Behavior genetics*, third ed. New York: W. H. Freeman and Co.

Popper, K. R. 1962. *Conjectures and refutations: The growth of scientific knowledge*. New York: Basic Books.

Popper, K. R. 1972. *Objective knowledge: An evolutionary approach*. Oxford, England: Oxford University Press.

Rice, G. et al. 1999. "Male homosexuality: Absence of linkage to microsatellite markers at Xq28." *Science* 284: 665-667.

Rottnek, M. (ed.). 1999. *Sissies and tomboys: Gender nonconformity and homosexual childhood*. New York: New York University Press.

Savin-Williams, R. C. and K. M. Cohen (eds.). 1996. *The lives of lesbians, gays and bisexuals: Children to adults*. Fort Worth, Tex.: Harcourt Brace College Publisher.

Searle, J. R. 1995. *The construction of social reality*. New York: The Free Press.

Searle, J. R. 1998. *Mind, language and society: Philosophy in the real world*. New York: Basic Books.

Seligman, M. E. P. 1994. *What you can change and what you can't*. New York: Alfred A. Knopf.

Sell, R. L., J. A. Wells, and D. Wypij. 1995. "The prevalence of homosexual behavior and attraction in the United States, the United Kingdom, and France: Results of national population-based samples." *Arch. Sexual Behavior* 24: 235-248.

Socarides, C. 1968. *The overt homosexual*. New York: Grune & Stratton.

Socarides, C. 1975. *Beyond sexual freedom*. New York: Quadrangle/New York Times Book Company.

Stein, T. S. 1998. "Social constructionism and essentialism: Theoretical and clinical considerations relevant to psychotherapy." *J. Gay and Lesbian Psychotherapy* 2: 29-49.

Swaab, D. F. and M. A. Hofman. 1990. "An enlarged superchiasmatic nucleus in homosexual men." *Brain Research* 537: 141-148.

Turner, W. J. 1994. "Comments on discordant MZ twinning in homosexuality." *Arch. Sexual Behavior* 23: 115-119.

Turner, W. 1995. "Homosexuality, Type I: An Xq28 phenomenon." *Arch. Sexual Behavior* 24: 109-134.

Weinrich, J. D. 1995. "Biological research on sexual orientation: A critique of the critics," pp. 197-213. *In* J. P. De Cecco and D. A. Parker (eds.), *Sex, cells, and same-sex desire: The biology of sexual preference*. New York: The Haworth Press, Inc.

Whitam, F. L. and M. Zent. 1984. "A cross-cultural assessment of early cross-gender behavior and familial factors in male homosexuality." *Arch. Sexual Behavior* 13: 427-440.

Whitam, F. L., M. Diamond, and J. Martin. 1993. "Homosexual orientation in twins." *Arch. Sexual Behavior* 22: 185-206.

Wright, W. 1998. *Born that way: Genes/behavior/personality*. New York: Alfred A. Knopf.

Zucker, K. J. and S. J. Bradley. 1995. *Gender identity disorder and psychosexual problems in children and adolescents*. The Guilford Press, New York and London.

Chapter 10

Homosexuality: A Call for Compassion and Moral Rigor

A. James Reimer

Development of Doctrine

The ethical issue of homosexuality apart from its intrinsic importance is also a useful test case for looking at how one interprets biblical texts. While the discussion of gay and lesbian sexuality is an important window into one's biblical hermeneutics, this is not the primary interest in the following essay. Rather, the focus here is on how one's understanding of doctrine, particularly the development of dogma, can help with dealing with tough moral and ethical issues like homosexuality in creative ways. Homosexuality then is a case example of ways of proceeding that should be applicable as well to other ethical problems like women's ordination, war, policing, social justice, euthenasia, bio-medical advances—issues which are not directly addressed here but could be, using the same general doctrinal approach. This is made possible through some notion of "doctrinal" development in the context of a discerning believing community led by the Holy Spirit [the church].

It is this developmental principle which is assumed in the discussion of homosexuality below, based on an essay which first appeared as an article in the *Mennonite Reporter* in 1987[1] and reflects my treatment of the subject in various venues in the 1980s and 1990s, including a lecture to Conrad Grebel College students,[2] an adult

174

Sunday school class at Rockway Mennonite Church, a presentation to Brethren/Mennonite Council for Lesbian and Gay Concerns,[3] and my work as chair of the Theological Concerns Council of Mennonite Conference of Easter Canada (MCEC) in 1993-94.

In the Council we spent a good deal of time discussing the issue and planning a workshop on the subject for MCEC Executive Board, Pastors, and other groups with an interest in the topic. Most recently, I was invited to respond to a United Methodist study of homosexuality.[4] This Methodist study used the traditional fourfold set of authorities—Bible, tradition, reason, experience—to examine the issue, which although not without its own problems, is surely an advance over a purely biblicist method of determining divine will in given situations.

The Catholic "development of doctrine" way also has its set of dangers—it still begs the question of how authentic development is to be distinguished from inauthentic development—but presupposes a high view of tradition and the church (church history becomes the history of biblical interpretation) that bears some resemblance to the high ecclesiology of Anabaptist-Mennonite theology. Catholics and Mennonites both have a high view of the church— moral and ethical issues need to be addressed not on the basis of *individual* hermeneutics, reason, or experience but corporately in the context of the church. Where they differ is in the nature of their church polity—the way they go about determining what is divine will in given situations.

Universal Affirmations and Specific Applications

I continue to find helpful John H. Yoder's characterization of believers church decision-making. For Yoder, ethical discourse in the church, as understood by Anabaptists, is characterized by four indispensable elements: the Spirit, the gathering of believers, the Scriptures, and the moral challenge of the situation. Taking seriously these four elements in determing God's will is what constitutes the "hermeneutic community."[5] My own emphasis on the "dogmatic foundations for Christian ethics" in this essay is not meant to replace Yoder's method. Rather, I mean to add a higher regard (than Yoder has) for the importance of doctrinal tradition and development; to spell out how confession, doctrine, catechesis, dogma, and creed function within this "Yoderian" process of reading the Bible and interpreting the moving of the Spirit within the believing community. It allows for diversity within unity on divisive issues such as homosexuality. What the confessional/dogmatic/creedal approach does is distinguish between the universal language of faith which ties all Christians together everywhere and ethical particulars on which sincere Christians disagree.

This is why the ancient creeds do not become as ethically specific as one might wish. What they do is give expression to the most fundamental affirmations of faith—faith in God the Creator, Christ the redeemer, and Holy Spirit the consummator—the theological/ontological foundation for all human ethics. The 1983 "Pastoral Letter on War and Peace" by the National Conference of Catholic Bishops makes the further distinction between universal moral principles and specific applications of these as follows:

> In doing this we realize, and we want readers of this letter to recognize, that not all statements in this letter have the same moral authority. At times we state universally binding moral principles found in the teaching of the Church; at other times the pastoral letter makes specific applications, observations and recommendations which allow for diversity of opinion on the part of those who assess the factual data of a situation differently.[6]

In applying to homosexuality the distinction between universal affirmations of faith and ever more specific applications of this faith to moral and ethical issues on which believers genuinely disagree, I draw the following conclusions for the Mennonite church. The ultimate criterion for belonging to the church within the believers church tradition, is to be baptized on the basis of a personal confession of faith in Jesus Christ and a commitment to living a regenerated life as far as is possible in the context of a fallen world in which all forms of sexuality are imperfect.

Our congregational church polity—and in this we differ from the Catholic traditions—allows for local congregations to deal with ever more concrete applications of this confession, especially in areas of morality and ethics, in freedom within certain agreed upon limits. This is where I end up in the following essay: namely, that it is on the local level, where believers of different sexual orientation confront each other face to face, that divine leading on such divisive issues will need to be discerned. It is dangerous for some centralized body to make authoritative pronouncements on matters of concrete application, and as a rule such denomination-wide "decrees" should be limited to affirming more general, universal, confessional principles and leaving detailed application to the local congregation.

Compassion and Moral Rigor

The extensive public airing of the controversial topic of homosexuality in the Mennonite press, at conferences, and in a variety of study documents indicates the extent to which the Mennonite community is willing to face openly one of the tough issues of our time.

When I read the poignant pleas for acceptance and understanding by gay persons and those close to them, on the one side, and the sincere and passionate arguments against homosexual activity, on the other—both using biblical texts and persuasive reasoning—I recognize the difficulty the church faces.

What is required, in my judgment, is compassionate listening to all members of our community, an openness to all the empirical, social-scientific data available, a serious reading of the biblical materials, sound theological thinking, open public debate, and prayerful receptiveness to the leading of the Holy Spirit. We're into the long haul here. The church is called to make moral judgments but we ought not to make them prematurely.

The first distinction we have to make is between compassionate solidarity with suffering persons (with those who represent "the other") and the developing of moral positions. I call these the "priestly pastoral" and the "prophetic-ethical" tasks of the church, respectively. Both are necessary, but they are not the same. Charity for those who suffer, particularly the stranger, takes precedence over "correct moral positions." In fact, a commitment to charity is itself a moral imperative.

This does not, however, absolve the church from the difficult task of developing biblically based moral positions on an urgent issue like homosexuality. The public debate about homosexuality points out the need to re-examine in a fundamental way our method of biblical interpretation and some of the basic tenets of what we believe.

I want here not so much to offer a definitive position of my own but to ask some basic questions of belief and offer some suggestions on how we might approach the issue. My observations grow partly out of a Pastor's Theology Seminar on homosexuality which I conducted at Conrad Grebel College from September to May 1987.

The biblical texts that refer directly to homosexuality are quite meager and open to a variety of interpretations. What this demonstrates is the need to move beyond quoting and exegeting isolated verses and passages. We need to read the Bible as a whole and find a thematic way of weaving together the variety of biblical materials and relating these to the present situation in a dynamic way.

The most fruitful way of doing this is by seeing the Scriptures as a drama of salvation with a three-fold structure: creation (created nature), sin and the Fall (fallen nature), and redemption (redeemed nature). What does God intend in creation? What is the nature and extent of the Fall? How and when does redemption take place? These questions are difficult to answer and in fact drive us to the very foundation of what we believe and hold dear.

Simply collating texts that have to do with homosexuality is inadequate. For one thing, the texts are diverse and subject to different interpretations. For another, we do not consider all parts of Scripture of equal value. New Testament texts, particularly for Mennonites, supersede in importance Old Testament texts. For Christans, Old Testament texts are read through the lenses of New Testament texts, which means that Jews will read the Hebrew Scriptures somewhat differently than Christians (which is not to assume their reading is inferior).

Further, even within the New Testament, certain theological or interpretive decisions have to be made. Christ's own life and teachings are generally considered to be for us the definitive Word of God, the norm by which we evaluate the rest of the Bible. For our position on war and peace, for instance, we begin not with Old Testament "divine warrior" texts, even though these need to be taken seriously, but with Christ's ethic of nonviolent love. In the end, we need a kind of hierarchy of normative values by which we interpret the Bible and make moral judgments, including judgments on the issue of homosexuality. [I should add here that my thinking has evolved further than when I first wrote this piece, as shown in my chapter on "God is Love but Not a Pacifist," in my book, *Mennonites and Classical Theology*.]

Created nature

We believe God created the world and that what God created was, and to a large extent remains, good. Part of this good creation and what it means to be human is human sexuality. But what kind of sexuality did God intend in creation? The answer to this question is not as clear as it might first appear. First of all, where do we go to find an answer?

Traditionally, Roman Catholics, for example, have maintained that we can discover God's intent in creation by looking both at revelation (Scriptures) and nature (natural law). Sex, they said, is for procreation and by looking at nature we can conclude that homosexuality is unnatural since procreation is impossible. A certain reading of the Genesis account supports this understanding of natural law.

The problem is that nature is ambiguous. The argument from nature can be used to support both heterosexual and homosexual ethics. One of the central claims made by the gay community is that homosexual orientation is such by nature. This is not to deny the importance of considering nature for Christian ethics. In addressing the issue of homosexuality, as well as other urgent moral issues, we need to take into account all the available empirical (including biological) data.

Protestants, and particularly Mennonites, have at least in theory given less credence to natural law and restricted themselves more to the Scriptures themselves as the source for norms on ethical questions. Unfortunately, this has its own set of problems. For one thing, the biblical text itself is ambiguous.

The Genesis account of creation presents at least two models for the purpose of human sexuality: procreation and companionship. A biblical case for homosexuality from Genesis, if one wanted to make one, would have to be made on the basis of the second model—unless, of course, advances in medical technology would make possible male conception.

A straightforward reading of Genesis, not to mention other parts of Scripture, in my opinion clearly places sexual activity (both for procreation and for companionship) within a male-female context. The problem, however, is that male/female language itself has become ambiguous for us today. Medical possibilities make male/female differentiation increasingly fluid. Potentially, at least, males can be made into females and females into males.

There is a further consideration. When we speak of God's intent in creation, do we speak about God's original creation, as represented in the Genesis stories, or do we include God's ongoing creation (the creation of each unique individual, for instance)? Surely, Christians want to say—and there is good biblical support for this—that God continues to create, and what God creates is good.

Individuals with a self-perceived homosexual orientation from as early as they can remember could, then, persuasively argue that they have been created with a particular orientation, and that this is a created good; and to deny this would be to deny the goodness of God's ongoing creation. Here the crucial question, of course, is whether the gay person has perceived himself or herself correctly. Surely we are all masters at self-deception. Has the homosexual in fact been born (or created) with a particular orientation, or is it in the end all a matter of psychological or social conditioning, some of it perhaps prenatal? Here, in my opinion, the empirical data is consequential but not conclusive at present.

For Mennonites, who place such a high premium on the life and teachings of Jesus, there is, however, something strange about beginning chronologically with Genesis to discover God's intent for sexual ethics. Ought we not begin with Jesus and read backwards and forwards through his eyes?

What a christological approach to ethics does, I believe, is put the emphasis not on what "is" the case but on what "ought" to be the case. In other words, the central question becomes not what we are, or how we were born, but what we can and ought by God's grace to become. This applies to heterosexuals and homosexuals alike. What would our redeemed natures look like? Before we address that question, we need first to examine the reality of the Fall.

Fallen nature

Even if we were to know clearly what God's intent in creation was, we believe that creation is fallen in an impersonal sense (evil and "original sin") and in a personal moral sense ("personal sin"). The implication here is that all human sexuality, whether in orientation or in activity, whether heterosexual or homosexual, has been distorted. None of us can live up to God's intent completely until the whole order is redeemed. To say this is not to excuse all sexual behavior. It is, nevertheless, to recognize that none of us is unblemished sexually, and that to identify homosexual activity as the one supreme example of the Fall, sexually speaking, is hypocritical.

How we understand the Fall—whether total or partial—will determine to some extent how we look at homosexuality. If we believe in the total depravity of the created order (as Lutherans and Calvinists traditionally do), then the orientation we are born with must be seen as much more fateful in determining our sexual behavior. Whether homosexuals can be held accountable for their orientation in a situation where their own freedom to choose an orientation does not exist then becomes highly questionable.

If, on the other hand, we believe with traditional Catholics and most Anabaptists that the Fall is only partial—that substantial amounts of human freedom have remained intact despite the Fall—then individuals shoulder a much greater degree of responsibility in choosing sexual behavior, for instance, regardless of how they were born. In short, initial orientation, whether viewed as a "created good" or the consequence of "original sin" is then less of a determining factor in sexual activity.

The really important issue, however, is how we view the church. For Mennonites, with their historic belief in a pure redeemed church, the pervasiveness of sin in all human life and activity, even after regeneration, is a central problem. If homosexual orientation is seen as a departure from God's intent, and homosexual practice as freely chosen sinful behavior, then it follows that a pure church cannot allow practicing homosexuals within its ranks.

How the Mennonite church is to deal with members of its communion who either (1) do not share some of the dominant values or beliefs of the members, or (2) have "fallen" from the normative position, is proving to be increasingly problematic on a wide range of issues (divorce and remarriage is another example). Our tendency in the past has been to exclude them. We are finding more and more, however, that the concept of the pure church is no longer adequate for our growing conviction that the church is not only a redeemed but also a redeeming community, in which individuals are not expected to be immediately perfect but are gradually nurtured to a fuller realization of God's intent.

Redeemed nature

We come now to what is perhaps the most difficult question. What does regeneration and ultimate redemption mean for human sexuality? We believe that Christ is the alpha and omega of creation, that in the life, work, and teachings of Jesus Christ, creation in general and individuals in particular have begun to be restored to God's initial intent. What this suggests is that the redemption of human sexuality is on the way but not yet perfected both for the heterosexual and the homosexual.

There are a number of possibilities. We could hold the position, for instance, that in Christ our fallenness is forgiven, but our natures will not be restored until the end of time. Behavior that falls short of the ideal, then, could be seen as tolerable within the church although not normative, waiting for final redemption. Or, we could maintain (a view closer to the Anabaptist position) that in Christ we are not only forgiven but our natures can be transformed (either suddenly or gradually through the Holy Spirit) already in the present, although not perfected until the end of time.

If we accept the normativity of heterosexuality within the second of these two options, then we might argue that the homosexually oriented person can not only be forgiven for his or her orientation and practice, but can gradually be changed in the context of the church toward heterosexuality through God's grace, pastoral care, a loving community, therapy, and so on.

If, on the other hand, we believe that heterosexuality is not the standard for all persons, but that some are in fact created by God with a homosexual orientation, and that redemption has to do not with giving up a particular sexual orientation but with mutuality and self-giving love in human relationships, then the task of the church is to foster fidelity within a monogamous relationship of whatever kind.

Of paramount importance is recognition that when we speak of the redeeming process of God's grace we are talking not only about the transformation of individuals but also of the entire created order. It is my firm conviction that the final transformation of individuals cannot take place separately from the redemption of the whole of creation. In short, we cannot expect individuals to be perfect until the total context has been perfectly restored.

What final perfection, when applied to human sexuality, will look like is, of course, a mystery, especially when we consider enigmatic biblical passages such as the one in Luke 20:34-36:

> Those who belong to this age marry and are given in marriage, but those ... considered worthy of a place in that age and in the resurrection from the dead neither marry nor are given in marriage. Indeed they cannot die any more, because they are like angels and children of God, being children of the resurrection.

Practical Implications: Three Options

In the light of all of these questions, what are we to do as a church? We have a number of options.[7] We can continue to maintain what the church has traditionally held: namely, that homosexual activity is intrinsically evil and must therefore be rejected. According to this view, biblical revelation teaches that God created human beings male and female and that sexual activity, whether for procreation or for companionship, is legitimate only within a monogamous heterosexual marriage. A homosexual orientation must in this view be seen as part of imperfect nature and homosexual activity as sinful.

For theologian Karl Barth, homosexual activity represents "the physical, psychological and social sickness, the phenomenon of perversion, decadence and decay, which can emerge when man refuses to admit the validity of the divine command. . . ."[8] While our heterosexuality or homosexuality does not determine our ultimate destiny—God's objective grace in Christ justifies regardless of orientation, inclination or activity—homosexual practice cannot be condoned by the church.

Implicit in this position is the assumption that change can occur through repentance, forgiveness, and God's transforming power, including therapy. Whether or not change in orientation does occur, however, celibacy for the homosexual is imperative. I think the church should take this first point of view with utmost seriousness. It does reflect the historic position of the church; it is one legitimate historic reading of the biblical text; and it does represent the need for the church to take strong moral positions against trends in society which it considers wrong. Further, it does emphasize the legitimate place of celibacy in the Christian life—something which we as Protestants and Mennonites have tended to undervalue in our traditions.

The weakness of this position, however, is that it does not adequately reflect the diverse interpretation of biblical texts on this and related issues. In addition, it does not sufficiently take into account the empirical and historical data on the subject.

There is a second option which considers homosexual acts as intrinsically imperfect, as a departure from the biblical view, but is willing to consider making exceptions under certain extreme conditions. Helmut Thielicke holds this view. According to him,

> The fundamental order of creation and the created determination of the two sexes make it appear justifiable to speak of homosexuality as a perversion—in any case, if we begin with the understanding that this term implies no moral depreciation whatsoever and that it is used purely theologically in the sense that homosexuality is in every case not in accord with the order of creation.[9]

Thielicke's conclusion is that when change is possible (according to empirical evidence, in most cases it is not) it should be actively sought. If change is not possible, homosexuals ought to sublimate their desires and not act on them. In certain exceptional cases, where sublimation seems not to be possible, ought homosexuals not at least be expected to structure their sexual relationships " in an ethically responsible way" without idealizing them as the standard? he asks.

The third option is to view homosexual activity as morally neutral, to be evaluated only in terms of its relational integrity. This position holds that God's intent is determined not primarily in terms of (1) divine command in Genesis, or (2) some static notion of natural law, but on the basis of a relational Christology.

Sin is seen primarily as the exercise of power and domination over others and applies equally to heterosexual and homosexual activity. Homosexuality is inherently no more prone to such domination than is heterosexuality. The church, in this view, needs to recognize homosexuals as an oppressed group in our society who need to be accepted for who they are. Both heterosexuals and homosexuals need to find an equal place within the church where they ought to be encouraged to grow in their mutual, loving, permanent, monogamous relationships.

This is what I take Gregory Baum's position to be when he says that

> the important question . . . is whether homosexuality is open to
> mutuality. Is the homosexual orientation capable of grounding
> friendship that enables the partners to grow and become more
> truly human? This is the crucial question. For the structure of
> redeemed human life is mutuality. There are gravely damaged
> sexual inclinations, e.g., sadism, masochism, and paedophilia,
> which may not be acknowledged without a struggle, for they
> exclude mutuality. They bind the participants in a cruel game
> of possessor and possessed. The important question, therefore,
> is whether homosexuality is open to mutuality. Can it be integrated into the kind of human life to which God summons us?[10]

What I find appealing in the third alternative is the weight it places on the sin of domination and the importance of mutuality. What I find less convincing is the too easy disregard of what I consider the biblical emphasis on the "normativity" of heterosexual monogamous relationships. This is why I find myself, at this point at least, leaning toward the second option, although I have some difficulty with the use of the term *perversion*. This view recognizes the diversity of homosexuality itself. It assumes that some homosexuals can change in their orientation while others cannot. For those who cannot change, for whatever reason, and find themselves unable to practise celibacy, it asks of them as of heterosexuals that they structure their sexual behavior responsibly.

What impresses me as I read the literature on the subject is the diversity of views and approaches that are present in the current debate. I support this diversity, at least at this stage of the discussion, and would caution the church against closing off the conversation prematurely through some kind of rigid, unilateral declaration. The subject is too complex.

At some point the church will need to make judgments about what it believes, but hopefully these declarations will have a tentative tone to them, reflecting an openness to new insights from all quarters. Most important of all, heterosexuals and homosexuals need to discover each other as human beings on the local level where they must learn to live and worship together.

Notes

1. A. James Reimer, "A Forum on Homosexuality," in *Mennonite Reporter* (June 22, 1987), 7-9. This essay was discussed later that year at a Conrad Grebel College Faculty Forum. A recent version has also been released in my book, *Mennonites and Classical Theology* (Kitchener, Ont.: Pandora Press, 2001), and the variant appearing here, in *To Continue the Dialogue*, is used by permission.

2. An open lecture to students at Conrad Grebel College given on November 12, 1986.

3. My talk, entitled "Theological Perspectives on Homosexuality," was given upon invitation at the International Convention (with the theme "Journey Toward Wholeness") of the Brethren/Mennonite Council for Lesbian and Gay Concerns in Toronto, Ontario, October 7-9, 1988.

4. The occasion was a discussion of "homosexuality" as part of the Lakeside [Ohio] Peace and Justice Week, August 3, 1999, a session chaired by Rev. Grayson Atha, pastor of King Avenue United Methodist Church in Columbus, Ohio.

5. John Howard Yoder, "Radical Reformation Ethics in Ecumenical Perspective," in *The Priestly Kingdom: Social Ethics as Gospel* (Notre Dame: University of Notre Dame Press, 1984), 117.

6. *The Challenge of Peace: God's Promise and Our Response: A Pastoral Letter on War and Peace*, May 3, 1983 National Conference of Catholic Bishops (Washington: United States Catholic Conference, 1983), i.

7. For the following categories, the various approaches to homosexuality,

and their representatives, particularly the views of Karl Barth, Helmut Thielicke and Gregory Baum, I am indebted to the work of Edward Batchelor, who in his helpful book *Homosexuality and Ethics* (New York: The Pilgrim Press, 1980), gathers the writings of numerous theologians on the subject. See especially Roger L. Shinn's opening essay, "Homosexuality: Christian Conviction and Inquiry," 11-13.

8. Karl Barth, "Church Dogmatics," in Batchelor, 49.

9. Helmut Thielicke, "The Theological-Ethical Aspect of Homosexuality," in Batechelor, 100.

10. Gregory Baum, "Catholic Homosexuals," in Batchelor, 23. I take this to be the position of Mennonite academics, church leaders, and others who signed or endorsed the statement, "A Welcoming Open Letter on Homosexuality," *Mennonite Weekly Review* (Feb. 17, 2000), 7. It is evident my own approach to and position on the delicate issue of heterosexual, homosexual, and lesbian sexuality differs in significant ways from this most recent statement by a sizeable group of Mennonites.

Chapter 11

Six Perspectives on the Homosexuality Controversy

Theodore Grimsrud

*I*N SEEKING DISCERNMENT CONCERNING THE CONTROVERSY over same-gender sexuality, we must learn better to understand points of view different from our own. This essay represents my attempt to do so. I will be describing the main arguments of several contemporary scholars who, in general, may be seen as reflecting two different viewpoints.

I am using terms for each of these viewpoints, *restrictive* and *inclusive*, that I hope are essentially value neutral. I use restrictive and inclusive especially to characterize viewpoints concerning how the church should respond to gay and lesbian Christians.

The common ground that makes it meaningful to put the first three writers under the rubric of the restrictive position is their view that the Christian churches should not affirm gay and lesbian sexuality. That is, the churches are called to restrict the involvement of gay and lesbian Christians. Inherent in the restrictive position is some sense that gay and lesbian relationships are morally deficient.

For the second set of writers, the church is called to be inclusive of gay and lesbian Christians involved in same-gender intimate relationships. My focus in the summaries that follow will be on biblical interpretation and theological viewpoints.[1]

The "Restrictive" Case

Stanley J. Grenz[2]

Stanley Grenz's position rests on his interpretation of biblical texts of two sorts, the handful of texts he understands directly to address same-gender sexual activity and the overall understanding the Bible gives of marriage as rooted in the creative intent of God. He believes the fundamental issue in the debate boils down to how much respect one is willing to give to the teaching of the Bible. For those who uphold the authority of the Bible in the church, Grenz asserts, rejecting the moral validity of all same-gender sexual activity is the only option (89). To understand any type of same-gender sex as acceptable simply means one is not giving the Bible its proper place as the source of normative Christian ethical directives.

Grenz understands Old Testament morality concerning sexual relationships to be reducible to one basic principle. Family and married life is inviolate. The overarching focus of Old Testament sexual ethics is to defend family and married life. The Holiness Code in Leviticus 17-26 argues that any sexual activity outside of the context of heterosexual marriage is a threat to the institution of marriage and hence is an abomination (46).

In Leviticus 20:13, men having sex with other men leads to the ultimate sanction—the death penalty. Grenz argues that even though this extreme punishment no longer should be enforced by Christians, the invocation of the death penalty still has relevance for Christians. The extremity of the punishment for same-gender sex reflects the seriousness of its violation of God's intent for human sexuality. Even if we do not use the death penalty for such offenses any more, we nonetheless should recognize that when it is prescribed we are facing a breach of God's intent for human life. The prohibition remains normative for us today, even if the punishment does not (47).

Concerning the New Testament, Grenz argues that in the first chapter of Romans Paul echoes the concerns of the Levitical Holiness Code in rejecting same-gender sexual activity as contrary to God's intentions for humans. For Paul, only the model of male/female marriage as the one legitimate context for sexual expression is natural and fits with the Creator's design. Sex outside of this context is "against nature" and brings upon itself God's anger (56).

Grenz asserts numerous times in his book that the role of the Bible is foundational for Christian ethics in large part because our reasoning is distorted due to the radical, all-encompassing impact of our fallenness. Even to claim that love is the core criterion for Christian ethics is not adequate unless we rely on the Bible for normative guidance about what love entails (97).

In responding to claims by inclusivist thinkers, Grenz rejects the idea that love as the core Christian ethical criterion should lead the church to affirm same-gender covenant relationships as expressions of that ultimate Christian value. For Grenz, love must be understood in the context of the overall biblical message of God's intentions for human social life. If God's order is being violated, it is not a loving response to condone that violation. The key issue, then, for Grenz, arises in relation to God's intention for human beings. What is our purpose, our goal, the direction we are to go (100)?

The creation account in Genesis provides us with crucial information in relation to these questions. Our direction as human beings may be seen in the fact that God created human beings as male and female (Gen. 1:27; Grenz, 103). Furthermore, Genesis 2:18 tells us that simply as male, the first human being was incomplete. To be complete, human living must include both genders, different from one another yet complementary.

Grenz understands the creation stories to provide the normative model for marriage—male and female, complementing and completing each other. From this portrayal, he concludes that sexual intimacy is meant only for people in an opposite-gender marriage. Sexual intimacy is meant to address our incompleteness—the incompleteness that God resolved by creating women to join with men (104).

Sexual intercourse has profound symbolic meaning for Grenz. It is always a symbolic act with three central messages at its core:

(1) Sexual intercourse symbolizes the exclusive bond between husband and wife, reflecting the biblical confession that the person of faith has an exclusive bond with God.

(2) Sexual intercourse symbolizes the mutuality of the marriage relationship, with each partner finding pleasure in the intimacy and seeking to foster the other's pleasure.

(3) Sexual intercourse symbolizes the married couple's openness to new life emerging from their relationship through the birth of children (108).

Grenz argues at length that same-gender covenant relationships simply cannot share in the richness of this symbolism. He believes legitimate sexual intimacy must always be symbolic in these ways,

and that the institution of marriage is meant to foster such rich symbolism. In doing so, marriage serves as a crucial element in the life
of the faith community.

Should the community affirm same-gender covenant relationships that include sexual intimacy, the community would be under-
cutting the meaning of marriage and in that way subverting the spiritual vitality of the community. Same-gender relationships cannot
fully reflect the marriage symbolism most obviously because they
cannot be open to the possibility of new life (children) stemming
from the relationship.

In Grenz's view, same-gender relationships also are incapable
of fully manifesting the other elements of the marriage symbolism.
He understands such relationships to be, by definition, manifesta-
tions of informal friendship, not the male-female bond of marriage
(113). He argues that friendship is a type of non-permanent, inclusive love (114). In that sense, homosexual relationships cannot be
exclusive in the same way that marriage is meant to be.

For Grenz, probably the most fundamental reason same-gender
covenant relationships among Christians should not be affirmed is
that they devalue marriage (141). He understands monogamous,
male-female marriage to be the foundation for Christian communal
spirituality. This sacred institution must be properly understood
and affirmed for the Christian church to have any hope of faithfully
carrying out its God-given mandate to be a light to the nations and
mediator of salvation to a spiritually needy world.

Thomas E. Schmidt[3]

Thomas Schmidt's starting point is his understanding of the
Bible. He sees the Bible as the normative authority for present-day
discernment of Christian sexual ethics. Experience, tradition, and
reason all play important roles, but all in subordination to the Bible's
teaching (18).

In Schmidt's view, the basic message of the Bible stems from
and elaborates on the teaching of the creation story in Genesis 1 and
2. Our understanding of appropriate human sexual expression
should follow from Genesis. The creation account makes four crucial points regarding sexuality: First, Reproduction is good. Second,
sex is good. Third, marriage is good. Fourth, male and female are
necessary sexual counterparts (43).

Normative human sexual expression follows from the order of
creation. God endorses sexual expression as the means for populat-

ing the earth. The only context for appropriate sexual expression is established from the very beginning: the marriage relationship of one man with one woman. The centrality of opposite-gender marriage follows from the basic complementarity of the two genders in the creation story.

The following are the crucial elements in the relation of male to female.

(1) The two were created as complementary. This is the intent of the sovereign, creator God for human life from the very beginning.

(2) Genesis 2 tells us that Adam is not given a mirror image when God made a companion for him. Rather, Adam is given a *her*—one who is different while also similar.

(3) The union of these two distinct yet similar beings is necessary to overcome the incompleteness of Adam by himself.

(4) From the very start then, human beings are infused with a created (or, "natural") drive for males to leave home and cleave to females. This new relationship then becomes the one legitimate context for sexual intercourse and childbearing (43-44).

(5) The complementarity of males and females is seen in their physical make-up itself. They are created for opposite-gender sexual intercourse (and same-gender couples can only simulate this physical complementarity; 45-46).

Same-gender sexual relationships, according to Schmidt, are problematic in a fundamental way. They reflect an implicit rejection of the very order of creation—and in doing so they reflect a rejection of God. Same-gender sexual relationships undermine the sanctity of opposite-gender marriage. They declare that a different expression of sexuality outside of the God-created intent for human beings is good (48). Such a rejection of God's will has to be unacceptable for all Christians who accept the authority of the Bible.

The biblical teaching against same-gender sexuality in all the rest of the Bible presupposes the Genesis portrayal of normative marriage and is consistent with that portrayal. The main reason the Bible speaks so clearly about sexual activity which occurs outside of opposite-gender marriage is, in Schmidt's view, because illicit sexual activity is a threat to the very social foundations of the Bible's faith communities.

Leviticus 18:22 and 20:13 give us the most direct teaching in the Old Testament proscribing same-gender sexual relationships. These two verses have normative force, even though they are surrounded by other commands which present-day Christians no longer consider binding. Their normativeness follows from their rootage in the creation story. The sexual prohibitions against same-gender sexual intercourse, including bestiality and incest, have the force of abiding moral law, not simply temporal purity regulations that Christians understand to have been superceded in Jesus Christ (90).

The enduring validity of the same-gender Levitical commands can also be seen in their being the basis for Paul's New Testament statements. Paul obviously did not see those commands as having passed away with the coming of Jesus—nor should we (91).

For Schmidt, Paul's writings reflect the creation order of human sexuality. The key texts are to be found in Romans1:18-27 and 1 Corinthians 6. Both passages begin with references to idolatry as the root cause of the immorality that the verses that follow address (53). Schmidt argues that, in Romans 1, Paul points to an inherent connection between idolatry and homosexuality. Paul singles out same-gender sexual activity because he seeks a vivid image of humankind's primal rejection of the sovereignty of God the creator (67). Since God's intent for opposite-gender marriage is the only appropriate context for sexual relationships, denials of the exclusivity of this context implicit in same-gender relationships mean rejecting God.

Another key element of Paul's teaching for Schmidt is the notion that human beings are profoundly fallen. We are dominated by the power of sin and prone to self-deception. For this reason, our experience in life cannot serve as a normative basis for sexual ethics. On this basis, Schmidt dismisses the possibility that the experience of "fully loving, life-enhancing . . . homosexual relationships" legitimates those relationships as morally appropriate (83). Christians must trust the clear word of God over human experience when these seem to be in tension.

Schmidt understands Paul to be teaching in Romans 1 that homosexuality is a paradigmatic case of human beings' distorted sense of their self-identity due to idolatry. Living in a same-gender relationship is to be in revolt against God. When people live in revolt against God, their lives inevitably will be corrupted, with alienation and brokenness as the consequences (85).

Schmidt goes into some detail outlining how present-day "homosexuals" are living evidence of this dynamic of revolt against God. The revolt is manifested in their rejection of the God-ordained pattern for sexual expression, and the fruit of the revolt is to be seen in the present-day brokenness of most homosexuals (122).

Paul's teaching against same-gender sex also found expression in 1 Corinthians 6:9 and 1 Timothy 1:10. Paul uses a term here which, according to Schmidt, he likely coined. The Greek word *arsenokoites* comes from the Greek translation of Leviticus 18:22 Paul would have used. Leviticus uses two words (*arseno* = "men" and *koiten* = "lies with") which are combined by Paul, presumably to evoke memories of the teaching of Leviticus that forbids "a man lying with another man as he would with a woman" (95-96).

As in Leviticus, Paul in these two places does not make any distinction among different types of same-gender sexual intimacy. Schmidt interprets this as evidence that Paul's inclusion of same-gender sex on his list of abominable behavior should be understood to apply to all expressions of same-gender sexual relations (96).

Schmidt concludes that the biblical teaching is being confirmed in our present day as we observe the self-destructiveness of same-gender sexual activity. This is what Paul's teaching in Romans 1 would lead us to expect. Idolatrous behavior is invariably self-destructive as God "gives up" idolaters to the consequences of their rebellion against God (100-130).

Richard B. Hays[4]

Richard Hays admits that the Bible rarely refers directly to homosexual behavior; however, he asserts, we must recognize that each rare reference is totally negative. The two references in the book of Leviticus (18:23; 20:10) establish the basic tone. Their unambiguous prohibition of same-gender sexual relationships sound the universal rejection of such relationships in Judaism (381).

Hays focuses most of his attention on pertinent New Testament texts, especially Romans 1:18-32. Before turning to Romans, though, he briefly treats Paul's comments in 1 Corinthians 6:9-10. The context in this initial letter to the Corinthians finds Paul criticizing people in the church for acting as if they were above moral rules due to their profound spiritual experiences (382). Paul seeks to ground the Corinthian Christians in a demanding moral ethic.

In articulating this ethic, Paul challenges his readers with a list of behaviors that are not morally appropriate for Christians. Included in this list are two terms that relate to same-gender sexuality. In Hays' view, these two terms, *malakoi* and *arsenokoitai*, refer to two different aspects of male/male sexual activity.

Malakoi appears often in Hellenistic Greek as a term for the "passive" partner in sexual intercourse, the male being penetrated. Paul,

Hays says, likely has the same idea in mind in 1 Corinthians 6:9, especially since *arsenokoitai* appears to be drawn from the Greek translation of Leviticus. So this latter term could well be referring to the "aggressive" partner (382). If so, Paul in 1 Corinthians 6:9 is challenging Christians not to be involved in any type of same-gender sex with his double (and, hence, all-encompassing) reference.

Romans 1 plays a special role in Christian sexual ethics because it is the only place in the New Testament that explains the Christian condemnation of homosexual behavior in an explicitly theological framework (383). Underlying Paul's theology here is his reference to God as creator. This reference grounds Paul's discussion of sexuality in the story of creation in Genesis which portrayed male/female sexuality as the norm (386).

The practice of same-gender sex, in Hays's account, may be understood as a type of "sacrament" for the counter-faith of those who reject God as creator and ruler of the universe (386). Faith in God includes, by definition, acceptance of the order God has created. To blatantly deny the exclusive normativeness of male/female sexuality hence is par excellence an expression of the refusal to honor God as God which Paul sees as the core problem with pagan idolatry.

According to Hays, Paul singles out homosexual intercourse because it so graphically reflects the way in which human rebellion against God is expressed in blatant distortion of how God created things to be. For Paul, same-gender sex is "against nature," by which he means that it is going against the order of creation. Those who engage in sexual relations with people of the same gender are acting "against nature" in defiance of the Creator (387). When rebellious human beings "exchange" their created sexuality for same-gender sexuality, they are showing how sinful human beings have "exchanged the truth about God for a lie" (Rom. 1:25; Hays, 388).

For Hays, when Paul writes in Romans about same-gender sexuality, he is referring to *all* types of homosexuality. Paul is not arguing about only pederasty or cultic prostitution but that all types of homosexual activity reflect the alienation of human beings from God (389).

The created order, the "natural" pattern, points toward the exclusivity of heterosexual marriage as the context for appropriate sexual intimacy. The entire Bible supports this understanding. This normativity of heterosexual marriage provides the context for the Bible's unqualifiedly negative explicit references to same-gender sexual activity (390).

The Bible as a whole also provides a picture of the human condition as one in which we are in bondage to sin. One consequence of the pervasiveness of sin is that our human desires and impulses are not to be trusted. That is, the fact that some human beings might feel a strong sexual attraction toward people of the same gender is not to be understood as necessarily good and trustworthy because it is "natural" to them. That these desires and impulses happen to be involuntary is not evidence that they are appropriately acted on. Due to the depth of the power of sin in the human heart, even our involuntary impulses may well be corrupted (390).

Another factor Hays draws on in articulating his restrictive case is the history of Christian hostility toward same-gender sex. For more than 1900 years. Christian moral teaching has uniformly understood homosexual behavior as contrary to God's will (397). For the church today, this long tradition must carry significant weight.

Hays concludes that the unanimity of the biblical witness against same-gender sexuality remains normative for Christians. He mentions several other points that support what Scripture teaches. The ambiguity of scientific evidence provides no clear basis for overturning the biblical perspective. The ambiguities and confusions over sexuality that characterize our present Western cultural situation argue for the church to maintain a clear message of heterosexual fidelity. The fact that human beings are so good at deceiving themselves supports the need for respecting normative ethical teaching that originates outside of human subjectivity.

Hays recognizes that Christians with affectional orientation directed toward people of the same gender face difficult challenges if they seek to adhere to his directives. However, he argues, ultimately this is a profound example of the Christian vocation wherein all Christians are challenged to allow our "natural" impulses to be challenged and frustrated when they do not conform with the values of costly, self-denying discipleship (402).

The "Inclusive" Case

Daniel A. Helminiak[5]

Daniel Helminiak identifies what he believes to be the crucial divide between Christians who reflect on sexuality issues. The one side he characterizes as practicing "fundamentalist readings of the Bible." In this approach, biblical passages mean whatever they mean to present-day readers. The other side, those practicing "historical-critical readings," understand biblical passages to mean whatever they meant to the people who wrote them (25-26).

Helminiak's commitment to the historical-critical approach undergirds his fundamental point about the Bible's teaching related to homosexuality. That is, we must not draw strong conclusions about the applicability of biblical texts to present-day issues when we do not have adequate historical background to determine what the texts meant to their writers and first readers (32). This uncertainty applies to all the small handful of biblical texts that appear to address same-gender sexuality.

Further, Helminiak argues that from what we can tell about the biblical teachings concerning same-gender sexuality, it appears clear that the Bible was not addressing the same types of relations that are under scrutiny in today's context. The Bible did not know of homosexuality as a sexual orientation; only of homosexual acts. Hence, it gives no answer "about spontaneous affection for people of the same sex and about the ethical possibility of expressing that affection in loving, sexual relationships" (33).

In part, Helminiak raises these points to emphasize his view that biblical pronouncements in and of themselves are not enough to establish present-day morality. That is, an action is not wrong simply because a Bible verse seems to label it as such. "A thing is wrong for a reason. If the reason no longer holds and no other reason is given, how can a thing still be judged wrong?" (33). With these serious qualifications concerning the Bible's applicability in mind, Helminiak turns to consider the biblical passages that provide the foundation for many restrictive arguments.

He argues that Genesis 19, the story of the judgment of Sodom, tells of a violation of hospitality expectations, not of a society that is judged because of its tolerance of loving same-gender intimacy (40). Helminiak actually seeks to turn on its head the traditional application of the Sodom story as a basis for excluding gay and lesbian Christians from the community of faith. He asserts that the inhospitality of Sodom is in fact echoed in our day when people oppose and abuse homosexual men and women for being who they are (41).

The second Old Testament passage commonly referred to in discussions of sexuality is Leviticus' double mention of the prohibition of "men lying with men as with women" (18:23; 20:10). This proscription, he argues, stemmed from concerns about idolatry—not from scruples about sex per se (45).

The core of the book of Leviticus, the Holiness Code, takes up chapters 17–26 and includes the prohibition of male-with-male sexual intercourse. According to Helminiak, the Holiness Code sought to prevent acts associated with Israel's pagan neighbors. The Code reflected a deep fear that Israelite identity as a distinct people would be severely compromised should the Israelites take on the ways of the "nations."

The prohibitions in the Holiness Code include a wide variety of actions which have in common their being characteristic of other nations. Many of these actions were not understood to be wrong in and of themselves but because they were connected with Gentile, and not Jewish, identity. Hence, Helminiak asserts, "no thought is given [in Leviticus] to whether the sex in itself is right or wrong" (46–47).

Male/male sex is called an "abomination" in Leviticus 20:13. Abomination meant "impurity," Helminiak argues, or the violation of a taboo. It is not called something wrong in itself. It is not a "sin" but rather a ritual violation (52). Helminiak concludes that the focus in Leviticus is on practical, historically particular concerns. Thus the prohibition here against male/male sex must not be seen as a timeless, absolute prohibition. Rather, it is time- and context-bound.

In turning to Paul's writings, Helminiak argues that Paul's concern in Romans 1:18ff focused on people engaging in sexual practices of a type not normal to them. That is, people who normally were heterosexually oriented were having sex with people of their own gender. He refers to Paul's use of "against nature" in Romans 11:24 (it is "against nature" for Gentile "branches" to be grafted on to the "tree" of Israel) to support the argument that when Paul uses that phrase in Romans 1 he has in mind simply that which is unexpected (65).

According to Helminiak, the key issue for Paul in Romans 1:27 is idolatry, people worshiping that which is not God, not with same-gender sex. Paul is making a point about various idolatrous practices among Gentiles, including people having sex in unexpected ways, sex of a sort they do not normally practice (77). If this is an accurate reading of Paul's intent, then the thrust of Romans 1 is not to provide a basis for present-day rejection of the moral legitimacy of loving, mutual, committed same-gender intimate relationships. Rather, Paul's words apply more to people engaging in sexual practices that are obsessive, out of control, promiscuous, and directly rebelling against godly values of commitment, mutuality, and respect.

Helminiak understands the other brief references to same-gender sexuality in Paul's writings (1 Cor. 6:9 and 1 Tim. 1:10) to be similar in meaning. The key term, used in both verses, is the Greek *arsenokoitai*. According to Helminiak, Paul uses this term (translated "sodomites" in the NRSV) to indicate a type of male/male sexual activity that is "wanton, lewd, and irresponsible." Paul does not mean to focus on the fact that this activity happens between people of the same gender so much as that its nature is exploitative and obsessive (85). That is, Paul is concerned about the harm done to people when they are out of control sexually, not about mutually edifying intimate relationships.

Helminiak challenges the traditional approach as putting too much weight on a small handful of passages that, on scrutiny, do not actually condemn present-day same-gender intimate relationships. The biblical texts that touch on homosexuality are all concerned with issues that do not apply to committed relationships among gay and lesbian Christians—namely, inhospitality, idolatrous religious practices, and abusive and exploitative treatment of others.

Martti Nissinen[6]

Martti Nissinen surveys in depth the attitudes of ancient Near Eastern cultures toward homosexuality. His treatment of biblical materials begins with consideration of the prohibition of male/male sex in the Levitical Holiness Code. He argues that the Holiness Code sexual regulations reflect a strong concern for strengthening the cohesion and identity of society, its integrity and growth. For the ancient Israelites, social cohesion was linked with strong gender roles and protection of family relationships. Anything that challenged gender roles or family relationships would have been seen as a terrible threat to the viability of the Israelite community. Taboos related to gender roles and sexual expression arose to protect this identity (41-42).

To underscore the importance of keeping these taboos and to sustain Israelite identity, the Holiness Code presents Israel's neighbors in quite a negative light. Though historical evidence indicates that this portrayal was inaccurate, the need for fostering a sense of distinctiveness was seen as crucial for protecting the identity of Israel in its fragile situation (42). The regulations on sexuality, including the prohibitions of male/male sex, must be understood in light of this quest of community survival.

Nissinen links gender roles with the prohibition of male/male sex. The Code focuses exclusively on males because it would have been impossible for female/female sex to challenge male domination (the domination being symbolized by the active, penetrating role males played in sex). What made male/male sex an "abomination" was one of the males taking the female role (being penetrated), thereby transgressing gender boundaries and confusing gender roles (43-44).

In tying the prohibition of male/male sex so directly to the particular context for which the Holiness Code was written, Nissinen means to deny its direct applicability to our present world. The Holiness Code prohibits such sexual activity because of a desire to maintain clearly distinct gender roles and because of a specific concern about rejecting non-Israelite religious practices. Neither of these concerns applies to modern-day Christians; hence, the prohibition does not have a direct application for us.

Genesis 19, the other main Old Testament text cited as pertinent to the discussion of homosexuality among Christians, has even less applicability to our sexual ethics than the Holiness Code, according to Nissinen. The story of Sodom is basically one of inhospitality, not of sexual behavior. The story makes this point by presenting two positive examples of hospitality, Abraham (18:1-5) and Lot (19:1-3), that contrast with the inhospitality of the Sodomites.

The specific expression of inhospitality was the attempt at gang rape of the visitors. Nissinen asserts that such practices were common in the ancient world as a means of one group exerting dominance over another. As with the Holiness Code, here too we see an underlying issue of male dominance. To rape men was to take away their masculinity. "The men [of Sodom] were motivated not to satisfy their sexual lust but to show their supremacy and power over the guests" (48-49).

Nissinen also briefly discusses two other Old Testament passages—the story of the murdered concubine in Judges 19 and the account of the close friendship between David and Jonathan in the books of Samuel. The Judges 19 story parallels the Sodom story in important respects and reinforces the point that the mob's concern was the expression of dominance not same-gender sexual desire (51). In this story, the mob asked for the male guest to abuse him, but instead were given his concubine. They abused the man's woman and left her for dead, which was another form of taking away his masculinity.

Ninissen calls the relationship David and Jonathan had "ho-mosocial" (a close friendship between men that may or may not have had erotic expressions; 17). He suggests their kind of friend-ship, based as it was on love and equality, may be "more compara-ble with modern homosexual people's experiences of themselves than those texts that explicitly speak of homosexual acts that are ag-gressive, violent expressions of domination and subjugation" (56).

In addressing Paul's writings, Nissinen states initially that in the Hellenistic world of Paul's day, same-gender sex was consid-ered "against nature" for two reasons. First, it did not lead to pro-creation. Second, it signaled a violation of sex roles wherein the male always was "active" and the female always "passive" (88).

Paul himself speaks of "nature" several times in his letters indi-cating "a matter of the common order of things as Paul had learned it." "Unnatural" or "against nature" means, for Paul, deviation from the normal order of things, the unconventional with overtones of disapproval. When he uses the term in Romans 1:19-32, he is not using it as a technical term with specifically Christian content. "Against nature" here simply means "unusual" or "not what one would expect" (62). Paul does not have "the created order" in mind when he uses "against nature." He is probably not alluding to Gen-esis 1–3 but rather adopting contemporary concepts like the "law of nature." He is simply reflecting contemporary Jewish and Hellenis-tic feeling that these people are "altering the conventional orders" (106-107).

According to Nissinen, Paul is not referring to homosexuals in our modern sense in the Romans passage. Quite likely, Paul would have been aware of people who did habitually engage in sex with people of the same gender—and there were terms used to identify such people. These terms, though, were never used by Paul. Here Paul simply refers to people engaging in same-gender sex. These presumably were people who normally ("by nature") were in op-posite-gender relationships (109).

Nissinen adds that Paul's central concern in Romans is not sex-uality at all. Paul uses the references to idolatrous sexual activity to raise the ire of his readers and to gain their approval of his condem-nation of what his readers would have seen as typical Gentile sin-fulness. Paul does this, though, not to add to the sense of righteous-ness that his readers may have had in reading these words, but ac-tually to turn the tables. Paul's use of Romans 1:18-32, as it turns out, is to drive home his point about the problematic self-righteousness of his readers. Paul, in the end, is challenging his readers not to be judgmental (111).

In concluding his treatment of Paul's writings, Nissinen asserts that the specific meaning of the terms used in 1 Corinthians 6:9 and 1 Timothy 1:10 that are often translated as referring to same-gender sexuality is actually quite obscure. In both passages, though, the context makes it clear that both *arsenokoites* and *malakos* are examples, along with numerous other terms used in these verses, of the exploitation of persons. Paul is concerned with the wrong that people do to others, not with unharmful intimate relationships (118).

Nissinen argues that the use to which present-day Christians put the Bible depends on their assumptions. In contrast to those who focus on violated purity and draw condemnatory conclusions from the Bible for same-gender sexuality, he suggests that a different starting point would lead to different conclusions concerning the Bible's relevance. "If homosexual people are seen as a historically oppressed and despised minority yearning for its rights, then quite different texts predominate other than those that describe sexual orgies and idolatry" (126).

He concludes that love should be the central hermeneutical principle when applying biblical teaching to the present world. The most fundamental question, in this light, is not "why is this person's sexual orientation something other than purely heterosexual?" Rather, the question is, "Why is the other person's different gender identity a problem for me and my society?" (140). That is, if love is the central focus, we will start with examining ourselves and accept that our most fundamental vocation is finding ways to treat all other people with love.

Letha Scanzoni and Virginia Mollenkott[7]

According to Letha Scanzoni and Virginia Mollenkott, the core message of the Bible is the command from Jesus to love one's neighbor as oneself. The possibility of treating others with love requires that we love ourselves. The ability to love ourselves follows from having a deep sense of God's love for each of us (8). Our sexual ethics must be understood in light of the love command—both in terms of how we relate to others sexually and of how we relate to others' sexuality.

With the love command as central, the authors point our attention to the Acts 10–11 story of the change in which the early Christians began to welcome non-Jewish Christians as full members of

the church. With Acts 10–11 as our model, they assert, we will realize that we may be called to transcend rules and simplistic readings
of Scripture in order consistently to live in light of the love command (17).

Scanzoni and Mollenkott believe the gospel calls on Jesus' followers to be partisans and advocates of marginalized people (39).
When the love command is the starting point in approaching the
Bible, we will place the highest priority on biblical texts that call
upon us to welcome the lowly and outcasts. This benefit of the doubt
toward compassion for the outcast challenges followers of Jesus to
overcome the social gap between themselves as heterosexual Christians and homosexuals. This gulf is necessary for objectifying and
excluding (51).

Scanzoni and Mollenkott do turn to the traditional texts that
overtly refer to same-gender sex. They begin, however, by emphasizing that the context for the mention of same-gender sexual activity in Scripture is always that of other negative acts like adultery,
failure to propagate, promiscuity, violence, and idolatrous worship.
The sexual acts themselves are not condemned in isolation from the
other problems (56).

The story of Sodom in Genesis 19, for example, tells not about
same-gender sexual orientation and intimate loving relationships.
The story there is about heterosexual males who were bent on gang
rape (58). "The men were not looking for a sexual experience but
rather wanted a chance to express their violent impulses and their
desires to humiliate Lot's guests" (59).

A second example, Leviticus 18–20, reflects a deep concern for
ritual purity as a means of showing Israel's distinctiveness as a people set apart for God. Activities that reflected conformity with surrounding cultures, particularly their religious practices, understood
by Israelites to be idolatrous, were strictly forbidden. It appears that
Israelites associated male/male sex with such practices.

Also, Israel's Holiness Code paid special attention to the problem of men "wasting their seed." The prohibition of male/male sex
(along with bestiality and sex during menstruation) reflects this concern about the misuse of semen. Further support for this point can
be seen in the lack of reference to female/female sex in the Holiness
Code since no "seed" was wasted (64-65).

A third example of the Bible's references to same-gender sexual
activity being connected with other problems is seen in the New
Testament book of Romans. In chapter one, Paul says nothing about

homosexual love; rather, the focus is on sexual activity in the context of idolatry and lust (68). In this passage, Paul draws on the Wisdom of Solomon, a sacred writing well known in Jewish circles. Wisdom 13–14 gives a general catalog of Gentile vices, beginning with idolatry and its consequences. Paul presents nothing original or specifically Christian, but simply repeats common Jewish understandings of the problem of idolatry and corrupt living among Gentiles (69-70).

Scanzoni and Mollenkott point out that Paul speaks of people with a heterosexual orientation who are controlled by insatiable lust. "Relationships of loving commitment were not even under discussion." Like Wisdom, Paul links idolatry with the sexual immorality of which he writes—sexual immorality characterized by injustice and exploitation (72-73).

The final examples of the Bible's mention of same-gender sexual activity come in 1 Corinthians and 1 Timothy. In both of these cases, Scanzoni and Mollenkott argue, the writer is referring to particular types of sexual abuse, not to homosexual orientation in general (76).

Scanzoni and Mollenkott also challenge the argument that the story of creation establishes male/female sex as the only acceptable type of sexual expression. They argue that the core concern in Genesis 1–2 is to tell us how we got here (hence, the allusion to procreation), not to indicate that male-female intercourse for purpose of procreation is the only valid type of sexual expression. To say that procreative sex is the only morally legitimate form would not only condemn same-gender sex but also any opposite-gender sex known ahead of time not to include the possibility of procreation (81).

They argue further that in Matthew 19:4-6, when Jesus alludes to Genesis 2:24, he is challenging sexist divorce laws, not making a statement about the exclusive moral legitimacy of opposite-gender sex. Jesus is addressing an issue that would only have come up in the context of heterosexual marriage. Thus he implies nothing about such marriage being the exclusive context for sex (82).

The co-humanity of humankind as male and female finds expression in many ways other than genital intercourse, Scanzoni and Mollenkott argue. The intimate commitment of two people of the same gender in a permanent relationship does not restrict either of the two from sharing deeply in many ways with people of the opposite gender. They point out that "heterosexual men and women can relate authentically as male and female in a social group with-

out having genital relations with everybody of the opposite sex."
Single people may also affirm co-humanity without sexual intercourse (149). Likewise, homosexual Christians may still relate to
those of the opposite gender (150-151). This recognition of the
breadth and depth of maleness and femaleness, they argue, challenges the focus on sexual intercourse as the locus of gender identity, and underscores the invalidity of using Genesis 1–2 against acceptance of same-gender relationships by Christians.

What Are the Key Issues?

My concern in this chapter has been simply to summarize diverse theological and biblical perspectives on the issues related to
homosexuality. A number of key questions, then, arise from comparing the viewpoints reported above.[8]

Applicability of biblical materials

The two groups surveyed—restrictive and inclusive—seem
clearly to differ on how we should apply biblical materials, though
not necessarily on the authority of the Bible per se. One of the basic
issues here is how clear we understand the Bible to be on the issue.
Is it possible categorically to equate the biblical teaching with a
given present-day position? One side seems fairly comfortable with
such an equation, the other seems to be saying that when studied
carefully, the Bible does not yield a clear position. For these latter
writers, the approach is not to dismiss the Bible out of hand, but
rather to draw a different understanding from the biblical data.

Another issue concerning the applicability of the biblical materials may be framed as a question of how directly these materials
should be applied now. How seriously must we take the great distance in time, geography, language, and culture between the Bible
times and ours? What are the implications of this distance? One crucial text where this issue is central involves the direct prohibition in
the Holiness Code of Leviticus. One side understands that, even
when carefully considering the distance, the Levitical prohibition
does provide us with a clear and directly applicable directive; the
other side understands Leviticus as part of an ancient foreign context that at most gives it indirect relevance for Christians.

Meaning of core references

As we have seen, the handful of biblical texts that speak directly
of same-gender sex lend themselves to a variety of interpretations.

A central difference among the writers summarized above can be seen in their responses to the question whether or not these texts refer to relationships that are in any relevant way analogous to present-day same-gender intimate relationships. The differences in relation to this question may be the most substantial in this controversy.

Focusing serious energy on this issue of the extent that legitimate analogies may be drawn between the biblical texts and present-day cases is crucial to any rapprochement. I believe progress could be made, but this would require careful work in constructing criteria for what would constitute legitimate analogies and application of those analogies to the biblical materials.

Differences related to specific texts are also obvious. None of the three restrictive writers cited draws upon the Sodom story in Genesis 19 as central to their arguments, although many others certainly do. The inclusive writers all reject such an application.

The three texts whose interpretations are the most in conflict are Leviticus 18-20, Romans 1, and 1 Corinthians 6. Is Leviticus reflecting an underlying, universal, creation-based principle as the basis for the prohibition of male/male sex, or is it reflecting instead time-bound contextual concerns that no longer are directly relevant for Christians?

Is the first chapter of Romans relevant to *all* same-gender relationships or only to same-gender sex practiced by people who are heterosexual in orientation? Does the critique of homosexual sex as "against nature" in Romans 1 rest on an understanding of a God-ordained created order in which male/female sex is the exclusive norm, or does it rest on a more practical view that such sexual activity is unconventional and "unexpected"?

How certain can we be about the meaning of the Greek terms in 1 Corinthians 6:9 that have in recent years been variously translated in English as "homosexuals"? Are these terms referring to same-gender sex per se or rather to exploitation and moral laxity?

"Creation" and marriage
The restrictive writers understand the creation account of Genesis 1–2 and its later use by Jesus as crucial to establishing the exclusive normativeness of male/female marital sex. People on the inclusive reject that interpretation and application.

What is the significance of the portrayal of humans as "male and female"? Is this simply a descriptive statement saying that we come from procreative sex without the implication that such sex is the only morally legitimate sexual expression? Or is it to be taken as a normative statement meant to establish that male/female marital sex is the only kind that God endorses?

How should we apply Jesus' use of the creation story to speak to the divorce issue in a passage like Matthew 19:3-9? How much should be implied for a general sexual ethic from this teaching specifically on the legitimacy of divorce? Is Jesus presenting a normative portrayal of the only appropriate type of sexual intimacy? Or is he only focusing on male and female relations because that was the specific concern he was addressing?

Even if one understands the Bible to affirm the centrality of male/female marriage to human community lived before God, does it follow that all same-gender intimate relationships must be rejected as morally inappropriate? Does seeing male/female marriage as the norm mean that any alternative to that is a threat to the norm? Or are these actually two separate issues, with a small minority of Christians living in same-gender intimate relationships no more a threat to male/female marriage and procreation than are singleness and childless male/female marriages?

"Sin" and purity

The basic question under the rubric of sin is how one interprets the biblical moral thrust. Are the sins Christians should be most concerned about threats to the purity of the community and direct violations of biblical law codes? Or is the sin problem understood to be centered on mistreatment of marginalized and vulnerable people? That is, should the church be focused on the "sin" of the alleged misbehavior *of* homosexual people, or should the church be focused on the "sin" of the alleged misbehavior *toward* homosexual people?

Concluding Thoughts

To the extent that the controversy over sexuality lends itself to rational resolution, we would do well to devote more energy to finding common ground in biblical interpretation. I do not believe the differences are so much based on different understandings of biblical authority as they are on different approaches to and meanings in the texts. Hence, in theory we should be able to progress toward some common ground.

To do so, we need to take each other's good faith attempts to grapple with the Bible seriously. Perhaps our biggest challenge is to make the effort to understand one another before launching into our critique. Rather than treating this controversy as an argument to win or lose, we would do much better to think more in terms of a puzzle to solve, in which case we all have a contribution to make. No one benefits from the acrimony of the current impasses in which the churches find themselves.

Notes

1. This essay is written in a spirit similar to that of a recent book: L. R. Holben, *What Christians Think About Homosexuality: Six Representative Viewpoints* (North Richland Hills, Tex.: BIBAL Press, 1999). However, whereas I have elected to focus in some depth on a few representative writers, Holben offers a more synthetic approach drawing upon many different writers.

2. Stanley J. Grenz, *Welcoming but Not Affirming: An Evangelical Response to Homosexuality* (Louisville: Westminster/John Knox Press, 1998), 89.

3. Thomas E. Schmidt, *Straight and Narrow? Compassion and Clarity in the Homosexuality Debate* (Downers Grove, Ill.: InterVarsity Press, 1995), 18.

4. Richard B. Hays, *The Moral Vision of the New Testament: A Contemporary Introduction to New Testament Ethics* (San Francisco: HarperCollins, 1996), 381.

5. Daniel A. Helminiak, *What the Bible Really Says About Homosexuality* (San Francisco: Alamo Square Press, 1994), 25-26.

6. Martti Nissinen, *Homoeroticism in the Biblical World* (Minneapolis: Fortress Press, 1998), 41-42.

7. Letha Dawson Scanzoni and Virginia Ramey Mollenkott, *Is the Homosexual My Neighbor? A Positive Christian Response* (San Francisco: Harper-Collins, 1994), 8.

8. 8. For further reading, I suggest the following materials. Two books that collect strong essays from each perspective are Robert L. Brawley, ed., *Biblical Ethics and Homosexuality: Listening to Scripture* (Louisville: Westminster/John Knox Press, 1996) and David L. Balch, *Homosexuality, Science and the "Plain Sense" of Scripture* (Grand Rapids, Mich.: Wm. B. Eerdmans, 2000).

Books from a restrictive perspective include Marion L. Soards, *Scripture and Homosexuality: Biblical Authority and the Church Today* (Louisville: Westminster/John Knox Press, 1995); James P. Hanigan, *Homosexuality: The Test Case for Christian Social Ethics* (New York: Paulist Press, 1988); and Donald J. Wold, *Out of Order: Homosexuality in the Bible and the Ancient Near East* (Grand Rapids, Mich.: Baker Book House, 1998); Richard F. Lovelace, *Homosexuality and the Church* (Old Tappen, N.J.: Fleming H. Revell Company, 1978); Christopher R. Seitz, *Word Without End: The Old Testament as Abiding Theological Witness* (Grand Rapids, Mich.: Wm. B. Eerdmans, 1998).

Books from a non-restrictive perspective include Gary David Comstock and Susan E. Henking, eds., *Que(e)rying Religion: A Critical Anthology* (New York: Continuum, 1997); L. William Countryman, *Dirt, Greed, and Sex: Sexual Ethics in the New Testament and Their Implications for Today* (Minneapolis:

Fortress Press, 1988); Robert E. Goss and Mona West, eds., *Take Back the Word: A Queer Reading of the Bible* (Cleveland: Pilgrim Press, 2000); John J. McNeill, *The Church and the Homosexual* (Boston: Beacon Press, 1993); and Walter Wink, ed., *Homosexuality and Christian Faith: Questions of Conscience for the Churches* (Minneapolis: Fortress Press, 1999).

Chapter 13

What Can We Do
When We Don't Agree?
Christian Tolerance in
Romans 14:1–15:6

Reta Halteman Finger

*T*HE THESIS OF THIS CHAPTER IS THAT IT IS MORE appropriate to apply the message of Romans 14:1–15:6 to the contemporary issue of homosexuality than to apply Romans 1:24-27. Issues of sexual orientation and practice threaten to tear apart the merging Mennonite Church USA today, just as issues of ethnic background and religious practice threatened the survival of the early church.

The most explicit reference to same-sex sex in the New Testament does lie in Romans 1, where Paul sees this inversion of sexual expression as a result of idolatry: the inversion of worshiping creature instead of Creator. Because of this, Paul is viewed as the New Testament's strongest champion of heterosexual sex as the only ethical option for Christians.

However, though it is important to grapple with the signficance of Romans 1, such open-and-shut interpretation risks missing the overall purpose of Paul's letter. Romans 1:24-27 is a subpoint of Paul's first proof of his major argument—one example among many of what he sees as human sin that results from idolatry. Paul first discusses pagan (Gentile) sins (1:18-32) but then moves on to condemn law-observant Jews for doing things that are just as evil (2:1–3:20). It is necessary for him to denounce all sin equally so he can drive home his triumphant conclusion in 3:22-24 that "there is no distinction, since all have sinned and fall short of the glory of God; they are now justified by his grace as a gift."

Paul provides additional proofs and elaborations in 5:1 through 15:13 on his major thesis that both Jews and Gentiles are made righteous before God through faith (or trust in the faithfulness of Jesus Christ) and not by any scrupulous observance of religious ritual. If we knew how to read Paul's letter as one single argument (though buttressed by many subproofs along the way), we could then see 14:1 through 15:13 as its final ringing climax: a vision of harmony and tolerance among squabbling Jewish and ex-pagan believers whose divergent convictions and lifestyle practices were driving them apart.

A major challenge of the first-century church was to figure out if believing Jews and Gentiles could be part of the same church. Huge questions loomed: Do Gentiles have to become Jews before they can be Christians? How can God be faithful to the original covenant made with Abraham and Moses if God accepts Gentiles *as Gentiles* who do not obey the Torah? How can these disperate peoples get along when their lifestyles and deep-rooted beliefs are so different? There was no question but that law-observant Jews had both Scripture and the honor of God solidly on their side.

Paul acknowledges this, but he has had long experience with Gentiles who have received the Holy Spirit apart from the law. By the time Paul has reached Romans 14, he has addressed the theological aspects of these questions, but now he must give his attention to the practical details of how his vision of unity can be lived out. Romans 14:1–15:6 recognizes the deep emotional and scriptural roots of the controversy but urges strenuous tolerance of others' lifestyles and practices.

Though struggles of eating meat and observing holy days seem trivial to us today, they were monumentally important when this letter was written. Similarly, issues of sexuality do not seem trivial in our highly sexualized society. Yet I believe they are no more crucial than was the Jew/Gentile hurdle in the early church.

The Story Behind Paul's Letter to Roman Christians

Until a generation ago, Romans was seen as a theological treatise, a "last will and testament" of Paul, the settled summation of his theology after the rough-and-tumble of missionary life. But the face of biblical scholarship has changed radically since then, and all biblical writings are now subjected to intense sociological, anthropological, political, and literary analysis. A simple question asking what a text meant to its original readers or hearers before we figure out what it means today has produced much fruit and has provided unexpected theological interpretations of many texts. Even though Romans is full of theological language, it also contains many clues to the actual, historical situation of both Paul the author and the Roman Christians as recipients.

According to Romans 15:22-33, Paul writes this letter from Corinth just before he sails for Jerusalem in spring A. D. 56 or 57.[1] He asserts he has finished his missionary work in the East and feels called to move west to Spain, to preach the gospel where no one yet has heard of Christ (15:18-21). Rome is on the way to Spain, a good stopping point in the capital of the Empire. Here Paul can be refreshed and hopefully draw from the skills and support of the Roman Christians in his efforts to reach a pagan people who speak Latin or Spanish dialects rather than Paul's Greek.

That is Paul's part of the plot that underlies this Romans letter. The other part is the rather troubled history of the fledgling Roman churches. The gospel seems to have reached Rome early. Acts 2 states that visitors from Rome were at Pentecost and heard Peter's sermon announcing Jesus' death and resurrection. Jews from Rome then would likely have returned to their native city, bringing the good news with them to the numerous synagogues in the capital city. "Jews-for-Jesus" would then have worshipped alongside other Jews in these synagogues. And, as in other cities noted in Acts, interested Gentiles embraced the Jesus message as well.

But the status of Jews in any of the Greco-Roman cities of the Empire was always tenuous. They tended to be contentious and politically active where their religious practices were concerned. In Rome in A.D. 49, things seemed to have come to a head when Claudius was emperor. The Roman historian Tacitus writes about Jews rioting over "Chrestus," which some have taken to be a misspelling of "Christus." Claudius, who tended to be anti-Jewish anyhow, issued an edict expelling Jews from Rome. Many of them fled to the East, and in Acts 18:2 we find two Roman citizens, Priscilla and Aquila, in Corinth for that very reason.

Paul apparently met a number of other Jews from Rome during his travels in Macedonia and Achaia (now modern Greece). Though never having visited Rome, he names at least sixteen persons in Romans 16:3-16. Some of them had become his coworkers and some were even his relatives.

Meanwhile, back in Rome, what was happening to the Jesus-believing Gentiles and Jewish slaves who were left behind? According to a number of scholars, they began forming house- or tenement-based churches, since Claudius had closed down Jewish synagogues. Here Gentiles would have moved into leadership, and the character of these groups would have begun to change. With less knowledge of Scripture, Gentiles may have ignored much of Mosaic law, including circumcision, food laws, and the observance of Jewish Sabbath and festival days. The tenor would likely have become more charismatic, with Gentile emphasis on experience of the Spirit.

But when Nero ascended the throne in A.D. 54, he allowed Claudius's edict to lapse, so Jews began returning to their native city. Christian Jews found the character of "church" quite changed under Gentile leadership. This sets the stage for some serious conflict over Scripture and lifestyle practices.

The Rhetoric of Romans

One advance in Romans scholarship over the last few decades has been in understanding Greco-Roman writing styles. Though Romans is a letter with typical greetings and conclusions, the body of the letter is a speech meant to be delivered publicly and orally. Paul's particular writing style in Romans is conciliatory, not combative as in Galatians. Clearly Paul is aiming toward reconciliation of conservatives and liberals in Rome.

This is important for him for two reasons. First, it is the nature of the gospel to unify disperate peoples. God is the God of *both* Jews *and* Gentiles (3:29); Jesus redeems *both* Jews and Gentiles *equally* (3:24). Second, Paul cannot get the good will and support he needs for his Spanish mission from the Roman Christians if they are not unified. It would be like Billy Graham planning an evangelistic campaign in a city and only getting one denomination to support his efforts while the rest blocked them.

The entire letter, then, is a masterpiece of balance, anticipating and answering objections by either group, seeking to draw them together into one unified body.

Eating Meat and Observing Days: An Identity Issue

Romans 12:1 to 15:13 comprises the fourth section of Paul's thesis that both Jew and Gentile are made righteous before God by faith—the ethical implications. "Therefore, brothers and sisters, because of God's mercies [the grace of God explained in chapters 1-11] I appeal to you to present your bodies as a living sacrifice." After the more general ethical instructions in chapters 12 and 13 of how to do this, Paul wades into two delicate matters that are preventing community: what kind of food to eat or avoid, and what kind of special days to observe or not observe.

Next to circumcision, nothing else marked out Jewish diaspora communities so clearly as dietary rules and special days outlined in the Torah. These customs affected Jewish social and business relationships more than any others. They became the boundary-markers separating Jews from Gentiles. Those who observed these rules were part of the people of God; those who did not were outside.

But Paul had dedicated himself to bringing the gospel to Gentiles and to breaking down the walls between Jew and Gentile—and this involved abandoning the boundary-markers of circumcision, food laws, and observance of sabbaths and special religious days. This would have been little problem for Gentiles who had never practiced these laws, but for those whose very identity was bound up with them, the crisis must have been monumental.

Thus Paul fears a split and even disintegration within the house churches of Rome. The conservatives may be so horrified by the loss of the "fence" of the law protecting them that they entirely lose their faith in Jesus Christ. The liberals may become insensitive to and contemptuous of the concerns of the conservatives and turn away from them. Amid such antagonisms, Paul's advice in 14:1–15:6 is sensitive and pastoral.

The "Strong" and the "Weak"

In 14:1-3, Paul first addresses the "strong" by telling them to welcome those who are "weak" in faith. It is clear that the strong are those whom we would call liberal—those who are not bound by these identity markers—and the weak are law-observant. Though we today might use the terms in opposite ways, Paul calls the conservatives weak because they are depending less on God's grace and putting more weight on the outward form of their faith. Yet he is equally tough on both. The strong who eat meat must not despise those who abstain. The weak must not pass judgment on those who eat. This shows Paul's keen psychological insight. Almost any social group has "strong" people who think themselves more open-minded and mature than the more "narrow-minded" traditionalists they end up despising and scorning. On the other hand, the traditionalists judge the liberals as acting like outsiders and, in this case, of not even being Christian.

In 14:3c-5, Paul reminds the judgmental weak that God is bigger than their idea of God, that God accepts people whom they think are unacceptable. He wants them to accept people who differ from them in fundamental ways.

The second piece of advice, in verse 5, is that "all should be fully convinced in their own minds." Paul recognizes that Christians will disagree with each other in fundamental ways, but they should not let another's position intimidate them. Hold to your own position and realize that both factions can be accepted by God. However, there is a crucial qualification: both lifestyles should be lived out in honor of the Lord and in thankfulness to God (v. 6).

Paul is quite evenhanded in his conclusion of this section: *all* of us will stand before the judgment seat of God, so each will answer for themselves as to whether they have been passing judgment on others or despising others (vv. 10-12).

A Word to the Strong

In his next paragraph, 14:13-23, Paul is primarily addressing the strong. Though they may be convinced nothing is unclean in and of itself, their guiding principle within the Christian community must be love. Paul himself asserts emphatically ("I know and am persuaded in the Lord Jesus") that he himself takes the "strong" position. He proclaims a law-free gospel. Yet such freedom from the rules must not cause the ruin of others within the church, others for whom Christ died. Christ himself is the pattern of that love, since he died for us even when we were his enemies (5:10).

Paul clearly wants to sensitize his liberal readers to the more conservative persons among them. "Do not let what you eat cause the ruin of one for whom Christ died" (14:15). If the liberals were so scornful and insensitive toward the conservatives that the latter were in danger of forsaking Christ and returning to normative Judaism with its typical boundary-markers of circumcision, food laws, and sabbath observance, the liberals would be held responsible for ruining their lives.

It should be noted, however, that Paul is using forceful terms like "injured" and "ruin" to describe the effect of the despising behavior of the strong. Those who already have sensitive consciences about hurting the feelings of others or offending them should not overreact to this counsel. Paul is speaking to a situation where the conservatives are in the minority and where their actual salvation or relationship with God is at risk because of the callous behavior of the liberals. As James Dunn puts it: "Paul has no intention of encouraging the weak to exercise undue pressure on their own behalf—to blackmail the strong by professing grief or hurt.[2]

In verses 19-21, Paul moves the discussion from the individual to the whole congregation. Not only must law-free persons be responsible for how they relate to more traditional individuals, but they must also be aware of how this is affecting the church or congregation as a whole. This is not merely the absence of friction, but positive, proactive peacemaking. The behavior of those who are in the majority and who do not religiously observe Mosaic laws must contribute to building up, not tearing down, the church.

What does Paul mean when, speaking to the strong in verse 22, he reminds them, "The faith that you have, have as your own conviction before God. Blessed are those who have no reason to condemn themselves for what they approve"? Freedom from law observance, Paul reminds his listeners, comes only through faith, an unconditional trust in God's ability to make one righteous apart from works of the law. The danger is that such liberty can lapse into carelessness and an attitude of I-can-do-whatever-I-want. This is a reminder that the liberty of the strong is tied directly to their active faith in God to save them.

At the same time, Paul encourages the conservatives in verse 23 to stick to their own convictions. If they truly have a conscience against eating ritually unclean meat, they will be condemned if they eat it. They should not feel forced by the pressure of those more liberal within the community to do something they sincerely believe is wrong. In fact, if they do go against their conscience by eating meat, they will not be doing it because of their faith (as the liberals presumably are). For them, then, the very act of eating meat would be sinful, since "whatever does not proceed from faith is sin" (v. 23).

Paul's Conclusion on the Weak and the Strong

The chapter break here is unfortunate, since Paul concludes his seamless discussion of eating meat and observing holy days in 15:1-

6. This is actually the first time (v. 1) that Paul calls the law-free individuals "strong" (and again identifies himself with this group). Verse 5:1 literally reads, "We the powerful ones (*dunatoi*) ought to carry the weaknesses of those without power." The word used for "weak" in 14:1—*asthenoi*—is now changed to *adunatoi*, whereas their "weaknesses" are *asthenemata*, from the same root as *asthenoi*. The word change here suggests that the liberal position is also the majority position within the Christian community and thus politically stronger than the position of the conservatives.

That is why the strong must carry the actual weaknesses of those in a politically weaker position. This is how the principle of love operates. The strong do not need to agree with or approve of the position of the conservatives, but they do need to identify with them. According to Dunn,

> the balance which Paul calls for, between disapproval of the attitudes, and sympathetic identification with those who hold them, is presumably modeled on the identification Christ achieved with sinful flesh with a view to its destruction (8:3).[3]

Paul concludes his long discussion of this major divisive issue in the Roman churches with a prayer for harmony, "so that together you may *with one voice* glorify the God and Father of our Lord Jesus Christ." Here Paul is not looking for a tacit or grudging "agreement to disagree," but an active mutuality that fully accepts the other as a child of God, regardless of different attitudes about a fundamental issue.

Romans 15:7-13 is the final summary to Paul's long argument which began in 1:16. "Welcome each other, just as Christ welcomed you, for the glory of God!" (v. 7). This concerns the overall issue of Jews and Gentiles working and worshiping together as one church. Paul buttresses his argument by stitching together Scriptures which affirm the inclusion of the Gentiles along with the Jews, the traditional people of God.

Connections to the Current Issue— Can Gay and Straight Live Together in the Church?

It is always easier to solve problems when they are someone else's, or to trivialize arguments between groups that one is not a part of. Unless we understand the depth of the ethnic-religious problem in the early church, we can look down our noses at first-century conflicts about diet and holiday observance as trivial indeed. Why did they argue over food when unity was so important?

In our day the comparable question of how to handle different beliefs about homosexual behavior in our churches confronts us. As with similar developments in a good many other denominations, a few of the smaller, less-conservative Mennonite congregations begin accepting gay and lesbian Christians as members on the basis of their faith, regardless of sexual orientation. The conferences or larger denominational bodies of which they are a part struggle with what to do: should they force them to change their position or be disfellowshiped from the conference?

In addition, given recent attempts of two denominational streams to merge, another complex dynamic arises: because of some differing emphases and church polity between the General Conference Mennonite and the Mennonite Church denominations, completing the planned merger has proved a challenge. The attempt at unity risks foundering primarily because of this controversial topic.

What can we learn from the conflicts of liberals and conservatives within the Roman churches and from Paul's counsel to them? Much, I believe, but there are also differences. Let's begin with the differences.

When the "Weak" Are Strong

It appears that the more liberal, law-free position concerning the Jewish boundary-markers of circumcision, food laws, and sabbaths was the more powerful, majority position in the Roman churches. The "weak" were not only those who needed the extra security of traditional observances to supplement their faith, but also those who were in a politically weaker position within the church.

Today, however, a more conservative position regarding homosexuality is the majority position as well as one that is typically politically stronger. Not only is the practice of same-sex genital sex considered sinful, but probably many Mennonites (and other Christians) see the orientation or identity itself as a choice and thus one that ought to be forcefully repudiated by those who struggle with this temptation.[4]

In that sense, then, whatever Paul says in Romans 14:1-15:6 that relates to strength from a majority position applies to today's conservatives on the topic of homosexuality. If the simplistic instruction to "love the sinner, hate the sin" is to have any teeth, it must mean that the conservatives "carry the weaknesses," or identify with the struggles, of Christian believers who are gay or lesbian (Rom. 15:1).

If indeed they believe that the very orientation is a choice and a temptation, conservatives must identify with those who struggle with this issue, knowing that each of them is struggling with other areas of temptation just as serious. (Paul's primary point in Romans 1:18-3:31 that all have sinned equally should remind conservatives that the issues with which they are tempted are no more or less serious than the issue of homosexuality.)

Trivial or Fundamental?

Let us now examine some of the similarities, places where our current controversy parallels that of the controversy within the Roman churches.

First, neither controversy concerns trivial issues. Laws governing diet and observance of sabbaths were the very practices that set Jews apart from pagans and the very practices (along with circumcision) that pagans had often insisted Jews must forsake.[5] The struggle during many centuries of maintaining these practices was what preserved the people of God as adherents of a faith distinct among pagans. The Scriptures were clear and specific about honoring the Sabbath and eating ritually clean food.

Similarly, the condemnation of same-sex genital sex, at least between males, is also fairly clear in the Hebrew Scriptures and is assumed to be sinful or pagan by Paul in Romans 1:24-27 and possibly in 1 Corinthians 6:9. In addition, the church has traditionally frowned on homosexual practice and for centuries has refused to perform gay and lesbian holy unions.

But Christians have often ignored other biblical commands that are far more explicit and reiterated far more often.[6] This topic goes beyond "the-Bible-says-it's-wrong." Our sexuality is also part of the unconscious, irrational aspect of our personhood. The vast majority of people are hardwired for physical and emotional attraction to the opposite sex, and our feelings about this go much deeper than conscious, intellectual reason. Additionally, given the highly sexualized nature of our present culture, our current controversy is one which is hardly trivial.

Therefore, if in both cases, believers are disagreeing on fundamental issues, Paul's principles should apply to both situations. The conservative, law-observant Jewish believers of Paul's day would compare with traditionalists today who believe all forms of homosexuality are sinful. The law-free liberals parallel those self-affirming Christian gays and lesbians today, as well as those who advocate a position of accepting them as full members of the church and supporting monogamous gay relationships.

The reader can then go back through the above discussion of Romans 14:1-15:6 and make the necessary connections. Here I will simply highlight a few points.

Challenges for Both Sides of the Controversy

1. Traditionalists need to recognize that their interpretation of this issue may not be the only right one. Even though no biblical statement on homosexuality is positive, there is not a one-to-one relationship between the sexual practices of Paul's day with that advocated for and by Christian gays and lesbians today. A concept of sexual orientation did not exist then; everyone was assumed to be naturally heterosexual, and Paul could then argue that same-sex genital sex was "against nature" (though he also argued in 1 Corinthians 11:14 that men wearing long hair was against nature, even though this is untrue and he really meant "against custom"). But a case can be made today that a small minority of people are naturally attracted to those of the same sex and that this has nothing to do with idolatry, which is the basis of Paul's argument in Romans 1:18-27.

Furthermore, the concept of faithful monogamy within same-sex relationships would have been foreign, or certainly not the norm for homosexual liaisons, in Paul's day. Though Jews did not practice same-sex sex, Paul would have been familiar with non-Jewish traditions of extra-marital and promiscuous homosexual sex. For example, one of the "job descriptions" of slaves of both genders was to be sexually available to masters or whoever masters allowed to rape them.[7]

Various other arguments by Christians have been made recognizing the existence and validity of homosexual orientation and the practice of monogamy within same-sex relationships. My point here is simply that traditionalists need to acknowledge that, even though they may be firmly convinced in their own minds that their position on this issue is the correct one, other positions are held by sincere Christians. If "God has welcomed them, who are you to pass judgment on servants of another?" (14:3-4).

2. On the other side, there are just as important cautions given to the liberals in Romans 14. They are not to despise or scorn the

more traditional brother or sister. When an issue becomes as polarized as homosexuality is today, those on the more open or accepting side can become impatient and scornful. They can tolerate any persons, it seems, *except* more conservative ones, those who will not tolerate their position. Some years ago, I offered to present a paper similar to this one at a consultation supportive of gay and lesbian relationships. This was rejected, and I found out later that the committee had been quite scornful of the mediating position I was advocating.

Granted, an attitude of accepting those who do not accept you or your behavior is difficult. It is especially so when your position is a minority one within a larger church, and when it feels like a fundamental rejection of one's very person. Nevertheless, it seems that is what Paul says must happen if the church is to truly be the church. The "strong" are to pursue what makes for peace and mutual upbuilding by loving and respecting even those who condemn their way of life (14:19). In doing this, the liberals become models of Jesus for the rest of the community. Also in a minority position among his own people when arrested, "Christ did not please himself; but, as it is writen, 'The insults of those who insult you have fallen on me'" (15:3).

Paul comments in 14:21 that "it is good not to eat meat or drink wine or do anything that makes your brother or sister stumble." Does that mean that liberals on our current issue should not come out as gays or lesbians, if that happens to be their orientation, or should remain sexually celibate? Perhaps the key here is found in the strong word *stumble*. Other ancient manuscripts of Romans add, "or be upset or weakened." And we must remember that earlier, in 14:15, the terms *injured* and *ruin* are used. These terms are stronger than simply to offend someone else by one's behavior. It is unlikely that a minority of self-affirming and loving Christian gays and lesbians today will drive traditionalists from the church and cause them to lose their salvation.

Nevertheless, a rigid and despising attitude by those who advocate for gay and lesbian rights can be detrimental to the church as a whole. Paul says conservatives are condemned if they are pressured by others to do something they feel is wrong (14:23). Whatever freedom believers have must come from their faith in Christ—a trust that only through him can they be made righteous before God. This would hold true not only for heterosexual conservatives, but for persons who realize they have homosexual attractions but believe it is wrong to act on them. A place must be made in the church for such persons. Conservatives must recognize their orientation and struggle, and liberals must respect their scruples.

Conclusions for a Unified Church

No doubt many more parallels can be drawn between the struggle of the Roman churches and ours today. But the location of these detailed instructions at the culmination of Paul's powerful argument that Jews and Gentiles are made righteous together—on the basis of faith and not boundary-marking works of the law—argues for its importance. We can affirm unity in the abstract. We can affirm salvation by faith alone. But when it comes to the nitty-gritty details and specific sore spots, we will fall into the sins of despising the conservatives among us or judging the liberals among us unless we seriously heed Paul's inspired, evenhanded counsel.

Notes

1. This chronology is derived from careful examination of Paul's letters, the book of Acts, and clues about sailing schedules and political events in extra-canonical literature

2. .James D. G. Dunn, "Romans 9-16," *Word Biblical Commentaries*, vol. 38B (Dallas, Tex.: Word Books, 1988, 835.

3. Ibid., 842.

4. When I bring up this topic in my first-year college class in biblical studies, asserting that both the Bible and Messiah College only refer to *practice* and not orientation, the resistance from students is immediate and strong. Many insist that orientation is a choice, and to even think about being attracted to the same sex is sinful or even "of the devil."

5. The most obvious example is the Maccabean Revolt of 167-168 BC, when the Syrian prince Antiochus IV was determined to wipe out this "barbarian" religion by prohibiting parents to circumcise their sons and sacrificing a pig on the Temple altar.

6. These include, among others, charging interest for loans, wearing head coverings for women when they pray, and even figuring out ways to get around the clear teachings of Jesus forbidding divorce or the use of violence. Conversely, some things are viewed as sinful today that are not stressed in our scriptures. Slavery is now considered immoral and unlawful, even though no New Testament writer condemns it. There are also statements in both testaments that if used today would be seen as clearly racist.

7. See Robert Jewett, "The Social Context and Implications of Homoerotic References in Romans," in *Homosexuality, Science, and the "Plain Sense" of Scripture*, ed. David L. Balch (Grand Rapids, Mich.: Wm. B. Eerdmans, 2000), 239, who refers to the normalcy, in that male-dominated society, of intercourse between male masters and male slaves.

Bibliography

A variety of resources have helped shape the above understanding of Romans. Key ones follow.

Donfried, Karl P., ed. *The Romans Debate*. Revised and expanded edition. Peabody, Mass.: Hendrickson, 1991.

Dunn, James D. G. "Romans 9-16." *Word Biblical Commentaries*, vol. 38B. Dallas, Tex.: Word Books, 1988.

Finger, Reta Halteman. *Paul and the Roman House Churches: A Simulation*. Scottdale, Pa.: Herald Press, 1993.

Jewett, Robert. *Christian Tolerance: Paul's Message to the Modern Church*. Philadelphia: Westminster, 1982.

Jewett, Robert, "The Social Context and Implications of Homoerotic References in Romans" in *Homosexuality, Science, and the "Plain Sense" of Scripture*, ed. David L. Balch. Grand Rapids, Mich.: Wm. B. Eerdmans, 2000, 223-241.

Chapter 13

Fruit of the Spirit or Works of the Flesh? Come Let Us Reason Together

Mark Thiessen Nation

*"T*HERE WAS ONCE AN ART CRITIC, I HAVE BEEN TOLD, who had a sure way of identifying ancient Maltese art objects: he found himself crying before them."[1] So begins the wonderful story of Magda and André Trocmé and the parish of Le Chambon in southern France and how, amid the terrors of World War II, these three thousand or so people, led by a pacifist pastor, saved the lives of thousands of Jews from the Nazis who wanted to kill them. This opening sentence reflects Philip Hallie's own response when he first read the story of Le Chambon: he found tears streaming down his cheeks.

By opening his book this way Hallie intends to suggest there are emotions appropriate for certain experiences, certain realities. Here those emotions relate to the excellence and moral goodness embodied in Le Chambon. Today many emotions are connected with the varied realities surrounding homosexuality: anger, fear, disgust. Amid such feelings, I do not know how we can address this subject in the church without considerable pain. As I approach the issue I am reminded of Walter Brueggemann's statement that "theology that is 'pre-pain' must be treated with suspicion."[2]

In relation to this issue, there must be pain because there are still "ministers" of the gospel who attend the funerals of prominent gay people carrying placards saying "God Hates Fags." Pain because adult children tell wrenching stories of being disowned by their families when they come out, reporting that they have been gay or lesbian for as long as they can remember. Pain because of sitting in the presence of someone who has repeatedly wished he were dead due to living in a world that tells him he must be straight—yet after years of yearning to be, of seeking help to be, he isn't. Pain because those who claim to be brothers and sisters within the church want to know why they cannot be fully a part of this church that is as much a part of their lives as anyone else's. Pain because this issue continually threatens to divide denominations. Pain because in fact the church (including the Mennonite Church) through more than two decades of struggle, has still not really moved forward on this complicated and only partly understood issue.

One reason we cannot move forward is that we are polarized, which is not uncommon with this sort of emotionally charged subject. Many of us, after some period of agonizing, believe we cannot live in mid-air forever. Therefore, with considerable discomfort, and aware of remaining questions and areas of ambiguity, we take positions. We are, when all is said and done, for or against homoerotic relations.[3] From that point forward we are mostly identified by our public stance.

This chapter is, in part, an attempt to do in essay form what practitioners of conflict resolution do in relation to such polarized issues. It attempts to help people realize that, although many of us have taken positions on homoerotic relations, that does not necessarily mean we are at polar opposite places. In point of fact, most of us, even after having taken positions, are somewhere along a spectrum. We agree with many others on a variety of issues, including those who may have finally taken a different stand on homoerotic relations.

I will attempt to display this spectrum and name what continues to separate us through four steps. First, I will delineate a number of issues about which I believe most of us agree. Second, I will name issues I believe cause some in this debate to reach for strong rhetoric. Third, I will provide glosses or annotations on what I have named in the first step. These glosses are an invitation to people who disagree to hear the potential inadequacies in their own positions as well as to hear the views of others. Finally, I will offer some thoughts to keep in mind which, I hope, will help us to move forward in ways that are potentially helpful for the church.

In all of this discussion, I am not pretending to be neutral. I have attempted to read widely and listen carefully to many voices in this debate over the last sixteen years or so. But I am aware of my own views. However, throughout most of this essay I am attempting to keep my views in the background.

What Can We Agree On? Naming the Spectrum

I am under no illusions that *all* of us agree on the following matters. Some of us are at opposite ends of the spectrum. However, we should not assume that the majority are at opposite extremes, because activists, who are most vocal, tend to represent the opposite extremes. I suggest that most people within Mennonite churches (and also the larger church) would agree on the following:

(1) The social and biological sciences have raised complicated questions about how people come to be gay and lesbian, questions that present puzzles we do not pretend fully to understand.

(2) We affirm that the Bible is centrally authoritative in defining the Christian faith and thus, among other things, provides instruction in what it means to live morally.

(3) There are only a few biblical texts that speak directly to the issue of homoerotic relations. Those few which do address the subject, taken at face value, speak negatively.

(4) Any discussion of homoerotic relations within the Bible must include a more comprehensive biblical framework that would include not only other texts related to sexuality, but also a broader understanding of Christian theology and ethics. Furthermore, this discussion should be placed within an overall framework of what it means to be Christian.

(5) We have something to learn from the various ways the church throughout its history has dealt both with sexuality in general and homoerotic relations in particular, as we seek today to wrestle with these matters.

(6) We believe Christians are commanded to love their neighbors as themselves. This would include repudiating any cruel behavior toward people (certainly including friends, family members, and coworkers) who are engaged in homoerotic relationships. Moreover, it would also include being loving toward gays, lesbians, and people who believe homoerotic behaviors to be wrong.

(7) We believe it is important to support and nurture heterosexual married couples (and their children). Moreover, if the church

were to shift positions on homosexual relationships, what is being suggested for adoption is a parallel monogamous arrangement for gays and lesbians.

(8) Homoerotic behavior is really the issue we are wrestling with. Of course this issue can neither be separated from the lives of the people who are in homoerotic relationships nor disconnected from broader issues related to sexuality.

It is important that we not pass lightly over this list (and perhaps other items should be added). If I am right that most of us would agree on these things, then it is important to note this common ground, perhaps more common ground than sometimes appears to be the case amid the strong polarizing rhetoric. If I am right that most of us agree about this much, then why do we not only disagree on the issue of homoerotic relations but even have substantial disagreements sometimes connected to oppositional rhetoric? Let me name, in the next section, three possible reasons.

Supercharging the Rhetoric

(1) The first reason that may help explain the strong rhetoric connected with homoerotic relations is that this is not just an "issue" but is connected to people. We are talking about family, friends, and brothers and sisters in Christ—in short, relationships. If anyone fails to understand why parents of gay or lesbian children, even parents who are theologically very conservative, come to have strong feelings about this issue, then they have a failure of imagination—or compassion.[4]

In fact, I would guess that this debate may be more painful within a context like the Mennonite Church than in some other denominations (not to minimize the intensity in other churches) precisely because we are in some ways (including literal) an extended family. Families have a commitment to one another and, of course, have closer relationships to each other than to those outside their families. It is also the case that because they trust each other and have granted power to the other family members, they can cause each more pain than anyone else can. As Philip Yancey has said, "Troublesome issues like divorce and homosexuality take on a different cast when you confront them not in a state legislature but in a family reunion."[5]

The next two reasons are mirror images of each other and are related to what George Lakoff identifies in his book, *Moral Politics*.[6]

Lakoff examines the way in which such issues as gun control, feminism, and abortion are connected to worldviews. Therefore, the issues are symbolically related to larger concerns, convictions, and moral commitments. In times of significant cultural shifts and transitions, worldviews can be under significant challenge, whether perceived or actual. In such contentious times, specific issues assume important symbolic roles. Fears, heightened concerns, become attached to these issues. They become plugs in the dike. If the plugs do not remain, who knows? The whole dam that is presently holding back a flood of evil may come crashing down.

(2) Some who affirm homoerotic relations have fears about those on the conservative side. Within the church they fear fundamentalists may take over. Something like what has happened among Southern Baptists could happen in the Mennonite Church. A rigidly defined orthodoxy would be enforced. Pastors and teachers in colleges and seminaries would have to be constantly looking over their shoulders worrying about whether someone was going to haul them before a disciplinary body for not believing and teaching the right thing. Or perhaps the fear is of a more specific Mennonite variety: we will return to our own earlier days (not that terribly long ago) when a set of beliefs and practices were rigidly enforced.

Furthermore some who affirm changing the church's position on homoerotic relations fear that the Religious Right is already too powerful in larger North American society. We do not want them taking over more and more of society.[7] In fact, matters of sexual (including homosexual) behavior should be a private matter, not something the state should monitor and enforce.

Finally, often the affirming folk perceive that the traditional folk have the bulk of the power. They are in the majority of the positions of power within the church and society. This makes the affirming folk feel rather powerless.

(3) On the other hand, some who endorse the traditional stance of the church believe the debates over this issue demonstrate that there is reason for concern about moral decline. Within the church, there is cause for worry about moral and theological confusion and spiritual sickness. Homosexuality issues are not the first sign of such confusion. They are merely indicative of a more wide-ranging confusion, and if properly resolved, might provide a beginning point to rectify the spiritual deterioration.

Many would argue that in the larger society there is also more moral confusion than there needs to be. And although it it is inappropriate for the state to monitor what are appropriately private sexual acts, nonetheless it is acceptable to have certain laws that serve not only to restrain but also to educate. Society, with its diversity, can decide it is appropriate, for instance, only to sanction heterosexual marriages or to forbid curricular materials for schools, intended for young children, that affirm homoerotic relationships.[8]

Glosses on Areas of Agreement

In this section I offer some glosses on the items listed in the section in which I tried to name things about which most of us agree. In doing this I hope to help us name the differences within the agreement so that, once named, they can perhaps be more accessible as points of discussion/debate. Also I want to call for greater honesty about the nature of disagreements.

(1) *Social and biological sciences.* I list and discuss this first not because I think it most important. I do not. But in many formal and informal discussions, the science related to how people become gay and lesbian assumes a significant role. In fact it often becomes a trump card, preventing honest conversations about difficult issues.

My central point here is simple: questions have been raised about how people become gay and lesbian which present puzzles no one has really solved.[9] The questions make it clear that sexual identity is complex and includes the interaction of genetics, familial relations, and the social environment beyond the family. Exactly how these factors interact is complicated, different for different individuals, and, I believe, not fully understood by anyone.

It has been intriguing to me to notice that many who affirm acceptance of homoerotic relations within the church seem to presume an essentialist view of sexual identity, i.e., "they have no choice," "that is just who they are." On the other hand, many who affirm the traditional Christian approach to homoerotic relations often assume a social constructionist view of sexual identity. That is to say, they presume a substantial plasticity to our sexual identity. Otherwise, why worry that our children might become gay or lesbian if their social world communicates in multiple ways that homoerotic relations are every bit as legitimate as heteroerotic relations?[10] Much of the public rhetoric that has pulled at heart strings has been essentialist: How can you raise moral questions when they *cannot* be any other way?[11] Yet the recent trend in much secular writing about gays and lesbians is social constructionist in orientation.[12]

What in my view is disingenuous—or reflective of inadequate reading—is to suggest that science provides clear data that make it impossible for us to raise moral questions about homoerotic relations.[13] Or, similarly, that we know enough about homosexuality today, through what science has taught us, that we can be confident that what the Bible is talking about in Leviticus or Romans is not what *we* are talking about. It goes without saying that the writers of the Bible did not use modern scientific models to study sexual identity or behavior. However, it does not follow that this silences the Bible's voice on the subject. Furthermore, we need to be more circumspect about our own "clear" knowledge. Science does not provide those in the know with a trump card in these discussions (which is not the same as saying that it is not a part of the conversation).

(2), (3), (4) *The Bible and Christian theology and ethics.* First let me speak to those in the church who are not biblical scholars or theologians. It is important for us all to be honest about the complexities surrounding this issue. There are the scientific complexities just discussed. There is also the complexity of interpreting some of the relevant texts.[14] It is true that Leviticus 18:22 is straightforward when it says, "You shall not lie with a male as with a woman; it is an abomination." But then Leviticus is also straightforward when it says, "You shall not let your animals breed with a different kind; you shall not sow your field with two kinds of seed; nor shall you put on a garment made of two different materials" (19:19).

Why is it that one text matters a great deal to us and the other not at all? There are (quite legitimately) difficult matters of interpretation here.[15] We should not invoke the complexity simply as a way to dismiss or relativize the texts, but rather be honest about the need for those who study such matters to help us know how to interpret such texts.[16]

Furthermore, we should be honest in asking why the question of homoerotic relations has assumed such importance. Money—and our temptations to serve it—assumes a much larger role in the Scriptures (and in the wealthy U.S. this has considerable relevance). Why is that not exercising us as much, if what we care about is the authority of the Scriptures?

Now a word to us biblical scholars and theologians. It is important that we not, directly or indirectly, communicate contempt for sincere Christians who seek to take the Bible and the call of Christ to discipleship seriously. We cannot expect most Christians to read the Scriptures in the way scholars would. I am grateful for those Mennonites who have refused to kill enemies during America's wars because of their commitment to take the Bible seriously and to faithfully live out Jesus' teaching to love enemies. That these same people do not understand the complexities of biblical interpretation related to the wars in Joshua or the violent imagery in Revelation is not something for which they are blameworthy (as if any of the rest of us fully understand these complicated matters). They are called to be faithful Christians. It is our job as teachers and pastors to provide adequate instruction for members of our churches, even as we accept that they need never be scholars.

Furthermore, it is imperative that we be honest about the complexities and diversity of opinions regarding the issues around homoerotic relations and biblical teaching. I have often heard it implied by theologians (Mennonite and otherwise) that no serious Scripture scholarship supports the traditional view (or that only fundamentalists do). That is simply not true.[17] It is true that for a while in the 1980s many were under the sway of the readings of the Bible provided by John Boswell.[18] However, beginning in the mid-1980s and continuing today, there are serious scholars who come to various conclusions.[19]

Moreover, since there are various academically respectable views, it is important that we scholars not overestimate our role. I believe we do have a crucial role in these conversations. But it will not do to imagine that we can invoke the word *scholarship* as a trump card to short-circuit full conversations with contributions by various people, including biblical scholars and theologians.

(5) *Church history.* More than a few believe that our central learning from the church on this topic, as with sexuality generally, is a negative learning. That is to say, the church has so often gotten it wrong, been overly negative about the body and preoccupied with sexual behavior, that—except for learning what not to do and say—we can largely ignore much of what has been done and said in relation to sexual and homosexual behavior throughout church history. There is truth in this. We can find numerous quotations and incidents to support the claim. There is much we need to learn by looking at mistakes of the past.

However, might we also have other important things to learn from the church on this subject? I believe we do. The stereotype of Christian sexual repressiveness from the outset is at best an exaggeration.[20] As renowned classicist Paul Veyne has said,

If any aspect of ancient life has been distorted by legend, this is it. It is widely but mistakenly believed that antiquity was a Garden of Eden from which repression was banished, Christianity having yet to insinuate the worm of sin into the forbidden fruit. Actually, the pagans were paralyzed by prohibitions.[21]

Similar things could be said about other periods of church history.[22] Again, this is not to say one could not find writings and actions regarding sexuality by church leaders that would be objectionable (though such texts should be read contextually, not anachronistically). This is simply to say that other voices—from the history of the church—can provide guidance, guidance that is much needed in our time.

I believe Linda Woodhead has it just right in saying that "When 'Christianity and 'the Christian tradition' come under attack, it often seems that what detractors have in their targets is not two thousand years of Christian history, but the Christianity of their youth and of the previous generation."[23] For Mennonites this is relevant to much more than sexuality. Many currently living have memories of overzealous church leaders seeking to enforce codes of conduct on a whole church or an area conference in ways that were experienced as oppressive and may often have been unwise.[24] These memories should provide a caution. And they should counsel us to desire wisdom. But the caution and counsel should not equal moral or doctrinal neutrality. Nor do they negate either the authority of Scripture or the riches that can be gained from drawing on Christian history.

(6) *Love of neighbors.* I believe it should be obvious to any Christians that—as people called to love our neighbors as ourselves—we are not to be cruel to anyone. This "anyone" certainly includes those engaged in homoerotic relationships. Moreover, our love should express itself in tangible, positive ways toward our neighbors. However, it is more than that, is it not? Mennonites (as a group) believe that following Jesus entails, among other things, being peacemakers—being committed to peace, justice, inclusion, and welcoming the marginalized as Jesus did. Does this not exclude rejecting those engaged in homoerotic relationships?

This question deserves brief exploration. Some have made much of the fact that Jesus said nothing about homosexuality. However, there are many issues to which Jesus never spoke. If, as Martti Nissinen and others have said, the Judaism Jesus knew was rather unequivocally negative on the matter of homoerotic relations, then Jesus had no reason to say anything if he agreed with the consen-

232 / TO CONTINUE THE DIALOGUE

sus.[25] In fact, given the consensus, it might be significant that Jesus didn't challenge convictions and practices firmly in place that denied the legitimacy of homoerotic relationships.

At a more abstract and principled level, one might argue that Jesus welcomed the marginalized; he was inclusive. But stating it this way begs the question. Adulterers (especially women) were marginalized in the world of Jesus and although Jesus (according to John 8) prevented the stoning of a woman caught in adultery, he nonetheless asked her to "go and sin no more." As Croatian theologian Miroslav Volf has put it,

> Jesus was no prophet of "inclusion". . . for whom the chief virtue was acceptance and the cardinal vice intolerance. [He did scandalously include many who were normally excluded, but he also] made the "intolerant" demand of repentance and the "condescending" offer of forgiveness.[26]

In short, an argument either from Jesus' teaching on peacemaking or his silence on the specific issue of homoerotic relationships in no way provides an endorsement of homoerotic relations.

(7) *Support for heterosexual married couples.* I do think it is important to note that most of those who want the church to affirm homoerotic relationships intend not to undermine heterosexual relationships or families. Quite the contrary, they wish them well. However, whether or not the formal affirmation of homoerotic relationships does in fact in some ways undermine the future of heterosexual identities and relationships is an open question.[27] It depends on how gays and lesbians come to be gay and lesbian or, put differently, how their gay and lesbian identities are formed (about which, I believe, we are still unsure). And it depends on what specific proposals for affirmation are suggested and accepted.[28]

Moreover, there are two other complicating issues. First, the debate about homosexuality is happening when there is not consensus in society, church, or the theological world about sexual relationships and monogamous marriages.[29] Second, many who write theological books or essays about homoerotic relations argue for non-traditional ways of structuring relationships, to put it most neutrally.[30] It is not clear to me that most of the relevant parties to these conversations distance themselves from, say, non-monogamous relationships. If that is indeed the case, then it needs to be stated.

(8) *Homoerotic relations and broader issues of sexuality.* I am certainly in agreement with those who say that it is inappropriate to

reflect on homoerotic relations without dealing with the contexts within which we discuss such relations, including broader issues related to sexuality. We need to discuss cultural and social contexts within which we live our lives, contexts that cannot help but shape our understandings of sexuality and our concepts regarding appropriate and inappropriate sexual attitudes and behavior. As Christians we also need to name biblical teachings and Christian convictions rooted in the Scriptures that serve to shape our lives, leading us to embody our convictions faithfully, including how we conduct ourselves sexually. And in fact contexts and convictions are interrelated for us. But what are the contexts to be named? And what are the convictions?

In 1991 a committee of the Presbyterian Church USA produced a document on human sexuality.[31] Early within this document the relevant contexts related to human sexuality were named as "patriarchy, heterosexism, and homophobia." It is important to name abusive patterns of authority and structured forms of injustice. Likewise, it is vital that we acknowledge stereotypes as well as hateful attitudes and behaviors toward gays and lesbians. However, only to name this one set of contexts ignores too many other relevant elements of our context. For instance, Walter Brueggemann, hardly conservative, at the beginning of an insightful recent essay says that "we may as well concede at the outset that we live, all of us, in a promiscuous, self-indulgent society that prizes autonomy."[32] Might these elements of our context not also be relevant for our deliberations about sexuality?

It is not particularly surprising that, when "patriarchy, heterosexism, and homophobia" are the only contexts named, then the only substantive moral guidance given by the Presbyterian document is a commitment "to an inclusive, egalitarian ethic of common decency," or what is elsewhere referred to as the criterion of "justice-love."[33] Our Scriptures certainly implore us to pursue justice and to embody love. However, there are also admonitions regarding sexual immorality, lust, passions, the works of the flesh, and self-control—concerns more at home with Brueggemann's reminders.

I worry that many of us, because of our reticence to be morally clear about sexuality, have been unwilling to take seriously this latter set of concerns that respond to other dimensions of our context. We have, for instance, allowed the conversations about sexuality to be hostage to the public rhetoric about "safe sex." But as Kari Jenson Gold has said, "Surely the words are ludicrously contradictory! Sex can be many things: dark, mysterious, passionate, wild, gentle, even reassuring, but it is not safe. If it is, it's not likely to be very sexy."[34]

Camille Paglia, an ex-Catholic, offers some devastating and insightful criticisms of the Presbyterian document just mentioned that I think can instruct us all as we approach sexuality.[35] She—herself approving of all manner of dissident sexual conduct—does not want Christians to be naive about the realities of sexuality. As she puts it, the document

> reduces the complexities and mysteries of eroticism to a clumsy, outmoded social-welfare ideology. The old-style Protestant suppression of the passions, torments, and untidy physicalities of the body is in fact still abundantly evident in the report, which, in its opening premise of "the basic goodness of sexuality," projects a happy, bouncy vision of human life that would have made Doris Day and Debbie Reynolds—those '50s blond divas—proud [p. 24]. . . . "Eros," says the report's glossary, is "a zest for life." Is this a soap commercial? Eros, like Dionysus, is a great and dangerous god. The report gives us vanilla sex, smothered with artificial butterscotch syrup. In its liberal zeal to understand, to accept, to heal, it reduces the grand tragicomedy of love and lust to a Hallmark card. Its unctuous normalizing of dissident sex is imperialistic and oppressive. The gay world is stripped of its outlaw adventures in toilets, alleyways, trucks, and orgy rooms. There are no leathermen, hustlers, or drag queens. Gay love is reduced to a nice, neat, middle-class couple moving in next door on "Father Knows Best." . . . This is censorship in the name of liberal benevolence [p. 25] . . . .[36]

Moreover, given the complex, powerful realities of sexuality, Paglia thinks Christians make a serious mistake when we strip ourselves of our own best resources:

> The report assails the "influential tradition of radical asceticism" in "Western Christianity." . . . It assumes that eremites and monks were not contemplatives but killjoys, neurotics, and misogynists, scowling while the rest of the world caroused, footloose and fancy free. The report complains of "our cultural captivity to a patriarchal model of sexuality and its ethic of sexual control," as if sexual rules and taboos were not prevalent in every culture [p. 24]. . . . The institutional religions, Catholic and Protestant, carry with them the majesty of history. Their

theology is impressive and coherent. Efforts to revise or dilute that theology for present convenience seem to me misguided [p. 27].[37]

Is there something "impressive" and "coherent" about our theological traditions—even in relation to sexuality and homosexuality—that we ignore at our peril? Are there cautions here that we should heed?

Revision for Present Convenience?
Some Closing Comments

I believe it is reasonable for Christians—simple believers or academics—to ask, with Paglia, whether revisions regarding our approach to homosexuality (and sexuality), currently under way in many circles, are "for present convenience." [38] Moreover, it seems reasonable to argue that the burden of proof is on those who would challenge the historical consensus within the church that the plain sense of Scripture on this issue is right, namely, that homoerotic behavior is not to be formally affirmed within the church.

However, that is not the same as saying that anyone should approach this subject with anything like certainty. Rather, for many of us it seems quite appropriate to approach it with an openness to learn, with humility, and with significant pain. I sense this, for instance, in the recent words of Kathryn Greene-McCreight:

> Let me say for the record that I am among those who wish they could be convinced that Scripture and tradition could be read to support the revisionist position, which would argue for the theological and religious appropriateness of homoerotic relationships for Christians who feel drawn to them. . . . While I have not yet been convinced by the revisionist position, I keep listening in hopes that someone will come up with something new.[39]

Furthermore, though I hope this essay has communicated that I want people at various places along a spectrum to hear each other, I nonetheless think it is a mistake to minimize the potential importance of the issues at stake in relation to this matter. No less a voice than that of the major German Protestant theologian, Wolfhart Pannenberg, has said that

> if a church were to let itself be pushed to the point where it ceased to treat homosexual activity as a departure from the bib-

lical norm, and recognized homosexual unions as a personal partnership of love equivalent to marriage, such a church would stand no longer on biblical ground but against the unequivocal witness of Scripture. A church that took this step would cease to be the one, holy, catholic, and apostolic Church.[40]

Lest someone imagine that strong theological claims are made only by theologians who affirm the tradition which stands against homoerotic relations, we should listen to Eugene Rogers Jr., another theologian. Rogers argues that if straight Christians do not move to affirm monogamous gay and lesbian marriages, then they are in danger of losing their salvation! In his substantial recent work, *Sexuality and the Christian Body*, Rogers makes the argument, offered also by others in recent years, that homosexuals are analogous to Gentiles in the New Testament.[41]

If there is anything that is central to many of Paul's theological arguments, it is that in Christ, Jews and Gentiles have been made one. Paul went to great effort and used strong rhetoric to indicate that Gentiles (which now includes almost all of us) are, in Christ, equal members of the people of God. Paul proclaimed this despite its offensiveness to many of those who, like himself, were Jews. In fact, to deny the inclusion of the Gentiles, said Paul, is to deny the gospel and the work of the Holy Spirit. Likewise, so this argument runs, in Christ, gay and straight have been made one.[42] If this is right, says Rogers, then "failing to accept faithful, monogamous gay and lesbian marriages may deny the work of the Spirit and put Gentile Christians [who are in the present denying what some Jews were then denying] in danger of their salvation."[43]

I think we do no one any favors if we forget that more than a few people share the views of either Pannenberg or Rogers. Each side can claim that profound theological issues are at stake—that the gospel and the future of the church are in the balance. And even if the theological stakes are not this high, we are still left with what seem irresolvable issues. We still need help moving forward when many tell us the stakes are this high. Thus this discussion should be taken seriously. We err if we take the questions related to homoerotic relationships with less seriousness than they deserve.

Whether Rogers' argument is convincing or not, he is at least attempting to do what needs to be done. That is to say, he is attempting to give solid, compelling theological reasons for his position, a position that seeks to overturn the consensus within the church.[44] Kathryn Greene-McCreight contends that "for traditional readers to be convinced of the righteousness before God of homo-erotic relationships, they would need to be convinced on 'tradition-alist' grounds. . . . Or the revisionist side must convincingly show how and why the rules must be changed."[45] It will not do simply to invoke words like tolerance, inclusion, or "our commitment to peace and justice." Properly understood, all of these ingredients are part of the discussion. However, they must be situated in a broader the-ological framework that includes the centrality of Jesus, the teach-ings of the Scriptures on homosexuality, sexuality, and what it means to be embodied persons while being faithfully Christian.[46]

As we continue to wrestle with these matters, we need to listen to each other. We need to speak honestly and humbly, with an open-ness to learn.[47] And we would do well to live with the apostle Paul's admonitions regarding "the works of the flesh" and "the fruit of the spirit" (Gal. 5:16-26).[48] We should not allow categorizations (for in-stance, liberal or conservative) to prevent any of us from taking se-riously Paul's admonitions regarding fornication, impurity, licen-tiousness, carousing, faithfulness, self-control, and "things like these" (Gal. 5:19-23). Nor, if we need to remind ourselves, should we allow these categorizations to prevent any of us from hearing Paul's admonitions regarding enmities, strife, anger, quarrels, dis-sensions, factions, love, patience, kindness, and gentleness (Gal. 5:19-23).[49]

Notes

1. Philip P. Hallie, *Lest Innocent Blood Be Shed* (New York: Harper & Row, 1979), 1.

2. Walter Brueggemann, "The Third World of Evangelical Imagination," in *Interpretation and Obedience: From Faithful Reading to Faithful Living* (Min-neapolis: Fortress Press), 26, n18.

3. An issue I have struggled with in this chapter is the use of language. It is perhaps impossible to use neutral language. I have usually chosen to use the term *homoerotic relations* as the matter being debated. It is the sexual be-havior of gays and lesbians that, for most people, is *the* issue. *Homoerotic*, a term used by various writers in this debate, seems to be as neutral as any word I can think of to refer easily to the issue at hand. A caution: though I have adopted this language, it is still imperative that we remember that the relationships between people who identify themselves as homosexual can-not and should not be reduced to the erotic or sexual component of their re-lationships. This is but a reminder that this "issue" is connected to a variety of complicated matters not adequately reducible to simple terminology.

4. See Roberta Showalter Kreider, ed., *From Wounded Hearts: Faith Stories of Lesbian, Gay, Bisexual and Transgendered People and Those Who Love Them* (Gaithersburg, Md.: Chi Rho Press, Inc., 1998). For a fuller narrative of one life see Mel White, *Stranger at the Gate: To Be Gay and Christian in America* (New York: Simon & Schuster, 1994).

5. Philip Yancey, "Why I Don't Go to a Megachurch," *Christianity Today* (May 29, 1996), 80.

6. George Lakoff, *Moral Politics: What Conservatives Know That Liberals Don't* (Chicago: The University of Chicago Press, 1996).

7. See Judith N. Shklar, "The Liberalism of Fear," in *Liberalism and the Moral Life*, ed. Nancy L. Rosenblum (Cambridge, Mass.: Harvard University Press, 1989), 21-38. On some of the reasons for the fear on this sort of contentious issue, see James Davison Hunter, *Culture Wars: The Struggle to Define America* (New York: Basic Books, 1991); James Davison Hunter, *Before the Shooting Begins: Searching For Democracy in America's Culture Wars* (New York: Basic Books, 1994); Didi Herman, *The Antigay Agenda: Orthodox Vision and The Christian Right* (Chicago: The University of Chicago Press, 1997); and as a challenge to some of these, see Christian Smith, *Christian America?: What Evangelicals Really Want* (Los Angeles: University of California Press, 2000).

8. In addition to most of the references in footnote seven, I would also refer to Ellen G. Friedman and Corinne Squire, *Morality USA* (Minneapolis: University of Minnesota Press, 1998) and Andrew Bard Schmookler, *Debating the Good Society: A Quest to Bridge America's Moral Divide* (Cambridge, Mass.: The MIT Press, 1999).

9. To get an overview of the subject, see Chandler Burr, *A Separate Creation: How Biology Makes Us Gay* (New York: Bantam Books, 1997); Jennifer Terry, *An American Obsession: Science, Medicine, and Homosexuality in Modern Society* (Chicago: The University of Chicago Press, 1999); and Vernon A. Rosario, *Science and Homosexualities* (New York: Routledge, 1999). Also see Stanton L. Jones and Mark A. Yarhouse, "The Use, Misuse, and Abuse of Science in the Ecclesiastical Homosexuality Debates," in *Homosexuality, Science, and the "Plain Sense" of Scripture,* ed. David L. Balch (Grand Rapids, Mich.: Wm. B. Eerdmans, 2000), 73-120, and their recent book, Stanton L. Jones and Mark A. Yarhouse, *Homosexuality: The Use of Scientific Research in the Church's Moral Debate* (Downers Grove, Ill.: InterVarsity Press, 2000).

10. In using "essentialist" and "social constructivist" language, I realize I am using language from the social sciences. Though such language is useful and instructive, it is also important to remember that theological language regarding, for instance, creation, sin, and corruptibility, are more determinative for Christians.

11. In case I have not been clear, let me say that I think it is a complicated mixture; thus the truth, I believe, of my previous paragraph.

12. The literature is vast, but see David F. Greenberg, *The Construction of Homosexuality* (Chicago: The University of Chicago, 1988); and Marjorie Garber, *Vice Versa: Bisexuality and the Eroticism of Everyday Life* (New York: Simon & Schuster, 1995).

13. Among other things, the way in which "choice" often figures into

these conversations is overly simplified in important ways. For some very insightful theological reflections that are relevant to these matters, see Michael Banner, "Prolegomena to a Dogmatic Sexual Ethic," in his *Christian Ethics and Contemporary Moral Problems* (Cambridge: Cambridge University Press, 1999), 269-309, and especially on choice, 295ff.

14. Among the many debatable points is the naming of immediately relevant texts. Most would agree that Romans 1:26-27 and Leviticus 18:22 and Leviticus 20:13 are among them. Others would include the lists in 1 Corinthians 6.9-10 and 1 Timothy 1:10. Many would concede that there should at least be discussions of Genesis 19:1-8; Judges 19:16-30; 2 Peter 2:6-7; and Jude 7, if only to set them aside as irrelevant. Finally, many would say that Genesis 1-2 serves as a backdrop to all of the Bible's teachings on sexuality. Even if one includes all of these, it is a small number of texts. But more significant is the fact that none of them, except Genesis 1-2, have any central importance in the contexts within which they appear.

Let me also mention one essay that is remarkable for being as clear and neutral (and in brief compass) as any I have read in laying out the issues in regard to reading the Scriptures on this topic: Walter Moberly, "The Use of Scripture in Contemporary Debate About Homosexuality," *Theology* 103, no. 814 (July–August 2000): 251-258.

15. For one of the most thorough, recent studies, and as a guide to other literature, see Jonathan Klawans, *Impurity and Sin in Ancient Judaism* (New York: Oxford University Press, 2000).

16. The person who has shaped much of the debate within the last twenty years is John Boswell. See his *Christianity, Social Tolerance, and Homosexuality: Gay People in Western Europe from the Beginning of the Christian Era to the Fourth Century* (Chicago: The University of Chicago Press, 1980). Some of the other writings worth taking seriously that attempt to wrestle with the relevant texts and that come to conclusions that would make those who affirm the Church's traditional stance uncomfortable are Bernadette J. Brooten, *Love Between Women: Early Christian Responses to Female Homoeroticism* (Chicago: University of Chicago Press, 1996); L. William Countryman, *Dirt, Greed & Sex: Sexual Ethics in the New Testament and Their Implications for Today* (Philadelphia: Fortress Press, 1988); Martti Nissinen, *Homoeroticism in the Biblical World* (Minneapolis, Minn.: Fortress Press, 1998); Robin Scroggs, *The New Testament and Homosexuality* (Philadelphia: Fortress Press, 1983); and Michael Vasey, *Strangers and Friends: A New Exploration of Homosexuality and the Bible* (London: Hodder & Stoughton, 1995).

17. See Robert A. Gagnon, *The Bible and Homosexual Practice* (Nashville, Tenn.: Abingdon Press, 2001); Richard Hays, "Homosexuality," in *The Moral Vision of the New Testament* (New York: HarperCollins, 1996), 379-406; idem, "Relations Natural and Unnatural: A Response to John Boswell's Exegesis of Romans 1," *The Journal of Religious Ethics* 14, no. 1 (Spring 1986): 184-215; Thomas Schmidt, *Straight & Narrow? Compassion & Clarity in the Homosexuality Debate* (Downers Grove, Ill.: InterVarsity Press, 1995); Mark D. Smith, "Ancient Bisexuality and the Interpretation of Romans 1:26-27," *Journal of the American Academy of Religion* 54, no. 2 (Summer 1996): 223-256; and David

F. Wright, "Homosexuals or Prostitutes? The Meaning of *Arsenokotai* (1 Cor. 6:9, 1 Tim. 1:10)," *Vigiliae Christianae* 38 (1984): 125-153. It should also be mentioned here that Willard Swartley has two unpublished essays that move in the same basic direction.

Finally, mention should be made of two excellent essays on hermeneutics. Anthony Thiselton, who probably knows as much about hermeneutics as anyone in the world, has written, "Can Hermeneutics Ease the Deadlock?" in *The Way Forward: Christian Voices on Homosexuality and the Church*, ed. Timothy Bradshaw (London: Hodder & Stoughton, 1997), 145-196. Also see this important essay: Kathryn Greene-McCreight, "The Logic of the Interpretation of Scripture and the Church's Debate Over Sexual Ethics," in *Homosexuality, Science, and the "Plain Sense" of Scripture*, 242-260.

18. As mentioned above, this is Boswell's 1980 book, *Christianity, Social Tolerance, and Homosexuality*. More recently he published John Boswell, *The Marriage of Likeness: Same-Sex Unions in Pre-Modern Europe* (London: HarperCollins, 1995, published in the U. S. with the title and subtitle reversed). For critical responses, in addition to some of the references to Boswell's biblical interpretations mentioned in an earlier footnote, see Bruce A. Williams, O. P., "Homosexuality and Christianity: A Review Discussion," *The Thomist* 46 (1982): 609-625; and Brent D. Shaw, "A Groom of One's Own? The Medieval Church and the Question of Gay Marriage," *The New Republic* 211 (July 18 and 25, 1994): 33-41.

19. Rather than list more writings here, let me simply mention the bibliographies in two important recent books (which themselves have very different views and approaches): Stanley J. Grenz, *Welcoming But Not Affirming: An Evangelical Response to Homosexuality* (Louisville: Westminster John Knox Press, 1998), 187-201 and Bernadette J. Brooten, *Love Between Women: Early Christian Responses to Female Homoeroticism* (Chicago: University of Chicago Press, 1996), 363-372.

20. For one instance of a recent book that helps rescue Paul from this claim see Francis Watson, *Agape, Eros, Gender: Towards a Pauline Sexual Ethic* (Cambridge: Cambridge University Press, 2000). Also see Raymond F. Collins, *Sexual Ethics and the New Testament* (New York: Crossroad Publishing Co., 2000).

21. Paul Veyne, "The Roman Empire," in *A History of Private Life*, ed. Philippe Ariès and Georges Duby, I: Paul Veyne, ed., *From Pagan Rome to Byzantium* (Cambridge, Mass.: The Belknap Press, 1987), 202. See also Aline Rousselle, *Porneia: On Desire and the Body in Antiquity*, tran. Felicia Pheasant (Oxford: Basil Blackwell, 1988).

22. See, e.g., John Behr, *Asceticism and Anthropology in Irenaeus and Clement* (New York: Oxford University Press, 2000). For an overview of much of the history, with substantial bibliographical guidance, see Mary E. Wiesner-Hanks, *Christianity and Sexuality in the Early Modern World* (New York: Routledge, 2000).

23. Linda Woodhead, "Life in the Spirit: Contemporary and Christian Understandings of the Human Person," in *New Soundings: Essays in Developing Tradition*, ed. Stephen Platten, Graham James, and Andrew Chandler

(London: Darton, Longman, & Todd, 1997), 118.

24. One subject that should be revisited in this regard is the Mennonite understanding of church. Paul Hiebert has described what he refers to as three basic approaches to understanding church: the bounded set, the fuzzy set, and the centered set. To oversimplify, the Mennonite Church has often taken a bounded set approach, one that focuses considerably on boundary issues that define people in or out. The centered-set approach, in contrast, focuses mostly on the center, what it is that centrally defines the church. See Paul Hiebert, "The Category *Christian* in the Mission Task," in his *Anthropological Reflections on Missiological Issues* (Grand Rapids, Mich.: Baker Books, 1994), 107-136. This clearly has relevance for the debates about homosexuality, as is shown in Michael A. King, *Trackless Wastes & Stars to Steer By* (Scottdale, Pa.: Herald Press, 1990), 115-136.

25. As Martti Nissinen, who is affirming of homoerotic behavior, says: "To the extent that Rabbinic and Hellenistic Jewish literature sheds light on the norms of Jewish society in Jesus' time, it can be assumed that public expressions of homosexuality were regarded as anomalous, idolatrous, and indecent" (Martti Nissinen, *Homoeroticism in the Biblical World: A Historical Perspective* (Minneapolis: Fortress Press, 1998), 118. See also Robin Scroggs, *The New Testament and Homosexuality* (Philadelphia: Fortress Press, 1983), 66-84.

26. Miroslav Volf, *Exclusion and Embrace* (Nashville: Abingdon Press, 1996), 72-73.

27. For a theological argument for homosexual marriage, see David Matzko McCarthy, "Homosexuality and the Practices of Marriage," *Modern Theology* 13, no. 3 (July 1997: 371-97). See also Catherine M. Wallace, *For Fidelity: How Intimacy and Commitment Enrich Our Lives* (New York: Vintage Books, 1998) and the critique of Wallace: J. Budziszewski, "Just Friends," *First Things* 87 (November 1998): 60-63.

28. At least as a way to see what some of the issues are, consult David M. Estlund and Martha C. Nussbaum, eds., *Sex, Preference, and Family* (New York: Oxford University Press, 1997); and Christopher Wolfe, ed., *Homosexuality and American Public Life* (Spence Pub. Co., 1999), esp. Part III.

29. For some sense of the diversity within the theological world, see James B. Nelson and Sandra P. Longfellow, eds., *Sexuality and the Sacred: Sources for Theological Reflection* (Louisville: Westminster John Knox Press, 1994); and Elizabeth Stuart and Adrian Thatcher, eds., *Christian Perspectives on Sexuality and Gender* (Grand Rapids, Mich.: Wm. B. Eerdmans, 1996).

30. As examples, see Gary David Comstock, *Gay Theology Without Apology* (Cleveland, Ohio: Pilgrim Press, 1993); Kathy Rudy, *Sex and the Church: Gender, Homosexuality, and the Transformation of Christian Ethics* (Boston, Mass.: Beacon Press, 1997); Elizabeth Stuart, *Just Good Friends: Towards a Lesbian and Gay Theology of Relationships* (London: Mowbry, 1995); Gary David Comstock and Susan E. Henking, eds., *Que(e)rying Religion: A Critical Anthology,*(New York: Continuum, 1997).

31. *Presbyterians and Human Sexuality 1991* (Louisville: The Office of the General Assembly, Presbyterian Church [U. S. A.], 1991). A summary was

published by the chair of the committee, John J. Carey, "Body and Soul: Presbyterians on Sexuality," *The Christian Century* 108 (May 8, 1991): 516-520. I
name this document partly because it strikes me as offering, more or less,
what I would imagine some within the Mennonite Church and Church of
the Brethren would want.

32. Walter Brueggemann, "Duty as Delight and Desire: Preaching Obedience That Is Not Legalism," in *The Covenanted Self: Explorations in Law and
Covenant*, ed. Patrick D. Miller (Minneapolis: Fortress Press, 1999), 35.

33. See the excerpt of the Presbyterian document published as "Sexuality
and Justice-Love," *The Christian Century* 108 (May 8, 1991): 519.

34. Kari Jenson Gold, "Getting Real," *First Things* (January 1994): 6.

35. For other, more measured, critiques of the Presbyterian document,
see Gary L. Watts, "An Empty Sexual Ethic," *The Christian Century* 108 (May
8, 1991): 520-521, and Michael Banner, "Five Churches in Search of Sexual
Ethics," in his *Christian Ethics and Contemporary Moral Problems* (Cambridge:
Cambridge University Press, 1999), 252-268.

36. Camille Paglia, "The Joy of Presbyterian Sex," *The New Republic* (De-
cember 2, 1991): 24- 27; reprinted in Camille Paglia, *Sex, Art, and American
Culture* (New York: Vintage Books, 1992), 26-37. Also see Camille Paglia,
"Rebel Love: Homosexuality," in her *Vamps & Tramps* (New York: Vintage
Books, 1994), 67-92.

I have serious disagreements with Camille Paglia's own views on sexuality and think some of her over-charged rhetoric unnecessary. However, her
response to the Presbyterian document is an important one in at least three
regards. First, she refuses to let us forget the complex emotional, relational,
and physical dimensions of sexuality. Second, if, with the document she criticizes, a church is going to offer an affirmation of sexual (and homosexual)
behaviors without simultaneously offering moral guidance regarding right
and wrong behaviors (other than those connected to oppression and injustice), then we need to be honest, as Paglia is, as to the range of behaviors
available in the larger culture (most of which, incidentally, she affirms).
Third, despite her own self-proclaimed pagan views, she wants the church
to be honestly, robustly Christian in its own views.

37. Camille Paglia, "The Joy of Presbyterian Sex," *The New Republic* (December 2, 1991): 24-27. For her general knowledge on the subject of sexuality see Camille Paglia, *Sexual Personae* (New York: Vintage Books, 1990).

38. Wendell Berry insightfully shows how well many contemporary approaches to sexuality fit with the general, consumerist *Zeitgeist*: Wendell
Berry, *Sex, Economy, Freedom and Community* (New York: Pantheon Books,
1993), 117-173.

39. Kathryn Greene-McCreight, "The Logic of the Interpretation of Scripture and the Church's Debate Over Sexual Ethics," in *Homosexuality, Science,
and the 'Plain Sense' of Scripture*, 245. On the other hand, read within the context of her whole essay, her words hardly represent a cavalier approach.

40. Quoted in Gilbert Meilander, "What Sex Is—And Is For," *First Things*
102 (April 2000): 44.

41. Eugene F. Rogers Jr., *Sexuality and the Christian Body* (Oxford: Black-

well Publishers, 1999), 28-66. It should perhaps be noted that this is only one component of Rogers' argument.

42. For other proponents of this argument, see Jeffrey S. Siker, "Homosexual Christians, the Bible, and Gentile Inclusion: Confessions of a Repenting Heterosexist," in *Homosexuality in the Church: Both Sides of the Debate*, ed. Jeffrey S. Siker (Louisville: Westminster John Knox Press, 1994), 178-194 and Stephen E. Fowl, *Engaging Scripture* (Oxford: Blackwell, 1998), 119-127. See also arguments against this approach in Richard Hays, "Homosexuality," *The Moral Vision of the New Testament*, 395-397, 399-400; Kathryn Greene-Mc-Creight, "The Logic of the Interpretation of Scripture and the Church's Debate Over Sexual Ethics," 253-260.

43. Rogers, *Sexuality and the Christian Body*, 52.

44. Rogers' book represents the most serious attempt I have seen to make a theological argument, on traditional grounds, for the affirmation of homoerotic relationships. This is not to say he is successful. For a review that suggests he is not successful, see Gilbert Meilander, "What Sex Is—And Is For," *First Things* 102 (April 2000): 44-49.

45. Greene-McCreight, "The Logic of the Interpretation of Scripture and the Church's Debate," 246-247. This is similar, formally, to what Luke Timothy Johnson suggests. See Luke Timothy Johnson, *Scripture and Discernment: Decision Making in the Church* (Nashville: Abingdon Press, 1996), 144-148. One could say that what Greene-McCreight is saying is vital for the ongoing integrity of the church.

46. There are many resources I would consult to wrestle with these issues. Along with writings listed in other footnotes, they would include William J. Abraham, "United Methodists at the End of the Mainline," *First Things* 84 (June/July 1998): 28-33; Michael Banner, "Prolegomena to a Dogmatic Sexual Ethic"; Rodney Clapp, "Tacit Holiness: The Importance of Bodies and Habits in Doing Church," in *Border Crossings: Christian Trespasses on Popular Culture and Public Affairs* (Grand Rapids, Mich.: Brazos Press, 2000), 63-74; Marva Dawn, *Sexual Character* (Grand Rapids, Mich.: Wm. B. Eerdmans, 1993); Robert W. Jenson, *Systematic Theology, Volume 2: The Works of God* (New York: Oxford University Press, 1999), 53-111; Gilbert Meilander, "The First of Institutions," *Pro Ecclesia* VI/4 (Fall 1997): 444-55; Oliver O'Donovan, "Homosexuality in the Church: Can There Be a Fruitful Theological Debate?" in *The Way Forward?*, 20-36; Ronald Rolheiser, *Seeking Spirituality* (London: Hodder & Stoughton, 1998); "St. Andrew's Day Statement: An Examination of the Theological Principles Affecting the Homosexuality Debate," in *The Way Forward?*, 5-11; Kiernan Scott and Michael Warren, eds., *Perspectives on Marriage*, 2nd ed. (New York: Oxford University Press, 2001); Rowan Williams, "The Body's Grace," in *Our Selves, Our Souls and Bodies*, ed. Charles Hefling (Cambridge, Mass.: Cowley Pub., 1996), 58-68; and Linda Woodhead, "Sex in a Wider Context," in *Sex These Days: Essays on Theology, Sexuality and Society*, ed. Jon Davies and Gerard Loughlin (Sheffield, England: Sheffield Academic Press, 1997), 98-120.

47. We could do worse than heed Luke Timothy Johnson's admonitions: "The church should not, cannot, define itself in response to political pres-

244 / TO CONTINUE THE DIALOGUE

sure or popularity polls. But it is called to discern the work of God in human lives and adapt its self-understanding in response to that work of God. Inclusivity must follow from evidence of holiness; are there narratives of homosexual *holiness* to which we must begin to listen?" (Johnson, *Scripture and Discernment*, 148).

48. On the fruit of the spirit see Philip D. Kenneson, *Life On the Vine* (Downers Grove, Ill.: InterVarsity Press, 1999).

49. I must thank the many friends who read and commented on an earlier draft of this essay: Jeremy Brooks, Alan and Eleanor Kreider, Phil Kenneson, Wayne and Leabell Miller, Martin Shupack, J. R. Burkholder, Margo Houts, Ted Grimsrud, Jeremy Thomson, Tim Foley, Willard Swartley, Nik Ansell, Gordon Preece, Brian Haymes, John D. Roth, Alastair McKay, Stanley Hauerwas, Fran Porter, Michael A. King, and C. Norman Kraus. I hope I haven't forgotten anyone. Of course, they have varying opinions about my essay. They are certainly not to be held responsible for my approach to this issue. However, all of them have improved the essay through their comments. Thanks.

Chapter 14

Commanded to Keep Wrestling and Wrestling and Wrestling[1]

Carolyn Schrock-Shenk

*I*T WAS DURING MY SECOND YEAR OF COLLEGE that I came to know a gay person well. We were good friends long before I knew he was gay, though in retrospect I remember him dropping hints along the way. He told me he was gay just before we went home for our extended Christmas break. And he told me he had tried to "go straight" many times but had never succeeded. He had never, however, pursued a relationship with a woman as part of that process. He liked me a lot as a person, he said, and thought perhaps he could go straight if I were willing to try a romantic relationship with him. Would I think about it over break? Then we parted.

There are numerous compelling formulas for producing angst in the life of a young person. This was one. I had been raised in the Conservative Conference of the Mennonite Church. I knew with complete clarity that "it" was wrong. Now I had the opportunity, perhaps the responsibility, to help "one of those" get on the straight and narrow path. It was a profoundly disquieting Christmas break.

It was also the beginning of a transformation process for me personally. This was the most intense encounter I had had up to that point with someone considered very "other." More "other" than people from the city or another ethnicity or a different religion. This was an "other" in a foundational kind of way. Yet he was still "Carl," someone I knew and loved. Knowing he was gay did not change that. I remember being glad I knew him well before I knew him as labeled.

I did not recognize at the time what a gift he gave me by telling me. I did not know then how risky it is for a Christian to come "out of the closet." Now I know. Now I remember Carl with a deep gratefulness—for taking the chance on me, for believing and hoping that I would love him anyway.

It was more than fifteen years later that I ventured into the thicket of issues surrounding homosexuality and church membership. I was director of Mennonite Conciliation Service (Akron, Pa.) and had avoided getting involved for some years. It felt too risky, for one reason. And looking in from the outside there did not seem to be a way through. A significant part of me believed, however, that there had to be a third way we as a church could choose. After six years of being involved in various aspects of the struggle, I still believe that, but with much less certainty. This is a difficult path we are walking. How true it is, in this case, that there are no easy answers.

There are times I wonder if Mennonites and other Christian denominations are crossing over some line toward self-destruction through our dealings with homosexuality; I wonder whether the train hurtling toward the cliff can actually be turned around. Has the contemporary church ever faced a more difficult issue than this? Has there ever been a denominational conflict quite so rancorous?

I do not know. I do not want to blow the conflicts we are experiencing out of proportion. I am young enough not to have a good sense of the intensity that may have surrounded other issues the church has worked through. And surely this issue is no more serious than some of those faced by the early church, whose members had to struggle with whether some scriptural directives long considered God's law would apply as well to Gentiles.

Nevertheless, I am deeply troubled by the nature of the conversation in our midst. I am baffled and dismayed by the reality that many people do not even feel free to express their own beliefs and convictions for fear of judgment or some kind of reprisal. While this seems to be more true for those on the "welcoming"—and minority—side, it also occurs for those on the "traditional" side. What have we as a church allowed ourselves to become if we can't talk to each other about our convictions? Where do we go from here?

I have helped guide in-depth processes related to homosexuality and church membership in a variety of places and at several levels, twice in extensive processes at the level of conflict between conference bodies and welcoming congregations. I am convinced, as are many on all sides of these two latter situations, that much good came out of these intense proceedings. Some fruitful dialogue took place. Understanding increased. People on each side were humanized in one another's eyes.

However, I have come away from each situation with a growing sense that we may simply need to stop it all and start over. We have built on a shoddy foundation, and the more we put on top of that faulty beginning, the more likely it is that it will eventually crumble. We simply have not built the necessary relationships, and we are making decisions in anger and bitterness. We have not understood and committed ourselves to a way of discerning together. What is the legacy we want to pass on to our children? Indeed, we may be handing them a "pure" church, whatever that may mean to any of us, but does this risk becoming the equivalent of carefully washing a piece of fruit then eating it with dirt-crusted hands?

What would it take to go back and rebuild that foundation? How do we clean our hands? I'd like to suggest several things for us to consider. They may seem overly simplistic, yet I'm reminded of one person's response when I expressed that fear. He said he and his wife, both professionals trained to help others through difficult situations, realize they often become two-year-olds in their own marital fights.

Understand Each Other's Fears, Reluctance, Suspicions

What is so difficult, frightening, or threatening about dialogue, about engagement with each other around homosexuality? Can we put those fears and threats on the table in an honest and direct way? Can we trust they will be heard and understood without judgment?

I believe we have not given sufficient attention to the gut-level reaction to homosexuality. We name it as a theological and moral issue, (and of course it is), but we have not sufficiently dealt with it as an emotional one. We are deeply reluctant to discuss the sexual dimension of our lives. This is especially true in congregational settings. Added to the general reluctance to discuss sexual issues is a strong sense of fear and aversion in many heterosexuals at the thought of physical intimacy with someone from one's own gender. One theologian talked about the need "to recognize the power of

this involuntary revulsion in many just as we recognize the power
of involuntary same-sex attraction in others."[2] Says another author,
"When it comes to considering homosexuality, until church members first come to terms with their guts, they will not be able to use
their heads."[3] We must acknowledge and address this powerful visceral response. We must find ways to talk together, without judgment or condemnation, about what lives in our gut.

Second, some of us who fear and resist dialogue do so out of a
belief that *dialogue* is simply a code word for "change your mind."
It is difficult to allow oneself to enter a dialogue process if one believes that the dialogue is expected to (and almost always does) lead
to more openness on the issue. This determines the path one is des-
tined to walk, removes the freedom of choice, and renders the
process manipulative. And who among us does not (and should
not) resist manipulation and freedom of choice?

There is a difference between fearing manipulation and fearing
change, though both fears are natural. Manipulation should always
be resisted, for it should have no place in the interactions of God's
people. Those of us who have pushed dialogue and dialogue
processes as a way simply to get the other to change, rather than as
a way to mutual understanding, must examine ourselves, our understanding of dialogue, and our tactics. Yes, the stories and the
conversations are powerful. Yes, they move us, as well they should.
But we must never let go of the understanding that one can truly
listen, understand, respect, and empathize without accepting as
one's own the views of the other. Some of us forget this.

Those of us who fear manipulation must be clear with ourselves
and with each other about this fear and about our commitment to
maintain a freedom to choose our convictions and beliefs throughout any formal dialogue process. We dare not allow our fear of manipulation to prevent us from listening deeply with our hearts or
turn into fear of change.

Those of us who fear change itself (all of us) must constantly remind ourselves that change is the essence of life. Without it we die,
physically, mentally, spiritually, and emotionally. To be truly alive
and faithful, we must open ourselves to change. If we truly believe
God will direct our change, we can relax and enter into dialogue
with less fear.

On the flip side, it is equally difficult to have dialogue when the
simple desire or request for dialogue is viewed as sin, as having
crossed over some line that separates the pure from the defiled.

Those willing to judge as sinful the dialogue process itself, as well as those who seek dialogue, must also do some serious self-examination.

Clearly there are many who see same-sex relationships as a non-negotiable and therefore any discussion seems not only pointless but wrong. However, just as those from the welcoming perspective must acknowledge that there are faithful Christians who believe there is compelling biblical rationale for condemning same-gender sexual activity, so must those with a traditional view acknowledge that there are faithful Christians who believe there is compelling biblical rationale for accepting same-sex committed relationships. We must stop casting each other out of the kingdom. Truly, that is not ours to do. This is a minimum requirement for dialogue.

Third, an enormous amount of peer pressure on both sides helps prevent dialogue. We fear going against the flow of those who generally believe as we do. We must face that pressure and resist it. There are many wonderful examples of people willing to take the risk of going against the pressure surrounding them. At one meeting, a college student gently challenged the prevailing tenor of a welcoming meeting by sharing his perception that "labeling" and "enemy-making" was happening. At another meeting, an older man shook his head after listening to a lengthy exchange about the wrongness of same-sex relationships and said, "I can't see it, I just can't. But neither can I say I never will. There are many things I see differently now than I did when I was a young man." These are examples we would do well to follow.

Fourth, there are fears related to relationships. Some of us fear losing or damaging relationships we do have. There are fundamental differences in many of our families of origin and our congregations, and we fear that open dialogue will damage our relationships, perhaps even split us. Is it possible to be both passionately and openly committed to an issue or belief—and to be equally committed to maintaining or building a relationship with someone just as passionately committed to an opposite view? I believe it is, but we don't have much practice at living out both.

There are others of us who fear building relationships across various boundaries. We tend to find essentially like-minded people who become part of our inner circles, those we allow to shape our understandings and daily activities. Many of us have not been well-served in this regard by growing up in quite insular communities, churches, and schools. We have learned from the moment of our birth to identify, and stay a safe distance from, the other. We simply do not act as if we believe the Quaker notion of "that of God in everyone." Miroslav Volf describes the essence of what we need as "the will to give ourselves to others and 'welcome' them, to read-just our identities to make space for them, is before any judgment about others, except that of identifying them in their humanity."[4] This is particularly critical admonition for those of us on the ex-tremes of either pole.

Finally, it is true that there has been judgment and silencing all along the spectrum. Many of us do not have clean hands. It is im-portant to remember, however, that those of us holding the tradi-tional view continue to have a great deal of power to silence. The "playing field" is not equal. A straight person's flinching at the thought of gay intimacy isn't the same as the dangers faced daily by gays and lesbians when they are honest about who they are. No pas-tor fears loss of credentials and no congregation fears expulsion be-cause they are not welcoming enough. Most of those who disagree with the traditional view do so hoping and praying that they are not silenced, expelled, or the cause of a split. This power imbalance militates against the possibility and promise of dialogue and is added rationale for stopping the process and starting over.

Recognize Our Finiteness

One of the first casualties of conflict is uncertainty. The more conflict escalates, the more certain we become of our rightness. And the more certain we become, the less we listen. Listening is often the second casualty. We are finite human beings and, as such, have a limited view on everything. To allow ourselves to give in to the temptation of believing that we have the final truth, the full under-standing on any particular issue, is to yield to idolatry. It is setting ourselves equal with God, forgetting that we all "know only in part" and all "see through a mirror dimly" (1 Cor. 13:9, 12).

It is no accident that this call for humility, for the "grace of un-certainty" comes in the middle of the familiar "love chapter." It is all about love, for if we truly believe we are not God on this issue, that our truth is incomplete, we can let go of our desperate need to be right, and we can be open to the other. Indeed, we become quite clear that we don't have it all figured out. Imagine how the Spirit could work if this attitude was spread throughout our congrega-tions!

This does not mean, however, that we have no truth or should be wishy-washy about our convictions. We *do* see in part and we must give witness to the part that we see and believe. As my well-traveled and well-educated grandma-in-law used to say, "Don't be so open-minded all your brains fall out."

Therefore our call is to balance any form of "knowing" with the deep awareness of our finiteness. That balancing, then, both clarifies our knowing and opens us to the truth of the other, to listening and respecting and holding the other in reverence even if—or especially if—the other's understanding is very different from ours.

The grace of uncertainty, the awareness of our finiteness opens us up in two critical ways. The first is a willingness to change our minds about the other. This is what happened over the weekend of October 23-24, 1999, in an amazing meeting between Jerry Falwell and Mel White, his former ghostwriter who is now a gay activist. Formerly they had been alienated, and Falwell had bitterly refused to enter into dialogue with White. But now they, along with 200 of each of their supporters, met to discuss their differences over homosexuality.

Falwell apologized for not always loving homosexuals and offered his hope that he would be found showing more love for homosexuals than in the past. He vowed never to "make statements that can be construed as sanctioning hate or antagonism against homosexuals."

White stressed his own readiness to see Falwell as a friend and not an enemy and, even while recognizing that Falwell was not changing his views on homosexuality, to reject efforts by those in the gay and lesbian community to demonize Falwell. Both Falwell and White then endured criticism from their own supporters for reconciling with the "enemy."[5] While I do not know what has happened since, that remarkable encounter ended with the two agreeing to disagree, to love and respect each other through their differences, and to work together to end violence toward gays and lesbians.

The second way the grace of uncertainty opens us is equally critical but perhaps even more difficult. It is a willingness to have our convictions and beliefs shaped and changed by the other and the Spirit working through the other. One sciologist calls this "the experience of alternation—opening oneself to the possibility that the alternative to what one presently believes is true may in fact be true." [6] Adds a Baptist pastor and writer, "To enter into dialogue is to accept the possibility that God could choose to reveal truth through our adversary, or through a new self-discovery as we reveal ourselves before the other, or through the interchange of convictions."[7]

True dialogue has more to do with the attitude we bring—the spirit of openness, humility and blessing—than with the mechanics of the discourse. True dialogue is not a life jacket when the boat is sinking. It is the boat itself; the very careful crafting required to hold it together when the storm of diversity crashes it about.

Commit to Staying Connected . . .

As a facilitator in the thicket of these issues, I quickly became aware of the dangers. The terrain was fraught with landmines and I needed to step very carefully. Was I perceived as neutral enough? Did I have an agenda? Could I be fair? The volatility, the risks, and what was at stake rapidly became apparent to me. There were two poles and the audible voices seemed to be only those at either end: One believed same-sex committed relationships could not be part of the church and any congregation believing otherwise needed to be expelled. Or one believed that same-sex committed relationships should be welcomed and nurtured in our churches. There was no sense of common ground and few voices willing to risk offering alternative paths.

Shortly into my initial involvement, two pastoral leaders renewed my belief that we could find a third way. One spoke with quiet passion in a small group session, the other preached with loud intensity in a conference setting. Their message was essentially the same. Both were clear that they did not agree with the stance of the welcoming congregation in their midst, though both had done extensive reading and study.

In the same breath, both were equally clear and more impassioned that the conference and the denomination should not cut them off. One reminded us that we were one body with a common faith and that cutting off this congregation that had carefully discerned their position represented "an evisceration of the body." The other laid out Paul's taking on the "conservatives" in Galatians and the "liberals" in 1 Corinthians. Then he quoted Ephesians 2:14: "He himself is our peace, who broke down the dividing wall of hostility and made the two one." Pounding the pulpit, he said, "Now when you don't find that verse in your Bible anymore, then we can part ways." This from two pastors who did not share the convictions of the welcoming congregations. From that point on I was no longer neutral in my facilitating. I became clearer with myself, and with those I worked, about my commitment to keeping them connected to each other.

I believe we can clearly disagree and stay connected. There is so much that we share, so many common beliefs, values, and perspectives. There is also much that is not clear about the Bible's application to our lives in the twenty-first century. Of course we will disagree, passionately so. And we must struggle with those disagreements. But the more I understand the life and mandate of Jesus, the clearer I am that we cannot cut ourselves off from each other or judge each other out of the kingdom. We preach love of enemy to the world. How can we do so if we have not even learned to love those in our own body with whom we disagree?

A commitment to stay connected, simply changing the question from *if* to *how*, fundamentally changes the rest of the story. It changes both how we "do" the discernment process and how we end up. This commitment is not about reaching agreement or figuring out who is right. It is not about how we feel about each other or the issue. It is a commitment of the will, a decision to love and respect and listen to the other in the same spirit that we want to be loved and respected and listened to, no matter what. There is a whole spectrum of connectedness, a range of ways to be in respectful, loving relationship with each other. We must find our place on that spectrum. And we must do so *together*, in loving relationship with each other.

I suggest, therefore, that before we as a church enter any kind of discernment process at any level in relation to homosexuality, we begin first with an examination of our relationships. Do they exemplify Jesus-love? Are we praying, worshiping, studying Scripture, talking, listening, eating, and playing with each other? If not, our task is clear.

If so, let us fashion a commitment at the front end to keeping that Jesus-love intact, to staying in close, loving relationship with each other through any kind of discernment process and beyond. This call is for all of us. For many of us on the traditional side, it will require reaching across the fear, the peer pressure, the visceral reaction. For many of us on the more welcoming side, it will require reaching across the passion of changed conviction, understanding that it is not progress or growth to open our hearts to some who need love and acceptance, only to close our hearts to others. This will take much effort and work from all of us. And it will require courageous leadership. But doing so will allow us to move forward with cleaner hands.

. . . for the Long Haul

This is where some of us really balk. We want to stop dealing with "it." We want the discussion to end. We are tired. We want closure. We want to focus on other things. Truly we do need to ease up on the tension, we need to relax, we need to take sabbaticals from the intensity. Certainly we need to focus on other things. We are about more than just sexuality. We can ease up and take breaks easily, I believe, if we agree together that we are committed to each other and to the struggle for the long haul. This issue—and the gays and lesbians among us—are here to stay. Indeed, there are congregations in good standing in their conferences who have many more gays and lesbians than some of the congregations that have been censured.

We will continue to have differences around homosexuality (and every other issue). We can't pretend otherwise. We must figure out how to engage each other with grace, justice, and patience whether we are part of the majority view on an issue or part of the minority. Indeed most of us will have a turn in both.

The pastor who pounded the conference pulpit continued his plea for staying together by saying that "we're commanded to hang in there with each other and keep wrestling with it and keep wrestling with it and keep wrestling with it." May God give us as a church what we need to keep wrestling, to listen openly to the fears of the other, to share our convictions with the grace of uncertainty, and to commit ourselves to each other for the long haul.

Notes

1. Portions of this chapter were adapted from Carolyn Schrock-Shenk, "Let's Talk: Thoughts on Dialogue," *Conciliation Quarterly* 15, no. 2 (Spring 1996), 1, 18-20; and "Due Process: Homosexuality and Church Membership," *Conciliation Quarterly* 18, no. 3 (Summer 1999), 18-20.

2. Walter Wink, ed., *Homosexuality and Christian Faith* (Minneapolis: Fortress Press, 1999), 91.

3. Beth Ann Gaede, ed., *Congregations Talking about Homosexuality* (New York: The Alban Institute: 1998), 25.

4. Miroslav Volf, *Exclusion and Embrace* (Nashville: Abingdon Press, 1996), 29.

5. Accounts of this meeting can be found in such sources as David Gushee, "Falwell, Gay Dialogue Is Welcomed," *Baptist Standard Online* (November 3, 1999), available at http://www.baptiststandard.com/1999/11_3/pages/comment_gay.html; Lynn Rosellini, "Jerry Falwell and Mel White Join Forces," *U.S. News and World Report* (November 1, 1999), available at http://www.usnews.com/usnews/issue/991101/white.htm; Deb Schwartz, "The Odd Couple," *Salon* (October 25, 1999), available at http://www.salon.com/news/feature/1999/10/25/falwell/index.html.

6. Peter L. Berger, *The Precarious Vision: A Sociologist Looks at Social Fictions and Christian Faith.* (Garden City, N.Y.: Doubleday and Co., 1961), 10, 17ff

7..Joseph Phelps, *More Light, Less Heat: How Dialogue Can Transform Christian Conflicts into Growth* (Jossey-Bass, San Francisco, 1999), 25.

Chapter 13

Making Theological and Ethical Decisions: Contextualizing the Bible

C. Norman Kraus

*I*N HIS CHAPTER ON HOMOSEXUALITY IN *The Moral Vision of the New Testament*, Richard B. Hays makes a nuanced distinction between exegesis and hermeneutics. After a careful exegetical survey of the New Testament texts on homosexuality, he concludes correctly that they are "entirely disapproving," but that is not his last word. Following this survey and conclusion he adds a section entitled, "Hermeneutics: Responding to the New Testament's Witness Against Homosexuality"[1] His own response is a conservative one; nevertheless, and this is my point, he recognizes that such a response must take into account evaluative factors other than the exegetical data and deals with the possibilities of different theological responses. Our "response" to the exegetical findings requires a theological-ethical judgment about how the textual material is to be made operational in our very different cultural settings.

It is this second step in the process of understanding how the biblical rules relate to us that has caused so much controversy. And it is this step that necessitates the continuance of churchly dialogue on ethical issues derived from the Bible. The Scriptures are very clear at the exegetical level about subjects like homicide, greedy accumulation of wealth, sexual indulgence, faithfulness in marriage, and vengeful retaliation for wrong done to us. How these basic religious-moral exhortations are to be given authentic "biblical" expression in our greatly varied cultural situations remains a continuing question.

This is the theological task of the church as it lives through the kaleidoscopic changes of history and human culture. Theologians are not trying to evade the "plain teachings of the Bible," as some suggest. Rather, they are recognizing the subtle but real differences in our contemporary societies that sometimes make literal transfers of meaning and application untenable. They are trying to take into account the new data—such as the age of the universe, the psychosomatic nature of human beings—and integrate it with biblical truth. Our physiological and psychological understandings are very different from those of the apostle Paul. Our moral convictions about the roles of husband and wife, and expectations in a Christian marriage differ considerably from those in his culture. Some would also argue that these same kinds of difference exist in the area of sexual definitions.

So the question becomes how we can be faithful to the "biblical" view of life in our twenty-first century western culture. On a subject as sensitive and tense as sexual self-identity, we need to be clear about the exact nature of the question that is being discussed and choose our terms carefully.

No one is arguing, for example, that same-sex erotic attraction is to be *normative* for the human family. Even if its expression in a monogamous covenanted context is recognized as moral, it can only be justified as an exception for a small minority.[2] There is, however, a question whether and in what sense it might be considered *normal*. It is obviously the orientation of only a small minority of the world's population, but we do not label minorities *abnormal*. Other minorities like left-handed people and white people are not normative for the human race, but they are not considered abnormal. Are hetero- and homosexual preferences like the preferences for the use of the right or left hand? This is a sensitive issue for the homosexual minority as well as the majority.

Even as we use words like *normal, abnormal, normative, natural,* and *unnatural,* they have a different meaning for us than they did for men and women in Paul's world. We define these terms by different standards. The ancients defined normal or natural by what seemed obvious—"the way it always was." Men's and women's roles, for example, had been shaped by ancient precedent designed to take care of physical and social needs and were assumed to be "the natural order of things." Contemporary standards for gauging normality include factors like statistical correlation, genetic causation, and pragmatic experience (whether caused by human manipulation or "natural forces"). Cultural relativity is recognized in the definition of the normal.

In the biblical culture the normative was defined by one's religious tradition—what was understood to be God's will. If God ordered distinction between clean and unclean animals and birds, that ordinance was binding because it came through the recognized divine authority (Lev. 20:25-26). No one asked what ethical principle lay behind it. People were simply to obey the commandment.

Of course we still speak of God's will as the norm for human behavior, but we generally determine what that will is by appealing to standards of righteousness/justice which we consider ethical rather than the other way around. We distinguish between a strictly *religious taboo* and an *ethical principle*, and we associate the divine imperative with the ethical.

This change in our presuppositions and modes of evaluation is just as characteristic of so-called theological conservatives as it is of liberals. Indeed, the argument between conservatives and liberals has been largely one of evaluating and adopting these present-day cultural presuppositions, values, and thought forms. These kinds of subtle differences complicate the theological-ethical process of identifying behaviors as moral and immoral across cultures.

Most scholars of the ancient Middle East agree that there was no recognition of homo- and hetero-"orientation" in what are generally referred to as "biblical cultures." In the case of homosexual behavior, the ancient writers, including those in the Bible, did not base their moral evaluation on the orientation of the individual but on the holiness taboo which demanded separation from the pagan cultures. They did not ask how God's people should treat people of same-sex orientation or what the *ethical* implications of such orientation might be.

Such relatively recent classification has raised a bevy of new questions, to which the biblical materials do not speak directly. How is a nonvolitional psycho-physical orientation to be rated on the normative scale? Is heterosexual orientation "normal" because the vast majority of people are heterosexual, and homosexual orientation "abnormal" because only a small minority belongs to this group? Does an orientation have a moral value? Should it be compared to inherited physical weaknesses or psychological tendencies like the tendency (which may also have physical roots) to alcoholism? How does an orientation affect the moral character and thus our evaluation of a behavior?

These are the kinds of considerations and questions theology works with. In some cases the transfer of biblical ideas and values across cultures is more simple than in others. In many of these "easy" cases the theological steps are mostly implicit. But implicit or explicit, simple or complex, we always have to make these intermediate steps in interpreting and relating the gospel for our time and society.

In the rest of this essay, therefore, I want to explore some of the factors we must take into account when we contextualize the biblical teachings on same-sex erotic relationships.

What is the Theological Task?

The general Council of Ephesus of 431 A.D. was called by the Christian emperor Theodosius II to settle the Nestorian controversy. The debate was about how Christ's humanity and deity are related. Central to the debate was the question whether Mary should be called "God-bearer" or "Christ-bearer." Given their presuppositions and definition of words, both sides were at least partly correct, but the issue was highly politicized and each side insisted its position was the only orthodox one. In this contentious atmosphere, as one author puts it, "Apparently neither party made the slightest effort to understand the other. In fact, each condemned the other for beliefs that the condemned denied, but which his accuser insisted were the implications of his position."[3]

In this Council the theological task was perceived to be formulating an infallible definition of Christ's nature, which all those who claimed the name catholic or orthodox would be required to accept. They understood the outcome of theological dialogue to be the "dogma," namely, what all members of the true church are required to acknowledge as truth. And "truth" was defined as that which always and in every place—universally—had been acknowledged by the church as the word of God. There could be only one universally true statement which was in no way affected by the great variety of cultures represented at the Council. They did not recognize their formulation of the "dogma" as a contextualization of biblical teaching, but as the only infallible interpretation of biblical teaching.

Today we recognize that Nestorians and Cyrilians, who were the protagonists at the Council, were very much men of their time and particular cultures. Their differences were in large part verbal. Their theological formulations were inescapably cultural contextualizations. Although Bishop Nestorius was rejected and banished from the realm, today those of us in the Protestant tradition agree with him that Mary should not be called "Mother of God." Indeed, the final statement of christological dogma, which was formulated at Chalcedon twenty years later, rejected both men's statements and settled for an ambiguous formula which allowed the theological (cultural) examination of the issue to proceed.

My point here is that the "truth as it is in Jesus" (Eph. 4:21) transcends the contextualized formulations of ecumenical councils. Theology is a process of contextualizing, i.e., finding the way to state and apply the truth in Christ to our many cultural contexts.

But why do I introduce this fifth-century theological debate about the formulation of doctrine into our discussion of an ethical interpretation and application of the Bible today? In the first place, to point out that all biblical interpretation across cultures is a *theological* process. And in the second place, to emphasize that the theological process is *culturally conditioned*.

These early church theologians far too naively identified their culturally conditioned theological orthodoxy with "the Bible says," and insisted that all the churches east and west had to affirm a uniform statement. To achieve this they used the power of the ecclesiastical and political institutions at their disposal. Thus they turned the interpretation of the Bible into a political power issue. Indeed, in 449 A.D., at the second Council of Ephesus, they actually came to blows. The winners imprisoned and banished their opponents. So long as the cultural nature of theological decisions is not recognized and only one final right position (orthodoxy) is insisted on, division into political majorities and minorities remains a real danger.

Our attempts to understand and apply ethical teachings of the Bible are, if anything, more culturally conditioned than the formulation of theological doctrines. Even within the New Testament itself, one can trace this culturally conditioned theological process. For example, while Paul states early on that women and slaves are equal to husbands and masters "in Christ" (Gal. 3:26-28), he does not make monogamous marriage or the manumission of slaves the only ethically acceptable practice in his first century world. Neither does he give any inspired advice about the limits of Christian participation in the political process or the military establishment, although he is very clear they should follow the pattern of agape as Jesus did. The church has had to make decisions on these subjects based on theological judgments drawn from Scripture, and it has differed in these judgments from time to time and place to place.

Those who believe that Christians shall not join the army cannot base their conviction on any one explicit prohibition. Nowhere does it say that followers of Christ cannot be police or military personnel. There are many teachings that give us a basis for the theological-ethical decision of the church to discourage its members from being a part of the modern military machine. However, there is no biblical text for making a dogmatic ruling that everyone who is part of the armed forces shall automatically be excommunicated from the church. In fact, we in the Anabaptist-Mennonite tradition have not followed such a rule or practice. Especially in our cross-cultural missions we have taken cultural-political differences into consideration as we tried to maintain the agapeic ideals of Jesus and the New Testament.

Likewise no New Testament teaching explicitly regulates the sexual relationship of homoerotic individuals. For example, there are no New Testament passages that say same-sex attraction is a sinful inclination resulting from the Fall of Adam. Or that people with same-sex attraction must either remain celibate or contract a heterosexual union. Or that they may not form intimate companionable unions. Or that they should not adopt and raise children.

There *are* passages like Romans 1:18-29, which we will consider later, that condemn pagan sexual perversions, and others that warn that *arsenokoitai* and *malakoi* do not belong to Christ's kingdom. (I use the Greek words because part of our problem is the proper definition of these words.) How this inspired advice to the first-century church is to be applied in the life of the twenty-first century church of North America is a valid and open question that needs careful theological consideration.

In both of these examples the church's decisions are not the result of a simple exegesis of scriptural passages. Both involve us in theological evaluation and contextualization, and given our human frailty, such theological activity cannot result in universal dogma. *Theology is the ongoing cultural vocation of the church. It is a dialogical process in which the clash of cultural and personal perspectives tests the validity of their partial truth.*

Hermeneutical Considerations
in the Theological Dialogue about Homosexuality

The context and nature of the biblical prohibition of same-sex sexual intimacy requires us to pay special attention to the hermeneutical rules that guide theological contextualization. The outright prohibition of same-sex genital activity is found only in the Holiness Code of Leviticus (18:22; 20:13), which is repeated in Deuteronomy as a law against cult prostitution (23:17-18). This context is significant for an understanding of the nature of the offense and its severe penalty.

The purity laws in the Mosaic Torah, referred to as the "Holiness Code," mark out the ethnic religious boundaries of Israel. They are based on the Lord's special deliverance from Egypt (Lev. 11:45). They define the distinctive guidelines for Israel's separation from the idolatrous cultures of the pagan nations and the special "holiness" required by Yahweh for his people. Their moral imperative is based on Israel's self-understanding as a nation separated unto the Lord. The laws regulating Israel's diet, sanitation procedures, cattle husbandry, and the like do not have a universal moral application as the prophets, Jesus, and Paul recognized. Such proscriptions have the force of religious moral tradition rather than rational ethical legislation for the well-being of the body politic.

The complication is that laws like "Thou shalt love thy neighbor" are also found in the Holiness Code. Some of the social-ethical rules for governing the nation given elsewhere are also included in the Levitical code. No clear distinction is made within the code itself, since its purpose is to define the difference between Israel and its pagan neighbors. However, the rules found exclusively in the Holiness Code have the character of cultural, ritualistic taboos that define the character of sacred space (temple) and time (worship). Indeed, they are given as ritualistic or ceremonial requirements for participation in the worship of Israel's God. They are proscriptions that set people and things apart for sacred purposes. Israel was to be God's holy (sacred) nation.

How are we to distinguish between religious taboo and ethical mandate? In the first place, the Torah itself and the Prophets treat these laws differently. The Holiness Code itself was not propagated by the prophets and officials of the body politic but by the priests as the direct instructions of Yahweh for his worship. It includes many social and personal regulations of everyday life that have no ethical parallel in our modern society. Some of the regulations, such as of family life and sexual activity, would even be considered morally questionable in our contemporary church communities.

To understand the religious and moral atmosphere that gave rise to such sacred taboos, one should note the story of Achan, who kept for himself some of the booty from Jericho which had been "devoted" to God and was to be destroyed (Josh. 7). Because he dared to hide in his tent "devoted things" set apart for God alone, all of Israel was defiled and needed to be cleansed and "sanctified" again. This required that the land be completely rid of Achan and all his family and possessions. So they were stoned and burned with fire to cleanse the land and its people of their desecration. Just so, the homosexual taboo prohibits an act that will defile Israel in Yahweh's sight and requires death to cleanse the land of an "abomination."

Homosexual behavior is associated with idolatry as a rejection of God's law spelling out the ritualistic separation of Israel from pagan neighbors. Along with other sexual conditions and practices we no longer observe, it is described as an *impure, shameful* practice, not as an *unjust* or *inequitable* one. We must make the hermeneutical decision whether all homosexual sexual activity is to be classified with ritual taboos or whether it belongs with other ethical admonitions also found in the code. Is it a "shameful" act or is it an "unjust" activity? We have made this a significant distinction in the contextualization of many ordinances in the Mosaic legislation.

It seems clear that same-sex genital activity among males is explicitly proscribed only as a holiness taboo. Of course same-sex sexual intercourse is denounced in other biblical references also, but there is every indication that the moral compunction behind its condemnation is essentially that of the holiness taboo. Homosexual sexual activity is condemned in the Bible as a matter of shame and defilement, not, for example, as an infringement of justice or as malicious injury. Its proscription has the character and sanction of a cultural taboo rather than of social ethical legislation. The moral compunction that enforces it stems from religious convictions. It is viewed as an unclean, degrading act that confuses the cultural roles assigned to the sexes and threatens the procreation of the race by wasting semen.

While it is severely condemned and its penalty is death, it does not have the same kind of ethical character and sanction as the laws defining political, social, and economic justice. Its offensiveness lies not in the injury it does to others but in society's repugnance and contempt. It is viewed in Israelite society as a desecration of one's self-awareness as a member of God's people.[4]

All this is not to argue that homoerotic sexual expression no longer has moral or religious implications. Rather, our point here is that for theological-ethical purposes of contextualization in today's society, the biblical proscription must be treated as a taboo of the Holiness Code, not as an ethical social principle based on scriptural fiat.

While homosexual sexual acts are prohibited only in the Holiness Code, their prohibition cannot be lightly dismissed like, for example, the rules about nocturnal emission of semen that made Israelite males unclean. They have social implications and effects which must be taken into account. But the fact that the sanction for the biblical prohibition is ritualistic separation (holiness), not personal-social moral consequences, requires us to reconsider their essential moral status when we apply the proscription in today's society. Its applicability to our contemporary church life must be evaluated and adapted like other purity regulations. If homosexual sexual acts are to be considered still as "unclean," defiling behavior, we must offer a theological and ethical rationale beyond the mere citing of biblical references.

This distinction between the cultic (religious) taboo and the ethical principle raises the question of theological and ethical contextualization. How shall we deal with cultic taboos of the Old Testament in our contemporary culture? And how shall we deal with the ethical commands? First, we observe that the concept of holiness is defined in ethical terms in the writings of the prophets and in the teachings of Jesus. The holiness of God is described not in terms of the divine otherness and sacred mystery, but in terms of God's righteous character—God's truthfulness, faithfulness, justice, and mercy.

Jesus challenged cultic and tribal tradition and set a new standard for human behavior. God's ethical character becomes the pattern for the meaning of holiness. To be "holy as God is holy," then, is defined by Paul as imitating God the Father, whose character was disclosed in Christ. The ethical and humane take precedece over tribal religious tradition, which in the New Testament is called "the tradition of the elders." Jesus' words, "The Sabbath was made for humankind not humankind for the Sabbath," are a good example of this.

According to this principle, therefore, the cultic taboos may be rejected, modified, or continued in their original form. This was the problem with which the New Testament church wrestled in the cases of circumcision and the clean and unclean taboos.

This leads to the question whether the taboo on homosexuality is to be rejected, modified, or continued. As said above, not all the laws in the Holiness Code are of the same moral weight, and in light of the almost universal deep-seated aversion to homosexuality the Levitical code should not be dismissed out of hand. Further, the strong condemnation of it in the first chapter of Romans has led some to feel it should be continued with minimal modification.

What then is the intense compulsion that lies behind the Levitical proscription? A number of things have been suggested. Certainly the definition of the male and female roles in the patriarchal cultures of the ancient Near East provide the context. Masculine self-identity as the dominant sex, and the association of penal penetration with that domination played a part. The passive role in male homosexual activity was considered the most shameful. Indeed, forcing the defeated foe to endure such abuse was a sign of one's power and victory.

John W. Miller has argued that the taboo is related to the growing sense of the male's fathering role in the family and the father's progressive realization that the female mothering function is a counterpart of his role. Miller writes, "For this same reason sexual conduct disruptive of marriage (rape, incest, adultery, homosexuality, transvestitism, sodomy) was identified and opposed to a degree unprecedented in the ancient Near East."[5]

Following this same line of reasoning, the taboo may also have been for protecting sons, and or fathers from abuse by their fathers or sons. (Note the story of Ham's disgracing of his father, Noah.) Perhaps it was also for the protection of the wife's rightful place in the family, and of her sexual and inheritance rights. In the first-century Roman world it was not unheard of for a husband-father to bring a male sexual partner into the family circle. This translates into the contemporary fear that any modification of the taboo will threaten "family life." Along with this there was a strong reaction against pagan idolatry and its worship patterns, which included manipulation of the forces of nature through ritual prostitution, both hetero- and homosexual.

All these reasons make it clear that the proscription of homosexual acts was not simply an arbitrary taboo to be dismissed in an enlightened contemporary culture. Even though its prohibition should continue to be viewed as a holiness taboo, as I am arguing in this essay, theological and ethical evaluation of its moral character and pragmatic consequences must be taken seriously. The constitutive moral character of the prohibition should affect our hermeneutical methodology and possibly its final ethical and pragmatic resolution.

Evaluating Sexual Offenses

In our evaluation of the sins prohibited in the Levitical purity code, we have traditionally made clear distinctions between ceremonial or ritualistic proscriptions and ethical rules. We have dismissed the ritualistic legislation as part of the old covenant and have retained the ethical regulations which are also found elsewhere in the Covenant Law. Sexual aberrations like fornication, adultery, incest, and prostitution have been classified as ethical regulations and enforced as part of our moral code. Other sexual functions, such as menstruation and involuntary excretion of semen, are no longer considered defiling. They are simply ritualistic regulations like the rules about eating blood or unclean meat, or touching a corpse.

Homosexual sexual intimacy and masturbation have for centuries been placed in a class by themselves. They were classified as "unnatural" acts and thus immoral. Like birth control, which was also considered unnatural, these acts of ejaculating semen prevented the possibility of procreation, and procreation was the end and justification for sexual gratification. More recently, masturbation has been declassified by many as a moral offense, but homosexual acts have retained all the moral opprobrium that they carried as religious taboos in a shame culture. Indeed the word *unnatural* connotes the same feelings of revulsion and shame that the impurity codes evoked.

In today's Western society we have little memory of when even in our own culture social and religious taboos played a large part in regulating social behavior. Certain actions and physical conditions were considered shameful and wrong, not necessarily because they were strictly unethical, but because they were "strange." They "just were not done!" The *taboo* had a strong *moral* sanction.[6]

Because we have forgotten, we tend to dismiss the seriousness of the biblical taboos of the clean and unclean. Biblical purity taboos have little significance in modern Western culture, where the moral impact of shame is no longer experienced as a social compunction. We reduce them to ceremonial legalisms since we no longer feel the compulsions of shame which enforced them, and this inevitably trivializes the moral standing of the holiness taboos.

This has led us to underestimate the moral significance of the ongoing struggle in the New Testament church about what is "clean" and "unclean." Thus we have failed to see the moral significance of dealing with homosexual behavior under the holiness rubric. Since we did not appreciate the moral gravity of the Holiness Codes, we reclassified homosexuality into categories of social ethics to give moral sanctions to our feelings of repugnance. This in turn has led to dealing with homosexual activity as criminal action.

In our society social violations are assigned ethical status and classified as crimes to be given moral gravity. Traditionally homosexuality has been dealt with in this way. Thus the decriminalization of homosexual practice among consenting adults has opened the way for its moral re-evaluation in the minds of many.

However, for many others who take the biblical injunctions seriously, the moral scandal remains. They take the homosexual taboo literally as a sweeping ethical prohibition. These biblically sensitive Christians have simply assumed that the weight of the homosexual taboo is to be given an equivalent ethical meaning and sanction in our social morality.

While their position should be taken seriously, it is our contention that both of these positions represent a theological or contextual shortcut that reduces the moral gravity of the question and leads to inappropriate solutions. We should neither trivialize the problem of homosexuality, on the one hand, by lightly dismissing the holiness taboos, nor, on the other hand, over-evaluate its moral status by a simplistic identifying of the taboo with personal and social ethical mandates. We should not dismiss the biblical categories of "purity"—shame and uncleanness—and substitute today's categories of rational morality when we evaluate the ethical character of homosexuality.

Neither should we translate the definition into terms of "transgressing the law of nature," or classify homosexuality with social ethical sins of prostitution, adultery, fornication, or kleptomania, all of which involve deceit and abuse of other people. The Old Testament discusses same-sex sexual acts in terms of shameful, unclean behavior. When we contextualize the Levitical categories of sin, we must evaluate the nature of the offense and the reasons they are assigned such harsh sentences before we evaluate their moral and religious gravity for the church today.

The writers of the New Testament did not dismiss the moral gravity of unclean and defiling behavior. Rather, they profoundly redefined the religious and moral values which enforced its prohibition. Both Jesus and the apostolic council at Jerusalem retained the moral categories of shameful, dishonorable, defiling, and unclean, but they redefined the moral parameters of impurity (Mark 7:21-33). Thus our controlling guideline should be whether *homosexual sexual intimacy is "unclean" according to the standard of holiness laid down by Jesus and the New Testament church.*

Defining Holiness in the New Testament

What is the new rationale and character for holiness in the early Christian community? What makes a thing or action unclean—unholy and displeasing to God? What makes an act shameful or unclean? We must ask how holiness is redefined in the New Testament based on the new revelation in Christ.

In Romans 14:14, 20 (cf. 1 Cor. 6:12-13) Paul lays down the principle that nothing is unclean in itself (cf. Mark 7:19; Luke 11:39-41). The unclean is identified as "works of darkness" and described with words like carousing, drunken dissipation, sexual excesses, indecent conduct, quarreling and jealousy (13:13), not with specific acts or social regulations. For example, husbands and wives are to love and respect each other as a matter of "righteousness and true holiness," but the patterns of family structure are not legislated. While some even in Paul's day twisted this "freedom from the law" to cover obvious immorality (Gal. 5:13; 1 Peter 2:16), the principle must be taken seriously, especially in the crossing of cultures with their different perspective and values.

The same external behaviors do not necessarily have the same moral meaning in every culture.[7] For example, in an earlier period of European history, sexual intercourse between couples anticipating marriage was generally acceptable as a test of the woman's fertility. Few couples were virgins when married. Or in biblical culture a man, even if married, was required to impregnate his sister-in-law if his brother died before his wife had born children.

This same kind of difference in cultural perspective and moral evaluation can be observed with reference to homosocial behavior. Cultures of Africa and Asia vary considerably in their tolerance and moral rationale of same-sex expressions. The same has been true in the history of the "Christian" West. Such cultural variations do not establish the ethical principle, but they do demonstrate the need for sensitive contextualization, and they suggest that we should not expect a single, universal application of the purity taboos with reference to pagan cultural practices.

In 2 Corinthians 6:14–7:1 we have a good example of the way Paul defines and applies the concept of religious purity or holiness. He quotes from Leviticus 26:12 and a medley of other Old Testament passages admonishing the church members to keep themselves separated from that which is unclean in pagan culture (v. 17). He exhorts them to "cleanse [themselves] from every defilement of body and of spirit making holiness perfect in the fear of God" (7:1). In this context he indicates that the unclean, which he identifies with "darkness," is associated with idolatry, lawlessness, and unbelief. This is quite consistent with the concept in the Mosaic Torah but without the accompanying social codes.

By way of comparison, in 1 Corinthians 6 Paul gives a concrete example of being "mismatched" with unbelievers and wrongdoers. The Corinthian Christians were actually submitting disputes to the judgment of such "unbelievers." This, he says, is shameful—a basic category and sanction of holiness regulations (v. 5). Then he lists a number of offenses that characterize the "wrongdoing" of those who do not belong to "the kingdom of God."

The list begins with fornicators, idolaters, and adulterers (v. 9). These are the classic Hebrew categories of unholiness. The idolatry of Israel is described as adultery, meaning in this context unfaithfulness to God. And fornication, as Paul defines it in the following verses, is joining the members of Christ with a prostitute. Bodies of Christians are temples of the Holy Spirit, and prostitution desecrates that temple. Fornication, which he describes as prostitution, is the controlling metaphor for unholiness in this passage. In Paul's world such prostitution was both homosexual and heterosexual without distinction between the two. Unholiness is depicted with the metaphors of "fornication and adultery," which are acts of idolatry.

The next word, *malakoi* (NRSV, "male prostitutes") is also associated with idolatry. Temple prostitutes, both male and female, were in some eras part of the ritual manipulation of fertility. They were serving as priests and priestesses of idolatrous gods attempting to control the creation process. Thus Paul may be describing unholiness with the same kind of idolatrous sexual metaphor.

The word *arsenokoitai* refers to sexual aggressors who take advantage of weaker males like slaves and youthful pupils (pederasty) to demonstrate their superior power and satisfy their lust.[8] Whether this classification of unbelievers is to be understood as also associated with idolatry or is a kind of transition to a new classification of the "unholy" is not entirely clear. The words that follow describe antisocial, harmful behaviors, which are also characteristic of "unbelievers and wrongdoers." If the latter association is intended, the emphasis is then on the abusive nature of the act. In any event Paul returns to the case of fornication at Corinth to continue his admonition to holiness.

Thus it seems clear that, for purposes of contextualizing this passage, we cannot make a simple identification of *all* homoerotic behavior with unholiness. Obviously all idolatrous and harmful antisocial behaviors are unholy according to our passage. It is not so obvious whether all homoerotic attraction and consensual expression is idolatrous and antisocial. In fact, except for the Levitical code, the Bible does not enumerate concrete rules for homoerotic behavior. We are left with the task of applying broader principles and parallel instructions for heterosexuals to our modern situation. Our task of theological contextualization cannot be one of simply applying a literal translation of this ancient text to a vastly changed modern culture.

In Ephesians 4: 24 we have the clearest example in the New Testament of the shift that has taken place in the definition of the holiness. Christians are exhorted to clothe themselves "with the new self, created according to the likeness of God in true righteousness and holiness." Here true righteousness and holiness merge into one picture of the godly life. No longer are the ritual taboos of the Holiness Code definitive for Christian behavior. The behaviors which "grieve the Holy Spirit of God" (4:30, 5: 3-5) are fornication, impurity, obscene and vulgar talk, and greed, which is identified with idolatry.

Holiness is defined in ethical terms of righteousness. Impurity is identified in verse 19 with "licentiousness" (unrestrained, lascivious sexual indulgence, what we today would identify as sexual addiction) and debauchery (excessive indulgence in sensual pleasure). In verses 25ff the unholy is described as anger, unfaithfulness, deceit, abuse, taking selfish advantage of others (stealing), giving priority to physical desires such as eating, drinking, self-indulgence (laziness), hostility, angry quarreling, malicious talk, and so forth.

Thus we conclude that the moral gravity of the Holiness Code which enumerates the acts that God despises is in no sense to be minimized. *It is, however, disassociated with the ritualistic taboos and given a thoroughly ethical definition based on the example and teaching of Jesus.* Holiness is "truth [as it] is in Jesus" (v. 21). It is following the pattern of Christ (v. 20). "True holiness" defines the moral image of God with which the new self is identified (v. 24).[9]

When the New Testament writers approach the issues of sexual ethics this way, they redefine the parameters of holiness (the "clean" and "unclean"). For example, castration no longer bars one from God's people. Eunuchs are welcome in the kingdom of God. Celibacy is even recommended as a special calling. Polygamy is discouraged, and concubinage becomes unacceptable. Sexual intimacy of the marriage bed is to be kept undefiled by fornication and adultery (Heb. 13:4). Its legitimacy is not defined by menstrual cycles or the possibility of procreation.

This shift in the moral classification of behaviors raises the question of the holiness taboo on same-sex sexual intimacy. Does the taboo define an essential ethical boundary? Is all homoerotic arousal a sinful temptation and the physical expression of such sexual attraction sin? Or is the taboo to be evaluated and regulated according to a new understanding of holiness? Does that which sanctifies heterosexual intimacy also sanctify homosexual intimacy? And vice versa, do the same things that make heterosexual intimacy unholy also make homosexual intimacy unholy? This is the shape of the theological-ethical question we face, and there is no one text that can infallibly answer it for us. We must make cultural adaptations based on all the best information that we have at present, and we must remain sensitive to the leading of the Holy Spirit as we move from culture to culture.

Romans 1:18-29: A theological crux

The broad intent of the passage in Romans 1:18-29 is quite clear. Exegetically, little is in dispute in this passage. Our questions arise from the fact that Paul makes a broad cultural judgment without being behavior-specific. Thus the question of what Paul is condemning in our own society becomes a matter of theological-ethical judgment. Granted that promiscuous, seductive, hedonistic, abusive, exploitative homoerotic behaviors, such as are indicated in verses 28-29, are both sinful and immoral, but do such adjectives characterize all homoerotic intimacy in today's society?[10] Given our more recent understanding of the origins and involuntary nature of same-sex attraction in a small percent of the population, does Paul's condemnation include chaste, monogamous, socially responsible same-sex intimacy for such people?[11]

As in other texts where he uses rabbinical thought patterns and arguments to make his point, in this passage Paul is using the language and patterns associated with the Jewish purity code. He describes same-sex erotic expression as "impurity" (*akatharsian*), "shameful" (*atimias*), and "unnatural" (*para physin*). Each of these modifiers comes directly out of the purity codes which defined pagan uncleanness and marked the boundaries for Israel's cultural assimilation with the surrounding cultures. His own implicit list of illicit behaviors is culturally conditioned, and he assumes that his readers share his own cultural perspective. Thus we must associate this passage with Israel's Holiness Code and bring those interpretative assumptions and methods to bear upon it.

Following the common pattern of Jewish anti-Gentile propaganda, Paul describes the condition of "unrelieved darkness" (Dodd) in Gentile society as the inevitable and instinctual consequence of idolatry. Like other first century Jewish writers, such as the philosopher Philo, he condemns Gentile culture as vile, malicious, deceitful, insolent, "God-hating" (vv. 28-29). As a result of such wickedness, God has given them up to degrading passions among which are perverted sexual practices. He names passion for same-sex genital acts as an expression of God's "wrath" against paganism, and his disgust is obvious. However, he does not elaborate on the precise customs and practices to which he is referring. He assumes that the amplification of specific homoerotic behaviors included in the condemnation will be obvious to the reader. Thus for us such specific definition becomes a matter of theological-ethical judgment.

For the purposes of making ethical decisions, recognition of this cultural character of Paul's argument is significant. It suggests that we must treat this passage like other culturally conditioned doctrinal and social teachings in the Pauline epistles, such as teachings on women's place in the church, slavery, marriage and divorce. Just as we have contextualized these teachings, adapting our specific behavior patterns to preserve their intent, so we must wrestle with the contextualization of Paul's teaching in this Romans passage.[12]

Two specific aspects of Paul's argument need careful consideration. The first is whether this condemnation along with the precise word *arsenokoites*, used in 1 Corinthians 6: 9, reaffirms the Levitical blanket prohibition of same-sex intercourse as a continuing New

Testament regulation. The second is the meaning and moral sanction against same-sex intercourse as "unnatural" (*para physin*). We shall look at these briefly in this order.

Those who hold that the Levitical proscription of any and all homoerotic sexual intimacy remains in force for Christians base their position on two lines of thought. The first is etymological, having to do with the origin of the word *arsenokoites*. Its use by Paul is the first known use in the early church. Whether or not he coined the term, it is traced to the literal translation of a Hebrew term describing the Levitical prohibition. Thus it is argued that Paul's use of the term most likely "presupposes and reaffirms" the Levitical prohibition and gives it a New Testament endorsement.[13]

This conclusion is reinforced by the fact that the Romans passage clearly reflects the character of the Holiness Code, as we noted above. The scandal and sanctions of homoerotic behavior which Paul castigates in the first chapter of Romans have the shame orientation and characteristics of the purity taboos which separated God's people under the old covenant from their pagan neighbors. And Paul is undoubtedly trying to draw the lines of separation between Christians and their contemporary Gentile neighbors.

In and of itself the etymological connection of *arsenokoites* with the Greek translation of the Levitical prohibition, although interesting, hardly establishes the legal purity taboo as a New Testament moral requirement. The word, whatever its etymology, has its own meaning and association in the first century ethical writings, and these suggest that it refers to coercive, abusive homosexual activity.

The argument from Romans 1:16-27 would be more persuasive except for the fact that there is a crucial theological change in the polemical rules of engagement. For Paul, the "righteousness" that separates followers of Christ from unbelievers is a *faith righteousness* (Rom. 1:16-17), not that "of the law." "Holiness" has been redefined as we noted above. We are not tied to the letter of the Levitical prohibitions.

This new freedom from the law must be defined. It does not mean that we are free to sin (6:1). We are not free to live lives of ungodliness and idolatry which characterize the pagan world under God's wrath—a wrath which manifests itself as a life doomed to self-destroying wickedness (1:29). Indulging in physical passions of greed, gluttony, or malicious anger; degrading our bodies in compulsive, licentious sexual behavior, whether heterosexual or homosexual, is beyond the pale of holiness. And clearly the homosexual

274 / TO CONTINUE THE DIALOGUE

patterns Paul refers to in this passage transgressed precisely these spiritual boundaries. But we are left with the task of defining the parameters of sexual behavior that fall within the boundaries of holiness redefined. Hence it is not in the spirit of Paul's gospel to simply transfer the legal, blanket proscription of homosexual intercourse in the Levitical code to the New Testament.

The second aspect of Paul's argument that needs elaboration is his use of the word *physis*. According to both the NRSV and the NIV translations of verses 26-27, Paul says that same-sex sexual intercourse is "unnatural" (*para physin*). The question is what he means by "natural" when he appeals to *physis* (nature) as his authority.

The translation of *physis* as "nature" and the description of same-sex intercourse as "unnatural" can easily leave a wrong impression in our context with its biological and evolutionary concepts of "nature." On the one hand, it might leave the impression in the minds of those who do not make clear distinctions between "orientation" and "act" that Paul labels homosexuality as a biological abnormality. In that case "unnatural" suggests that homosexuality is a genetic accident, and the unfortunate person should be pitied. More likely, among conservative readers it suggests a perversion of the created order and thus a moral abnormality. Translated into theological jargon, it is viewed as a result of Adam's fall. "Nature" is understood as God's intended order for creation, and homosexual orientation is a phenomenon of "fallen nature."

We might note here that this understanding of the problem makes it difficult to maintain a clean distinction between the sin of orientation and the sin of practice. The usual comparisons for orientation in this case are inherited physical and psychological weaknesses like alcoholism, kleptomania, and inability to control one's temper. The orientation itself is understood as a species of lust and temptation to do evil which must be kept strictly under control. In those traditions, like the Mennonite, where sin has been more narrowly defined as a voluntary act of yielding to temptation rather than as the condition of our human existence, the distinction between orientation and practice has seemed an ideal solution. However, we need to be reminded that heterosexual attractions are also a part of "fallen nature," and they are not equated with lust. When we identify same-sex "attraction" with lust, a "fallen" or "unnatural" passion, we are putting it into a special "sinful" category.

Others with a more psychological orientation have understood "unnatural" to refer to what is natural or unnatural to the individual. Thus, they argue, same-sex genital relations are not unnatural to one of homosexual orientation. Those who interpret this way point out that Paul is describing an unnatural practice on the part of ungodly heterosexuals who exercise their perverted sexual passions. Therefore, they hold that the passage really does not speak to our contemporary issue of what is natural for those who by nature have homoerotic rather than heteroerotic sexual attractions.

The problem with this interpretation of "natural" is that Paul is describing a prevalent social condition, not an individual psychological one. He is describing in general terms what he believes to be the perversion of gender roles in the ancient society. Women are acting like men, (note he mentions this first!) and vice versa men are submitting to the debauchery of acting like or using men as women. This is what is so "unnatural," and he roundly condemns it as an example of what happens when humankind refuses to recognize the sovereignty of God and his intended order for society.

In traditional Roman Catholic theology, nature and natural have been equated with the order of creation (*ktisis*). Many in the Protestant tradition who would not follow the full natural theology of Catholicism still hold to this equation of "nature" and "creation" in this context. Accordingly it is held that here Paul is arguing from an intended creation pattern much as he did in 1 Corinthians 11:7-10 where he bases the relation of men and women on his reading of the creation account. Thus it is asserted that, according to Paul, homosexuality is "unnatural"—a perversion of the created order of nature and, by extension, a desecration of God's image.

This identity of the natural with the creation order gives Paul's words a theological import in our modern culture which is dubious. By *physis* Paul is appealing not to a biological order as we understand it in the modern world but to the traditionally recognized conventions of his Jewish world, which he understands to be the natural order of creation. In this passage he does not mention *ktisis* (creation) although he may be implicitly alluding to it, and he does not, as he does in 1 Corinthians 11, use it as justification of his point of view. As Martti Nissinen puts it,

> In antiquity, *physis* expresses a fundamental cultural rule or a conventional, proper, or inborn character or appearance, or the true being of a person or a thing rather than 'nature' in a genetic-biological sense, as a modern reader would perceive it. Accordingly, "unnatural" is a synonym for (seriously) unconventional.[14]

This does not give the passage less weight. It simply underscores the necessity of treating it as a contextual word, and not as a divine oracle defining a universal fiat of the Creator.

There can be no question that Paul disapproves of same-sex practices as he knew them in the pagan world of his time. Indeed, many pagan writers also disapproved! The *physis* to which he appeals is itself a Stoic concept. The question is whether the homosexual practices condemned in the ancient pagan society—which included pederasty, involuntary use of slaves, husbands bringing a male consort into the marriage relation, cultic prostitution, rape of subordinates, and all kinds of promiscuous behavior—encompassed all possible forms of intimate homoerotic behavior.

Certainly Paul's condemnation of all then-known same-sex behaviors would include those promiscuous, profligate, irresponsible, dissolute sexual behaviors which in the popular mind have been associated with a "homosexual lifestyle." Paul's condemnation would include any behavior which harms or takes advantage of another person's weakness for one's own pleasure. But does that condemnation include homoerotic intimacy between consenting, covenanting, same-sex attracted adults functioning responsibility within the societal framework? It seems doubtful that Paul knew or was speaking about this kind of a situation.

My own conclusion is that we best follow the pattern of interpretation we have used in the contextualization of Paul's direct instructions in 1 Corinthians 11:1-17 to tackle what Helmut Thielicke calls this "complicated and basically insoluble problem."[15] Granted, the two issues are not commensurate. Neither does Paul give explicit instructions on homosexuality in the Romans passage as he does to the Corinthians, but the hermeneutical method required to understand his position and contextualize his admonitions is the same. Both passages appeal to *physis* as understood in the ancient culture, and Corinthians also appeals explicitly to *ktisis*. Except for those groups which still insist on a literal interpretation of both Paul's theological argument for a hierarchical pattern in male-female gender roles and a literal application of the symbol of covering the head, we have taken considerable liberty to adapt both his theological argument and his cultural application.

I have argued in this chapter that it is the role of theological dialogue to interpret and apply or contextualize the biblical text, and that answers to the questions that cluster around homosexuality require a theological and ethical *judgment* in our present cultural context. Such an evaluation requires us to find right questions as well as right answers.

I have suggested that questions such as the following are important for contextualizing the biblical teachings: What lies back of the Levitical proscription that gives it legal and moral sanction, and how does this rationale relate to today's issues? How is *holiness* redefined in the New Testament? Knowing what we do today about the physical and psychological nature of homosexuality, how should it be classified—as pathological affliction, arrested social development, spiritual rebellion, moral perversion, minority bio-psychological trait? Is "orientation" a kind of lust, temptation, moral or psychological weakness, or simply a minority "normality"?

Answers to such questions cannot be read as a simple matter of exegesis from the text. That is why a continuing dialogue seeking further understanding and consensus continues to be necessary. For the present "dialogue" may be the only form consensus can take.

Notes

1. See Richard B. Hays, *The Moral Vision of the New Testament*, (New York: HarperCollins, 1996), 394ff.

2. Not only is it a matter of continuing the human race, the vast majority of the world's population are incorrigibly heterosexual in their preference of sexual partners, and the question is not about the moral legitimacy of *bisexual* sexual intimacy. Thus to make same-sex erotic intimacy normative for more than the small minority of those people so orientated would involve multiple partners.

3. Jerald C. Brauer, ed., *The Westminster Dictionary of Church History* (Philadelphia: Westminster Press, 1971), 301.

4. Jacob Milgrom, a Jewish biblical scholar and author of the *Anchor Bible* commentary on Leviticus, has made an exhaustive study of the Holiness Code. He concludes, "The common denominator of all the [sexual] prohibitions, I submit, is that they involve the emission of semen for the purpose of copulation, resulting in either incest and illicit progeny or, as in this [homosexual] case, lack of progeny. . . . In a word, the theme . . . is procreation. . . . Semen emission, per se, is not forbidden; it just defiles, but purificatory rites must follow. But in certain cases of sexual congress, it is strictly forbidden, and severe consequences must follow"; see *Leviticus 17-22: A New Translation with Introduction and Commentary* (New York: Doubleday, 2000), 1567.

At the end of his analysis of these regulations, he concludes, "Finally, it is imperative to draw the logical conclusion of this discussion for our time. If my basic thesis is correct that the common denominator of the entire list of sexual prohibitions, including homosexuality, is procreation within a stable family, then a consolatory and compensatory remedy is at hand for Jewish gays (non-Jews, unless they live within the boundaries of biblical Israel, are not subject to these laws; see chapter 20 COMMENT D): if [Jewish] partners adopt children, they do not violate the intent of the prohibition"; *Leviticus 17-22*, 1568.

5. See John W. Miller, *Biblical Faith and Fathering* (New York: Paulist Press, 1989), 253.

6. An interracial marriage, or even an ancestor from the wrong social class, was simply not mentioned! A mentally disabled child or a child with a birth deformity was hidden away from sight. A family member suffering from "insanity" was locked up or "put away" in an asylum. Left-handedness was an embarrassment and children were forced to write with their right hands. Most things associated with sex were "hush hush," especially irregular physical conditions, and epithets like "sissy," "tomboy," "old maid," "strange," and "queer" were actually control mechanisms in the community. All of these are examples of *taboos* of more or less serious moral implications. Homosexual behaviors were dealt with according to this moral classification.

7. See Gilbert Herdt's article on "Homosexuality" in *The Encyclopedia of Religion*, vol. 6, ed. in chief Mircea Eliade (New York: Macmillan, 1987), 445-453 for a good survey of the anthropological data on this point.

8. See Donald Blosser's chapter in this book.

9. In his article, "The Rationale of the Laws of Clean and Unclean in the Old Testament," Joe M. Sprinkle concludes that

> Nevertheless, arguably some principles of the purity laws and sacred space are still applicable. Even in the OT cleanness and uncleanness metaphorically symbolized moral purity and impurity, and moral purity is still a Christian ideal. . . . The evangelical Church would benefit if it devoted more attention to themes underscored in the laws of clean and unclean. . . . Though separation from Gentiles is obsolete for Christians, separation from the world is not. . . ." *Journal of The Evangelical Theological Society* 43, no. 4 (December 2000): 636.

10. Richard Hays has written a definitive exegesis of the Romans 1 passage with which I fully agree—this despite whatever final contextual position one might take. Attempts to read Paul as uncertain or ambiguous about the practice of same-sex coitus seem doomed to failure! Or to read his use of "natural" to include those whom we now know to be same-sex attracted "by nature" seems disingenious. Further, there is no evidence that Paul himself changed his mind on this point as he did in the case of the acceptance of Gentiles. Nevertheless, the question of a contemporary critical contextualization remains as it does also in the 1 Corinthians 11 passage. See Richard B. Hays, "Relations Natural and Unnatural: A Response to John Boswell's Exegesis of Romans 1," *The Journal of Religious Ethics* 14, no 1 (Spring 1986), 184-215.

11. People indulge in same-sex genital intimacy for a variety of reasons. Many, if not all, of these reasons cannot be morally justified. In these cases "reorientation," which is the basic meaning of the Greek word for repentance, is indicated. The crux of the ethical issue arises in the case of the 1-3 percent of the population that are biologically and involuntarily disposed to

same-sex attraction by genetic and early childhood conditioning. Is it justified, e.g., to assume that such an involuntary orientation should be treated
as a call to celibacy?

In his paper on "Jesus and Paul on Homosexuality," Willard Swartley
also recognizes this point. He writes, "Whether the gap [between biblical
and modern culture] also extends to homosexual practice in any and every
form now is the issue of current debate, i.e., is practice now to be regarded
differently than it was in Scripture?" (Unpublished paper, 6.)

12. It should be noted that some scholars have argued that Paul's use of
the regulations of the Holiness Code's condemnation of homosexuality
should be read as the New Testament's affirmation of its continuing moral
relevance for Christians. This is a possible theological position which should
be carefully considered. I have offered a possible alternative hermeneutical
approach which, so far as I know, has not been carefully considered in Mennonite circles. It is these kinds of theological and cultural considerations that
need to be evaluated in coming to a final position.

13. See Hays, *The Moral Vision of the New Testament*, 382. Hays refers to
Robert Scroggs' earlier work, *The New Testament and Homosexuality* (Philadelphia: Fortress Press, 1983) to substantiate the etymological connection.

14. Martti Nissinen, *Homoeroticiam in the Biblical World, a Historical Perspective*, (Minneapolis, Minn.: Fortress Press, 1998), 105.

15. Helmut Thielicke, *The Ethics of Sex* (New York: Harper & Row, 1964),
291.

Chapter 16

Responses

Mary Schertz, John A. Lapp, Willard M. Swartley, Sheldon Burkhalter, Richard A. Showalter, Elsie Steelberg and Donald Steelberg, Elaine K. Swartzentruber, George R. Brunk

Courage to Continue

Fifty years is a substantial part of one life but a blink of an eye on the stage of church history. Still, in the fifty years that have constituted my life thus far, I have witnessed several "revolutions" or turns in the tide of how and why we do things in the church. The first was the completely bloodless revolution, rhetorically speaking, of the disappearance of the covering on the heads of churchwomen in what was then known as the Old Mennonite Church. Although there were a few attempts to stem the tide, for the most part the covering just disappeared, quietly and permanently.

Divorce and women in ministry were other revolutions—neither of which can be characterized by the word *bloodless*. There were instances of angry rhetoric, of intense difference gone awry, leading people on many sides of the issues into sins of thoughtlessness and pride—on conference floors, in congregations, and in our church institutions. With time, of course, one forgives or forgets some of that intensity. The anger fades, the hurts dissipate, the past begins to look better than it was in reality.

But even allowing for the softening effects of passing years, neither of these instances equals the present debate on homosexuality for sheer rage. The names we are calling each other and the way we are talking to and about each other, the dismissing of each other's convictions out of hand, and even demonizing each other have reached the point of apparent impasse. There is open despair among us. We are not sure whether there is a way through the morass of feelings and ideas to a solution with which we can live together in peace. We wonder if there is hope.

The essays in this book represent an attempt to find a way through that confusion, and the writers and editors are to be commended for the clarity of the content and the calm tone. A friend moving into conference leadership told me recently that his vision for his new responsibilities in the emerging church is to be a "non-anxious presence" in these troubling times. That goal seems to me to be a worthy one and one to which this book also contributes. If we are to find a way through this Slough of Despond, it will be through reducing the anxiety and continuing the dialogue. The major strength of this group of essays is that they shine the light on some other paths we might take in the journey. They provide hope that there are trails out of the bog and that we can, if we choose, explore the hills together.

I have three responses to these chapters, responses which, unfortunately, do not seem to fit neatly under a common theme.

Several of the writers call for a "safe place" to continue the dialogue. I want to say a simple "Amen" to that call. We must both crave and insist on common safety as the first necessity. What it will take to achieve that goal may well be the most difficult part of the journey because we will need to put the common safety before our own safety. For instance, there is safety in numbers, but the numbers who are willing to speak to this issue are not high.

Common safety would require those of us who have taken personal safety in silence to speak. Common safety would also require those of us who have taken personal safety in encamping with those who are like-minded to risk opening our minds and enlarging the circle. Finally, common safety would require us to live by ground rules that guide and limit our conversations. C. Norman Kraus, in his introduction, suggests that dialogue calls for suspension of an ultimate resolution, the recognition of all participants as full members of Christ's body, granting freedom of conscience under the lordship of Christ, and reliance on grace.

To make serious use of these suggestions would mean letting go of our own assumptions of how we think the church should proceed with this dialogue. To make serious use of these guidelines would also create a healthier and kinder conversation, one in which we might all find safety. These are costly suggestions, demanding personal and corporate courage. Is our collective commitment to the church sufficient to engage in such dialogue?

My second response is a "thank you note" for the historical perspectives that have been made available in this book. Chapters 5, 6, and 7 recount and analyze the stories that lie behind the Mennonite denominational Saskatoon and Purdue statements. Many of our attempts to understand and live with these resolutions have been reductionistic. It is very helpful, crucial even, to carry a deeper awareness of this history into our continuing dialogue.

I was, however, disappointed that the document *Human Sexuality in the Christian Life* did not receive more attention in this recounting of the history. This document preceded the resolutions that were passed by the assemblies and was intended to be a guide for studies undertaken by congregations in continuing the dialogue. I have yet to discover a congregation that actually used the document, though there must surely be some. I have used this undervalued book in teaching seminary classes and because it is genuinely and broadly dialogical it has been very helpful to students. It is a worthy forerunner and companion piece to consider alongside *To Continue the Dialogue*.

My last response has to do with the Bible—I am, after all, a biblical scholar. I am pleased and grateful that David Schroeder, Don Blosser, and Reta Halteman Finger have worked directly with the biblical texts and that other authors have incorporated textual concerns and issues into their hermeneutical and theological work. It is such careful work that will eventually help us live faithfully with the biblical witness and lovingly toward each other.

I am also concerned, however, about how lay people read the Bible and take ownership in discerning its guidance and wisdom on contemporary questions. In addition to the kind of work presented so powerfully here, we also need to think hard about how the conversation about the Bible in congregations and other settings can move beyond Bible "soccer," where we concentrate on getting the ball and scoring points. Some of our creative energy and hard thought needs to center on how people understand the Bible and live with it canonically.

One of the exercises that has been useful in the seminary classroom is to ask students, before they wrestle with an ethical issue, to name the ten biblical passages "without which they cannot live." It is a simple question to ask, less simple to answer, but it has a rather remarkable effect on the conversation. We not only learn how people think about the Bible, but we understand better the commonalities and differences among us. Whether that exercise would be helpful in a congregation, I do not know. But I think we need to put as much energy into such practical matters as we do into the larger matters of hermeneutics and theology.

I am glad this book is being published. It represents a courageous next step in the journey. It also models, in many ways, what needs to happen more widely and at more levels. Certainly there is more to be said and more to be done. But what is said and done from this point will benefit greatly from the courage and integrity of these writers and these essays. The journey we may well be walking for the rest of our lives is enriched by these efforts.

—*Mary Schertz, Professor of New Testament,*
  Associated Mennonite Biblical Seminary

Questions and Considerations to Keep in Mind

When I was in first grade I started to stutter. In the days before speech therapists were readily available, my parents took me to the family physician. He asked, "Are you trying to make your son write with the right hand?" My parents admitted to such. Dr. Paul, as we called him, thought there might be a connection. I started writing with my left hand. The stuttering stopped. I have wondered whether homosexual orientation might be like left-handedness, though of course with more far-reaching implications.

From these essays I have learned more about homosexuality and the debate surrounding it than I previously thought necessary. My personal interest continues to be more with the character of the welcoming and discipling church than with homosexuality per se.

When I told a friend about this book, he expressed a doubt that "any book will bring the debate to an end or even improve it. I think people have stopped listening to each other."

If this is the case, how will a book premised on the necessity of dialogue get partisans involved in the conversation? Will these chapters capture the attention of those who pray for "help to be the kind of persons God wants us to be"? Will these essays also address those who pray expecting "God to help us solve our problem"? Different approaches to spiritual wisdom are as much part of this dialogue as is understanding sexual diversity.

One of the most important ingredients for attracting church people to this dialogue is a healthy dose of traditional Mennonite humility. There is so much we do not know about this topic and many others. At its best the Mennonite tradition has practiced a humble willingness to accept some differences and yet be one peoplehood. We have been separated by geography and conference affiliations while maintaining a shared set of convictions and practices.

Reading such a volume stimulates many questions, more than can be addressed here, but here is an initial list:

(1) Why is this issue so conspicuous at this moment of history? Why didn't churches feel compelled to address this issue before the 1970s?

(2) How does homosexuality compare as a priority concern with other contemporary moral concerns in our congregations?

(3) What does it mean for the church to be focused on a single issue apart from other dimensions of moral discernment?

(4) What are the implications for worldwide church relationships when one sector of the church adopts a moral position different from those held by the majority church overseas?

(5) Where is the locus of discernment on such an issue in the church? Do traditional church polities help us in this regard?

(6) How can the beloved community of God be lovingly accepting of people with differing lifestyles and orientations?

There is a story making the rounds of a group of pastors discussing how to deal with a gay church member. Most of the pastors wanted to draw a sharp line and forbid membership. Another pastor asked, "What are the other behavioral practices on which you are disciplining members?" There was an embarrassed silence!

This story illustrates a basic issue raised by this debate. Are we indeed disciplined bodies of the faithful? Perhaps if we had a coherent set of understandings for church discipline the discussion of homosexuality would be easier.

I am apprehensive that by focusing on a single issue of moral discernment, we may unwittingly make the church into a special interest group. To avoid this we need renewed clarity that the church is a community, the body of Christ, committed to making the way of God known in the world. For participants in this community their first and primary commitment is to be obedient to Jesus the Christ. Specific moral concerns ought to be addressed as part of the continuous struggle to be obedient rather than as occasions to draw boundaries for new distinctions.

Dialogue should be a normal process of church life, an expression of a living community based on mutual respect and trustful relationships. If we are committed to one another, then we cannot stop listening to one another. We cannot avoid dealing with complex issues. I have wondered whether homosexuality is the real issue or whether it has become an easy and convenient boundary marker for congregations and conferences who are in danger of losing the capacity to be disciplined communities of obedient disciples.

One of my current preoccupations is to reflect on the globality of the church. What does the worldwide character of the church mean for local and regional congregations in their definition of faith and practice? If the majority of Mennonites are African, Asian, and Latin American (the South), how do we take their convictions and insights seriously in the development of doctrine and practice in North America? This gets difficult when there are conspicuous differences, even gaps, in experience and understanding (in both directions).

The worldwide Anglican communion discovered such a gap at their most recent (1998) Lambeth meeting of bishops. British and North American bishops have welcomed practicing gays and lesbians in their congregations while the majority of bishops in the South reject homosexual practice and strongly oppose same-gender unions. I suspect, based on anecdotal evidence, that Mennonite church leaders in the South share many of the same convictions as do the Anglicans in the South. (These differences are also evident among the several ethnicities in North American churches). One reason for considering homosexuality a local congregational or conference issue is to keep it off the denominational and hence international agenda.

How do we in the North deal with these differences? Will we have the patience and magnanimity to listen to the concerns of the South before moving persistently ahead? I am not comfortable having North American definitions or solutions imposed on sisters and brothers who have not been party to the conversation. Neither am I comfortable with the church in the North ignoring convictions from the South by acting unilaterally.

Discussion of this issue is made more difficult because homosexuality has become so highly politicized in Western culture. There are aggressive groups who want to make acceptance of homosexuality a public right. There are equally aggressive groups who insist that a stable society requires shared cultural norms and that homosexuality does not fit these. These points of view are advocated by well-organized and well-financed pressure groups representing different social classes, different cultural markets, and different religious alliances. Congregational discussion and that of the larger church is much impacted by contemporary cultural dynamics. I also wonder if the sexual promiscuousness of our culture has something to do with the contentious character of this debate. In such an environment should not abstinence or celibacy be considered an option for true holiness, whether heterosexual or homosexual?

The burden of this volume is not to bring premature closure to the search for Divine light on this discussion. We should indeed "continue the dialogue," with the goal of enlarging our capacity to be both welcoming (evangelistic) and covenantal (disciplined) congregations and conferences. I hope many congregations and conference groups will find the spiritual resources and take the time to work through the process suggested in appendix two of this volume as well as several chapters on how discernment might unfold. Authentic dialogue will require Spirit-led discernment, a Christ-like love of the church, and the Father's self-giving desire for the reconciliation of all people.

—*John A. Lapp, Executive Secretary Emeritus,*
  Mennonite Central Committee

Binding the Spirit-Powers

The week during which this response was to be written, to meet the publisher's deadline, was also the first week of a forty-day fast undertaken by our congregation to pray for the wounds of our conference and wider church surrounding membership and homosexuality issues, and for our congregation's long-range planning as well. Fasting itself was defined in a variety of ways—not food only, since for some of us it would be unwise to fast from food. So during the first day I sought to discern how and in what way I was to fast. I was also pondering what type of response, if any, I should make to this volume.

On the second fast day, as I wept to discern both what my fast should be and how to respond to this book, it became clear to me that my fasting should be a prayer, to be prayed in the morning and evening, and as often during the day as possible. It came to me in these words: "Lord God, in the name of Jesus Christ I bind those spirit-powers that agitate and confuse, incite dissension and division. Pour out upon us, O Lord, your Spirit to create love, trust, and freedom to be your faithful people."

This book is entitled *To Continue the Dialogue*. The title is a bit presumptuous, since it could be questioned whether dialogue has been occurring. The title may also connote the notion that positions are set, that those from both sides need to dialogue with each other. My sense is that a different stance might be more fruitful. That is a call to *discernment*. I suggest that the articles in this book that will help the discernment process most are those by Schroeder, Reimer, and Nation. Others may give helpful background information. Kraus's first chapter risks trivializing the issue by comparing it to other issues from the Mennonite past. But this issue plagues all Christian denominations. Nonetheless, Kraus's concluding five points are helpful.

As I put it about a decade ago to a gathering of conference leaders on this topic: what we have before us on this issue is the task of adjudicating between four sources of moral authority:

Holy Spirit

Scripture   **Experience**
                                                                          (including Reason)

**Teaching and Tradition
of the Church**

For Anabaptist-Mennonites, the faith-community, with appeal to Scripture, is also a source of authority. But on this issue the community is divided. Scripture and church tradition clearly regard same-sex genital relationships to be morally wrong. Even if one were to accept interpretations of the key Scriptures that neutralize these texts in relation to current same-sex practices (see Blosser and Grimsrud, part B; material which for me at some crucial points is quite a stretch to interpretation with integrity), it is not possible, in my thinking, to construct a *biblical* case authorizing same-sex genital relations as morally right. In that regard, this issue differs from the slavery, war, and women issues I wrote about in 1983.

Numerous voices from experience call for rethinking the issue, highlighting the need for (pastoral) support of homosexual people and their families (e.g., Smucker). Some voices, also from experience but not represented in the volume, speak of possible transformation of same-sex desire-practice to heterosexual desire-practice.

Often it is said that science (see Keener and Swartzentruber in this volume) in its various forms—biology, pyschology, and so forth—is another source of authority. On this I demur. Science can provide helpful information but does not determine moral authority. *Is* does not produce an *ought*. To put this matter simply: the inventions of the automobile or of the Internet have revolutionized our way of living, but they have not altered the moral authority of the ten commandments.

We continue to search for the leading of the Spirit on this matter. I propose an experiment to help in this discernment: for same-sex partners to read and prayerfully reflect on Romans 8:1-27—a text that connects us to the Holy Spirit in multiple ways—and seek to discern what happens to the desire. Reporting from a dozen cases, where both partners confess Christian identity, would be helpful. This would be practical field research to illumine further Nation's article.

When all is said and done, what matters most in our living and dying is whether we are "in Christ" and led by God's Spirit. This is *the* important issue about our identity, not sexual identity. Sexual identity should not be a core-identifying feature of those born again by the grace and power of God. Whether we live or die, *who we are in Jesus Christ* is what really counts.

Missing from the volume is analysis of Western culture, which may indeed be the kingpin in this whole debate, since our church brothers and sisters in other cultures do not perceive this as an issue in the way it has afflicted Western churches. Wouldn't a critical analysis of our own culture represent the distinctive role that Anabaptism might play in this contemporary debate? To what extent is this phenomenon a Western urban cultural construct, exported to other cities worldwide, as David Greenberg, sociologist at University of Chicago, has argued? Is it possible that our sex-sated culture has provided the crack through which the demonic enters in this matter—and that this is why the issue is so divisive? Compare Walter Wink's view on the myth of redemptive violence and the domination system that characterizes American culture.

Finally, on the fifth day of my fasting, when this response was to be submitted, my scheduled Scriptures included Hebrews 4:12, a key text on discernment, fastened itself on my mind:

> Indeed, the word of God is living and acti ve, sharper than any two-edged sword, piercing until it divides soul from spirit, joints from marrow; it is able to judge the thoughts and intentions of the heart.

So, let the discernment, and possibly dialogue, be bathed in prayer-command that frees us from agitation, confusion, dissension, and division, and let it be empowered by the living and active word of God. Let us also remember what many of us learned early on in Sunday school, "Love one another." That love extends to accepting—even if we do not affirm the practice of—those who understand themselves to be homosexual, as well as those who disagree with us in construing how the moral authority of Scripture and church bears on this issue.

—*Willard M. Swartley, Professor of New Testament*
Associated Mennonite Biblical Seminary

Freedom to Discern

I heartily welcome this first effort among Mennonite scholars to publish a book-length resource examining biblical, theological, and pastoral issues about homosexuality. Chapters about discernment process and recent history in the Mennonite Church's struggle to be faithful and compassionate amid intense conflict are also revealing. While some readers at either end of the spectrum may wish for more inclusion of their voices among the chapters, I applaud the effort made here to bring careful scholarship and love for the church to our continuing discernment. My prayer is that this publication will encourage further scholarship and refinement of conviction as we earnestly seek God's will for the sake of Christian unity, compassion and faithfulness.

We expect Christian scholars and academics to be responsible; they also need freedom and space if their gifts are truly to serve the church. Such freedom is especially difficult in a situation of polarization and fear as seems to mark today's debate over homosexuality. We need to remind ourselves that ever since creation freedom and responsibility have gone together hand-in-hand in the Judeo-Christian faith. From the first humans in the Garden, through the prophets, Jesus of Nazareth, the apostles, and the reformers of the church, freedom and responsibility have been risks and gifts God chose to offer humanity. This book finds its place in this tradition. Spiritual renewal and growth occur where faith is examined, challenged, lived and shared.

As a pastor and delegate to the 1987 Mennonite Church biennial assembly at Purdue, Indiana, I expected leaders to help the church with published materials to "continue in loving dialogue." I had found the Mennonite study guide, *Human Sexuality in the Christian Life* (1985), very helpful, especially in placing homosexuality in the broader context of sexuality and in identifying key questions and issues for further study. I remember reading a host of books in the late 1980s such as by Boswell, Nelson, Scroggs, Furnish, and Smedes (noting the significantly different ways authors treat the biblical text) to sort out my own convictions. For a time, I regularly visited a gay Mennonite who was dying of AIDS.

I looked for resources and settings within the Mennonite church where biblical interpretation and pastoral experiences could be examined and tested. To my surprise, almost nothing of a scholarly nature appeared in our church papers or in book form. Meanwhile the debate in the church turned to polity issues, as conferences weighed whether or not to discipline congregations that dissented from church statements. While I sympathized with the conferences' struggles, it felt to me like actions toward congregations were being taken on the basis of a short list of "proof-texts," two-minute conference speeches, letters to the editor, and two lines in a confession of faith. Without scholarly resources, it also felt like we were telling our students and young adults, "Don't ask questions or wonder why because denominational statements have told you so!"

Sadly, debate at this time hovers like a heavy cloud over the "final" (time will tell) stages of merger between two Mennonite bodies. *To Continue the Dialogue* makes no claim to be the final word; it is an invitation to a careful reading of the Bible and compassionate care. Christian freedom and integrity require this kind of process.

Without neglecting the importance of pastoral care and polity in the way the church lives out its faith in Christ, I want to underscore the essential role the Bible plays in our life together. As several of the authors in this book note, we must not weary of returning again and again to the biblical account nor leave it to scholars alone. As Christians who take ethics seriously and how Christ would have us live, we know the importance of reading the Bible carefully.

In my personal journey with ethical issues I have often noticed that the emphasis one places on particular texts, or the neglect of others, determines how one chooses to believe and to live as a Christian. If one relies on a proof-text approach, this becomes all the more problematic in relation to such an issue as homosexuality, since it seems evident that only a handful of Bible texts speak directly to the issue. This is where biblical theology (the particular text understood in its immediate context as well as the entire Bible) becomes so important.

Let me illustrate with two issues about which Christians histor-ically have strongly disagreed. On graduating from a Mennonite high school, I thought my pacifist convictions were firmly rooted, so I could hold my own in a discussion with non-pacifists. "Armed" with several texts from Jesus' Sermon on the Mount and the injunc-tions of Paul like be "at peace with all," I went off to an evangelical college where most of my new friends were children of fathers who had served in World War II. The discovery that my friends had more Scripture texts in favor of their position than I could find (from war in the Old Testament to Jesus and the centurion and Paul's teaching that government "does not bear the sword in vain") led to serious doubts about what my church had taught me. Well into my studies at an evangelical seminary, I began to discover that biblical themes (biblical theology) from creation and the Fall (Gen. 1–6:6) to human reconciliation through Jesus' death on the cross enabled me to em-brace peacemaking and nonviolence as God's will for Christians.

A similar controversial subject in relation to which we see the possibility of handling texts in a variety of ways is the role of women in the Bible. Those who emphasize male "headship" and female "submission" come out on one side while those who argue "neither male nor female" come out on the other. Since Paul referred to the creation story when using these words, I discovered a biblical theol-ogy that portrayed both male and female created "in the image of God." They then share as caretakers of the earth and as partners who cherish and complement each other. Not until the Fall de-scribed in Genesis 3 do we read of hierarchy, in the warning that "'he shall rule over you,'" which surely is not prescriptive (see my "Male and Female: Hierarchy or Partnership?" *Gospel Herald*, Octo-ber 14, 1975, 725-728).

Returning to homosexuality, much attention has been given to the several commonly used proof-texts, and appropriately so in light of the uncertainty of what some of the Greek words mean. For example, Paul's use of *arsenokoitai* in 1 Corinthians 6:9, often trans-lated "homosexual," is so rare in ancient Greek literature that its meaning is not clear two millenniums later. Blosser in his chapter sees significance in the appearance of the word in lists implying "economic exploitation," even as he does not elaborate on the seem-ingly closer meaning in the Jewish-Greek translation of Leviticus 18:22 and 20:13: a man should not lie "with a man as with a woman."

Nevertheless, I suggest that biblical theology offers essential foundations and guidance for understanding the teaching of the

292 / TO CONTINUE THE DIALOGUE

Bible regarding homosexuality. Here again a careful reading of the creation account I believe is crucial. "Male and female" in the creation story is about much more than reproduction and survival of the human race. Instead the text in Hebrew poetic parallelism emphasizes the divine image in the creation of male and female. In other words, our male and female sexuality somehow reflects God's image. The second creation account in Genesis 2 moves in a similar direction: for the male "there was not found a helper as his partner" until God brought a woman (*isha*) to the man (*ish*), someone like him but uniquely different.

How are we to understand homosexuality, and how then shall we live? I suggest we must continue with biblical theology by examining the major themes of the Bible, such as the Fall, redemption, justice, welcoming the marginalized, holiness, mercy, grace, spiritual transformation, self-control, mutuality, and community. As with the questions of war and the role of women, biblical theology enables us to move beyond selective proof-texts regarding homosexuality to discern God's will.

The task of biblical interpretation and scholarship is not easy. So the church must exercise patience and allow responsible freedom for our gifted scholars to aid us. *To Continue the Dialogue* calls us to this process and offers us a language with which we can talk with each other.

—*Sheldon Burkhalter, Director of Church Relations, Goshen College*

Let's Not Continue the Dialogue.

I speak for those many of us who are weary of "dialogue" as apparently assumed in this volume. Even a cursory reading of the preceding chapters leads me to the conclusion that in general, the writers have no conclusions. Or if there are conclusions, they remain either hidden or partly disavowed.

Therefore, I do not accept dialogue as an accurate description of these essays. They might be termed reflections, historical observations, tentative new directions, subtle (or occasionally not-so-subtle) challenges to the confessed faith of a community. But "dialogue" is, I believe, a potentially dangerous misnomer.

The fact is that "I have no standpoint except that point where I stand" (Lesslie Newbigin, *The Open Secret*, Eerdmans, 1995, 163). Neither does anyone else. As an evangelical Anabaptist who is part of a particular witnessing community gathered around Jesus, I engage freely in open interchange with all kinds of people, but my primary stance is that of a witness. Insofar as I engage in fruitful dialogue, I can do so only with clarity about where I stand.

However, not only do I have an individual place to stand, but also I have entered into a corporate place to stand: "in Christ" or "in the body of Christ." As a body, we have freely confessed our faith in Christ who died for our sins and rose again, the power of the Holy Spirit to transform lives, our acceptance of the authority of the Word of God, our eternal hope, and our commission to share with the world in suffering love.

As part of that historic and contemporary confession, we recognize the pervasiveness of sin in personal and corporate life in every culture, including our own. For us, this includes homosexual behavior. This is not a greater or lesser expression of our fallenness than other sins. It is not a sin to be especially highlighted or judged. It is not connected with a "phobia" of some kind. But it is sin.

With some exceptions, the overarching intent of these essays appears to be to question that understanding. If so, the dialogue is not within these pages, but it will have to be with many others, like me, who are not well represented here. The reality is that millions of ordinary believers like me around the world have been engaged for many years in such interchanges with many in our cultures. We rejoice more and more strongly in the One who has demonstrated again and again his power to change lives, including even (though not always) "orientations."

So those who are looking for some new place to stand, something different from what I have outlined briefly here, may rightly be exasperated with our apparent intransigence. Please forgive us. We do not mean to be stubborn, to function as judges of all others, or to reject association with those who are different from us.

Rather, our greatest joy is to herald the freedom and new life which we have found in Christ. We do become weary of invitations to "dialogue" which seem in some way to invite us away from that freedom.

"To continue the dialogue"? If by that is meant, "looking for a new place to stand," I have no enthusiasm. Indeed, I'll probably normally just say, "No, thank you." But invite me to understand, then witness? You bet.

—*Richard Showalter, President, Eastern Mennonite Missions*

294 / TO CONTINUE THE DIALOGUE

It Could Be Even Better

It has been twenty-three years since I started as a resident in psychiatry and first began to think about same-gender attraction. The compelling reason was the homosexual patients I began to see whose lives were being seriously and negatively affected by society's treatment of them. As the years progressed, I learned that there is evidence that homosexuality is not chosen. There are biological components, some better defined than others. Although the roots are multiple, evidence clearly demonstrates a large biological component. The Keener/Swartzendruber chapter is excellent on this point. In my view this means that the church has to decide to reach out and embrace rather than exclude. Few churches are including.

Because of the theological emphasis of this book, I have asked my husband to join me from this point forward in our response to this book.

Elsie: Shortly after the 1980 General Conference Triennium (a churchwide gathering of the General Conference Mennonite Church, GC), I was asked to serve as GC representative on the committee that produced the sexuality study resulting in the Saskatoon/Purdue denominational statements. Our broad purpose was to study sexuality itself, so it was disheartening for the only consideration in those assemblies to be on homosexuality

As is noted in this book, the promise to continue dialogue and study has not been kept by the denominations. Unfortunately, "dialogue" has been limited to tiresome volleys in the church press. I recently had occasion to review my committee files and find that letters today have changed little from twenty years ago.

This book is good, but the gay voice is largely absent. We continue the dialogue without that voice despite the caution John Howard Yoder offered years ago. It is not enough, though good, to listen to the parents of gays or to read the diary entries of gays or lesbians. The last time denominational leaders asked gays to speak at an official assembly was in 1980 at Estes Park, Colorado, as part of the small groups. Leaders of various seminars at later assemblies did include these voices, but on their own authority, not on behalf of the denominations.

The book shows how spotty the reception of the Listening Committee's recommendations has been and how difficult for gay causes to have booths or a presence at assemblies. As we have learned through the addition of minorities in other conversations, discussions end differently when the minority voice is included. We have also learned from our African-American and other minorities that token representation of one voice is not enough. A community of voices is needed. Not to listen is to exclude.

Donald: Despite its best intentions, the book is not always dialogical in its tone or its reasoning. There are strong chapters on biblical word studies but the calculation seems to be not to offend Purdue/Saskatoon. So we have Camille Paglia, an admitted pagan, stereotyping homosexuals as she attacks another denomination's attempt to deal with the issue. We have negative descriptions like "genetic accidents" not set in quotation. Theologians Barth and Tillich and others are cited, writing twenty years before the scientific community's thought would have helped challenge their acceptance or received tradition.

Theodore Grimsrud gives a balanced reading of current biblical scholars' thinking on same-gender attraction. Against the whole, it does not make the book feel balanced. Paglia's reminder that Eros is a dangerous god is good and fits the Holiness Code's "abominations," but I fear Mark Thiessen Nations's inclusion of her remarks will be read only against same-gender attraction rather than as a warning to us all. David Schroeder's observation that neither the church nor the Christian homosexual community has worked out a "satisfactory" systematic theological rationale based on Scriptures is his opinion. Other theologians than Grimsrud cites have spoken to such a theology. What better place to have heard them than here, but most of the quoted sources are repetitiously traditional.

To develop a theology, one also needs to pay attention to the contextual culture of today, as Norman Kraus argues. It was out of Israel's experience of exile in Babylon that the Hebrew Scriptures were collated and reshaped. Why is it that in our culture homosexuality has become such a dividing topic?Walter Brueggeman has somewhere suggested that it is because the acceptance of homosexuality is such an obvious indication of the loss of Western males' hegemony, an exile as critical as the exile into Babylon.

This is a mirror way of stating, as John W. Miller does, that the original taboo may be related to the growing sense of the male's fathering role in the family. It is interesting that Miller can entertain a sociological origin for a belief held in Babylon when the usual interpretation is that the creation and holiness passages are God's sole inspiration. Where else might this contextualizing lead us? A comparison of how and why the church adjusted the words of Jesus on divorce would be a helpful exercise.

Our culture is strongly homophobic. Culture has affected and informed our Mennonite thinking, though Mennonites are often counter-cultural. If evidence points to biological components, why isn't it theologically engaged? If the preponderant scriptural concern is economic justice, is the concentration on homosexuality our way of avoiding the greater scriptural concern?

Elsie: Asking people to wait a long time while the church makes up its mind on how to deal with "them" is neither welcoming nor Jesus-like. I think I am past waiting for dialogue to happen. I am ready to accept diversity and difference of opinion that allows others to live with what they believe God calls them to. John Fortunato, an Episcopalian author, said already in a 1991 article in *Christianity and Crisis* that the

> appropriate response to injustice is outrage and protest—not polite dialogue. . . . Imagine, if you will, asking black clergy to sit on a Committee on Race and listen open-mindedly to a discussion of whether or not black people are by nature intellectually inferior to white people. . . . No one with a conscience would ask a black person to sit through that and no self-respecting black person would agree to do it.

We have a mission. The suicide rate of adolescent boys coming to terms with their sexual orientation is very high. They don't have mentors or role models. We know that psychologically it is best if gay/lesbian individuals can accept who they are and get on with their lives. Sexual orientation is only a small part of who we are, yet in the church we identify gay or lesbian persons as being only that. So we miss out on the gifts they can bring us.

There are excellent resources for study. Keener and Swartzendruber in their bibliography list a textbook edited by Cabaj and Stein and published by the American Psychiatric Association (1996). It is a very thorough reference. Mondimore (1996) is another.

I have changed my own thinking. Whereas I previously emphasized the studies that pointed to a biological or genetic cause of homosexuality—perhaps because I thought people might be more accepting of homosexual individuals if the cause were biological—I now recognize that the causes are multiple and perhaps not that important in influencing attitudes.

Donald: I take heart from the fact that the paradigm conference for deciding these things at Jerusalem (Acts 15) ends up with the first-century church, except for the ban on fornication, never again similarly addressing the strictures the Council mandated. May it be so with us.

— *Elsie Steelberg, Psychiatrist, Prairie View Regional Mental Health Center; and Donald Steelberg, General Conference Mennonite Church pastor now serving on an interim basis*

An Administrator's Quandary

As an adminstrator at an Anabaptist-related college, I find it risky business to go on record regarding a subject so highly conflictual in religious circles as homosexuality. I find it so risky, in fact, that I have asked the publisher to edit out identifiers and release this response anonymously.

Institutional leaders are frequently called on to exercise "leadership," but only, of course, so long as the exercise of leadership does not upset the delicate balance of power essential to the well-being of an organization. Any religious institution in existence for even a short time has established traditions and corporate culture. The success and health of an institution requires balancing the tension between the desire to exercise the independent free will of the institution with the perceptions and wanted expectations of the various stake-holding groups who may claim identity with the organization.

I am in just such a precarious position. Can I make any statement of response to this important discussion that will not be interpreted negatively by some constituents of the school I help serve? When should institutional leaders step up to the plate, so to speak, and be heard no matter what the consequences, and when should leaders refrain from comment for the public relations well-being of their institution? The current state of conversation regarding homosexuality in the life of Anabaptist-related denominations is so polarizing leaders often feel neutralized. A leader quickly perceives that condemnation will result no matter what position is taken.

My particular institution is a Christian college within the Anabaptist tradition. Our Christian faith and practice is derived from Anabaptist confessions of faith. Our common life as a Christian college is closely identified with traditions of Anabaptist faith and practice melded together from the many Anabaptist and Christian communities out of which our faculty, staff, and students originate. This wide diversity within the college necessitates dialogue on many issues.

A Christian college focused on the liberal arts, with its primary student body being traditional young adults, is continually challenged by the developmental issues of eighteen to twenty-four-year-old young adults. High on that list of issues is sexuality. North American Western culture brandishes sexuality in every aspect of life. Can a Christian college, in the context of sexuality blatantly being hoisted on everyone's consciousness day by day if not minute by minute, avoid discussing the pros and cons of various forms of sexual expression?

I believe Christian colleges—even church-related ones—must be permitted to have open discussions with young adults regarding the pros and cons of various sexual expressions. If a Christian college cannot have such discussions regarding human sexuality, where will the conversations occur? Where will the faith perspective be heard? Only in secular universities? Only in church? Where will the breadth of dialogue unfold?

I value the attempt of this book to engage in respectful dialogue regarding homosexuality. This volume is an attempt to struggle with the many aspects of homosexuality realizing there is still much to learn. If we are truly to be a community of Christian disciples interpreting the Scriptures together, we must listen to each other, opening ourselves to the Spirit of God, while acknowledging our intellectual human limitations. The examples of the church throughout the past 2000 years making difficult decisions on many types of issues ought to be resource material for our current day.

In short, I am not responding to a particular perspective in the debate. But I support conversation, study, and discernment together as a community seeking to follow the way of Jesus the Christ.

—*An Anbaptist College Administrator*

Who Belongs and Who Decides?

The chapters contained in this volume speak to the necessity of keeping open a dialogue about same-gender affection, faithfulness, and church discipline. There are no startling new insights or final answers here, but rather reflections on where we've been and suggestions for where we might go. If read by persons concerned about the future of the Mennonite Church, these chapters can help nurture an ongoing dialogue.

The heavy focus in this book on reading the biblical text implies that if only we could all interpret the Scriptures the same way, or if we could all realize that interpretation of the Bible is both necessary and inevitable, we would go a long way toward adjudicating the issues that divide us.

Having experienced a long and painful church discipline process that essentially left Atlanta Mennonite Fellowship dismembered from the larger Mennonite Church, I am less than optimistic about such adjudication. Re-reading or re-interpreting the biblical texts, especially those few passages that may or may not refer to same-gender affection orientation, seems ineffective in the thick of negotiations about same-gender affection, faithfulness, and church discipline. Though we are theoretically "people of the book," when push comes to shove we are very much "people of power politics," fighting more about turf than about theology. The fundamental questions in this dialogue seem to be quite simply, Who belongs? And who gets to decide who belongs?"

We have always had and will always have differences in the ways we understand what it means—theologically, ethically and spiritually—to be Mennonites. Such is the nature of a non-creedal, non-hierarchically defined ecclesiology. Perhaps we would do well to take a step back from the theological, ethical, spiritual, and even biblical questions to ask ourselves a more basic question. Why has the inclusion or exclusion of same-gender affectional persons become such a central and defining battleground for Mennonites (along with many other Christin groups) at the beginning of the twenty-first century? What about our self-understanding as Mennonites is so deeply threatened by either the inclusion or exclusion of same-gender affectional people that we are willing either to dismember our sisters and brothers or to be dismembered from a church that we all deeply love?

Among the many false dichotomies set up in such dialogue is one between a kind of bland tolerance that welcomes any and all behaviors, beliefs, and ethics into the church on one hand, and faithfulness to Anabaptist-Mennonite principles of church discipline on the other. A rising generation of Mennonite church leaders and scholars without visceral memories of being denied communion because our coat had buttons on it or thundering from the pulpit about the sinfulness of women cutting their hair might pause before romanticizing the redemptive possibilities of church discipline.

While we should resist morphing into liberal Protestantism, we need not cede all elements of tolerance, love, and justice to Christians living nearer the center of mainstream culture than we'd like.

We should be wary of any sort of church discipline that serves to reaffirm our own correctness and our own strong and sure identity as members at the center of the Mennonite fold while marginalizing any who are not just like us. Surely faithfulness demands more of us than that!

— *Elaine K. Swartzentruber, Assistant Professor of Religion Wake Forest University*

Resources at a Watershed Point

Throughout church history, on a sporadic but regular basis, issues have arisen that become watershed points in the church's discernment of faith and ethics. These issues rise above the usual debates that reflect the constant tension between progressives and conservatives. They cut across the normal party lines, release exceptional energy and passion, cause sharp division and schism, and can take generations to reach some degree of resolution and consensus. Slavery in the nineteenth century is a relatively recent example of such an issue, an issue that has come full circle with the reunification of some denominations that divided over it. (With this example I do not mean to imply that the new perspective is always right.) The clarity of discernment comes only in painful struggle and with the aid of hindsight.

From all appearances we are now amid such a time with the issue of homosexuality. In my opinion, however, the watershed issue here is not just homosexuality but the larger range of sexual questions sometimes referred to as "the sexual revolution." In the second half of the twentieth century and into the twenty-first, we are witnessing on these questions a huge shift of social reality in society and church. Conservatives and liberals alike, in the Western world at least, have changed in viewpoint and practice on sexual ethics. Not just homosexuality but sexuality in general is "out of the closet."

What this means, amazingly enough, is that only in our time, after two thousand years of church life, are we able to do the kind of thorough "discernment of spirits" in the realm of sexuality that the church has done in many areas of human experience long ago. (This not to deny that the basic framework for sexual ethics goes back to the biblical resources.)

There can be no doubt that much of the sexual revolution reflects human sinfulness. At the same time we cannot exclude that some new understandings of the line between right and wrong will result from this new openness and awareness. Indeed, it appears to have happened already, for example, in the nearly universal acceptance of recreational sex in marriage as pleasing to God. The central challenge is to distinguish between those changes in sexual mores that reflect an increasingly neo-pagan culture (and therefore to be resisted) and any changes that reflect new insight in to the freedom of the gospel.

Given this understanding of our present situation, I welcome the publication of this book with its dialogical style. What we need are resources which inform us of the widest range of facts, experience, and perspectives. These chapters provide just such a range in a well-informed, insightful and, given the complexity of the subject, quite readable form. To have this kind of resource is the necessary beginning point for true discernment. Furthermore, we need wider distribution of resources to more church members since many of us have little experiential or theoretical knowledge on homosexuality. This is in contrast with divorce, for example, that has left few families untouched.

The "homosexual problem" for the church can be expressed as the question of how to respond to these facts: On the one side, Scripture and tradition have a single voice rejecting whatever is understood as same-sex activity. On the other side, there are persons who show the evidence of sincere faith, the fruit of the Spirit, and love for the church who find no essential conflict with entering same-sex, life-long, faithful relationships. It is the clash of these realities that calls the church to serious work of discernment.

From this follow several implications, as I see it. First, we need to own the ambiguous situation in which we find ourselves. To admit that we do not have a clear answer is uncomfortable and to sustain the accompanying insecurity is difficult. It feels like some kind of unbelief. What is demanded of us is a "courageous humility." In humility we acknowledge our ignorance and refuse to hurt persons under the pretense of "having it all together." In courage we believe that God will lead us through the stumblings, even failures, of the present to more light.

Second, in the time of ambiguity we ought not cut loose from all the moorings. For this reason the church has done well to articulate a position on homosexuality that is in harmony with the tradition. However, such statements should not be used to deny the situation we are in nor to stifle the process of discernment.

Third, the church and society need to create the space within which the moral character of monogamous, same-sex partnerships can play itself out. What precise form this might take I do not claim to know. But this is nothing more than the freedom that God has extended to the human race at the price of a messy history. It is nothing more than the freedom our Anabaptist predecessors asked, but did not receive, to demonstrate the possibility of a new way of being the church in the world.

But someone is sure to reply that these implications are self-contradictory. Exactly! The only way to live honestly in an ambiguous situation is to embrace a certain degree of contradiction. This is not the same as a relativistic view of morality. It is the acknowledgment of the transitional situation in which we live together with the commitment to "discern what is the will of God—what is good and acceptable and perfect" (Rom. 12:2).

—*George R. Brunk III, Professor of New Testament*
Eastern Mennonite Seminary

Appendix 1

Report of Listening Committee for Homosexual Concerns

The Listening Committee for Homosexual Concerns was appointed by leadership groups within the General Conference Mennonite Church and the Mennonite Church to listen to the emerging voices on this increasingly volatile subject in our churches. It represents an incisive summary of Mennonite people's thinking on homosexuality in 1991. The committee's final report (here slightly abbreviated and with one or two subheads or the occasional format detail added or revised for clarity), is included in this book because it is the first study document to open fundamental issues related to homosexuality in its individual, social and churchly dimensions in ways not previously discussed in the church.

The report concludes with a strong recommendation that the denominations, both their institutions and congregations, launch a vigorous study process on homosexuality. The committee believed that without a responsible study process the issue might become dangerously explosive to the detriment of the church. As other chapters in this book document, denominational leaders did not follow through on this recommendation, although various groups coined policy statements and took actions on the subject in the intervening years. —C. Norman Kraus, editor

To: Commission on Education, General Conference Mennonite Church
Mennonite Board of Congregational Ministries, Mennonite Church
From: Joint Listening Committee For Homosexual Concerns
Date: August 20, 1992
Subject: *Final Report: Listening Committee for Homosexual Concerns*

"Is there any place for me in the Mennonite Church?"—To the Listening Committee by a lesbian Christian raised Mennonite and wishing to continue to serve in the church.

Introduction

The Listening Committee for Homosexual Concerns is a joint committee of the General Conference Mennonite Church and the Mennonite Church with its members appointed by the Mennonite Board of Congregational Ministries of the Mennonite Church and the Commission on Education of the General Conference Mennonite Church. It served a two-year term from July 1990 through the Triennial Sessions of the General Conference Mennonite Church in July 1992.

A. The Committee assignment, its interpretation of the assignment and this report's response to the assignment.

1. The "task of the committee" given by the Executive Officers of the appointing agencies (Everett Thomas, Ex. Sec. of MBCM and Norma Johnson, Ex. Sec. of COE), was outlined as follows:

> a. "To care for gay and lesbian persons and their families in the General Conference Mennonite Church and the Mennonite Church by listening to their alienation and pain in the church and society;

> b. To encourage and help dialogue between persons of various perspectives concerning homosexuality and to foster continued theological discernment in the church on this issue;

> c. To make recommendations to MBCM and COE regarding policy, program and church life to deal with alienation and hurt."

2. The committee interpreted this assignment essentially as follows.

> a. It was to listen to the general church (point 2), to gay and lesbian persons in our congregations (those who wish to share) and their families (point 3) on any and all matters they wish to discuss with us concerning homosexuality. This listening was to take place chiefly at the general assemblies, but not be limited to those occasions.

> b. It was to foster continued biblical and theological discussion and discernment on this issue in our church. This work began through seminar assignments on the Bible and homosexuality at the general assemblies of the two bodies, th[r]ough sharing written materials on the subject and through contributions in regional and congregational discussions on this subject.

> c. Make recommendations regarding policy, program and church life concerning this issue.

3. The report of the committee.

This report first reviews the history of discussions of homosexuality in our denominations and locates our present listening committee in relation to this history.

The committee's work with assignment (1) is a major part of this report. It summarizes what we have heard in our denominations on this issue. While doing this, the report also tries to bring a greater awareness and increased understanding of homosexuality as a physical, social and religious phenomenon.

In connection with assignment (2) we have tried to understand how Mennonites are interpreting the Bible on homosexuality and how we are reflecting theologically and ethically on the subject. This report includes some of our observations on these items.

In connection with assignment (3) we have examined and outlined perspectives and positions various congregations have taken or are taking on homosexuality. However, we have backed away from definitive biblical and theological interpretations or policy and program resolutions on this issue for our churches at this time. Why? Were we intimidated by the intense feelings or wide-ranging pluralism of positions we encountered? Perhaps we should have been more aggressive in outlining biblical and theological perspectives as well as "policy and program" concerning homosexuality for the church. In the totality of our work we may infer or imply certain directions the denominations may take in working with this issue, but we have not interpreted our mandate to set down those directions into recommendations. We do make a modest "program" recommendation along with several enabling recommendations at the end of this report.

B. Committee procedure

Our committee carried out its assignment the following ways.

1. We engaged in a committee and individual education process on this subject by:
   - committee members sharing their specialized expertise in an internally directed seminar on the subject.
   - interviewing gays and lesbians in committee sessions and in individual private settings.
   - listening to family members and friends.
   - reading books and periodicals on the subject.
   - interviewing and listening to lectures of several specialists in the field as individual members and once as a committee.

2. We listened to individuals and groups who wished to share with us on this subject for two years from July 1990 through the MC General Assembly, July 1991 and the GC Triennial Assembly at Sioux Fall, South Dakota, July 1992.

3. We attended several meetings of groups working with homosexual issues.

4. We carried on extensive correspondence with interested persons.

5. We served as consultants or speakers in Conferences and congregational study processes.

6. We developed our views concerning homosexuality: causes of it, biblical and theological perspectives on it and the relation of homosexuals to the Christian confession and Mennonite church life.

7. We prepared two reports: a two-page summary which provides a brief overview of our work and this report, which gathers together our listenings, observations and recommendations.

Funding was made available for expenses for two committee meetings and attendance by the committee members at the two assemblies (MC in 1991 and GCMC in 1992). No funds were available for any research, surveys, hearings and field work, attendance at specialized meetings, writing or staff time.

C. Committee observations

1. Our committee listened to each other and worked together as a committee. Here is a review of our committee work.

a. Our committee met first Nov. 16 and 17, 1990, at Newton, Kansas, in four sessions for orientation (getting acquainted, sharing experiences, understandings and perspectives on homosexuality and reviewing the history of this issue in our Conferences). We studied the committee's mandate, prepared recommendations for three seminars for the MC Oregon General Assembly and began to plan our committee's procedure to do its work at the Assembly. We listened to a lesbian's personal experience story, began plans for a committee self-education program at pre-Assembly committee sessions at Oregon, discussed our relationships with the Brethren/Mennonite Council for Gay and Lesbian Concerns and requested that MBCM approve the addition of two members of that organization to our Committee.

b. Our committee met a second time in four pre-assembly sessions at Eugene, Oregon, July 28-29, 1991. We shared (written and oral) studies from each member on "Our Understandings of Homosexuality," entered a committee process designed to help each member gain a heightened awareness of our personal sexuality, reviewed recent reactions in our churches (including written materials in the church press) on the homosexuality question, noted recent activities of committee members in this area, took note of various approaches congregations are developing to work with homosexuality in their congregations and set up plans for our work as a listening group (both in structured sessions and informal contacts) at the Assembly.

c. During the Mennonite Church's General Assembly our committee was very busy. We held two-hour open-discussion periods each day (except Thursday) to hear individuals and groups (including a two-hour session with the Students and Young Adults group at the Assembly) discuss their comments and concerns about homosexuality. We met privately with all groups and individuals seeking contact with one or more members of the committee. All committee members (when possible) attended the three seminars on this subject at the Assembly and the two public meetings planned by the BMC representation. The committee also held several committee planning and processing sessions during the week.

We did not hear as many personal experience stories from gays and lesbians or from family members in committee listening sessions at this assembly as we expected. Perhaps the public character of our committee work made it unsafe to share personal stories. We heard debate on whether, and how, the church should relate to homosexuality and the homosexuals among us.

d. Our committee had a third two-day meeting, June 12-13, 1992 at Germantown Mennonite Church, Philadelphia, during which we reviewed the activities of committee members over the past year (in listening to persons and groups involved in homosexuality issues, in sharing in retreats, lectures, workshops, and seminars on this issue), worked with plans for participation in the GC triennial sessions and worked at discovering our committee mind for our final report.

e. Our fourth meeting was in connection with the Triennial sessions of the General Conference, July 1992. We met in two closed-Committee sessions to make plans for our work during the triennial sessions, reviewed the individual work of committee members, interviewed AMBS President, Marlin Miller and AMBS Board Chairman, Darrell Fast, concerning recent actions of the Seminary with a homosexual student to understand their rationale for their action, planned our "listening" processes during the sessions, worked on recommendations of the committee to our appointing agencies and worked with the committee's final report. Committee members were available during the days in a designated room for conversation with interested persons. Members also shared in other planned meetings discussing homosexual concerns.

2. Our committee listened and observes that the work of our committee is linked to an extensive and convoluted history involving both GC and MC studies on sexuality and homosexuality.

We lay out some of this history here in order for you to see how our committee and its assignment fits into the shape and direction of previous discussions on homosexuality in our church. Here are some high points in that history.

A. A study on Human Sexuality was commissioned in 1980 by the GCMC, joined by the MC in 1981. Its goals were to: 1) "develop guiding principles which can help persons struggling with a broad range of sexual concerns; 2) speak forthrightly the mind of Christ (on this issue] amid the sexual revolution . . . in North American society; 3) clarify our position of

God-given sexuality with regard to premarital and extramarital intercourse and homosexual behavior. . . . "(p. 11., *A Working Document for Study and Dialogue: Human Sexuality in the Christian Life*). The committee considered its final report "a document for study and dialogue (in our congregations) . . . to help the church in looking at our attitudes toward human sexuality" (p.13, *Document*). The study developed its materials to serve as an educational piece for use by study groups in the congregations. It did not prepare its report to serve as a definitive statement by the denominations on human sexuality.

B. The final report of the Sexuality study aroused spirited discussion among the delegate bodies of both commissioning groups (GC in 1986 and MC in 1987) and precipitated a resolution including the following (GC) sentences passed (with slight modifications) by both bodies. "We understand the Bible to teach that sexual ("genital," [MC]) intercourse is reserved for a man and a woman united in marriage ("covenant . . . " [MC]) and that violation of this teaching [GC], ("even within this relationship, i.e., wife battering," [MC]) is a sin. It is our understanding that this teaching also precludes premarital, extramarital, and homosexual sexual activity." They also recommended the study of the SEXUALITY in the congregations.

C. These assemblies' resolutions affirmed but confused several points:

1. They received the Sexuality Committee's Report and encouraged congregations to study it.

2. They summarized certain positions concerning sexuality and homosexuality beyond the suggestions of the Sexuality Study itself, defining certain acts for both heterosexuals (premarital and extramarital sexual intercourse ["genital" and "wife battering," MC] and homosexual "sexual activity") as sin.

3. The assemblies furthermore seemed to project their resolutions as *official* positions for the denominations (an approach implied again by the "summary statement" passed by the MC General Board, July 29, 1991). But in what sense are the assembly resolutions, or the MC General Board's statement, denominational statements? Some interpret them as "official" denominational positions, others interpret them as "guides" to positions commended to congregations for consideration. This difference of interpretation on the authority of assembly statements vis-à-vis congregational (and conference) authority has caused some confusion.

4. When the assemblies accepted the sexuality committee's report and recommended its study in the congregations but nevertheless passed resolutions concerning homosexuality not in that report, a popular confusion emerged on whether the assemblies really wanted congregations to study the SEXUALITY committee's report on homosexuality or not for, as some have told us, "there is nothing to study, the assemblies have spoken." This confusion persists to the present time.

D. On the MC side specific questions concerning the relation of homosexuality to Christian faith and life and to church membership and participation arose in 1983 when Christian homosexuals, members of the Mennonite Church (associated with the Brethren-Mennonite Homosexual Council) who had publicly owned their homosexual preference and continued to claim Mennonite identity, actively sought recognition and discussion of the issue in the church. Homosexual Listening Committees were appointed first by the Executive Committee of Region V (now dissolved) and later by the MC General Board. This group "listened" at Assemblies at Bethlehem (1983), Ames (1985), Purdue (1987), and Normal (1989) and submitted a Report in 1989 detailing their learnings and giving their recommendations to the General Board. The Board received this Report, discussed at various times aspects of it but did not follow through with its recommendations. Rather it lodged further work on the homosexuality issue with MBCM and that Board appointed this committee with the mandate outlined above. The General Conference, in a somewhat similar process, lodged responsibility with their Commission on Education.

E. Through the years at least seven MC groups have become involved in the "homosexual issue": The General Board, the General Assembly, the Council on Faith and Life, the Board of Congregational Ministries, the Sexuality Study Committee, and at least two different Listening Committees for Homosexual Concerns. A somewhat similar multiplicity of processes occurred in the GC, though fewer groups were involved in work with the issue. Important comments on the subject of homosexuality have been made by these groups but the lines of communication, responsibilities and relationships among these groups tended to be confused, mandates unclear and overridden, and recommendations ignored or passed by.

3. Our committee listened and observes there are pervasive misunderstandings in the church on the status and mandate of the present Listening Committee.

The Listening Committee was to be "totally objective and impartial on the issue of [homosexuality] . . . it is not, it is biased . . . and has not been helpful."—from a letter to a co-chairman of the committee.

I . . . recommend . . . measures that would . . . dissolv[e] . . . the Listening Committee for Homosexual Concerns. . . . "—from a letter to the Council of Faith, Life and Strategy of the Mennonite Church.

The Listening Committee shall ". . . foster continued biblical and theological discernment in our church concerning this issue. . . . [and] make recommendations regarding policy, program and church life concerning this issue. Assignment to Listening Committee July 1990.

The misunderstanding of the role of the listening committee has many linkages. It is linked to a misunderstanding of the status of the Sexuality study committee's final report ("Is it an official position of the denominations"?), to a particular interpretation of the resolutions of the GC and MC delegate bodies concerning the sexuality study ("Do they also condemn homosexual orientation as sin or only homosexual sexual acts?"), to the role of the General Boards in continuing studies of homosexuality ("Are they saying and doing more or less than the delegate bodies intended for them to do?"), to the relationship of the present Listening Committee to the prior MC [district] Listening Committees ("why is there another Listening Committee?"), to the relation of the present Listening Committee to the content of the [Human] Sexuality [Study Committee's] report [of 1985] on homosexuality (some think that the Sexuality study committee developed a definitive position on homosexuality. It did not. It recommended continuing study of the issue), to the implication of the committee's title "listening" (it implies "neutrality"), to the mandate, personnel and process of the present listening committee (from "Why has the committee not supplied literature and helped the church work through this issue in our congregations?" to "You are undermining the church's historic stand against homosexuality by your presence as a committee"; or, from "The committee must develop a definitive position on homosexuality for our church" to "The committee should be abolished").

It seems that the presence of a "listening" committee which has "listened" to the same issue for eight years gives several distinctly different impressions to our constituencies. . . .

4. Our committee listened and observes there is a widespread, apprehensive concern on the subject of homosexuality in our church.

". . . some topics are truly too hot to handle. In the Mennonite Church today homosexuality is one of these." *Gospel Herald* editorial, Nov. 5, 1991.

We see this apprehension among members who are gay or lesbian. We see it in their families, in our congregations, in pastors, in various denominational bureaucracies and in individuals and groups who carry a particular position toward the issue. Some of this interest is expressed publicly, and a few describe it as a critical "flashpoint" issue in denominational life but more of this apprehension is tucked nervously and uncomfortably just beneath the surface of public discussion. Of course, this aroused interest goes beyond the specific subject of homosexuality. It awakens personal fears (subconscious and conscious) associated with our total sexuality.

Not all of this aroused interest is joined with a desire or willingness to work with the issue. Some among us strenuously reject the idea that a conversation on homosexuality should be opened or continued in the church. Others grieve because it is going on. Generally speaking these persons are certain that discussing homosexuality minimizes its (inferred) sinfulness or undercuts the social institutions of marriage and family life or confuses sexual ethical standards or stimulates unfortunate tension and strife in the church. But others grieve that so little work is being done or so little leadership is being given on this subject in our church.

When discussions are opened, reactions range from almost total ignorance of the issues to reflective and informed opinions in opposition to or in advocacy of the homosexual; from generalized, inarticulate nervousness to panicky, irrational and passionate outrage against or in defense of the homosexual; from rejection of both the homosexual person and his or her position to acceptance and moral support of both. Earlier, only the homosexuals themselves tried to open a discussion of homosexuality. Now other persons are beginning to share in the discussion and develop their views on it.

It appears however that many of our people, though uncertain, are cautiously willing to discuss this issue but are reluctant to do so because they fear rejection or censure from church members and leaders. They are asking our church leaders to lead them in it. There is reason to believe that this present nervous interest concerning homosexuality can be metamorphosed into constructive dialogue within and for the church.

5. Our committee listened and observes that this issue places many conscientious members of our churches at the painful, grinding edge between two cardinal emphases in our theology and practice: unconditional Christian care and love for persons, but particularly for socially marginalized ones, and confrontation with moral judgment on these persons for acts they consider sinful.

"A young man in our congregation returned home. He has aids. He is a homosexual. Our congregation has not talked to the young man or his family. What do we say? What do we do? I believe homosexuality is sin. . . . What do I do?" From a man in his sixties to the listening committee.

. . . . Many of our people feel they are on the edge of two fundamental theological principles underlying Mennonite theology and practice as these relate to homosexuality. The first is the Christian conviction that God comes and loves and cares for the marginalized, the misunderstood, the abused and oppressed persons of society irrespective of their situation. The second is a strong discipleship theology and tradition which carries an acute ethical sense, a strong moral judgment on what is right and wrong. This ethical sensitivity calls for rigorous action: to commend what is right, and to condemn what is wrong. Many feel pulled to love and condemn the homosexual at the same time. Some begin thinking on this issue from relational experiences with the homosexual as a person, others begin from rational— biblical, theological or ethical—perspectives. . . .

This complex theological and ethical dilemma provides a good setting for some individuals to proclaim that "the church is adrift, it has no position on this issue" and to demand the church accept their particular solution to the homosexuality issue by everyone else in the church.

6. Our committee listened and observes that members of our church are not sure what homosexuality is and do not share a common understanding of important words and ideas used in discussing the subject.

These different understandings cause confusion in our conversations. We are referring particularly to meanings for the terms "sexuality," "sex," "homosexual," "gay" and "lesbian" and the phrases "homosexual orientation" and "homosexual addiction. . . ."

Sexuality stands for the totality of what we mean by femaleness and maleness. It gathers up the constellation of feelings, self-perceptions, responses and actions which cause each individual to think of herself-himself as a female or male human being. This sexual quality of life is stamped on and intertwined with the fundamental reality of shared human identity underlying both maleness and femaleness.

Sex is understood biologically as those bodily organs which distinguish male and female gender and behaviorally as expressed in sexual intercourse.

A homosexual is a person who is attracted primarily to persons of the same sex rather than to the opposite sex.

However, the use of the title *homosexual* among us is more varied than the above definition suggests because it has gathered inferences from the causes of homosexuality (see point 7) and from popular speech involving homosexuals and sexual activities which give it additional connotations. For example. some use the word homosexual to stand only for those who experience same-sex sexual arousal. For others, homosexual stands for a person practicing same-sex genital sex; for them, all homosexuals are "that way." Some use the term in a descriptive sense without moral inferences, others use it with moral connotations only, usually condemnatory.

In more recent times the term *homosexual orientation* is being used to refer to a condition of self-identity which arises from genetic, biological or psychosocial causes and appears in an individual usually apart from that individual's intention or personal choice. . . .

Homosexual addiction is used by some people to stand for all forms of homosexuality. They believe the very presence of homosexual attraction is sexual addiction. Others use the term (homosexual) *addiction* to refer only to those persons who exhibit compulsive same-sex sexual behaviors. We prefer to reserve use of the term for the second sense, just as we would use the term *addiction* for heterosexuals who are similarly self-absorbed in compulsive heterosexual sexual relations.

Gay and *lesbian* are terms frequently used by homosexual men and women to refer to themselves. Sometimes "gay" is used to refer to both men and women homosexuals; but because of issues raised by contemporary sexism and from different life experiences, many choose to use "gay" for homosexual men and "lesbian" for homosexual women. . . .

7. Our committee listened and observes there are strong differences of opinion among us on the sources or causes of homosexuality.

The definitive causes for homosexuality have not been pinpointed by scientific research. At least six theories about its cause are proposed.

One theory is that homosexuality comes from a genetic "accident" taking place within the genetic processes. This accident causes homosexual orientation or a predisposition toward homosexuality.

A second theory is that homosexuality arises from hormonal accidents. For unknown reasons chemical irregularities occur in the developing zy-

gote or fetus in the early stages of pregnancy and result in an abnormal release of hormones, estrogen or testosterone, for example. This accidental
exposure triggers the condition, homosexual orientation. . . .

A third theory for the cause of homosexuality is that it is acquired
through defective socialization relationships between the child and parents. This theory arises from classic psychoanalytic Freudian theory. . . .

A fourth [theory for the] cause for homosexuality is situational. That is,
some homosexuals emerge from enforced same-sex physical relationships,
in prisons or in the army, for example, where the only human and sexual
relationships are with same-sex associations. In these contexts there may
emerge for some persons, not only a behavioral conditioning toward same-
sex behaviors but a form of same-sex orientation.

A fifth theory for homosexuality is that it is totally volitional and intentional. All homosexuals choose homosexual attraction and behaviors. There
is no such reality as unintentional homosexual orientation.

A sixth theory for the cause of homosexuality incorporates causes from
the previous ones. In different persons their homosexuality may arise from
genetic irregularity or from chemical influences on the fetus or from dysfunctional psychosocial relationships of early childhood, or from their enforced situations. This view suggests there are several possible causes for
homosexuality and not just one cause.

An important implication arising from this discussion of causes for homosexuality is this: if some causes of homosexuality are from genetic or
prenatal causes totally disconnected from the choice of a person, and are
intertwined with one's essential identity as a human being, then it needs to
be acknowledged and received by Christians as "an act of God" in birth,
similar to the way other birth irregularities are interpreted. Also, for homosexuals who have not chosen their sexual preference, the acknowledgment
and acceptance of this identity is one essential step for growth into human
(and Christian) wholeness. But if, on the other hand, one considers other
types of homosexuality to be acquired by choice or from behavioral conditioning or by the raising of psychological defense responses (voluntarily or
involuntarily given) to relational experiences, then homosexuality is, at
least in some of those instances, a psychosexual aberration which one must
confront to come to fullness of life, psychologically and spiritually.

It appears clear there are several precipitating causes for homosexuality and to attribute all types of homosexuality to one cause is inadequate to
account for the complexity of homosexual reality. Probably also there are
different intensities of homosexual feelings just as there are different intensities of heterosexual ones. If these observations are correct it means the
church needs to be open to more than one source or cause for homosexuality and therefore open to more than one path for homosexuals to find fullness of life. The limitation to one approach only for working with homosexuals is inadequate.

8. Our committee listened and observes that many in our church are hard

pressed with homophobic fears concerning homosexuality because our thinking on this subject has been shaped by popular myths about it. (The word *myth* is used here in the sense of a misconception or false impression concerning homosexuality.) [The committee listed nine myths.]

9. Our committee listened and observes there are homosexuals in our congregations and that there are more who do not reveal their homosexual orientation than who do.

If the percentage of homosexually inclined persons appears in our Mennonite MC and GCMC population as is present in the general population, then a conservative estimate of adult, homosexually inclined persons in our congregations approaches 10,000 persons.

These persons are located at all places along a line from secrecy about their sexual orientation to an open public acknowledgment of it; from fear, grief and anger about their homosexuality to an acceptance of it as God's mysterious creative activity with them; from rejection, isolation, and anger by family, former friends and the church community about this to a forgiving and loving spirit to these same people along with a love for Christ and a longing to work fully as his ministering servants in the church.

A relatively small number of same-sex oriented persons have "come out" and publicly acknowledged their orientation in our denomination. Those who have and who try to continue relationship with our church community have found it takes a great amount of spiritual and psychological energy to discuss and represent their position again and again.

10. Our committee listened and observes that people are asking: "What does the Bible say about homosexuality"?

"Homosexuality is a sin, the Bible is clear. Scripture is infallible. What is happening to the Mennonite Church [in discussing homosexuality]? If the Mennonite Church does not hold firm on this issue, I'll have to leave it." —A "straight" young man in his early twenties to the listening committee.

Our people look to the Bible as one source for guidance in working with all difficult issues concerning Christian faith and life. They are looking to the Bible for help in working with this issue too, but in doing so, they are discovering there is complexity in interpreting the Bible on this issue and there are different interpretations by equally honest and committed interpreters.

As a preliminary observation on this point, we have observed that our people are surprised when they pay close attention to sexual relationships in the Bible for they see different accepted patterns of relationships than is our customary modern one. For example, there are several models of heterosexual relationships—polygamy, concubinage, levirate marriage, plural marriages in the royal court, and monogamy. . . . Additionally too, our people can notice a diversity of understandings and teachings on sexual matters within the Bible itself. For example, Genesis 1 and 2 affirm the created goodness of sexuality, the wanted harmony of gender relations and the goodness of monogamy while Proverbs warns against the dangers of sexual enticement and relations. The Song of Songs celebrates the joys of sexual passion while Paul in 1 Corinthians regards sexual passion as a spiritual burden and recommends celibacy rather than marriage.

We also notice there are different approaches to interpreting the Bible's references to homosexuality developing among us. One approach is to find specific passages where homosexuality seems to be mentioned. . . . But a very perplexing thing happens with proof-text interpretative approach. Two opposite conclusions concerning homosexuality are declared by equally honest and sincere interpreters. One group says the Bible clearly teaches that all homosexuality is sin, both orientation and acts. A second group, using the identical proof-texts, concludes the Bible does not teach that homosexual orientation or that all homosexual acts are sin.

A second approach is to begin with the broad and overarching themes of the biblical message and interpret texts with homosexual inferences in relation to those themes. Examples of central themes used for this interpretative process are: the "orders of creation" as they relate to sexuality and sexual acts; God's grace and his judging, saving and forgiving acts; covenant theology and relationships which are based on covenant; the kingdom of God or the character of life patterned after "the mind of Christ." Specific stories and teachings in the Bible both are used to understand these broad themes and are interpreted in the light of these themes.

But here again, two opposite conclusions concerning homosexuality are arrived at by equally honest and sincere persons using this broad themes approach. . . .

This results in four lines of interpretation of the Bible on this subject in our church—two interpretations from the proof-text approach and two from the broad themes approach—with modifications in each and the interweaving of all four over and around each other.

Why does all this variety of interpretation occur? The answer to this question is too complex for us to try to answer here. . . .

Whatever the reasons, the fact of the matter is: there are opposite conclusions in interpreting the Bible on this subject in our midst. This accounts for the distressing bewilderment, even anger, many feel as they discuss the Bible's teaching on homosexuality. Does this mean we should stop studying the Bible on this subject? No. Rather, our committee believes we must continue to study the biblical materials on sexuality and homosexuality in our congregations much more than we have in the past, and trust God to lead us to greater consensus in interpreting its message for us.

11. Our committee listened and observes that our church is trying to figure out whether homosexual orientation is a sin or is not a sin.

* * *

One view among us is that homosexual orientation (and all homosexual behaviors) is sin. This position rejects the idea that there are any genetic or chemical-hormonal causes for homosexuality. Homosexuality is always a moral issue; it is never, from any cause or in any form, a normal or amoral psycho-physical condition. Some persons holding this view do not deny there can be congenital, acquired or relational factors involved with homosexual attraction, but same-sex attraction is not a fixed psychosexual trait, condition or orientation. The presence of homosexual attractions is not necessarily sin, but the acceptance of them as normal is sin. For God created all humans to heterosexual attraction.

In this view homosexuality is integrated with the theological idea called "total depravity" or "original sin" which says that humans universally share in an historical state and process infected by the pervasive reality of evil. This universal social, spiritual, and psychological reality is expressed in the broken incompleteness of all aspects of human and created life. All forms of homosexuality are a part of that sinful depravity.

A second view among us is that homosexual orientation is not morally sinful but homosexual sexual activities are sin. In this view homosexuality, which comes from prenatal causes and has no connection with the individual's choice, should not be interpreted as sin. From a theological perspective this sexual attraction belongs within the providential mystery of God's creative activity and must be acknowledged and worked with from that perspective.

An extension of this view by some among us includes the idea that even homosexuality precipitated by defective and dysfunctional family and social systems is not sin because it appears as the result of a child's innocent and immature involvement in the complex web of relational forces which resulted in homosexuality. . . .

To recap, this view holds that homosexual orientation is not a sin but homosexual sexual acts are sins. The route to Christian sexuality is to live as a celibate or live in heterosexual marriage (even though it may not include a totally honest sexual relationship with one's spouse).

A third view is that neither homosexual orientation nor homosexual sexual acts are sin if there is a covenant commitment to fidelity and love for the partner. Homosexuals can be Christians as sexual partners. Homosexuals, as heterosexuals, are responsible to nurture their Christian life. including the disciplines necessary to manage their sexuality and sexual practices. Homosexual actions, including homosexual genital sex, is sin when it is abusive and promiscuous.

12. Our committee listened and observes that those who accept the condition of homosexual orientation are trying to decide what homosexual behaviors are honorable and good and what behaviors are sinful and wrong.

If the fact of homosexual orientation is not sin, then the challenge to both Christian homosexuals and the heterosexual Christian community is to develop ethical standards for homosexual relationships, just as the church has developed for heterosexual ones. The church has a long history of making ethical judgments concerning acceptable and unacceptable heterosexual relationships, but it has not worked equally hard to create Christian ethical standards for various homosexual relationships.

These moral judgments would need to be developed all across the line of homosexual relationships: for homosexual social friendships, homosexual responses to erotic attraction, homosexual sexual acts and homosexual sexual addiction and promiscuity.

[Committee observations about people's reactions to such a suggestion.]

13. Our committee listened and observes that both our denominational leaders and our congregations are cautiously involved with several approaches to the questions raised by homosexuality and having openly affirmed homosexuals as members of our congregations.

"I know this is an issue the church must deal with, yet if I mention homosexuality, I'll lose my job." —A pastor's comments in a listening committee session. . . .

"This is going to be emotional. . . . As a straight male, I need the church to accept gay and lesbian persons . . . to be open . . . I need the church to be for me." —From a young man who sobbed and cried aloud ending with his arms outstretched to all in the room in a listening committee session.

The Approach of the Denominations' Leadership

Denominational leaders led assemblies to an ethically definitive statement declaring that homosexual genital acts are sinful (1980 and 1981) following the report of the SEXUALITY study, which included one section on homosexuality, but at the same time continued a Listening Committee to hear what the church was saying and to continue dialogue on the subject. In the GCMC neither its General Board nor COE officially commented further. In the MC its General Board issued Summary Statements (July 29, 1991) to clarify its "stance . . . on homosexuality." In those statements, it deplored "homophobic" reactions, supported "ministries which help persons who desire a change in sexual orientation" (thereby acknowledging the idea of a homosexual "orientation"), urged "members to avail themselves of these ministries" and called on conferences and congregations to "provide pastoral leadership in clarifying understandings and responding redemptively to homosexual people." MBCM has not commented further on these statements.

Congregational Approaches

At the present time we think we are seeing at least five approaches to homosexual persons present among our congregations.

318 / TO CONTINUE THE DIALOGUE

318 / TO CONTINUE THE DIALOGUE

318 / TO CONTINUE THE DIALOGUE

1. This first approach we may call the traditional one. This view sees the homosexual orientation/condition—relationships and sexual expressions—as sinful and prohibited by God. It is not a subject which needs more discussion congregationally. On a personal basis members reflect reactions to homosexuality which appear in our North American society. Many are repulsed by the issue or tend to reject both the openly confessed homosexual and homosexual relationships of any kind. (Occasionally among us a distinction is recognized between a homosexually oriented person who lives a life of ordinary human friendships excluding genital sexual acts and a homosexual who engages in genital relationships; Or between a homosexual couple who relate to each other as partners in fidelity of love and commitment, and homosexuals who do not do so. Most often however, these distinctions are not recognized or made. The terms *homosexual lifestyle*, *homosexual practices* or just *homosexual* come to stand for homosexual sexual activities and every homosexual is considered "this way." The recent church member profile of five Mennonite denominations reports that the percent of Mennonites who believe homosexual acts ("acts" are undefined) are "always wrong" has grown from 86 percent in 1972 to 92 percent in 1989 (*The Mennonite Mosaic: Identity and Modernization* by Leo Driedger and J. Howard Kauffman). The implication of this information may be that the question was too obscure or imprecise to be helpful, or that there is a hardening of resistance to homosexuals who have publicly identified themselves as fellow-Christians and members of the church.

2. Some Mennonite congregations are approaching homosexuals following the lead of such organizations as Exodus International. . . .

This approach acknowledges the reality of homosexual attraction and of persons who call themselves homosexuals. It considers all types of homosexuals and all forms of homosexuality sinful and calls for repentance from both the condition of homosexuality and feelings and behaviors of it. Some may consider homosexual orientation from biological or psycho-social origins as not sinful in itself, but any expression of it is sinful. The cure is to acknowledge and repent of its presence and its expressions and reorient one's affections to heterosexual affectional attraction and marriage. It is believed a cure of homosexuality (or at least expressions of it) will be achieved by a genuine Christian conversion with spiritual disciplines assisted by participation in a group support program and, as necessary, by appropriate psychiatric counseling. The congregation should aggressively reach out toward homosexuals, love and care for them as with all other sinners and, upon repentance and changed life patterns, welcome them as full participating members in the congregation.

3. Some congregations are approaching homosexuals by viewing homosexual orientation as a morally neutral condition. The sin of homosexuality is located in lustful eroticism and homosexual genital sex. Such persons are called to repent and renounce such sins, to respond in faith in Christ and grow in Christian character and witness as any other persons.

Furthermore, they must commit themselves to either celibacy or heterosexual marriage if they wish to be received as Christians and church members. This appears to be the position of those advocating and supporting the General Boards' resolutions.

4. Some congregations are working with homosexuals by using several approaches. They believe there can be several authentic Christian approaches to homosexuality in our congregations because there are several causes of homosexuality. Some homosexuals, oriented to their condition from congenital causes (and perhaps from some acquired ones), need to be accepted as homosexuals and allowed to shape a Christian lifestyle in their homosexual situation.

Other homosexuals (some who may be oriented to homosexuality from acquired psychological conditioning or have turned to same-sex relationships from intentional choice because of sinful reactionary impulses) must find the path to personal wholeness only through confession, renewed Christian experience and helpful counseling processes. This Christian renewal may involve a rejection of their homosexuality with reorientation to heterosexuality.

This more nuanced approach will call for a high level of spiritual depth, personal and emotional sensitivity, intellectual clarity and pastoral care in our midst to accept and work with these several understandings.

5. A final approach emerging in a few of our congregations is that Christian homosexuals can live in covenanted, monogamous sexual relationships and be full participating members of the church. This approach calls for the same level of commitment and fidelity from homosexual as from heterosexual unions.

Recommendations by the
Listening Committee for Homosexual Concerns

"I am fearful for our church on this question of homosexuality. . . . It could split our church. We have two roots for our present patterns of biblical interpretation and our theological reflections: the broad themes approach of Anabaptism and the propositional rules approach of Fundamentalism. No one has found good ways to dialogue across this chasm. When I work with congregations on such issues, it seems we can only agree to disagree." —Comments at a dinner discussion group of 30 persons by a professional Mennonite mediator.

We must find ways to study homosexuality in our congregations if we are going to be faithful to our vision of what church is all about and if we care at all for homosexuals in our congregations." —From a conversation with an older church member.

A. Program recommendation

The Listening Committee for Homosexual Concerns recommends that the Mennonite Church and the General Conference Mennonite Church intensify its efforts to help congregations study homosexuality to discern how homosexuals can relate to the church's life and ministry.

(This recommendation is focused primarily on the congregation but we also urge the study of this issue on all other levels and appropriate settings of church life: in conference district meetings, church agencies and institutions and general assemblies.)

The Rationale

1. There is much diversity of opinion an homosexuality among us on such subjects as: the interpretation of Scriptures on the subject, the causes of homosexuality, the appropriate ethical standards for homosexuals, and effective congregational approaches for working with homosexuals. The church needs to seek and achieve a more unified Christian resolution to these different opinions and convictions. We believe more intentional and structured discussions will help develop informed opinions and a greater common mind on the subject.

2. The general assemblies of the General Conference (1986) and Mennonite Church (1987) and the 1985 Human Sexuality study each urged continuing dialogue and discernment on the subjects of sexuality and homosexuality in our congregations.

3. The agonizing feeling of alienation and rejection now being experienced by homosexuals in our congregations, the confused pain of family members and friends, and the alarmed anxiety of persons who resist this subject—all these reactions cry out for more careful, sustained and disciplined study of this issue in our congregations. Since it is God's will that the church pursues peace and just relationships for all in the church, we believe pastors and congregational leaders (and church leaders on all levels of church life) must assume more responsibility to lead the church in working with homosexuality.

4. Our people are beginning to want to discuss this issue. There is much (sometimes intense) interest in this subject—even as there are efforts to ignore it or hide it under the table. We see indications of this interest in responses to our committee's activities, in the church press when it opens the subject and in the large attendance at seminars on this subject in both the MC Assembly at Oregon, 1991, and the GC Triennial Sessions at Sioux Falls 1992.

5. Our denominations have carried forward discussions of this subject on the General assemblies level for the past decade because this is where the issues were first focused. This has been a dramatic place to open discussion on the issue but it is not the best place to carry on sustained ones. It is time to move the dialogue on this issue to the congregation.

B. Enabling Recommendations

1. The Denominations' Role

We recommend that the General Boards structurally identify a place and a person in the denominations' organization (perhaps in COE and MBCM respectively) charged with responsibility to lead and help dialogue and education in the congregations and throughout the denominations on this subject by:

a. developing resource materials on all aspects on this subject (biblical, theological, ethical, scientific, pastoral) and making them available for the use of congregations and other study groups.

b. creating an information center where congregations and groups can find help in planning their own study processes and can learn of existing networks and structures which can help them in their studies.

c. planning for workshops on this subject at national and district assemblies.

d. opening conversations with Mennonite homosexual persons to hear their stories and elicit their contributions.

e. opening and maintaining contact with organizations working in this area and impacting our people and congregations with their viewpoints and materials.

f. listening to and focusing the church-wide conversation about homosexuality.

2. The Institutions' Role

a. We recommend that our seminaries (and other church educational institutions) assume more aggressive responsibility to study homosexuality—biblical, theological, ethical, scientific—and make their studies and skills available to help congregations and groups become informed on this issue and process it. Further, that they help pastors provide effective pastoral care for individuals impacted by homosexuality.

b. We suggest that the institutions of the church regularly review their policies to ensure that these policies are not discriminatory with regard to persons of same-sex orientation.

3. The Pastor and Congregational Leadership's Role

a. We recognize that most pastors or church councils do not want to propose or lead study processes on this issue, particularly if there is no congregational agitation to do so. The subject is too sensitive. Therefore we offer some initiating and processing suggestions. We suggest:

1) that our congregational leaders consciously and intentionally initiate contact and open themselves to homosexually oriented persons and their families in their congregations, hear their stories as homosexuals and gain sensitivity to their situations as fellow human beings and Christians. The

purpose of this initiative is primarily to gain a greater understanding of the homosexual as a person but also to use these learnings to sensitize the congregation to the personal dimensions or homosexuality, to correct misunderstandings of homophobic fears and reduce cruel comments and unloving attitudes expressed about homosexuals in our congregations and society.

2) that pastors and church leaders in our congregations (but also on denominational and conference levels) enter and lead this discussion with an upfront acknowledgment of their own biblical and ethical convictions they already hold on the subject but also commit themselves to a spirit and a process of openness, humility and patience to other viewpoints. Above all, we urge leaders to hold firmly to the assured conviction that the Spirit of Christ will lead us in discussing and seeking consensus on this issue.

3) that pastors make available sustained, sensitive, and caring pastoral services to gay and lesbian persons in the congregation without neglecting similar services for all other persons irrespective of the biblical or ethical positions they hold toward homosexuality.

4) that our pastors and congregational leaders work to develop a congregational climate and gathered context where persons are free to tell their stories of same-sex identity or involvement with homosexuals and share their thoughts, pain, fears, disgust, anxiety, prejudices, and convictions they have on this issue, whatever they are.

b. We recommend that the congregational process does not stop with study and discernment but that it include a summarizing their congregational resolution or views on this issue and at the same time continue to learn from and contributing to the discussions of other congregations and groups.

Appendix 2

Entering the Homosexuality Discussion: A Guide For Congregational Dialogue

Edward Stoltzfus and C. Norman Kraus

Introduction and Background

The question of the relation of same-sex oriented persons to membership in the Mennonite Church (individuals in the congregation, congregations in the Conference) became a live and public issue in the 1970s. Some members of the church associated with the Brethren-Mennonite Council for Gay and Lesbian Concerns publicly owned their identity and actively sought continuing recognition as full members in good standing in the church. At first the question was recognition of those who openly declared their same-sex orientation, but soon the further issue of homosexual "holy unions" was raised. In the early stages of discussion, most congregations were only indirectly affected by this turn of events as petitions were taken by the BMC to the national denomenational boards.

As several chapters in this book detail, the Mennonite Church (1980) and the General Conference Mennonite Church (1981) commissioned a study on human sexuality which produced a document called *A Working Document For Study and Dialogue: Human Sexuality in the Christian Life.* Several Mennonite conferences, including the Mennonite General Conference, appointed "listening committees" to hear what concerned individuals and groups were saying on the issues. Unfortunately, the relation and responsibility of the various committees tended to be confused in the mind of the church membership. Their assignments and the church's expectations were not uniformly understood, and their mandates were unclear or overridden. In the end their attempts to clarify the issues were largely ignored and their recommendations for further congregational study were simply passed by.

As explored in various chapters in this book, the delegate bodies of both (GC, 1986; and MC, 1987) passed similar resolutions stating, "We understand the Bible to teach that sexual ("genital," [MC]) intercourse is reserved for a man and woman united in marriage ("covenant" [MC]) and that violation of this teaching [GC] is a sin. It is our understanding that this teaching precludes . . . homosexual sexual activity." The MC statement also encouraged continuing study of the issue in the congregations. The status and authority of these resolutions in the two denominations were unclear. Some interpreted them as official positions, even as "laws," to be obeyed by all conferences and congregations. Others interpreted them as "guides" commended to congregations and conferences for consideration. There is historical precedent for both interpretations.

Through the years several congregations have been disciplined in one way or another by regional conferences, including expelling from conference membership. At the present time more members are openly identifying their same-sex orientation and more couples in same-sex unions are requesting membership or continuing membership in congregations.

This forces congregations to face the issues and decide whether or not they will accept them as members. Currently the status of congregations who accept members engaged in various types of same-sex activity has become a divisive problem in the Mennonite Church U. S. Below we provide a guide for congregations and groups interested in further discussion of the pertinent issues.

Getting Started

1. *Expectations:* What are we trying to do today?
   - Gather more information? What does the Bible say? What do the natural sciences tell us?
   - Clarify and unscramble my/our thoughts and feelings? Why do I/we feel conflicted and anxious about this subject?
   - Come to congregational consensus? Arrive at a working position for the congregation?
   - Have a general discussion and, if necessary, agree to disagree?

2. *Present understandings:* How do I feel about discussing the subject?—my fears, sensitivities.
   - Where have I/we acquired our present understandings? from church? school? the media? the anti-gay lobby? the "pro-family" advocates?
   - What kind of assumptions and possible biases do we bring to the discussion?

3. *Defining Terms:* How much do we agree on what we mean by the words we use in discussion the subject of homosexuality? Here are some definitions for discussion:

Human stands for that personal reality, often referred to as "the image of God," by which individuals grasp, shape and give definition to themselves in relation to each other and God in family and community. One's sexual self-definition is an important part of but not the essential core of one's humanity.

Sexuality stands for the constellation of feelings, self-perceptions, responses and actions that cause each individual to think of herself-himself as a differentiated female or male human being. In human beings this sexual self-definition occurs on a continuum between the poles of male and female. Each of us has both male and female characteristics. This sexual quality of life is intertwined with the fundamental reality of shared humanity.

Sex stands biologically for those body organs which distinguish male and female gender. Behaviorally it stands for those feelings and actions expressed in sexual activities and intercourse.

A *homosexual person* is sexually attracted to another person of the same sex, sometimes referred to as *homoerotic* attraction. Homosexuality is found in both men and women. Homosexual feelings vary in intensity in different individuals.

Sexual orientation is distinguished from sexual *behavior* or *practice*. Orientation describes the person's erotic sexual attraction to the opposite or same sex. A *heterosexual* orientation indicates that one by self-definition is erotically attracted to those of the opposite sex, and the *homosexual* orientation to those of the same sex.

Gay frequently refers to homosexual males (though sometimes to homosexuals of both sexes).

Lesbian refers to homosexual females.

Same-sex unions refers to homosocial and homoerotic monogamous unions analogous to heterosexual marriage.

Homosexual lifestyle is a loosely defined phrase often implying the promiscuous acting out of homosexual fantasies or addiction. Because of this association, it is probably best not used as a general descriptive term to define homosocial behaviors.

Sexual addiction can and does occur in both hetero- and homosexual individuals. It refers to obsessive-compulsive sexual behaviors in either case. Some who believe that same-sex attraction itself is sin refer to the orientation itself as an addiction.

Sodomy denotes coition, either heterosexual or homosexual, by anal penetration, but it is sometimes popularly used as a general term for male homosexuals.

Homophobia is the unreasoning fear and antipathy toward those of homosexual orientation.

4. *Understanding the tensions:* Why is homosexuality such a galvanizing issue for us at this time? Examples of some reasons:
- Because it has become a major moral, cultural issue in our society.
- Because it is a divisive issue among those in Anabaptist-Mennonite and other believers church traditions. Some individuals, couples, and congregations are being cut off from membership in the church.
- Because homosexual orientation/expression seems unnatural and disgusting, and we believe it should be repudiated.
- Because I/we believe that according to the Bible homosexual orientation/expression is a sin against God and others and must be condemned.
- Because some persons are being unfairly penalized by both society and the church for conditions over which they have little control.

5. *Causes of homosexuality:* At present there is no consensus among scientists in the fields of biology and psychology about the causes of homosexual *orientation*. (Note: There may be a number of causes for homosexual behavior.) Among projected causes are these:
- It stems from a genetic source—a variation in the genetic processes.
- It is caused by a hormonal imbalance during prenatal development due to chemical irregularities or injury occurring in the developing zygote or fetus during pregnancy. (There may be a parallel with other irregularities such as Down's syndrome, certain types of dyslexia, mental retardation, or some physical irregularities as blindness, deafness.)
- It developes from faulty psychological and environmental conditions between the child and parents or other adults precipitated by defective relationships occurring in the socialization process.
- It is fostered by segregation in a single-gender environment such as in prison, the military, or enforced religious celibacy (as in monasticism).
- It is the result of intentional and volitional choices, acting out erotic homosexual fantasies.

Homosexual orientation may be the result of a combination of the above causes.

6. *Discerning the moral dimensions:* All sexual relationships have a moral dimension—hetero- as well as homosexual. Heterosexual sin is plainly described in the Bible—lust, fornication, prostitution, adultery, etc. What is sinful in homosexual relationships? Is homosexuality sin in the sense of "actual sin," or is it what is called "original" or inherited sinfulness resulting from the Fall of Adam?
- Is the sin in the homoerotic attraction? (Is the attraction "lust"?)
- Is it in inwardly indulging the attraction (fantasizing, "yielding to temptation")?
- Is it in forming caring same-sex friendships?
- Is it in physical touching and caressing resulting in sexual stimulation and arousal?

- Is it in the promiscuous act? The abusive act? The act within a covenanted monogamous relationship?

6. *The biblical perspective:* What does the Bible say? There are a variety of approaches and interpretations of the biblical data. Following are several commonly held positions:

- The Bible condemns all aspects of homosexuality, both orientation and practice.
- The Bible condemns homosexual practice, but it does not speak to the question of orientation.
- The Bible condemns all kinds of promiscuous, abusive, licentious sexual behavior as sin, whether heterosexual or homosexual. It does not explicitly condemn consenting, monogamous homoerotic sexual unions.
- The New Testament considers the sexual regulations found in the Levitical Holiness Code, such as genital mutulation (eunuchs), menstrual uncleanness, and homosexual intercourse, to be on a par with other ritualistic taboos like the dietary rules (unclean and clean foods), touching dead bodies, circumcision, and so forth.
- The New Testament, particularly in Romans 1:18-26, upholds the Holiness Code prohibition of all same-sex genital sexual encounters and gives it a New Testament sanction.

These suggested topics and questions are intended to illustrate the wide variety of understandings among Christians and to help raise the issues that are in dispute among us. We hope this book will be helpful in further exploration of the questions so perplexing the churches today.

Along with this suggested guide for discussion, we recommend that church leaders may want to prepare by consulting *Congregations Talking about Homosexuality: Dialogue on a Difficult Issue,* edited by Beth Ann Gaede. This book deals with the preparations and procedures necessary on discussing hard subjects in a congregation, gives the experiences of a number of congregations who tackled the topic of homosexuality, and identifies difficulties in discussing controversial issues. It is published by the Alban Institute, Suite 1250 West, 7315 Wisconsin Avenue, Bethesda, Maryland 20814-3211.

The Contributors

Don Blosser, Goshen, Indiana, was a pastor for seventeen years in Illinois and in Atlantic Coast conferences of the Mennonite Church. He holds a Ph.D. in New Testament from the University of St. Andrews and has completed over twenty-two years of teaching biblical studies at Goshen (Ind.) College. He is author of *A Dictionary of the Literature of the Bible* (published in China, 1993), and contributor to *Jesus, His Life and Times* (edited by Thomas Schmidt, Publications International, Ltd., 1999).

Reta Halteman Finger, Harrisonburg, Virginia, and Grantham, Pennsylvania, was editor of the Christian feminist magazine *Daughters of Sarah* from 1979-1994. She received a Ph.D. in New Testament from Garrett Evangelical Theological Seminary/Northwestern University in 1997. She has taught as Assistant Professor of New Testament at Messiah College in Grantham since 1995. She is author of numerous works, including *Paul and the Roman House Churches* (Herald Press, 1993).

Lin Garber, Boston, Massachussetts, was born in New Paris, Indiana, in 1935. (Named Verlin, he adopted the shorter name for career purposes.) A 1957 graduate of Goshen College, he was a professional singer in New York City until 1983. Since 1991 he has lived in Boston, where he is active in the Mennonite Congregation of Boston. Baptized at age eight, he has followed with keen attention the flow of change over the years in his beloved faith community.

Theodore Grimsrud, Harrisonburg, Virginia, is Assistant Professor of Theology and Peace Studies at Eastern Mennonite University, Harrisonburg, Virginia. Before joining the EMU faculty in 1996, he served ten years as a pastor in Mennonite churches in Oregon, Arizona, and South Dakota. He is author of *God's Healing Strategy* and co-editor of *Peace and Justice Shall Embrace* (both published by Pandora Press U.S. in 2000).

Carl S. Keener, State College, Pennsylvania, is Professor Emeritus of Biology at Pennsylvania State University. With degrees from Eastern Mennonite University, University of Pennsylvania, and North Carolina State University, his professional work has been in systematic botany. He and his wife, Gladys Swartz Keener, have three children and four grandchildren. They are members of University Mennonite Church in State College.

C. Norman Kraus, Harrisonburg, Virginia, is Professor Emeritus of Bible and Religion at Goshen College. He has taught also at Associated Mennonite Biblical Seminary, the Baptist Theological College (Western Australia), Serampore Theological College (India), and lectured in other colleges and seminaries in the United States and abroad. He has served as a pastor of a Mennonite congregation and as a missionary teacher-pastor in Japan. He is author and editor of thirteen books and many published articles.

Michael A. King, Telford, Pennsylvania, is pastor, Spring Mount (Pa.) Mennonite Church; publisher, Pandora Press U.S.; and founding editor, *DreamSeeker Magazine*. He has been pastor in a variety of congregations in diverse settings and is author (with Ronald J. Sider) of *Preaching about Life in a Threatening World* (Westminster, 1987), *Trackless Wastes and Stars to Steer By: Christian Identity in a Homeless Age* (Herald Press, 1990), and of many articles.

Paul M. Lederach, Lansdale, Pennsylvania, was ordained to the ministry in Franconia Mennonite Conference in 1944. For twenty-nine years he served Mennonite Publishing House as Curriculum Specialist and Director of the Congregational Literature Division. He has been president of the Mennonite Board of Education, taught at Union Biblical Seminary (Puna, India), and written many books, including *A Third Way* (Herald Press, 1980) and *Daniel* (Herald Press, 1994) in the Believer's Church Bible Commentary series.

Mark Thiessen Nation, London, England, is Director, London Menonite Center, England. Beginning in autumn 2002 he will be Associate Professor of Theology at Eastern Mennonite Seminary. He is author of more than fifteen articles and co-editor of four books, most recently *The Wisdom of the Cross: Essays in Honor of John Howard Yoder* (Eerdmans, 1999) and *Faithfulness and Fortitude: In Conversation with the Theological Ethics of Stanley Hauerwas* (T & T Clark, 2000). His doctoral dissertation, *The Ecumenical Patience and Vocation of John Howard Yoder*, is in process of publication by Eerdmans.

A. James Reimer, Kitchener, Ontario, is Professor of Religion and Theology at Conrad Grebel College, University of Waterloo, and Toronto School of Theology. He is author of numerous articles and books, including *Mennonites And Classical Theology: Dogmatic Foundations for Christian Ethics* (Pandora Press, 2001).

Carolyn Schrock-Shenk, Goshen, Indiana, is Associate Professor of Peace, Justice and Conflict Studies at Goshen College. Earlier she was Associate Director, then Director of Mennonite Conciliation Service, Akron, Pennsylvania, for ten years. She has extensive experience as a mediator, trainer, facilitator, and conflict consultant for many individuals, groups, organizations, and congregations. She was editor of *Conciliation Quarterly* and has co-edited several books as well as written a number of articles. She is married to Dave Schrock-Shenk and is mother of Caleb and John.

David Schroeder, Winnipeg, Manitoba, originally from Altona, Manitoba, is an ordained minister (now retired). He has preached and taught extensively within the Conference of Mennonites in Canada and in the larger church. His Th.D. in New Testament is from the University of Hamburg. For thirty years, 1959-1989, he was professor in New Testament and Ethics at Canadian Mennonite Bible College.

Marcus Smucker, Bird in Hand, Pennsylvania, served as pastor in Portland, Oregon, for sixteen years and as a professor at Associated Mennonite Biblical Seminary for seventeen years, teaching in the areas of pastoral care, pastoral counseling, and spiritual formation. He is a certified pastoral counselor, spiritual director, and consultant to congregations in conflict.

Edward Stoltzfus, Harrisonburg, Virginia, is Professor Emeritus of Theology at Eastern Mennonite Seminary. He served as pastor of Bethel Mennonite Church, West Liberty, Ohio; First Mennonite Church, Iowa City; and on the faculty at Goshen College. He was a moderator of Mennonite General Assembly (MC). As co-chairman of the Joint MC/GC Listening Committee for Homosexual Concerns, he wrote its final report. He and his wife Mildred live in Harrisonburg.

Douglas E. Swartzendruber, Malibu, California, recently retired from the University of Colorado (Colorado Springs), where he was Professor and Chair of Biology. He is a graduate of Goshen College and the University of Colorado Health Sciences Center. His teaching and research have been primarily in the areas of cell biology, experimental pathology, and breast cancer. He is currently coordinating laboratories in the Natural Science Division at Pepperdine University in Malibu. He and his wife, Rhonda Willems Swartzendruber, have three children and are members of Beth El Mennonite Church.

Melanie Zuercher, Hesston, Kansas, was born in Germany and grew up in a Mennonite home in America. She is a graduate of Goshen College and Associated Mennonite Biblical Seminary, Elkhart, Indiana. Beside numerous freelance projects, she has served as writer and editor for *Festival Quarterly* magazine and Good Books in Lancaster County, Pennsylvania; a citizens' social justice organization in Kentucky; *The Mennonite* (in its original incarnation as the General Conference Mennonite Church magazine); and is presently employed by GCMC News Service.

The Editor

C. NORMAN KRAUS WAS BORN IN DENBIGH (Newport News), Virginia, February 20, 1924, to Clyde and Phoebe (Shenk) Kraus. He was baptized into the Mennonite Church at age nine by Bishop George R. Brunk. He attended Eastern Mennonite School (high school and college) Goshen College, and Goshen Biblical Seminary. Later he studied at Princeton Theological Seminary (1953-1954) and Duke University (1958-1961) where he received his Ph. D. in Religion.

He taught social science and history in high school at Eastern Mennonite School (1946-1949); and Bible and religion at Goshen College (1951-1980). He also lectured at the Associated Mennonite Biblical Seminary and taught at Serampore Theological College (India), Union Biblical Seminary (India), and Baptist Theological College of Western Australia. He was ordained to the ministry and served a congregation in Topeka, Indiana (1950-1953).

Interspersed with faculty assignment at Goshen College, he served with Mennonite Central Committee and Mennonite Board of Missions in various board and overseas teaching assignments. From 1980-1987 he served with the Mennonite Board of Missions in Japan, also lecturing and teaching in various other Asian countries.

Kraus is author of numerous articles and books, including *The Community of the Spirit* (Eerdmans, 1976, Herald Press rev. 1993), *The Authentic Witness* (Eerdmans, 1979), *Evangelicalism and Anabaptism* (editor and author, Herald, 1979), *Missions, Evangelism and Church Growth* (ed. and author, Herald 1980), *Jesus Christ Our Lord* (Herald, 1987, 1990), *God Our Savior* (Herald, 1991), *An Intrusive Gospel: Christian Mission in the Postmodern World* (InterVarsity, 1998), and more.

In 1988 he retired to Harrisonburg, Virginia, where he now lives with his wife Rhoda. He remains busy writing and teaching, having made several trips to Japan, China, and India to lecture.